# *Florence & Tuscany with Kids*

Second Edition - 2015

Ariela Bankier

**Second Edition, February 2015**

Photos are used by permission and are the property of the original owners. All photos credits appear at the end of the book. If your photo appears without a credit, or isn't credited properly, please let us know and we will fix it immediately.

Front cover photos: Nickolay Vinokurov/Shutterstock.com and LianeM/Shutterstock.com; Back cover photo: Francesco R. Iacomino/Shutterstock.com

Managing Editor and Author: Ariela Bankier

Senior Editor: Suzanne Klein

Associate Editor: Amy L. Hayden

Scientific Advisor and Contributor: Federica Caneparo

Fact Checking: Maya Szczupak, Simona Graffeo

Graphic Design and e-book Format: eBook DesignWorks, Melisa Coppola

Illustrations: Karen Dishaw

Maps: Jiban Dahal

# Table of Contents

# Disclaimer:

Although the author of this guide has made every effort to provide readers with the most accurate and up-to-date information (as of the date of publication), she accepts no responsibility for any damages, loss, injury, or inconvenience sustained by readers of this guide. The author makes no warranties or representations of any kind regarding the accuracy of the information (text or maps) listed in this guide, including the completeness, suitability or availability of the products and services listed, and does not endorse, operate, or control any of the products or services listed in this guide. The author is in no event liable for any sort of direct or indirect or consequential damages that arise from the information found in this guide. If you have come across any errors in this guide, please let us know so we can correct our future editions. If you have any comments or concerns, please write to this address: info@travel-italy.guru Thank you!

# General note:

Travel information tends to change quickly. In addition, the recent economic crisis has influenced many businesses and attractions, including restaurants and hotels. Shops may close without notice, and some sites may change, or reduce, their opening hours unexpectedly. For this reason, we recommend confirming the details in this guide before your departure, just to be on the safe side.

# Introduction

Tuscany is a dream destination, a pivotal stop in any tour of Italy, and it isn't difficult to see why. With its enchantingly simple beauty, ranging from fruit-filled vineyards to tiny medieval villages and picturesque rolling hills, Tuscany is the heart of Italian culture. Its capital, Florence, has been attracting crowds for hundreds of years, and smaller towns like Pisa, San Gimignano, and Lucca also draw visitors from around the world. Throughout Tuscany, travellers find delicious food, world-famous architecture and artwork, and—of course—heavenly ice cream. With all of this to offer, what's not to love about the area? The problem, at least for some families, is the mistaken belief that Tuscany isn't a family-friendly vacation destination.

"My kids will never last in all those museums", you may be thinking. However, we can assure you that it doesn't have to be that way. Tuscany can actually be a wonderful place for parents and kids alike (from toddlers to teenagers), and if you plan your trip correctly, it may even be one of your most memorable vacations yet. How can you do that? That's where we come in.

*Florence & Tuscany with Kids* is the most comprehensive guide for families travelling to this region. It contains everything you need to know to build the perfect vacation for your family, from practical tips on moving around Tuscany to information on B&Bs, beaches, adventure and amusement parks, medieval castles, kid-friendly museums, festivals, and great restaurants. We're also honest about which places aren't worth your time and effort, which places shouldn't be missed, and the best ways to navigate hilly terrain when you (and your kids) are short on stamina. You will also find several unique features in this guide, such as Kids' Corners (filled with interesting information), detective missions, insider's tips, money-saving ideas, and fun family events and activities. And all is presented in a friendly, easy-to-use format. In short, your next great vacation starts here.

Welcome to Tuscany, and have a wonderful trip!

Ariela Bankier

# How to Use this Guide

*Florence & Tuscany with Kids* is divided into 14 chapters. Each one is dedicated to a different geographical area in Tuscany and includes one or two easy-to-follow (but detailed) self-guided itineraries. At the end of each chapter you will find sections dedicated to the best family-friendly restaurants and hotels in the area, as well as special events and activities that might interest your family. The last chapter (chapter 14) includes a review list of the best activities, hikes, parks, beaches, and museums for the entire family.

## Q: Why is the guide divided into itineraries?

Several travel guides offer lists of all the attractions and sights in a given area, but they don't explain how to create a fun, sensible itinerary that everyone—even young children—will enjoy. Our itineraries, which are meant to give our readers a sense of which sights and attractions go well together, are built so that readers can follow them to the letter or use them as a general reference point, whichever they prefer. All of the itineraries are designed to be very easy to mix, match, or modify. And since the itineraries are organized by geographical order and proximity, you can build a day with your favourite activities from two or even three different itineraries.

The longest chapter is dedicated to Florence and includes information about the city's museums, parks, kid-friendly attractions, family restaurants, the best ice cream, and much more. The other chapters cover northern Tuscany (Pisa, Lucca, and the Garfagnana area), southern Tuscany (mainly Val d'Orcia, Montepulciano, Chiusi, and the Maremma area), eastern Tuscany (Arezzo and Cortona), western Tuscany (the Etruscan Beach) and central Tuscany (the Chianti region and the hill towns of Volterra, San Gimignano, and more). Each itinerary is filled with practical tips for navigating the area with children.

## Q: What unique features does this guide offer?

We have included a number of unique features in this guide to help get your kids involved and have a great time. **The first feature is our "Missions"**, a series of fun, detective-style missions that kids can complete when you visit a sight.

**A second feature is the "Kids' Corner"** that you will find at the end of most itineraries. These include fun facts, stories, and anecdotes, everything from how much the Pisa Tower weighs to techniques for training falcons and stories of pirates. These facts and stories are meant to get kids curious about their surroundings while having fun. Some kids still won't be interested and would rather just enjoy walking and exploring, which is, of course, perfectly fine. But if they do want to know a little bit more, all they have to do is turn a page...

**A third feature is the "Special Events in the Area" section,** which covers the main family-friendly events, from medieval feasts to jousting matches and carnivals. If you are travelling to Tuscany in July and August, there are at least 10 big events to choose from, and we highly recommend working one of them into your schedule. There is nothing quite like hearing drums beat in the background while a procession of men and women dressed in medieval clothes marches by, waving flags. Bigger events, like sporting contests, races, and jousting, will probably be one of the most memorable parts of the trip.

**A fourth feature is the "Special Activities in the Area" section,** dedicated to all the fun stuff kids and teenagers love to do: horseback rides, thermal springs, Italian cooking classes, adventure parks, amusement parks, and more. You will find several suggestions for every itinerary, and we highly recommend choosing a few activities and trying to work them into your schedule. A cooking class, for example, could be an exciting experience for teenagers, and a pony or horse ride might be the most-talked-about part of your trip for your 8- or 12-year-old. An adventure park, after a long day of sightseeing, can make all the difference between cranky kids who feel they "aren't doing anything fun" and happy kids who get to run around, tire themselves out, and then fall asleep early, letting you enjoy a quiet evening to yourself.

> **Tip:** If you plan on booking a special activity, always ask in advance whether it is appropriate for your family. Make sure, for example, that a riding tour/lesson is suitable for younger children and inexperienced riders before booking it, and make sure your travel insurance covers any extreme sports and riding tours. Take into consideration any health issues before booking an intense activity like horseback riding, quad tours, hikes, rafting, bike rides, extreme sports, and more. You may want to consult with your doctor before making plans to visit any thermal baths, as well. Thermal water has medicinal properties, and some doctors do not recommend those with health concerns or children younger than 12 to enter them.

## Q: Some towns in Tuscany aren't mentioned in this guide. Why is that?

It's true, not every single sight and town in Tuscany are mentioned in this guide (though the best and most important ones absolutely are). In fact, if you would call this guide opinionated, you wouldn't be wrong. If we think a medieval village is no more than average, we won't hesitate to say so, and if we believe a certain area or town isn't suitable for (most) families, we will express that clearly.

The reason for this approach is that we feel describing every single miniscule church and hamlet (and there are literally hundreds of churches and medieval villages in Tuscany) as wonderful, charming, and quaint is unfair to our readers. If you have a month to tour the Tuscan countryside, then discovering tiny, unknown areas can be a real treat. But if you have about a week in the area, like most travellers, you'll have to be picky about where you spend your time and money. There is no reason to drive 30 minutes to a pleasant but entirely unimportant town when just a few kilometres away sits a much more interesting sight that you and your kids will probably enjoy more. We know that you have worked hard to be able to take your family on this vacation, and we want you to have the best possible experience. We hope our recommendations will be able to help you do just that. We are, however, always happy and grateful to hear any comments and suggestions from our readers. If you believe we haven't covered a sight, town, or attraction that should be featured in the guide, please let us know.

## Q: I'm still not sure travelling to Tuscany with my seven- and nine-year-old children is a good idea.

Travelling with kids can be challenging, but it is also a wonderful adventure. Very few experiences in life are as character-building, eye-opening, horizon-expanding, fun, and instructive as travel. Seeing the heart of European culture with their own eyes and touching 500-year-old monuments will teach kids more about history and mankind than one hundred books or movies. The daily contact with different cultures, languages, and customs will help them develop as people and understand the world in a way that only travel can do. Even the more annoying aspects of travel have their advantages. Learning to handle complicated situations that require patience and thinking outside the box, adapting yourself to new situations, tasting new (sometimes weird and sometimes delicious) foods, living outside your comfort zone, and daring to try new things are all experiences that teach children to become more resilient, confident, and mature. It also helps them become more open to the world and curious about their surroundings. Travel can and usually does bring families closer, and the memories from the trip will stay with your kids long after they've left home for good.

In our experience, kids don't always get enough credit for what they are able to understand and enjoy on a trip. While it is true that most (okay, all) kids would pick a visit to the amusement park over a visit to the museum, there is no reason you can't do both. The fact that your nine-year-old probably won't spend four hours in the Uffizi Museum, expressing his thoughts about the art in the form of Haiku poems, doesn't mean that he can't enjoy a 40-minute tour of the art collection there, if properly prepared in advance.

## Q: Are the maps in this guide enough, or do I need a GPS/other maps?

You will find several maps in this guide, but we do encourage you to use a GPS or a detailed road map of Tuscany, as well as to pick up detailed city maps at the tourist information offices in cities like Florence and Siena. A good GPS/regional road map will be essential during this trip (don't rely only on the road signs), since our maps are meant to give readers a general sense of direction, but aren't enough for easy navigation. A detailed city map can be useful for one simple reason: Italian towns and villages are filled with tiny alleys and hidden piazzas that can't be shown with enough detail in our guide. In any case, you should also know that once you get used to the way Italian towns are built, you won't get lost; all of the attractions are usually concentrated in the historical centre—"centro" or "centro storico" in Italian—which is marked on road signs with a bull's-eye.

## Terms You Will Find Throughout The Guide

As you tour Tuscany (or Italy, for that matter), you will notice you keep coming across a few technical terms or words that are useful to know in advance:

Duomo—the central church/cathedral in town. Every self-respecting town, even the smallest ones, has a duomo, which is usually considered the focal point of the town. In most cases, if you are trying to get to the historical centre (the centro storico), ask where the duomo is.

**Fresco**—churches (and sometimes private homes, too) in Italy are decorated with frescoes (affresco, in Italian). This term refers to paintings painted directly on the plaster walls.

**Baptistery**—next to most duomos, you will find the baptistery (battistero, in Italian), where, you've guessed it, infants were baptised.

**Piazza**—town square. There are several piazzas in every Italian town.

**Piazzale**—a larger piazza.

**Palazzo**—though it sounds like "palace", palazzo actually means "building". In some cases, it means very fancy buildings and even small palaces. The plural of palazzo is palazzi.

**Ponte**—bridge. For example: Ponte Vecchio, in Florence, means "the old bridge".

**San**—saint.

**Borgo**—any small fortified medieval village.

**Uscita (pronounced "ushita")**—exit.

**Entrata**—entryway/entrance.

**Via**—road/street.

**Fermata**—stop (usually used for bus stops).

**Stazione**—station (usually used for train stations; pronounced "statsione").

# Planning Your Trip

Planning your trip in a smart way can save you time, money, and stress. Throughout this guide, you will find dozens of tips and ideas meant to make this trip as easy as possible. Preparing in advance, in our experience, can make a huge difference.

## Choosing when to travel

If you are travelling as a family, you are probably limited to travelling during school vacations. Most tourists visit Tuscany during the summer months (July is the busiest month in Florence). There are pros and cons to summer travel in Tuscany. The pros are that most of the cultural events and festivities take place in the summer, the days are longer (which means you can get more done), the fine weather permits you to spend some time at the beach and in the pool (an idea kids will appreciate), and opening times for attractions are longer, adapted for the influx of tourists. The cons are that everything is crowded and there are lines for every major attraction. Italians are on vacation too, so the beaches, pools, and amusement parks are absolutely cramped. The prices are higher (a family apartment can cost 35-40% more during the summer months), and well... it's hot (not surprising; summer tends to be that way, but it's still a consideration).

The loveliest period of the year to visit Tuscany, in our opinion, is in September and October, just before the Vendemia (the vintage or fall grape harvest), when the air has cooled down but the days are still long and most places are still open. After November, rain tends to spoil most of the fun, and several places close down or drastically reduce their hours until April or May. Spring is also quite pleasant, and in May and June you will enjoy, for the most part, great weather (although some rain is still possible).

## Documents you'll need before leaving

If you are a EU citizen, you will just need your ID card. We also recommend bringing your national health certificate with you, which allows you to receive free emergency medical treatment if needed. If you are travelling from outside the EU, you will need to bring a passport. Passports must be valid for at least six more months from the date of your entry into Italy. If you plan on entering Italy in July and your passport expires in September, for example, then you should renew it before leaving or you might have problems getting in. Kids need passports, too (check your national guidelines). As a precaution, bring vaccination documents and health insurance documents as well as any other documentation that might be needed in case of a medical emergency.

We also recommend making photocopies and virtual copies (scan the documents and email them to yourself, or save them on a USB, or both) of all your important documents in case anything gets lost or stolen.

If you plan on renting a car, you will need a driver's license (most companies require at least two years of experience) and a credit card (which must be under the same name as the driver's license).

You may also want to print out driving instructions to your hotels (or at least the hotel where you'll be staying your first night).

If you've booked your ticket (or rented your car) online, print out the confirmation letter and the e-tickets you were sent. Some companies require just the code you were sent; others require the actual printed ticket/voucher (especially if there is a barcode on it).

If flying with low-cost companies (like Ryanair and Easyjet), carefully read about their check-in process to avoid any unpleasant surprises (for example, do you need to check in online before arriving at the airport?).

## Local money

Like the rest of the EU, prices in Italy are in Euro (1 euro = about $1.40, and 1 British pound = about 1.8 euro). You can change money in the airport and in most city centres. If you have an international credit card (very useful; contact your bank for more information) you can also simply withdraw money, in the local currency, from ATMs across Italy (check first what the commission will be for the withdrawal and for the conversion from dollars/pounds to Euro).

Don't forget to notify your bank that you will be using your credit card abroad, or they might block it automatically, thinking it was stolen.

When changing money (either in Italy or in your home country), ask for bills no higher than 50 euros; 100-euro bills are hard to break, and 500-euro bills will arouse suspicion.

## Fraud

Two of the most common frauds involve false bills/coins and identity theft. The probability that you will be given a false 20-euro (or even 100-euro) bill is extremely low. This trick is mostly used in stores when trying to scam the owner.

False coins, however, are a popular trick in markets; check the 2-euro coin you're given as change to make sure it really is a 2-euro coin and not an old 500-lire coin (which looks very similar but is worth nothing). Identity theft happens when thieves attach a small camera to ATMs to steal PIN numbers. Simply cover your hand with your other hand or a scarf while entering the code to avoid any problems.

## Crime

Tuscany is a very calm area, and even though there are criminals (like any other country in the world), it is rare for tourists to feel unsafe. You probably shouldn't pick the darkest corner of the train station and stand there all alone holding cash at 03:00, but other than that, you probably won't encounter any real problems. The biggest hassle is pickpockets (see our advice in the Florence Itinerary). Apply common sense to avoid unpleasant events. Don't carry all of your money in one purse, so that even if you do get targeted, you won't lose $600. If your hotel has a reliable safe, leave some of your money there. Don't put your wallet in your pocket or in the outer (or side) pockets of your backpack, where it can be pulled out without you even noticing. Don't put your documents and your cash in the same wallet (that way if your wallet is stolen, you will still have your passports and tickets, and your vacation won't be ruined). Keep a piece of paper with the emergency number of your credit card company so you can call immediately if your credit card is stolen, and take extra care when standing in touristy, crowded spaces, such as the train station or night trains. There is no metro system in Tuscany, but if you plan on travelling from Tuscany to Milan or Rome, know that pickpockets love the metro systems in both cities. If you do get robbed, you will need to file a complaint at the police station, so they can help you get new documents (if they were stolen) and for insurance purposes.

## Insurance

Consider taking out some sort of travel and luggage insurance. There are several options available, and a quick search online will yield affordable results.

## Emergency Numbers and Medical Emergencies

Call 113 from any phone to reach the police (or 112).
Call 118 for an ambulance.
    If you need a pharmacy or a hospital (or any other shop or service), and

there are no locals you can ask, you can call 1254 (a sort of yellow pages service), where an operator will help you find whatever you are looking for. Alternatively, use this website (for English, change the language on the top right corner of the page): www.paginebianche.it. If you need a pharmacy, type "farmacia" or for a hospital, type "ospedale".

If you suffer from any medical problems, make sure you pack enough prescription drugs to last your entire trip (plus a few extra), since Italian pharmacies may not carry the medicine you need. We also recommend that when travelling with kids you pack some basic medicine (cough syrup, allergy medicine, analgesic medicine, a syrup to bring a fever down) you're familiar with, instead of trying to figure out which of the local brands is most similar to the stuff you know from home. This, of course, in no way means that you shouldn't go see a doctor if you or your child are unwell.

## Doctors in Florence

A visit to the doctor costs between 80-100 euro; a higher fee may be charged if you show up without an appointment. If there is an emergency, go directly to the hospital. You won't be turned away, even if you don't have insurance, and it may even cost less than a private doctor.

**Dr. Stephen Kerr** is a general practitioner/family physician trained in Britain. Office hours: weekday mornings and afternoons (by appointment); weekday afternoons, 15:00-17:00 (without appointments). His clinic is in Piazza Mercato Nuovo 1, Florence. Tel and Fax: 055.288055, Cell: 335.8361682, www.dr-kerr. com

**Dr. Francesco Porro** specializes in Paediatrics. He offers home visits, too. Visits by appointment. Available for emergency calls 24 hours a day at 338.8203612. Home address: Via S. Francesco di Paola 20, Florence, Tel: 055.222036; Office address: Medical Service, Via Lorenzo il Magnifico 59, Florence; Tel: 055.475411

**Dr. Fabio Romboli** specializes in Paediatrics. Office hours: Tuesday, Wednesday, Friday: 15:00-18:00. His office is in Via della Robbia 53, Florence; Tel: 055.579327. His home phone number, in case of an emergency, is 055.587766.

**Dr. Giovanni Fazi** is a dentist, trained in the US. Office hours: Monday-Friday, 9:30-13:00, 14:30-19:30. His office is in Via A. La Marmora 22, Florence. Tel: 055.583258

To find a full list of doctors in all of Tuscany, Google "doctor Tuscany American embassy". Both the American and the British Embassies offer updated lists of English speaking physicians.

Another usedul website to consult is: www.medicalservice.firenze.it

## Calling Home and Using the Internet while in Italy

In this day and age, with so many easy-to-operate apps and services allowing you to talk with your family back home (and navigate online), 21-digit long-distance calling cards seem like a thing of the past.

To call home (using your computer or smartphone), try Skype or WhatsApp.

Skype has been around for many years, and it is still a good option. If your friends and family have Skype, too, you can speak for free through your Internet connection. Alternatively, you can buy minutes and call landlines from your computer. WhatsApp is probably the most popular communication app today, compatible with just about any smartphone. Check their new offer, WhatsApp SIM, too. Google Hangouts is another useful (and free) option.

If you want to make calls within Italy (to other Italian numbers), and more importantly, use your phone for Internet (especially for map apps, like Google Maps), the best solution is to buy a local SIM card. This will work, as long as you have a GSM-compatible, unlocked phone (which means it will work in Europe), and your phone allows the use of SIM cards other than the original one. If you don't have such a phone, you can buy one in Italy for as little as 30 euro for a basic phone and slightly more for a phone with Internet. An Italian SIM card costs 5-10 euro and is already charged with that amount of money. You can add more money to it and activate an Internet service that will allow you to use your phone (and more importantly—the internet) for a very low fee during your entire trip in Italy. You will need an ID or passport to buy a SIM card (the shop will photocopy it for legal reasons), and within 24 hours, you will have an Italian phone and Internet. You can buy a SIM card at any of the main cell phone operators' shops, which can be found in the main street in the larger towns or better yet, directly at the airport. There are a number of local operators, we recommend TIM and VODAFON.

Ask for a "ricaricabile", which means a "pay as you go" offer, and ask the shop to activate the cheapest Internet offer they have (usually around 9 euro per month, but check and see what special offers they have.

Other free apps worth looking into are Viber and magicJack. We also recommend the services of www.xcomglobal.com, which will give you web access for a flat, pre-paid and reasonable fee.

One last thing to remember - if you are travelling with your own SIM card, make sure you disable cellular data roaming before you leave for your trip. Otherwise, a very hefty bill will wait for you when you return home.

# Packing and Luggage

The two best pieces of advice we could give you regarding packing are: keep it light and make sure to pack essential items you won't be able to find abroad.

**Essential items:** Your list of essential items may change, based on your specific needs and the ages of your kids, especially if you are travelling with babies, but it usually includes an extra pair of glasses (especially if you are the driver), music for the car (if you plan on renting a car, and you have younger children), any special foods you may need (specific baby formula which may not be available in Italy, kosher food, gluten-free food, etc.), vitamins, and any medicine that you use regularly (assume you won't find it in Italy) or that you might require. A transformer (adaptor plug) is important too. Note that the European electrical system is different than the American and British system (220 volts). In fact, you may want a few adaptor plugs, since you will likely be travelling with at least two phones and one computer. Knowing what to pack when travelling with kids can be stressful. Since the exact list of what you need greatly varies depending on the age of your children, we recommend learning from the experience of other parents and Googling "what to pack kids abroad" or "packing list abroad" to find endless lists of suggestions online. You'll find ideas that you hadn't even considered, from the best brand of backpacks to essential baby formula tips, from portable high seats and strollers to medicine, from baby wipes suggestions to space-saving ideas.

**Keeping it light:** The truth is, if you can hardly lift your suitcase when you're still at home, you certainly won't manage (easily) to carry it to the train and to your hotel. You should know that most train stations and under 3 star hotels don't have elevators, so you will have to lift your suitcase constantly.

Before packing, check the weight allowance for luggage on your flight. Most companies allow you to bring one suitcase that weighs up to 20 kg (we've tried and the answer is no, they won't let you bring two bags weighing 10 kg each). You may also bring a handbag that is no bigger than 55 cm x 40 cm x 20 cm (some companies also limit the handbag weight to 8 or 10 kg).

Low-cost companies (like Ryanair and Easyjet) are VERY strict about letting you take only one item on board. They are also very strict about the measurements of your handbag, and they actually do measure it before they let you on the flight. You won't be able to get on the plane with a handbag and a personal bag, plastic bag, camera bag, computer bag, or anything else (except for the duty-free shopping you bought in the airport after the security check). Other companies are less strict, but they will require you pay for overweight luggage, which may be pricey (at the end of your trip, if you know you've bought too many souvenirs, consider popping by the post office and sending yourself a package instead of paying extra for your luggage).

## Packing Extra Stuff for Activities and Fun

In addition to the usual packing, you will also need to bring accessories for the activities in this guide. They won't take up much space, but they are essential for carrying out the missions in the different itineraries. You'll need:

1.  Crayons

2.  A notebook where kids can paint (preferably A4 size)

3.  Another notebook for writing (a journal or notepad)

4.  Binoculars—this may seem like an excessive item, but it is absolute-ly not. It not only helps kids feel like detectives or spies but also helps them see things better. One of the reasons kids get so bored in churches is that they can't see; everything is too high or too far away. With binoculars, your little detective can see the expression on the saints' faces in the frescoes in Florence or check out the detail on the dome of the Duomo.

Additionally, we recommend packing some basic craft materials to help toddlers and young children survive long flights and car rides. Wikki stix, reusable stickers, Lego kits, portable DVD players, an etch-a-sketch, glitter pens and colorful paper for origami are all useful. Tablets loaded with ebooks or audio books are also a big hit. If you plan on doing any crafts during your flight, remember that certain materials are not allowed on airplanes for security reaosns (scissors, naturally, but glue and clay might also be a problem. Check your airline's guidelines).

# Getting Into Italian Mode

## Opening Times

As time goes by, more shops and museums are adopting what is known as "orario continuato", which means they are open all day long, but this is not yet the norm for Italian businesses. Many places, especially in smaller towns, still operate according to traditional business hours.

**Shops**: Monday-Saturday: 09:30/10:00-13:00 and 15:30/16:00/17:00-19:00/19:30. Sunday: Most shops are either closed or open during the morning only. Some shops are also closed on Monday mornings. In smaller towns, it is common to find that all shops are closed for no apparent reason on a specific weekday, and that weekday changes from town to town (though it is usually either Monday or Tuesday).

**Banks**: Monday-Friday: 08:30-12:30/13:00/13:30 and 14:00/14:30-15:30/16:00/16:30. Many banks are open on Saturday too.

**Trains**: There are very few trains after 22:00 and virtually no trains between 24:00 and 05:00 (except for a few night trains which cross the region and make a number of stops).

**Museums**: It depends on the specific museum, but several museums are closed on Mondays.

## National Holidays

Everything, including museums, attractions, and most shops and restaurants, will be closed on:

| | |
|---|---|
| **1 January** | New Year's Day |
| **6 January** | Epiphany |
| **Monday after Easter** | Easter Monday |
| **25 April** | Liberation Day |

| **1 May** | International Workers' Day |
| **2 June** | Republic Day |
| **15 August** | Assumption Day |
| **1 November** | All Saints' Day |
| **8 December** | Immaculate Conception Day |
| **25 December** | Christmas |
| **26 December** | St. Stephen's Day |

## Phone numbers

What may seem at first as a complicated system, is actually quite simple.

**Home and office telephone numbers** have an area code, followed by the number. Rome's area code, for example, is 06. Milan's is 02. Most towns in Tuscany have an area code that begins with 05. Florence's code, for example, is 055. Pisa's is 050. Let's say you wish to call your hotel in Florence, whose number is 055.999999. Whether you dial this number from within Italy or from abroad, you will have to dial the same number, including the zero at the beginning of the area code. If you are dialing from abroad, don't forget to add the International Call Prefix (00) and Italy's Country Code (39) before the number (for example: 00.39.055999999 or 00.39.329444444)

**Cell phone numbers** begin with 3. For example: 338.2222222 or 329.4444444, etc.

## Addresses

Addresses in Italy are written like this: Via Rossi 22, Lucca. This example address is located on Rossi street (via = street) number 22, in a town called Lucca. Since Lucca happens to be the main town in Lucca Province, there is no need to specify the province. If it weren't the main town, they would have probably specified the province too, like this: Hotel Ciao, Via Dante 4, Altopascio (Lucca). This means that the hotel is located on Dante street number 4, in a town called Altopascio, and the town of Altopascio is located within the province of Lucca. The reason the province is added to the address is that you will find several towns by the same name in all of Italy, and without specifying the province, people won't know which town you are talking about.

In some cases, especially when looking for hotels, agriturismi, and restaurants that are located in the countryside, you will encounter this type of address: Hotel Buongiorno, Via Puccini 14, Loc. San Giuliano Terme, Pisa. Loc stands for località, and it simply means a suburb, or a small village, that technically is part of the town (in this case, Pisa) but is located outside the town itself. Some places don't bother to write down 'località', but it is inferred. For example: Ristorante Amore, Via Dante 2, Montefiorale, Greve in Chianti. In this case, the Ristornate Amore is located in Dante Street number 2, in a small suburb/village called Montefiorale. Montefiorale is very close to the larger town of Greve in Chianti, but it isn't actually part of the town itself. Needless to say, you will need a car to reach most località addresses.

# Arriving in Tuscany

## BY PLANE

The main airport in Tuscany isn't the one in Florence, as many would believe, but the Galileo Galilei Airport in Pisa. Thanks to several low-cost companies that have diverted their flights to Pisa in recent years, the airport has significantly grown and improved. It is modern, small but efficient, very close to town, and close to the highway. All of the major car rental companies also have offices on the premises. If you are arriving from Europe, you'll find the best deals with low-cost companies like Ryanair and Easyjet, who both fly to Pisa. If you are flying from the USA, there are daily direct Delta flights from NY to Pisa (and non-direct flights with Alitalia and several other companies, too). Find out more here: www.pisa-airport.com.

Naturally, The Florence airport offers a number of low cost flights, too. AirBerlin, Meridiana and Vueling are just a few of the companies that fly to Florence. Find out more here: www.aeroporto.firenze.it.

If you plan to rent a car, we recommend renting one at Pisa's airport, or at the Florence airport, and not in Florence city center, for two reasons. First, the airports offer more comfortable offices, with all the leading companies gathered in one space connected by shuttle to the airport. Second, and more importantly, many rental companies in Florence are located inside the city centre (not in a ZTL area, but near one. See explanation below about what a ZTL is and why it should be avoided). This means that once you get your car, while trying to drive out of the city centre and get on the highway, you might find yourself accidentally entering a ZTL area. The airport rental car offices, on the other hand, are just a few metres from the main highway.

If you are moving around using public transportation, getting from the airport to the city centre is quite easy.

To reach Florence city centre from Florence airport, take 'BusItalia'. Buses leave every half-hour, between 5:00am and 8:00pm. Find out more here: www.fsbusitalia.it. Alternatively, take a taxi. The airport is only 15 minutes from the city centre, and taxis are obligated to charge a flat fee of about 20-23 euro. (However, you will pay extra for luggage, or if you are travelling at night, or on a holiday).

To reach Florence from Pisa airport, either take the direct train with trenitalia (the train track is located right next to the airport exit), or use the services of a private bus company called Terravision. Bus fare might actually be cheaper than the train. Tickets can be bought in advance. Find out more here: www.terravision.eu.

## BY TRAIN

Florence can easily be reached by train from just about any major city in Italy. There are several trains a day from Rome, Milan, Venice, Bologna, Torino and other towns. With the Freccia (high speed) train from Rome, for example, you can reach Florence in less than 90 minutes. The Freccia train from Milan will take just under two hours. Tickets can be bought online in advance (enabling you to not only pick your seat, but also save quite a lot of money). If you haven't booked a ticket in advance, and you are looking for a cheaper option, consider the regional trains. They take about twice as long as the Freccia trains, but they are also much cheaper. Find out more here: www.trenitalia.com

# Moving Around in Tuscany

One you've decided where you want to go and the main towns you plan to visit, the inevitable question arises: **How will we get from place to place? Should we rent a car? Or can we travel by train and bus?**

In short: yes, you should rent a car. Without a car, it will be very difficult to visit anything off the beaten path; the natural reserves, parks, adventure parks, and some smaller villages will all be off-limits without a car. You won't be able to book your stay in charming little agriturismi and B&Bs that are not serviced by public transport, either, and you will have to depend on the sometimes erratic bus schedules (especially difficult on Sundays and holidays) to get to hill towns. You also won't have the option of leaving at least some of your luggage in the car while walking around the city. Most of the itineraries in this guide are built on the assumption that you will be travelling with a car.

### When don't we need a car?

When travelling in Florence, Pisa, Lucca, and Siena, driving a car is not only unnecessary, it's actually a bad idea. These are all towns whose historical centres (centro storico) are considered ZTL (limited traffic zone). That means they are closed for non-residential traffic. Drive into a ZTL area without a permit and a hefty fine will arrive by mail (around 100 euros). Since all four major towns are easily accessible by train, and their historical centres are small enough to be visited by foot, a car isn't necessary. If you plan on visiting only these four destinations, and nothing else, you can do very well using only public transportation.

## Driving, Parking, and Renting a Car in Italy

### Driving in Italy

If you are a EU citizen, your driving license is valid in Italy, and you need no other documentation. If you are travelling from the USA or Canada, you need to obtain an international driving permit before leaving for Italy. Driving in Italy is just like driving in any other country (don't be intimidated by stories of horrifying and insane Italian drivers; they are not true, for the most part). Our best advice is that when travelling between destinations, stick to the high roads, which are far easier to navigate. When you are travelling inside an area or driving along the countryside and hoping to see some pretty scenery, try the scenic little roads. Be aware, however, that it will take more time to get to your destination.

There are two kinds of highways in Italy: free and toll. Those with a toll are called "Autostrada", and they are marked with green road signs. The free roads have different names but are always marked with blue road signs. The advantages of the toll Autostrada are that the maximum speed limit is higher (up to 130 kmph) and there are fewer speed cameras. When you enter the Autostrada, you will find an automated booth, that will issue you a ticket. Keep that ticket, and hand it over when you leave the Autostrada, so the operator can calculate how much to charge you. When you exit the autostrada, make sure you don't line up for the toll booths marked TELEPASS (which are reserved for Telepass subscribers). Instead, pick the booths with an illustration of money. If you prefer to pay at a booth operated by a human being, not a machine, pick the booth with an illustration of a hand on it.

**Drinking and driving:** The maximum amount of alcohol permitted in your blood is 0.5 mg/ml. This is especially relevant if you plan on doing any wine tasting in charming little vineyards during your trip.

The **ZTL** (zona traffico limitato) is an issue that many tourists aren't aware of, but is very important. Most towns in Italy protect their historical centre, which is where most of the attractions are, by defining it as a ZTL, a limited traffic area, where only residents can drive and/or park. There are security cameras at the entrance to any ZTL area that register your vehicle number and send you, or your rental company, a fine (which, together with handling fees charged by the rental company, will be about 100 euro).

Stories about tourists who got confused and entered the same ZTL area three times in less than 10 minutes, getting a fine each time, are more common than you think. Our best advice is to simply avoid driving in the city, especially Florence. Most town centres in Tuscany are so small you don't really need a car anyway. If arriving with a car, park in a lot outside the centro storico and walk or take a bus to the centre. You will usually find very accessible parking lots, especially in touristy towns.

What does a ZTL sign look like? A white circle surrounded by a red ring and next to it another sign saying ZTL (or zona traffico limitato). If you are still not sure and want positive ID of the culprit, Google "ZTL" in Google Images and look your enemy in the eye.

## Parking in Italy

Look at the parking lines on the road. White lines (or no lines, unless there is a road sign saying otherwise) mean parking is free. Blue lines mean you have to pay for parking: look for the parking meters around the parking lot, decide how long you will stay, and put the appropriate amount of change in the machine.

Take the receipt the machine prints out, and put it, facing out, on the dashboard of your car, near the steering wheel. If the parking space is marked yellow, you can't park there.

## Renting a Car in Italy

The major rental companies in Italy are Avis, Europcar, Sixt, and Hertz. We suggest looking into all four before booking a car. We also recommend checking websites such as www.autoeurope.com, www.rentalcars.com and www.skyscanner.com to find the best deals. You can rent a car in Italy if you are over 21 and have had a license for more than two years (some companies require only one year of experience). When renting a car, you have to present a document (passport or I.D card for EU citizens) and a credit card (NOT a debit card), both belonging to the person who is renting the car. You can't rent a car with Mr Smith's license and pay with Mrs Smith's credit card, for example. There are a number of insurance options, but we recommend taking the most comprehensive one. Regardless of the type of insurance you have, mark every scratch and bump on the car. Some insurances say they are all inclusive, but the small print reveals that damage to mirrors, for example, or lower parts of the car or wheels, is not covered.

You should know that most cars in Italy have a hand gear (stick). If you don't feel comfortable driving such a car, make sure you specifically order a model you are comfortable with. Cars based on diesel (and not fuel) will save you money.

Always fill up the gas tank when returning the car; you will be charged extra if the company has to fill it for you. You will also be charged extra for returning a very dirty car (you don't have to take it the car wash; just make sure it's acceptably clean), for returning the car at a different office than the one you picked it up at, and for accessories such as a GPS, snow chains, baby seats, etc.

GPS units are very useful, and we highly recommend using them with this guide, but if you plan on renting a car with a GPS for a week or more, it's probably cheaper to buy your own GPS, as long as it has European maps on it. You can walk into any "Mediaworld" or "Euronics" or "Unieuro" shop in Italy (the three largest chain stores for electronics) and buy a GPS for about 100 euro, and then take it back home with you.

Snow chains are obligatory by law if travelling between November and mid-April in Tuscany. Rental companies never seem to mention this fact, but if you are stopped by the police, and don't have either snow chains or winter tires you will have to pay the hefty fine, not the rental company.

If you are travelling with younger kids, by law they are required to sit in child car seats or booster seats. Children under 36kg (80 pounds) or under 150 cm can choose between a booster seat and a child car seat; children under 18 kg must have a child car seat. Book these in advance when renting a car, or buy one when you reach Italy and then take it home with you; they are really not that expensive.

One last thing: try not to fill your car with gas on Sundays. There usually is no one manning gas stations on Sundays, so you will have to use the automatic machine, which is easy but the machine doesn't always have exact change.

## Moving Around in Tuscany on Public Transport

### Trains

Trains are a great way to move around and reach the main towns (Florence, Siena, Pisa, Lucca, Grosseto, Livorno, etc.). The central station will either be called "Stazione Centrale" (pronounced "statsione chentrale" and marked like this: FS) or it may simply be based on the city's name: Pisa Centrale, Siena Centrale, Lucca Centrale, etc. There are a few exceptions to this rule. Florence's main train station, for example, is called Firenze SMN (Firenze Santa Maria Novella; Firenze is the Italian name for Florence).

Trains are a great option for families: you don't have to drive, you can relax all the way, and, unlike a bus, there is room to move around and toilets available, a perk parents with toddlers will appreciate (though sometimes these toilets can be dirty enough to put you off the idea of using them). Assuming you will be travelling only in Italy, and that you are not using a European railroad pass, you will need to buy a ticket every time you want to take a train somewhere. There are a number of train companies in Italy, but in Tuscany there is just one—Trenitalia (which is also the largest company in Italy)—and while other companies cover only parts of the country, Trenitalia covers every angle and spot. Find out more here: www.trenitalia.com.

The Trenitalia trains can be divided into two categories: regular trains (known as regional and IC trains) and high-speed trains (known as the Freccia trains). When travelling inside Tuscany, you will mostly be using the regional trains (the high-speed Freccia trains connect major cities, like Rome and Milan or Florence and Venice, not small towns like the ones in Tuscany). Freccia train tickets are more expensive and they have a specific time and place booking. Regional trains, on the other hand, have no specific booking restrictions—you just get on the regional train you want and sit wherever you find a free seat.

To buy a ticket in the train station, go to the ticket office (marked "biglietteria") or use the self-service machines (look at the illustrations on top of the machine; some only have an illustration of a credit card, which means they don't accept cash). The self-service machines are easy to use, and you can select a menu in English, too.

> **Tip:** If you are travelling a short distance, usually under 80 km, from Pisa to Florence, for example, you can get a generic "up to X km" ticket at the newspaper stand, instead of waiting in line at the ticket office. Just make sure this ticket covers the right distance (ask the vendor: "va bene per X?" meaning: "Is this ticket okay for reaching X?").

Always validate your ticket before getting on the train in one of the little yellow (or modern white and green) machines near the tracks. A ticket is valid for six hours from the moment it is validated. A non-validated ticket can lead to a hefty fine. Children under four years old don't have to pay for a ticket (but they can't occupy a seat of their own, either). Children under 12 are eligible for a 50% discount (the terms of this offer may change depending on your destination, and you may be required to present documentation proving your child's age). To be on the safe side, always ask whether your child needs to buy a ticket or not.

> **Tip:** Unlike the high-speed Freccia trains, where there is a difference between first and second-class, there is no difference whatsoever in the regional or IC trains (except that first class costs more).

Most train stations in Tuscany are rather small (Florence being the main exception). Tracks are called "binari" (binario in singular). In every station you will find two boards, usually electronic, like in airports: with one listing the arriving trains (marked: Arrivi) and one listing the departing trains (marked: Partenze). The two boards are almost identical, so when you check to see when your train leaves make sure you are looking at the right board.

When you look for your train on the board, you may notice that the train has a different name than you would expect. Let's say, for example, that you've just bought a ticket to Pisa at the Florence station. Your ticket says "Pisa" and the polite lady at the ticket office said the train leaves at 16:00 (this is a regional ticket, so there won't be an exact time of departure on the ticket itself). And yet, as you check the departures (Partenze) board to find out from which track (binario, sometimes marked: bin.) your train is leaving, you discover that there is no train to Pisa leaving at 16:00, only a train to Livorno. Don't be alarmed. Most trains make several stops along the way, and it is very likely that the stop you need to reach isn't the final destination of the train, which is why it doesn't appear on the board. Simply walk to the track and check the more detailed board on the track itself. It will list all the stops along the route. Alternatively, look for the yellow paper boards placed throughout the station (ignore the white paper boards). These list all the trains that leave from the station at all hours, as well as all the stops they make along the way. You can also, of course, ask the personnel.

## Urban Buses

Every town and city has its own bus system (except for tiny towns in the same area, which are serviced by the same company). This means that a bus ticket you bought in Florence won't be valid in Siena and the bus ticket you bought in Pisa is useless in Lucca. The easiest way to buy a ticket is at a newspaper stand. There is always a newspaper stand in medium-sized and large train stations. Ask for a bus ticket: "un biglietto per l'autobus per favore" (pronounced "oon bilieto per l'aoo-tobus, per favore"). If there is no place to buy a ticket, try buying one on board (it will be more expensive though, and the driver will ask for exact change. It is unlikely he will be able to break any bills).

Like the train, you must validate your bus ticket once you get on the bus. While the validating machines for trains are outside the train, on the track, the validating machines for buses are inside the bus itself. There are usually little machines at the front and back of the bus. Bus tickets are valid for about an hour (it depends on the city) from the moment you validate them.

## Extra-Urban Buses

Most towns can be reached by train or by bus. Other towns (hill towns, for example) can be reached only by bus (trains can't climb the high paths). These busses are called extra-urban busses, and they usually leave from the train station or a block or two away. Extra-urban busses from Florence, for example, leave from the station just two minutes away from Santa Maria Novella (stand with your back to Santa Maria Novella, turn right, and walk along the street until you see the busses).

# Eating and Drinking in Tuscany

Food is one of the greatest perks Italy has to offer: from pasta and pizza to gelato, everything is tasty. Italian food served outside of Italy can be quite different from the original version. Italian restaurants in the USA, for example, tend to prepare heavier, creamier versions of the traditional Italian food, so it might take a few tries to get used to the new flavours.

The three main meals are colazione, pranzo, and cena. Colazione (breakfast) is usually eaten at the bar (a bar in Italy isn't a place that serves alcohol but a place that serves coffee and snacks in the morning). Italian breakfast is very limited (which is often a big surprise for guests expecting a large breakfast at their B&B). Some B&Bs got the message and started serving more European or American breakfasts; others stick to the traditional cappuccino, brioche, and marmalade plan. Pranzo (lunch) is usually served between 12:30-14:30. You will find very few (if any) restaurants that serve lunch later than 14:30. Cena (dinner) is served between 19:30-21:30. Most places (unless they are a pizzeria) won't sit you at a table after 21:30-22:00.

## What should we order?

**In the morning:** If you ask for "un caffe", you'll get an espresso. Alternatively, ask for a cappuccino, or a caffe latte (which is closer to the Starbucks version of coffee, with a lot of milk), or a macchiato (an espresso with a touch of milk foam). Our personal recommendation for the hot summer months is to ask for a "shakerato" (cold coffee, shaken with ice cubes. If you want it sweetened, ask for: "con zucchero"). Accompany that with a brioche or croissant; there are plenty to choose from, and they are all on display near the counter. If you eat standing up by the bar, as most Italians do, you will be charged less than if you sit down at the table and order.

**Lunch/dinnertime:** Traditionally, a meal consists of an antipasto (a selection of meats and cheeses and little bites that will awaken your appetite), a primo (first dish, usually pasta or soup), a secondo (main dish, usually meat or fish), a contorno (side dish, usually vegetables or French fries), a dolce (dessert), and coffee (only caffe, never order a cappuccino after lunch or dinner). This is followed occasionally, at dinnertime, by an ammazzacaffe (a liquor, like limoncello, to help you digest). Clearly, you won't be able to order this much food every time you sit down to eat. What most Italians do is choose either a primo or a secondo and add to that something small—an antipasto (which can be shared), a contorno, or maybe just dessert.

**What to order?** If you are anything like us (curious foodies), you'll want to try everything Tuscany has to offer. Pasta is the obvious choice—best if it's homemade and served with a traditional sauce. There are so many sauce options it would be impossible to list them all here, but trust your instincts and read the menu to find out what the ingredients are. Most restaurants will offer a menu in English too. Be brave; don't be afraid to try things like gnocchi, pasta with truffle sauce (delicious), or pappardelle (flat, wide pasta, usually served with ragu).

If you love meat, Tuscany is the place for you. The most famous steak in the region is the "Fiorentina", a huge ordeal, priced by weight and served bloody (seared on the outside, raw on the inside). If you like your meat well done, or even medium, this is not the dish for you. Other local favourites are anything with cinghiale (boar), tagliata (sliced steak, usually served with parmesan or mushrooms), and trippa (a cow's stomach). Tuscans aren't shy about eating internal parts; their most famous sandwich is called "Lampredotto" and is made with different parts of a cow's stomach. They say it's tasty. We prefer taking their word for it.

If you are vegetarian, avoid most soups, which are usually based on meat or chicken stock, and feast on pastas and pizzas. If you are not sure, just ask: "Sono vegetariano, c'e' carne o pesce?" (pronounced "sono vegettariano, che carne o peshe?"). Most hard cheeses are produced with caglio (rennet, produced from cows), and you should avoid anything containing "strutto" and "lardo" (both mean lard). It might seem strange, but strutto is sometimes found in breads, focaccias, and pastries.

Kids tend to love lasagne and cannelloni. They might also enjoy two of our personal favourite traditional Tuscan dishes: papa al pomodoro (a mushy and delicious tomato stew) or ribollita (a vegetable and bread soup/stew. It tastes much better than it sounds. The best one in Tuscany is served in Trattoria Marione, in Florence, by the way (the rest of the dishes aren't that exciting. We come just for the ribollita). Side dishes are also a safe bet with kids; go for the pattatine fritte (French fries) to keep everyone happy. If you want a plain plate of pasta for fussy toddlers, ask for "pasta bianca, senza condimenti, per favore" (pronounced as it is written). If you want to ask for a plate of pasta with simple tomato sauce, ask for "pasta con salsa di pomodoro, senza altri condimenti, per favore".

If you are looking for a lighter lunch, try a sandwich from a bar or a Panini shop, a slice of pizza, or even a doner kebab (a relatively new concept in Italy, brought in with immigrants from the Middle East; this is basically pita bread filled with meat, salad, and some sauce).

> **Tip:** Choose pizzerias that advertise themselves with the magic words "forno a legna" (real wood-burning stove). Avoid restaurants that are too close to monuments (difficult in Florence, where it's hard to find anything which isn't close to something or another), or those that have menus with photos in them. Avoid restaurants with waiters standing outside trying to convince you to come in, restaurants with no one in them, restaurants with menus in six languages, and restaurants with food on the outside (like a sculpture of a man holding an actual pizza, for example). After a while, you will develop a sort of sixth sense and know which restaurants promise an excellent culinary experience and which ones should be avoided.

## Tipping

Restaurants in Italy charge what is called "coperto", which means a fixed fee for "opening the table". Contrary to what many tourists believe, it has nothing to do with how much bread you eat or whether you ask for water or not. Water is charged separately. You may wish to leave a 10% tip at the end of a dinner, if you were pleased with the service, but you don't have to. A 20% tip is considered very generous. Tipping in taxis, hotels, etc. is absolutely up to you; it will be appreciated, but it isn't considered a huge faux pas if you don't do it. The one case in which tipping may be a good idea is when someone goes out of their way to help you, in which case a tip is the best way to show your appreciation.

## Booking in Advance

If there is a specific restaurant you want to try out, we highly recommend booking in advance. During the summer months restaurants in towns like Florence, Siena, and San Gimignano are always full.

# Sleeping in Tuscany

One of the most difficult choices for a tourist is picking a place to sleep. There are thousands of hotels, beds-and-breakfasts (B&Bs), agriturismi and resorts in Tuscany. Most of the recommendations in this book are for B&Bs and agriturismi (which is a B&B with a farm or an active agricultural business attached, like a vineyard or an olive grove). This is because we feel that these small, family-run establishments represent the spirit of Tuscany and give you a better feel of the Italian lifestyle and charm. If you are not interested in charm but in air conditioning, elevators, and an attentive reception desk, then these probably aren't for you, and you'd better choose a hotel.

## A few useful tips when choosing a place to sleep:

- Hostels, budget hotels, and 1- or 2-star hotels are a great option for saving some cash, but they almost never have A/C, are often located in buildings without elevators, and won't have many (or any) amenities in the room. The really cheap ones may not even have a private toilet and bathroom in the room, though that is quite rare (except in hostels, where it's common).

- Check out the hotel's/B&B's website to get a feel of the place. One photo is better than one hundred words.

- Note that European family rooms are smaller than American rooms. If you are travelling with one toddler, a standard family room will be enough. If you are travelling with more than one child, you will probably need two rooms.

- If renting an apartment, ask what the price includes to avoid unpleasant surprises. Is there a minimum number of nights? Is it possible to get a crib for the baby? Does the price of the room include ALL cleaning charges? Will you be charged separately for electricity, gas, or heating? Does the price include a weekly change of linen and use of the laundry room and Wi-Fi (it usually does)? Does the price include parking? Is the apartment furnished? Will you find soap, kitchen tools, and other necessities to cook a family meal? Are there any additional expenses or bills? What activities are available? A pool and some sort of playing area are standard, but some B&Bs and agriturismi offer cooking classes, riding lessons, playgrounds, organized hikes, bikes for rent, and more.

- There are advantages and disadvantages to every choice. The main disadvantage of agriturismi and out-of-town B&Bs are that they are often located in little villages in the countryside or on a farm in the middle of nowhere. This means they may be more challenging to find, and you'll have to drive for 15 minutes (or so) every time you need something from the store or want to go into town (for dinner, for example).

- If there's a specific B&B or agriturismo you are interested in and have heard a lot about, book well in advance, as the good places tend to fill up rather quickly. That said, don't be quick to dismiss the less famous B&B. There are dozens of excellent options, and they are often cheaper and less crowded.

Another thing to take into consideration—especially if you plan on choosing one or two places to stay and taking day trips from these "home bases"—is how accessible your lodging is and whether it's sufficiently close to main roads. Finding a remote little farm can be fun for the first couple of nights, but later on you may discover it isn't very comfortable to travel to and from on a daily basis. Our recommendation for those who plan on making day trips from one or two central lodging locations is to avoid apartments and B&Bs located deep in rural areas, such as the heart of the Chianti region (Radda in Chianti, Gaiole in Chianti, etc.), the heart of the Val d'Orcia (Pienza, Montalcino, etc.), and the Maremma area. Instead, choose an easily accessible location relatively close to a main road. This, of course, isn't necessary if you plan on touring an area and spending just a night or two there before moving on to the next town.

## Finding an Apartment

Renting an apartment is a popular choice for families. There are a number of websites that will help you find the right apartment.

www.tuscanyaccommodation.com

www.ownersdirect.co.uk/

www.bbplanet.com

www.tuscanyfinerentals.com

www.casevacanza.it

www.friendlyrentals.com

www.waytostay.com

www.gowithoh.com/vacation-florence-apartments/

## Should we pick one place and sleep there for the entire time we are in Tuscany?

It all depends on the places you plan to visit. If you are planning on touring just one area of Tuscany for example, spending your entire time in Florence or at the beach, then yes, renting an apartment for the entire week makes perfect sense. However, if you plan on touring various areas of Tuscany, sleeping in just one place means several hours of driving each day, often on narrow winding country roads, which can be stressful both for the driver and the kids in the back seat. We suggest that for a seven to eight day vacation, you pick a minimum of two focal points to sleep in, depending on the areas you intend to visit. If, for example, you plan on seeing Florence (days 1 and 2), Pisa and Lucca (day 3), San Gimignano and Monteriggioni (day 4), Siena (day 5), Montepulciano and Chiusi (day 6), and the Etruscan Beach (day 7), you can sleep in Florence the first two nights and south of Siena for the rest of your trip.

# Travelling with Kids

There is much to say about travelling with kids, and some books are dedicated entirely to this subject. We'd like to offer a few general tips we've found helpful.

## Slow down
When travelling with children, time must be a flexible concept. You want to see as much as you can, but everything takes longer with kids (especially younger ones). Unless you plan on becoming the family sergeant and rushing everyone along all day, accept that you won't be able to see every single thing there is to see in Tuscany. Focus on fewer attractions and really enjoy the ride. If there's anything we can learn from the Italians, it's the charm of taking things slowly. Decide on a reasonable number of sights and attractions (no more than three a day, for the most part). We promise you will still have a great time and won't feel like you are missing out on anything, and the added bonus is that getting from place to place will be a fun adventure, not a hysterical race against the clock.

## Enjoy the fact that you are together and that you are on vacation
It seems so obvious, but sometimes we forget that the best vacation memories aren't of the exact view you saw from the tower in Siena, or the artwork in room number 5 in the Uffizi Museum. The best memories are more personal, like the time Dad dropped his ice cream on that little boy's head, when a pigeon attacked Mom, or when someone's shoe was eaten by a goat at the farm. In other words, this vacation is also your chance to just enjoy your family.

## Combine serious activities, like museums, with fun activities
Balance your days by combining sightseeing with fun activities your kids will enjoy, like trekking, bike riding, going to the beach, horseback riding, or visiting an amusement park. If you spend the morning touring Siena, spend the afternoon doing something more active, like a cooking lesson or touring the park. After visiting the Uffizi Museum in Florence, don't rush off to see another museum. Instead, do something fun, like climbing up the Duomo's dome, running around the Boboli Gardens, or even going to the pool in the Cascine Park. Stop for lunch and ice cream, and then squeeze in one more sight you want to see.

## Get kids of all ages (from toddlers to teens) involved
Encourage your children to read more about Tuscany, mark places they are going

to see on the map, and figure out how far they are about to travel. Have them read about the sights online, or at least look at online pictures, and decide if there are any special places that THEY are interested in seeing (and then insert these places into your itinerary). Encourage them to learn a few words in Italian, using one of the free basic online courses (Google "learn Italian") or watch an Italian film together (like *Cinema Paradiso* or, if they are older, *La Vita e' Bella*).

## Set aside a budget for buying knick-knacks
What may seem like useless rubbish to adults may mean a great deal to a seven-year-old boy or girl, who loves to fill pockets with "treasures". For the price of just one dinner at a restaurant (about 25-35 euro), you can budget an entire week of knick-knack shopping, including the little prizes kids get for completing the missions in this guide.

## Give kids some economic freedom
Give your kids a few daily euro to budget their own purchases. Younger children adore having "a lot of money" (i.e., lots of coins in their very own purse; lots of ten-cent coins are much better than just one 1-euro coin, of course...). Older kids love the sense of independence and maturity that comes from having their own money.

## Encourage kids to communicate
Most Italians love kids, and they can't get enough of sweet kids trying to speak Italian. Most children will enjoy the attention and affection they will receive if they try to be communicative and friendly. This is another good reason to have them learn, in advance, how to say a few basic Italian words and phrases, like "Hello", "Thank you", "Excuse me", "Good-bye", "Where is...?", "How much does it cost?", "My name is...", "I am X years old" etc.

## Get your child a cheap camera
Whether you get a disposable or digital camera, there are several inexpensive options on the market. Disposable cameras are cheaper but developing the film instead of downloading the photos will probably end up costing more than the camera itself. A child with his own camera (assuming he is interested in taking his own photos) will feel more independent and be more interested in his surroundings. Yes, it might slow you down sometimes, especially when he wants to take yet another photo of that tower (which won't be that different from the 50 photos that came before it), but it's worth it. Your child's photos can also be used to update the family's digital travel blog (see more on that under "Travelling with

Teenagers and Older Children"). Of course, you should also carry your own camera, but once you get home, try to incorporate a few of the photos your child shot into the family album. He will be very proud.

### Use games to combat boredom while standing in line

Ten out of ten scientists will tell you that kids don't like standing in line. You will find tips on how to avoid the lines in the itineraries themselves, especially in Florence, Siena, and Pisa, but when you do find yourself stuck in a line, use that time to master activities that don't require moving. For example, before leaving for your trip, watch YouTube videos that demonstrate yo-yo tricks. Then, while standing in line, pull out a yo-yo and let the kids practice the tricks. Do the same with magic tricks that don't require much moving. Braid your child's hair in Renaissance style (see the Florence Itinerary for the technique) or, if you are brave, do some face painting for the toddlers. All you need are a few colourful eye pencils, a few eye shadows, and some lipstick. Cleansing wipes clean it all off once it's your turn to go inside. Play games like "I Spy" or "Guess What Famous Person I Am Thinking Of (21 questions; yes or no only)". Ask, "What would you do if ..." and insert some funny or gross hypothetical questions. Our personal favourite is "What's worse?" questions like "What's worse: falling into a swamp or eating a bug?" or "What's cuter: a puppy or a baby Koala?" If you don't mind people staring, you can create a massage chain (Dad massages Mom, who massages one of the kids, etc.) or play a game of "Guess that Word" (Dad writes a word on Mom's back with his finger, Mom writes the same word on the first child's back, who in turn writes it on the second child's back, etc.). You can also carry games around to pass the time, anything from PSP to Etch-a-Sketch. Soap bubbles are another popular activity for toddlers. Encourage your kids to make friendship bracelets, take pictures of their surroundings with their cameras, or check out how far away they can see with their binoculars.

## Travelling with Teenagers and Older Children

For a 15-year-old teenager, being "stuck" with his/her parents and little brothers or sisters for a week in a foreign land, away from his/her friends, and with no privacy, may be a difficult concept to digest, no matter how wonderful the vacation. Try to offer things teenagers can enjoy and later brag about to their friends. For example, take your teenage daughter to a great spa with thermal waters. You don't even have to book a massage; you can just use the thermal pools. A massage or a beauty treatment would be a huge bonus, though. Italians have been keeping themselves pretty for thousands of years thanks to these springs. If you are looking for a place, we recommend the Petriolo Spa Hotel, an hour from Siena (www.atahotels.it/petriolo) or Giusti Spa, in Monsummano Terme, about 50 minutes from Florence (www.grottagiustispa.com), but there are several other options as well. Add activities such as late night strolls along the river, open air concerts, dinner in a jazz club, horseback rides, quad tours and cooking classes, to keep everyone happy. You will find several suggestions and ideas throught this guide.

If you have younger kids, you can try to divide and conquer. Dad can take the younger kids to an adventure or amusement park near Pisa (there are a few to choose from), while the older girls can have some alone time. This idea works for older boys, too. A teenage son might enjoy a soccer match so, while Dad takes him there, Mom can take the younger kids to an amusement park.

While younger kids are (relatively) easy to please with adventure parks and swimming pools, teenagers are a tougher crowd and might be more receptive to "adult-style" activities. Allow them time to do the activities that they love, like shopping or visiting museums they find interesting. Try the popular leather market in Florence or even outlet shopping malls such as 'The Mall' and 'Barberino del Mugello'. Both outlets are situated about 30 minutes north of Florence. Find out more here: www.mcarthurglen.com/it/barberino-designer-outlet/it and here: www.themall.it. If they are responsible, consider letting older teenagers venture on their own for a few hours (especially if they have a cell phone with them). Florence is a safe city (except for pickpockets), and the "alone time" will be much appreciated.

Give your teenagers (and pre-teen) some responsibilities. Put them in charge of the family travel blog, appoint them as official camera operators, or encourage them to learn some Italian before the trip and be the official "save-the-day translator" for the whole family. Not all teenagers may love this additional responsibility, though. Carefully consider your teenager's personality, and if this will make him/her feel stressed or ruin his/her vacation, don't do it.

Technology is a huge part of the average teenager's life. Use that to your advantage. Get teenagers to download travel apps to their smartphones that will help you during the trip (most of them are free). Here is a partial list of apps and the ways your teenager can use them to make your trip successful (you can find more by Googling "cool travel apps", "travel apps kids", and "Italy apps").

1. Encourage teenagers to take photos of their surroundings and post them on photo sharing websites such as Flickr, Instagram, Tumblr or even Pinterest. They might just disocver they have a natural talent

and will draw the attention of new fans. If they are looking for apps to make the most of their phone/android cameras, 26 Camera+ is an app worth considering. We also recommend Camera Awesome, by smugmugg, and  Camera FV-5.

2. Instead of fighting and having to nag your teenagers about packing, get them to manage their own packing with an app, like **Triplist**. This app is also very useful for building the entire itinerary.

3. Appoint your teenagers Head Navigators, using apps like **Google Maps**, **Waze** (our personal favourite), **Maps2Go**, or offline map services like **Sygic** (the most popular offline GPS app), **MapFactor**, **Route 66 maps + Navigation** and the useful **MapsWithMe**. This is not only a good way to get them involved and responsible, it's also the easiest way to plan your itinerary and not get lost in town. Many teenagers and even pre-teens turn out to be quite savvy and re-sourceful when it's up to them to decide where to go and how to get there, instead of being led passively from one point to the other.

4. Ask your teenagers and pre-teens to search for extra information on the places you plan on visiting, using anything from Wikipedia to apps like **Triposo** (which works offline, too).

5. In their capacity as Official Translators, ask kids and teenagers to help with translating menus or instructions using **Google Translator**.

6. Check for hotels and reviews with the very popular **TripAdvisor** app, **Hotels.com**, **Booking.com**, and **Trivago**.

7. Learn some basic useful phrases with the popular **Tourist: Language Learn & Speak** app.

8. Ask your teenager to download a currency convertor and appoint them as the Official Treasurer of the family, helping you figure out what is and isn't a good deal and how much things really cost.

9. Have your teenager download audiobooks, Italian music, and cooking apps to help you all get into the Italian vibe. Maybe even consider cooking a real Italian dinner in your rented apartment, with groceries

you pick up in the market or supermarket.

## Travelling with Toddlers and Younger Children

It is easy to get toddlers excited about your trip, because just about everything will be new to them: the airplane and trains (both major hits among the toddler community), the tall buildings and the motorcycles everywhere, the pizza and the castles. Show them pictures of what they are about to see to prepare them and create anticipation.

When choosing where you want to visit, try to avoid villages that are full of stairs, as well as very steep towns (some hill towns have steep alleys that toddlers will have a difficult time walking up). Avoid places like Arezzo, Cortona, and even Montepulciano; stick to places like San Gimignano, Volterra, Siena, and Florence.

Add several breaks to your itinerary, especially in Florence (you will find a special box about gardens and playgrounds in the Florence Itinerary). If you are looking for toddler-suitable activities, check out the Pisa and Lucca Itinerary and the Populonia and the Etruscan Beach Itinerary, where you will find several suggestions (always under "Special Activities in the Area", at the end of the itinerary).

Make sure you pack plenty of surprises, such as travel size board games, portable DVD players and/or tablets with games and books on them, stickers, cooring pages, activity books and crayons. Binoculars, walkie talkies, and a loved toy from back home are always useful options.

**Tip:** Looking for the perfect book to read with your kids during your vacation? Try our popular Riddle Books! **The Great Book of Animal Riddles** is specifically designed to intrigue young readers with fun new facts and beautiful photographs of wild animals. Find out who is stronger: a grizzly bear or a tiger; whether some turtles really breathe through their behinds; which animal is even faster than the cheetah; how ants communicate with each other; and whether koalas really have fingerprints. Visit us at www.bankierbooks.com to find out more, and to receive a **free** gift for every purchase!

# How to Build a Trip
## Using the Suggested Itineraries

Here are a few examples of trips you could build based on the itineraries in this guide.

## Option 1

**Family of four:** two children, ages 6 and 10.
**Looking for:** some nature, a little bit of art, a couple of children's activities, and some low-key, relaxing fun.
**Duration:** Family has one week in Tuscany. They have never been there before.
**Sleeping:** The family will choose two or three focal points and then rent an apartment or book a room in a B&B or an agriturismo for each.
The first half of the vacation will be spent in central-northern Tuscany: Pisa, Lucca, and Florence.
The second half of the vacation will be in southern Tuscany: Siena, Montepulciano, Chiusi, and Maremma.

| Days | Itinerary |
|------|-----------|
| Day 1 | Florence; sleep in Florence. |
| Day 2 | Florence in the morning, family activity in the afternoon (adventure park, cooking class, or ice cream tour); sleep in Florence. |
| Day 3 | Pisa (the Leaning Tower) and Lucca (ride a bike on the ramparts; possibly an adventure park suggested in the Pisa Itinerary); sleep in San Gimignano. |
| Day 4 | San Gimignano or Volterra and Monteriggioni; sleep in San Gimignano or south of Siena. |

| Day 5 | Siena in the morning, spend the afternoon either in Siena or out of town (see Siena itinerary for ideas); sleep south of Siena. |
| Day 6 | Montepulciano and Chiusi (touring Etruscan secret paths); sleep south of Siena. |
| Day 7 | The Etruscan Beach (Populonia Archaeological Park or Follonica Water Park) or a hike/canoe tour of the Natural Reserve in the Maremma. |

# Option 2

**Family of four:** two children, ages 12 and 15.
**Looking for:** a few visits to hill towns and the main cities in the region, art, good food and wine.
**Duration:** Family has eight full days in Tuscany. They have never been there before.
**Sleeping:** The family will choose three focal points and book a room in a B&B or an agriturismo for each.
The first half of the vacation will be spent in Florence and the Chianti area (central Tuscany). The second half of the vacation will be in southern Tuscany: Siena, Montepulciano, Chiusi, and Maremma.

| Days | Itinerary |
|------|-----------|
| Day 1 | Florence (including a Segway tour of the historical centre); sleep in Florence. |
| Day 2 | Pisa (the Leaning Tower) and Lucca (relaxing, possibly even a bike ride along the ramparts); sleep in Florence. |
| Day 3 | Florence, possibly include a half-day cooking class and night tour of the city; sleep in Florence or Chianti area. |
| Day 4 | Tour of the Chianti area and a horseback riding trip; sleep in San Gimignano or Chianti area. |

| Day 5 | San Gimignano and Volterra; sleep in San Gimignano or Volterra. |
| Day 7 | Siena, afternoon in Monte Olivetto Maggiore (including the Gregorian chants); sleep around Val d'Orcia. |
| Day 8 | Val d'Orcia, including cheese tasting in Pienza. Alternatively, tour the Maremma area, focusing on Saturnia Terme, Pitigliano and Sorano. |

# Option 3

**Family of 4:** two children, ages 3 and 6.
**Looking for:** nature and a few basic museums and attractions suitable for younger children.
**Duration:** Family has six days in Tuscany. They have never been there before.
**Sleeping:** Family will choose three focal points and rent an apartment or book a room in a B&B or an agriturismo for each.
The first half of the vacation will be spent in central-northern Tuscany: Pisa, Lucca, and Florence. The second half of the vacation will be in southern Tuscany: the Etruscan Beach and the Maremma.

| Day | Itinerary |
|---|---|
| Day 1 | Pisa (Leaning Tower) and one of the adventure parks in the area (the Livorno Acquarium, for example, or Parco Pitagora); sleep in Florence. |
| Day 2 | Florence (mostly walking around the historical centre, no more than one museum, spending the afternoon at the Boboli Gardens); sleep in Florence. |
| Day 3 | San Gimignano (optional pony ride), or Volterra and Peccioli Prehistoric Park; sleep in San Gimignano or near Volterra. |

| Day 4 | Etruscan Beach and Cavallino Matto Adventure Park, or the Etruscan Beach and the Mines Museum and tour; sleep near the beach, bordering with the Maremma. |
| Day 5 | Maremma, including Capalbio Park (drive south via the Val d'Orcia, so you can at least enjoy the view even if you don't make a stop); sleep in the same place. |
| Day 6 | Maremma, including the Natural Reserve; sleep in the same place. |

# Option 4

**Family of 4:** two children, ages 10 and 12.
**Looking for:** nature, action, just a little bit of art and small charming towns, no museums (unless they are very special), no more than two churches, and only if they are impressive.
**Duration:** Family has eight days in Tuscany. They have never been there before.
**Sleeping:** Family will choose three focal points and rent an apartment or book a room in a B&B or an agriturismo for each.
The first half of the vacation will be spent in central-northern Tuscany: Pisa, Lucca, Florence, and the Garfagnana area. The second half of the vacation will be in southern Tuscany: Siena, Montepulciano, Chiusi, and Maremma.

| Day | Itinerary |
| --- | --- |
| Day 1 | Florence; sleep in Florence. |
| Day 2 | Pisa and Lucca, including the leaning tower and the bike ride along the ramparts; drive north and sleep in Bagni di Lucca. |
| Day 3 | Garfagnana tour, including the quarry and the Fosdinovo Adventure Park or Campocecina; sleep in Bagni di Lucca. |
| Day 4 | Garfagnana, including the Grotta del Vento and/or Orrido dei Botri; sleep in Bagni di Lucca. |

| Day 3 | Florence (possibly including a cooking class); sleep in Florence. |
| Day 4 | San Gimignano and Siena; sleep south of Siena. |
| Day 5 | Chiusi, and the Etruscans tombs; sleep near the Maremma. |
| Day 6 | Saturnia, Pitigliano, possibly a horse ride or an adventure park; sleep near Maremma. |
| Day 7 | Canoe tour of the Maremma Natural Park in the morning, Capalbio Park in the afternoon; sleep in the Maremma. |
| Day 8 | A relaxed day in Val d'Orcia, including Montalcino Fort, some cheese tasting in Pienza, and a dip at the fantastic thermal baths of San Filippo. |

# Option 5

**Family of 4:** two teenagers, ages 16 and 17.
**Looking for:** the most important sights, relatively interested in art but want some action and nature, too.
**Duration:** Family has eight days in Tuscany. They have never been there before.
**Sleeping:** Family will choose three or four focal points and book a room in a B&B or an agriturismo for each.
The first half of the vacation will be spent in central Tuscany: Pisa, Lucca, and Florence. The second half of the vacation will be in southern Tuscany: Siena, Val d'Orcia, and the Maremma.

| Day | Itinerary |
| --- | --- |
| Day 1 | Florence (including the major museums and churches, like the Uffizi, Santa Croce, the Accademia etc.); sleep in Florence. |
| Day 2 | Florence; sleep in Florence. |
| Day 3 | Pisa and Lucca; sleep in Lucca. |

| Day 4 | Chianti and a cooking class or horseback riding; sleep in the area around Radda in Chianti. |
|-------|---------------------------------------------------------------------------------------------|
| Day 5 | San Gimignano and Volterra; sleep near San Gimignano. |
| Day 6 | Siena, possibly include an outdoor activity in the afternoon; sleep south of Siena. |
| Day 7 | Val d'Orcia; sleep south of Siena. |
| Day 8 | Maremma, including Saturnia Terme and Pitigliano. |

# Map of Tuscany

# FLORENCE

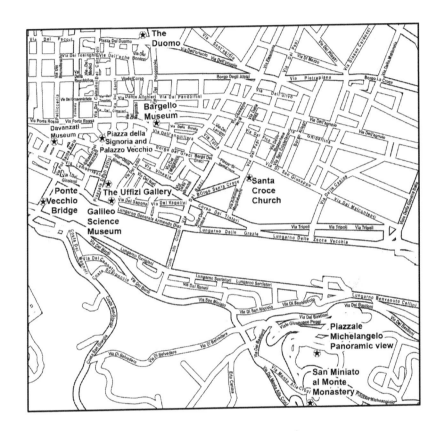

# Chapter 1

# Florence

What more can be said about Florence, a city about which so much has been written? Its beauty, fame, and vitality have been described for centuries in numerous books, films and poems. As the heart of Renaissance culture and a virtual living museum, Florence manages to enchant visitors even if they don't step inside a single monument. Travelling to Florence with kids can be a challenge—the city is so crammed with sights that it can be tiring and overwhelming, and in many cases kids are simply too young to appreciate the art and history around them, but it is far from impossible. If planned correctly, Florence can actually be a unique experience for the whole family.

The itinerary dedicated to Florence is the longest in this book, not only because there is so much to see and do, but also because we have added several missions, activities, and "Kids' Corners" that will help make this remarkable city more accessible to younger visitors.

Unlike subsequent itineraries, the Florence Itinerary isn't organized in any particular order. There are simply too many possibilities, and deciding which ones to pursue depends upon your family's tastes and interests. Instead, you will find detailed descriptions of the many attractions Florence has to offer (including a special section on the most kid-friendly museums), as well as tips and advice on how to combine them and make the most of your stay. We also recommend consulting the "Top 10 Activities in Florence" and "Planning Your Visit to Florence with Kids" sections in this chapter, to help you make the most informed decision. And since Florence houses one of the best-known museums in the world (the Uffizi), we have also included three additional mini-guides: "Uffizi's Insider's Guide" and "How Medieval and Renaissance Artists Worked—A look Behind the Scenes" (for adults) filled with information about the museum's best-known paintings, and "The Ultimate Guide for Art Detectives" (for kids), designed to help younger visitors understand the paintings around them through stories and anecdotes. All three can be found at the end of this chapter.

# Top 10 Family Activities

1. Climb up to the Duomo's dome to get a unique view of the city.

2. Be impressed with the artwork in one of the world's most famous museums—the Uffizi.

3. Hike or take the bus up to Piazzale Michelangelo to enjoy an incredible panoramic view of the city.

4. Say hello to David, one of the most famous sculptures in the world, in Galleria dell'Accademia.

5. Hunt for fashionable souvenirs in the leather market by Piazza San Lorenzo.

6. Walk along the Ponte Vecchio during sunset.

7. Run around and discover hidden corners of the Boboli Gardens.

8. Learn all about Galileo Galilei's scientific discoveries in the Galilei Science Museum.

9. Go back in time and discover what a typical Renaissance house looked like in the Davanzati Museum.

10. Tour the impressive armour and ancient sword collection in the Stibbert Museum.

# Florence

## GETTING THERE

**BY CAR:** From Rome, take either the A1 or the SS1 (depending on traffic, this will take three to four hours). From Milano, take the A1. From Venice, take the A13 and then connect to the A1. From Pisa, take the SGC (also known as the Fi-Pi-Li) or the A11. You can park in Florence, as long as you don't enter or park in the city's historical centre, which is almost completely ZTL.

**PARKING IN FLORENCE:** if you do arrive to Florence with a car, you will have to find a place to park it. Unlike other cities, we do not recommend parking on the street in Florence. Not only becuase of the ZTL problem, but also because every area has specfic cleaning days and other restrictions, and there's a chance your car will be towed. The simplest solution is to find either a garage, or a parking lot, and leave your car there. Garages are a popular choice. A number of garages in town have agreements with the city, which allow clients to enter the ZTL area in order to park in their garage. That means that you can, for example, book IN ADVANCE a parking space in a garage such as the Grande Ponte Vecchio (www.gragepontevecchio.it), the firparking garage (www.firpark.com), and Florence Parking (www.florenceparking.it). All of these garages ofer the same service: they will insert your license plate data into their list, enabling you to enter and exit the ZTL area on that specific day (read the specific regulations on their website). Parking isn't cheap - expect to pay more than 20 euro per day - but then again, train tickets aren't that cheap, either...

Alternatively, you can book a spot at the Santa Maria Novella parking lot. This is a huge facilty, situated just minutes from the Duomo. It is very conveniently located, but it does not offer the special ZTL offer, so be careful when you enter it. Slightly farther away from the center, but still within walking distance, is Parcheggio fortezza Fiera, which is located near the Fortezza di Basso. This large lot is just 10 minutes from the main train station, it is easily accessible (Piazzale Montelungo, Tel: 055.5030.2209). Pacheggio Sant'Ambrogio is another valid option, situated just 15 minutes from the Duomo (Piazza Lorenzo Ghiberti, Tel: 055.5030.2209). Parcheggio Oltrarno (10 minutes from Pitti palace and the Ponte Vecchio), Piazza della Calza, Tel: 055.5030.2209;

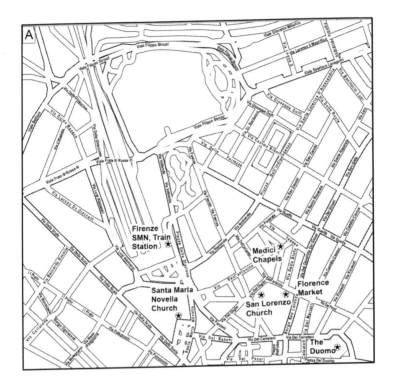

**BY TRAIN:** The easiest way to get to Florence is by train (get off at the central train station, called Santa Maria Novella station, or SMN). With a train, you don't have to worry about parking or driving onto a ZTL street and getting fined. Since the train station is just 10 minutes away from the Duomo, and there are several connections a day from Rome, Pisa, Milano, Venice, Siena, and more, a train is your best option.

**Tip:** Florence's main train station is quite useful: you will find a 24-hour pharmacy near the left exit of the station (in front of the McDonald's) and a number of cheap dining options (we recommend the pizza at the RossoSapore stand, inside the food court). Near Track 16, there is a luggage storage room that is open daily from 06:00-23:30 (hours may vary, double check before leaving your bags), perfect if you plan on staying in Florence for just a few hours and want to tour the city without schlepping heavy bags. (Note: even if you don't mind carrying your bags, many museums won't let you in with bags larger than a backpack, and most museums in Florence don't have proper cloakrooms).

**TOURIST INFORMATION OFFICES:** The main office is across the street from the SMN station 🕐 (open Monday-Saturday, 08:30-19:00; Sundays and holidays, 08:30-14:00; Tel: 055.212245). A secondary office is located near the Duomo, at Via Cavour 1r (open Monday-Saturday, 08:30-18:30; Sundays and holidays, 08:30-13:30; Tel: 055.290832). It's a good idea to stop by one of the offices to get a map of the sights for easy navigation, just in case your hotel doesn't provide you with one, as well as an updated opening times sheet for all the museums and attractions.

## GETTING AROUND IN FLORENCE

Florence's historical centre is small and almost everything is within walking distance.

From SMN to the Duomo: about 10 minutes
From the Duomo to the Uffizi: another 10 minutes
From the Duomo to San Marco and the Accademia: about 15 minutes

Piazzale Michelangelo and the Stibbert Museum are farther away; a taxi or a bus is the best option. From the SMN to Piazzale Michelangelo, take bus number 12; from the SMN to the Stibbert Museum, take bus number 4.

# Technical Things You Should Know Before You Leave

## PICKPOCKETS

- With nearly five million tourists visiting Florence every year, it's not diffi- cult to figure out why pickpockets are a problem in Florence. A few basic precautions will help ensure your safety.
- Never put your purse or wallet in your pocket, and never put it in an outer pocket of your backpack where it can be easily pulled out without you even noticing (the thieves of Florence can teach the Oliver Twist crew a trick or two, we promise you that).
- If your hotel has a reliable safe, leave your money there (but not your documents—you will need some sort of documentation on you through- out the trip).
- Hide a 50 euro bill in an unlikely place, so that even if you are targeted you will at least have enough money to get back to your hotel and call home (or the embassy, if your documents were stolen).
- Don't put your passports and your money in the same wallet. Thieves don't care about your documents. They will throw them out and keep the money, but it will be a terrible mess for you. Hide your important documents, cred- it cards, and travellers' cheques deep inside your bag, and use a smaller wallet with cash handy for your daily spending.
- Prepare in advance a list of numbers you'll need to call should your wallet be stolen. For obvious reasons, don't keep the list of numbers in your wallet. If you have been robbed, cancel your credit cards immediately and file a complaint at the police station. There's a police post at the SMN station, in front of McDonald's.
- Make a photocopy of all of your documents and store them in a safe place (such as your suitcase). If you want to be even safer, scan all of your docu- ments and send the file to yourself via email. That way you can always have access to a copy of your documentation.

A final word of warning: the Santa Maria Novella station and its surrounding area, the Duomo Piazza, and bus number 7 (going to Fiesole) are favourite spots for thieves, mostly because these are such crowded places that hardly anyone sees them coming.

# Opening Times and Days in Florence

Florence can be a bit of a nightmare when it comes to opening hours. All hours indicated in this itinerary were accurate at the time of publication, but to be on the safe side, pick up an updated sheet of hours for the town's churches and museums at the tourist office (across the street from the train station) when you

arrive. Watch out for museums like San Marco and the Medici Chapels, which have particularly strange hours. Check the list you get at the tourist office for attractions that may close early on the day of your arrival and start with those, so you won't arrive too late and find yourself standing in front of closed doors. You should also note that even though Stibbert Museum is open all day, tours only leave once an hour (and self-led tours are not allowed). Many Florence attractions are closed on Mondays (as are most museums in Italy), so plan to dedicate Mondays to outside activities. The best days to visit Florence are Wednesdays, Thursdays, and Fridays, when almost everything is open.

# Combination Tickets and
# Making Advance Reservations

The most comprehensive combination card for exploring Florence is the **Firenze card**, which costs 72 euro and is valid for 72 hours. The card includes free entry to almost every museum in Florence—without having to make reservations or stand in line—as well as access to free public transportation and free Wi-Fi access. If you are an EU citizen, the Firenze card will allow your children under 18 to get in free with you. However, you should note that at most museums EU citizens under 18 don't pay for their tickets anyway (or pay a reduced admission fee). In this case, the main advantage the Firenze card offers is that you won't have to reserve tickets or pay any reservation fees (attractions often charge for reservations, even if the tickets themselves are free). With a Firenze card, you can simply walk in.

If you are not an EU citizen, your kids won't get in for free using your Firenze Card, but they will still be able to enter the **state** museums for free (with or without a Frienze Card), and the Firenze card will give you access to most of Florence's museums without standing in line and without booking in advance. Whether the card is convenient or not depends on the number of attractions you think you might be able to visit in three days' time. If you plan on visiting just the Uffizi and the Accademia, you probably don't need the card (but make advance reservations at both places to avoid extremely long lines). If you plan on also seeing the Palazzo Vecchio and the Medici Chapels during your visit, a Firenze Card starts to make sense. If you plan on visiting additional attractions as well, such as San Marco, the Science Museum, Stibbert Museum, and the Pitti Palace, then the card is an excellent idea.

The main problem with the card, other than its hefty price, is that it doesn't cover the Duomo's dome (it does, however, cover Giotto's Bell Tower and the Baptistery, which means you can climb up Giotto's tower instead of the dome and save some time and money).

**Finding a Firenze Card:** You can buy Firenze cards at the tourist information offices, located in front of the Santa Maria Novella train station (SMN); near the Duomo at Via Cavour 1; at the Uffizi Gallery (next to the ticket line, door number 2); or online at www.firenzecard.it. If you choose to buy a card online, you'll receive a voucher and then pick up an actual magnetic card at one of the offices mentioned above.

> **Tip:** Remember that most museums in Florence are closed on Mondays (and on some Sundays, too). If you plan to spend those days of the week in Florence, you'll miss out on a great deal and if you buy a Firenze Card, it will be wasted as well. Also, note that several museums don't accept credit cards. Make sure you have enough cash on you, so you don't discover too late that you've been standing in line for 45 minutes in vain.

# Do I Need to Buy Tickets for My Children?

This is a very good question, and—like so many other things in Italy—the answer is: it depends. If you are **visiting a state or publicly owned museum** (most museums and churches in Florence fall into this category), then children under six usually won't have to pay admission at all, and children under 18 are eligible for free or reduced admission. However, you should know that some (popular) attractions will still ask you to pay a reservation fee for your children (which can be ridiculously high), even if the ticket itself is free. Some places require reservation fees only when booking tickets for kids over six, and some places require reservation fees for everyone, regardless of age. **If you are visiting a private museum or church,** the admission price depends on each museum's policy. A minority of private museums do not offer discounts for kids but most will offer at least some sort of reduced admission for kids under 12. **Our advice: always ask** whether your kids are eligible for free or reduced tickets, and always ask whether you'll need to pay any fees for your children when you reserve tickets in advance.

## Florence's History in 60 Seconds

Florence was built by the Romans, who gave the city its name (which means "wealthy and prosperous"). Throughout the Middle Ages, Florence was a moderately successful town, but it was only during the Renaissance that it became so powerful and influential. Not even the black plague, which killed more than 40% of Italy's population, managed to destroy this vibrant city, and with time its influence only grew. In fact, the florin, a Florentine coin, was once accepted as the international coin for all of Europe. Florence's position as a leader in the wool industry greatly contributed to its rise to power, and its banking families—led  by the Medicis (who were the Pope's bankers)—confirmed its position. Between the 14th and 16th centuries, Florence was one of the most important cities in the world, home to Europe's greatest artists and the birthplace of the Renaissance. The modern Italian language is based on a Florentine dialect, and Florence, whose historical centre was recognized as a World Heritage Site in 1982, is still considered a must-see destination visited by millions of people every year.

# **Planning** Your Visit to Florence with Kids

More than any other city in Tuscany, Florence requires planning in advance, especially if you'll be there fewer than three days and are travelling with kids who are easily bored by "artsy stuff". This doesn't mean you have to skip Florence. Absolutely not. It simply means that world-famous sights such as the Uffizi Museum, the Accademia Museum (Galleria dell'Accademia), Santa Croce, and the Medici Chapels need to be balanced out with kid-friendly museums and attractions, such as climbing the Duomo's dome or running around the Boboli Gardens. Other possibilities for kids include climbing Palazzo Vecchio's ancient tower, exploring the Science or Stibbert Museums, and climbing up to Piazzale Michelangelo for a view of the city (all described in detail in this itinerary). Here are a few general tips and ideas that will make your planning much easier:

**Decide in advance what interests your family most.** Describe the Florence itinerary to your kids and find photos on the Internet so they can see the possible options. Decide together what your favourite places are. If kids are involved in the process of deciding where they go and what they see, they will probably be more excited and cooperative. Older kids and teenagers can read up on the places you plan to visit and become "mini-experts" who can save the day by answering questions like real professionals, especially those posed by their inquisitive younger siblings.

**Add kid-friendly attractions to your itinerary.** As we've said before, balance is everything. Though the art in the Uffizi is incredible (and this guide does its best to get kids interested, so that parents can enjoy their visit, too), kids won't necessarily be that impressed. In addition to the sights already mentioned (the Duomo's dome, Palazzo Vecchio, Boboli Gardens, and Piazzale Michelangelo), there are other places kids might enjoy.

Minor museums, such as the Davanzati museum (see page 104) or the Costume Museum in Palazzo Pitti (with a few stunning dresses that little girls and even teenagers will adore), might turn out to be favourite stops. The Stibbert Museum (filled with beautiful armour) and the Science and Natural History Museums, as well as Leonardo da Vinci's Machine Exhibition, are all great places for kids. All of these museums have websites (detailed in the itinerary) that you can check in advance to see if you (and your kids) are interested in what they have to offer.

Ideally, organize your itinerary alternating between grown-up stuff and kid-friendly activities, so everyone leaves Florence happy. A visit to the Uffizi can be followed by an hour or two in the park and ice cream, for example. If your kids are older than 12, consider taking a Segway tour to explore Florence's historical centre. If they are younger than 12, consider hopping on a double-decker tourist bus to see the sights. (This is largely unnecessary in a small city like Florence, but kids love sitting on the open deck and looking at attractions from up high—and getting a chance to rest their legs!) If you have a car, you can even leave Florence altogether, spending part of the day exploring the countryside, visiting a local adventure park (see suggestions at the end of this chapter, under "Activities in the Area") or splashing around in your hotel's pool (or even the public pool in Cascine Park, a popular choice for families in the city, detailed later in this itinerary).

**Add teenage-friendly activities to your itinerary.**
Unlike children, teenagers don't want to run around and climb on things. They do, however, want to be impressed and have a good time. Segway tours of Florence, non-alcoholic drinks at the Excelsior Hotel Restaurant (with its stunning 360° view of the city) or a night out at a jazz club along the river will help earn you points with your teens. Shopping in the leather market around San Lorenzo, cooking classes, ice cream tours, and open-air concerts (check out events and concerts in Florence at the local tourist office) may also help.

**Save time on the annoying stuff.** We all know how impatient kids can get when they have to stand in lines for hours (but let's face it: so do adults), and with millions of tourists visiting Florence every year, there are sure to be quite a few lines. Minimize your queue time by booking everything in advance (especially the Uffizi and the Accademia Museums). Otherwise, by the time you go in, everyone will be tired and crabby. Booking in advance costs more money, but it really is worth the extra cost.

**Build a relaxed schedule, with as many breaks as possible.** Don't spend the morning dashing from the Uffizi to the Ponte Vecchio to the Pitti Palace to Santa Maria del Carmine, keeping everyone on a tight, military-style schedule. It won't work. Instead, you end up with cranky, nervous kids and exasperated adults. Assume you won't be able to see more than three attractions a day if travelling with younger children, four with older kids. That way, if you do end up seeing more sights, you'll be pleasantly surprised. Don't forget to take breaks; they are hugely important. Florence can also get very hot during the summer; it is filled with tourists and can seem, at times, like a giant bowl of human soup. Taking a few moments every once in a while to sit down, have a cold drink, and relax with some ice cream in a piazza can make all the difference (this is your hard-earned vacation, after all).

## Segway Tours

Segway tours are a unique way to explore the city and make for a special family adventure. Both easy to operate and fun to use, Segways are a cool way to get around that combines modern technology with century-old sights. **Italy Segway Tours** offers three-hour tours of the most important sights in Florence, led by an English-speaking guide. The tour includes a 30-minute Segway orientation to help you get used to the technology before you start zooming down the streets. Segways aren't for people weighing less than 45 kg (about 100 pounds) or more than 113 kg (about 250 pounds). Children under 18 must be accompanied by an adult. Self-led tours with an audio guide cost around 75 euro, while guided tours cost around 90 euro per person. Tours leave from Via dei Cimatori 9r. April-October, daily tours leave at 09:30 and 14:30; November-March, daily tours leave at 09:30 only; advance reservations are required. Tel: 055.2398855, www.italysegwaytours.com

## Shopping

With so many opportunities to explore Italian fashion, Florence makes shopping easy. If you are looking for high-end stores, such as Gucci and Prada, head towards Via Tornabuoni and the area around Piazza della Repubblica. If you are looking for leather goods, head to the leather market near San Lorenzo Church. Regular shops (which teenagers will love) are scattered just about everywhere in the historical centre. If you are looking for some more serious retail therapy, **Barberino del Muggello**—an outlet mall 40 minutes north of Florence—features both well-known Italian and international brands. Check out their website at www.mcarthurglen.com/en/our-outlets/italy/barberino-designer-outlet for information about the shops and the bus service they operate from SMN to the outlet village. The bus is pricey, but if you don't have a car it's your only option for getting there. Another popular and more exclusive shopping destination is **The Mall Outlet Village**, featuring such names as Fendi, Gucci, and Bottega Veneta. See more at their website, www.themall.it. The Mall Outlet Village is located 30 minutes from Florence and offers shuttle service that will pick you up from your hotel (for a price, of course).

**Use our suggestions to engage even children who go crazy after more than 10 minutes in a museum.** If you think your kids will hate any sort of museum or church, there are several other activities to enjoy. Climb to the top of the Duomo for an impressive view of the city, walk around the beautiful Piazza della Signoria, or pop in to see Palazzo Vecchio. Let them run around between the baroque statues of the majestic Boboli Gardens, peek into the life of monks in San Marco Museum and ex-monastery, or organize an ice cream tour (try several flavours of gelato at several ice cream shops, and then decide which was best. Repeat if necessary...). In addition to the Science and Stibbert Museums, the Archaeological Museum or the Anthropological Museum are also kid-friendly stops. You can also cut back on the number of days you spend n Florence and head out to more "active destinations" (the Pisa and Lucca Itinerary and the Garfagnana Itinerary are excellent destinations for more active kids).

**Use the extra activities suggested at the end of this chapter.** Yes, they require a bit of a splurge, but they can be the most memorable parts of your trip, if you choose carefully. Spending half a day in Florence and the other half taking a cooking class in a real Italian villa or riding horses in the Chianti region can be an incredible experience and memory, something kids and teenagers will tell their friends about with pride.

**Reward kids for the missions they complete with little gifts and souvenirs.** There are several missions throughout this guide that help get kids involved and interested while letting adults enjoy their visit without having to entertain children the entire time. We highly recommend setting a small prize or reward for every few missions successfully completed to make kids feel that their efforts aren't futile. We hope you won't look at it as bribery or a waste of money. You'll be surprised how meaningful these little prizes can be for kids.

**When possible, try not to be too strict about food.** Florence is very hot during the summer, and the combination of heat and walking for hours on end can be hard on your body. Allowing everyone to have two ice creams a day is actually reasonable, and, yes, even an occasional Popsicle (or two) is fine. Also—make sure your kids are drinking enough (and not just water) so that they don't dehydrate, which is much more common than people think.

**Let Mary Poppins be your inspiration.** A bag full of surprises can be a real lifesaver. Several missions in this book require binoculars, so make sure you buy at least one pair (since you can easily find a pair for less than 15 euro, consider getting one for every child). This might seem excessive, but binoculars work for two reasons: they are cool, and they let your kids actually see the exhibits, which are often hung too high or are too small to be easily seen. Also, pack tiny games kids can play to pass the time while waiting in line or sitting in the park (patty for younger kids, travel-sized box games for older kids, or even a PSP or iPad can be helpful). Yo-yos, Slinkies, and mp3 players loaded with audiobooks—all of these can be useful, as well.

**Get the right gear.** Kids (and adults) need hats to protect them from the sun; choose cool hats so that everyone looks good in photos. Sunscreen, sunglasses, and comfortable walking shoes are a must. If you plan on visiting churches, make sure you have a shirt with sleeves and that you are not wearing excessively short pants or skirts, or the churches may not let you in (most churches offer a poncho or scarf to cover your body when you walk inside, but not all of them).

# Here's an example of a reasonable, but fun-packed, three-day itinerary in Florence:

1. The **Uffizi**, followed by **Piazza della Signoria** and **Palazzo Vecchio**, including a climb to the top of the tower (allow more time if you've booked the family-guided tour; see itinerary for details). Cross the **Ponte Vecchio** and have lunch in the Oltrarno (around **Piazza Santo Spirito**). Check out the **Boboli Gardens** until dinner (alternatively, skip the gardens and head to **Galileo Galilei's Science Museum**).

2. The **Accademia Museum** (Galleria dell'Accadmia, to see Michelangelo's David) followed by a short visit to **San Marco**, then reserve some time for vegging out in Piazza Santissima Annunziata or in a park. Have lunch, climb to the top of the **Duomo's** dome and/or Giotto's Bell Tower, and then spend the rest of the afternoon in a park or a pool (alternatively, squeeze in a visit to **Santa Croce**, if you want).

3. Check out the **Medici Chapels** (you can skip the San Lorenzo Church) and get some shopping done in the **leather market** around Piazza San Lorenzo. Have lunch, and spend a couple of hours in the **Stibbert Museum** (if you love armour) or **Davanzatti Museum** (to see how people lived in medieval and Renaissance Florence). Towards 17:00-17:30, take a bus or cab to **Piazzale Michelangelo** to hear the Gregorian chants in San Miniato a Monte Church around 18:30 and then enjoy spectacular views from Piazzale Michelangelo at sunset.

## An example of a two-day itinerary with toddlers and younger children:

1. Start your day at the **Duomo**, admiring its magnificence and comparing it to **Giotto's Bell Tower** (you won't be able to climb up with toddlers, but don't worry, you'll find great city views accessible to everyone in a minute). Then walk up to **Piazza della Signoria** and check out the fountain and David's replica statue (entry to the **Uffizi** is optional; if you do enter, you can skip most rooms and focus on the big names in rooms 10-14, 15, and 35). Cross the **Ponte Vecchio** and head for the **Boboli Gardens**. Have an early pizza dinner.

2. Explore **Stibbert Museum's** collection of armour and then spend an hour or two in the adjoining **park**, running around on the grass and between the trees. Alternatively, spend the morning at the **Science Museum** and then take a long walk along the river. After a light lunch, it's time to take the bus or a taxi to **Piazzale Michelangelo** to explore the relaxing **San Miniato al Monte Church** and cemetery, hear the Gregorian chants by the monks, and enjoy the wonderful view from Piazzale Michelangelo.

## An example itinerary, if you only have one day in Florence:

Unlike other destinations in this guide, Florence has more than enough attractions to easily fill up three or four days. But if you have just one day to spend in the town, try to visit the **Duomo** (even just from the outside, it's very impressive). Then visit one of the museums, such as the **Accademia**, to see Michelangelo's *David* or the **Uffizi**, to see Renaissance masterpieces. Next, cross the **Ponte Vecchio**, the oldest bridge in Florence, and take a cab (or a bus, but that will be more time consuming) up to **Piazzale Michelangelo** to see Florence in all its glory. Spend your evening in the area around **Piazza della Signoria**, Florence's most impressive piazza (after the Duomo, naturally). Make sure you book a good restaurant for dinner and then go out for ice cream. If you only have one day (or two, for that matter), **booking your tickets for the Uffizi and the Accademia in advance is crucial**. Otherwise, you'll find yourself spending three hours standing in line instead of touring the city itself.

# The Uffizi

The Uffizi is one of the most famous museums in the world—and rightfully so. Originally designed by Giorgio Vasari as the Medici family offices (hence its name), the small and inviting space is home to some of the most exquisite paintings of the Renaissance, including works by Leonardo Da Vinci, Botticelli, Giotto, and Michelangelo. Unlike the Met, the Louvre, or the Prado, the Uffizi can easily be toured in 90 minutes, or even 45 minutes if the kids are getting impatient. If you have very little time, focus on the famous rooms: 3, (note that due to recent rennovatios, the contents of rooms 3-7 have been temporarily moved to rooms 43-45); 8, 10-14 (Botticelli); 15 (Leonardo da Vinci); 35 (Michelangelo); 66 (Raffaello); 83 (Titian) and 90 (Caravaggio). During your visit, don't forget to stop at the Uffizi's terrace and admire the view. Alternatively, **to make the most of your Uffizi tour**, check out our "Uffizi's Insider's Guide" (for adults) and "The Ultimate Guide for Art Detectives: How to Read a Painting" (for children) sections found at the end of this itinerary. If you have ever wondered why medieval paintings look so strange, why they are covered in gold, what the Lily flower symbolizes, if the colour red has any hidden meanings, and how Leonardo da Vinci started off his career, these guides will give you all the answers you are looking for.

🕑 Opening times: Tuesday-Sunday, 08:15-18:50 (ticket offices close at 18:05). Closed Mondays. You can enter using the Firenze Card (go directly to door number 2) or book your ticket online in advance at www.ticketsflorence.com or www.b-ticket.com/b-ticket/Uffizi. Pay for and print your voucher, and then exchange it for a ticket 10 minutes before your scheduled visit (go to door number 3). Alternatively, tickets can also be booked by phone (a reservation fee of 4 euro per ticket applies) at this number: 055.294883. Kids between 7 and 18 years old enter for free, but still have to pay for advanced reservation. Kids under 6 years old enter for free and don't have to pay for advanced reservation.

**Tip:** Tour the Uffizi's courtyard, too. It is filled with art students, street artists, tourists, and souvenir stalls to help you get in a festive mood. You can draw your kids' attention to students attempting to paint the masterpieces and suggest they do the same (bring crayons and paper in advance).

# The Duomo

Florence's Duomo (main cathedral) is one of the most
famous churches in Italy and is
surrounded by three additional must-see attractions: the
Duomo Piazza, the Bell Tower
(known as Giotto's Campanile,
which you can climb to see a
lovely view of the city), and
San Giovanni's Baptistery (the building with the golden doors). For many families, the best part of the visit is climbing up the Duomo's dome to enjoy a bird's
eye view of Florence from the top of this majestic cathedral. One little problem
can spoil the fun, however - the endless lines you have to stand in if you want
to climb up.

### DUOMO TICKETS AND AVOIDING LINES
To avoid lines, book tickets in advance online. A 10-euro combo ticket is
available (free for children under 6 years old), that will grant you entry to the
Duomo, the dome, the bell tower and the rest of the attractions. To book in
advance, visit www.operaduomo.firenze.it. Read the instructions carefully regarding the voucher you will receive, what you must do with it, and where to
pick up your tickets. Alternatively, buy your ticket directly at the ticket office.
There are three ticket offices - one inside the Duomo, by the crypt, one by the
bell tower's door, and one in front of the baptistery, at the entrance to the Art
and Congress building (at number 7, the door next to the Buca San Giovanni
restaurant). We find that the line is shortest at the Art and Congress building,
and, to save time, there are also automatic ticket machines, in addition to the

regular ticket office.

The combo card allows you to visit quite a few attractions, but personally we recommend that families with kids focus on one big attraction that can be climbed on (the most popular one is the dome, but the bell tower has its fans too, especially if you bought the Firenze Card) and the Duomo itself. The other attractions can be easily admired from the outside. Since both the dome and the bell tower require climbing more than 400 stairs each, it is unlikely you'll want to visit both on the same day.

## ⊙ OPENING TIMES FOR ALL THE ATTRACTIONS IN PIAZZA DUOMO

**The Duomo**, open daily, Monday-Wednesday, Friday, 10:00-17:00; Saturday, 10:00-16:45; Sunday, 13:30-16:45; Thursdays: May-October, 10:00-16:00; January-April and November-December, 10:00-16:30; July-September, 10:00-17:00. Opening times may change during religious holidays. Check website before arrival. **Bell Tower (Campanile)**, open daily, 8:30-19:30 (until 18:50 off-season). **Dome**, Monday-Friday, 08:30-19:00; Saturdays, 08:30-17:40; closed Sunday. Off-season closes at 18:20. Closed: the three days before Easter, Easter, 24 June, 15 August, 8 September, as well as on regular national holidays. **Baptistery**, open daily, 11:15-19:00; Sunday and the first Saturday of every month, 08:30-14:00; Off-season closes at 18:20; entrance is free on 24 June. **Duomo Museum**, the museum is currently closed for rennovation. Updated opening times can be found here: www.operaduomo.firenze.it.

**FLORENCE'S BEAUTIFUL DUOMO** was begun by Arnolfo di Cambio (the same architect who built Palazzo Vecchio and Santa Croce) in 1296 and was built on top of the city's former cathedral, Santa Reparata (named after Saint Reparata, the co-patron saint of Florence, together with Saint John the Baptist).

The word Duomo, by the way, comes from the Latin "domus", meaning "house", because the Duomo is considered to be God's house.

Though the Duomo was impressive from the beginning, no one knew how to finish it, and so the city found itself with a 45-meter-wide cathedral with no roof (and no façade, but more on that later). In 1418, a competition was organized to solve this problem. Among the architects who took on the challenge were Lorenzo Ghiberti (who had won another competition 17 years earlier to create the Baptistery's golden doors) and Filippo Brunelleschi, one of the most renowned architects in the city. Both were eventually elected as co-headmasters of the project, but Brunelleschi, who had hated Ghiberti ever since he lost the Baptistery golden-door design competition to him, would hear nothing of it. He pretended to be ill, leaving Ghiberti to deal with the complicated project on his own. Once Ghiberti admitted he was in over his head, Brunelleschi returned triumphant to design this incredibly complicated dome by himself, thus becoming one of the most famous architects in history.

## Brunelleschi's Dome

Brunelleschi's work and ingenious solution are considered, even today, to be a remarkable achievement. For inspiration, Brunelleschi travelled with his good friend Donatello (yes, THAT Donatello) to Rome, where they thoroughly studied the Pantheon's slightly smaller dome. The solution he came up with was basically a double dome. First, he laid the "skeleton", which you can still see if you stand inside the Dome and look up, and then he filled the space between the "bones" with bricks set in an interlocking pattern, so that the dome supported its own weight. The inside part of the dome was decorated with a majestic fresco, Giorgio Vasari's *Last Judgment* (once you are inside, take out your binoculars for a better view).

One of the most impressive features of the Duomo is its façade, but (surprisingly) it was only built in the 19th century, cleverly designed in a style to match the rest of the cathedral. The façade was supposed to be Lorenzo the Magnificent's baby project, a mark he would leave on the city, to demonstrate that he wasn't just a skilled politician and mighty ruler but also a patron of the arts, like his grandfather, Cosimo. However, the project soon spun out of control and was abandoned halfway through. It was only some 400 years later, in 1876 that the façade we see today was started (and completed a decade later).

Enter the Duomo to admire its interior decorations. To your right stands the funerary monument to Filippo Brunelleschi, created by his pupil and adopted son, Andrea Cavalcanti. To be buried in the Duomo, and with such a monument (and not just a tomb slab in the pavement), was a great and unprecedented honour for an artist and a clear acknowledgement of Brunelleschi's civic role in Florentine society. If you are wondering what Brunelleschi looked like, head to the Duomo's museum, where you will find his death mask (look in the Kids' Corner later in this itinerary to find out more about this unique custom). There are two more note-worthy funerary monuments in the Duomo: to your left, you will find two frescoes depicting two "capitani di ventura" (mercenary captains), men who led the Florentine army in battle (in this case against Milan). The first fresco depicts Sir John Hawkwood, a notorious English mercenary (1320-1394), and the second depicts Italian-born Nicolò da Tolentino (1350-1435).

**Mission 1:** Can you find a fresco of a man wearing red, holding a book, and with a crown of leaves around his head? He is important enough to be painted on the walls of the Duomo. Who do you think he is?

# The Baptistery

This beautiful example of Romanesque architecture is actually one of the oldest religious buildings in Florence. It is first mentioned as far back as the 10th century, when it served as a (somewhat humble) cathedral for the city. The Baptistery, where Dante and many of the Medici family members were christened, is well known both for its exterior and interior décor. Outside, you will find the Baptistery's golden-bronze doors, known as the Gates to Paradise, a name given to them by Michelangelo, who was impressed with their beauty and craftsmanship. Designed by Lorenzo Ghiberti when he was only 21 years old, the elaborate and priceless doors took more than 20 years to complete. Several artists competed for the honour of designing the prestigious entryway (including a woman, whose name is unknown, although she probably came from a local family of artists, the Gaddis). Ghiberti's proposal swept the jury, however. The doors are divided into 28 panels, describing the life of Christ, scenes from the New Testament, and the evangelists. Upon completion in

1452, the doors immediately became an international sensation, so much so that Ghiberti was invited by Pope Nicholas V to come work for him in Rome. Note that the doors currently on the Baptistery are actually a copy; the precious, original doors were moved to the Duomo Museum. The interior of the Baptistery is stunning as well, especially the overwhelming mosaic ceiling covering its dome and apse.

**Mission 2:** Take a photo of yourself in front of the doors while holding out your arms to make the letter "L" (for Lorenzo) and then "G" (for Ghiberti).

## Giotto's Bell Tower

Despite the name, Giotto only made the drawings for the impressive bell tower by the Duomo. He died three years after work began, so the task was carried out by another great artist, Andrea Pisano (1290-1348). Together with other sculptors such as Nino Pisano (his son), Luca della Robbia, and Donatello, Pisano created the tower's hexagonal and diamond-shaped panels with stories from Genesis, images of men's labour, and niches with statues of prophets. The choice to decorate the tower with scenes of working men wasn't incidental: the bell marked time, calling people to work and duty (like Mass or the fighting field) and was a reminder that manual labour kept people away from sin.

# The Duomo Museum

Though often ignored, the museum does offer a few interesting surprises for visitors, including the original Ghiberti doors, one of Michelangelo's pietas, and number of beautiful gothic sculptures.

# Piazza della Signoria and Palazzo Vecchio

Named after the governing body of Florence (the Signoria), Piazza della Signoria is one of Florence's best-known squares. Located just a few meters from the Uffizi and a half-block from the Ponte Vecchio, the piazza is a perfect place to stop for a break, enjoy the view, let the kids run around, or sip a cold drink in one of the area's many coffee houses (check the prices first, most places overcharge). Dominating the piazza is Palazzo Vecchio, Florence's impressive 700-year-old town hall.

For hundreds of years, Piazza della Signoria was the beating heart of Florence and a favoured location for most public events, including festivities, games, religious devotion processions, carnivals, preparations for war, and even executions (read more about the fanatic monk Savonarola, the most famous man executed here, in the San Marco Museum Itinerary).

**Mission 1:** There is a mark on the floor around the centre of the piazza at the exact point in which Savonarola was executed. Can you find it?

**Tip:** Would you like to know how many iPads it would take to make a row as long as the Duomo's dome? Or find out more about the (slightly gruesome) tradition of death mask making? If so, check out our Kids' Corner at the end of this itinerary!

**Tip:** Would you like to tour Florence on a horse-drawn carriage? During the high-season, you will find several carriages waiting for you near the Duomo!

# Raging Bulls and Roaring Lions - Past Events in Piazza della Signoria

Our culture's definition of dramatic public events has changed greatly since medieval and Renaissance times. In those days, violent feasts were the preferred ways to pass holidays. Live hunting matches were organized in which wild animals, such as lions (who were raised as pets by influential clergymen and noble families), were brought in to hunt bulls and boars that had been released in the piazza. For other events, such as the carnival celebrations, exotic animals (including elephants and giraffes) were paraded in front of the shocked crowds. Another common celebration in the 15th century was the (somewhat horrifying) bull festival (reminiscent of today's bull fighting in Spain), in which bulls were slaughtered as a sign of the organizer's masculinity and power. This festival was accompanied by songs and dancing.

The row of statues in the open-air arched gallery next to Palazzo Vecchio is known as the Loggia dei Lanzi. Once a space that housed Cosimo I mercenary soldiers, it is today considered an important cultural meeting point and remains decorated with some well-known artwork, like Benvenuto Cellini's famous *Perseus with the Head of Medusa* and Jean de Boulogne's *Rape of the Sabine Women*.

**Mission 2:** How many statues are in the Loggia? How many statues are of animals?

**Mission 3:** Take a picture standing in front of the Palazzo Vecchio, pretending to be the ruler of Florence.

On the other side of the piazza stands a famous replica of David (the original is in the Galleria dell'Accademia) and Neptune's Fountain, which was vandalized a few years ago when a tourist cut off Neptune's finger.

**Mission 4:** Take a picture in front of the fountain, imitating Neptune's pose.

**Mission 5:** Neptune's Fountain is decorated with a number of statues, but one of them is a statue of an animal. What kind of animal is it?

**Mission 6:** Take a picture standing in front of David's statue, imitating David's pose.

# Palazzo Vecchio

Though overlooked by some families, Palazzo Vecchio ("the old palace") is actually quite interesting, and its Grand Hall (Sala dei Cinquecento) is impressive enough to make you sigh. Kids will love climbing the palace's ancient tower, and the Palazzo staff organizes regular activities for families, which last about an hour and focus on life during Renaissance times: parties, costumes, and toys, as well as the crazy adventures of Cosimo I, his wife (Elenora of Toledo), and their 11 children. These tours are popular and must be booked in advance. Find out more about the tour schedule here at www.museoragazzi.it or make your reservation via email (info. museoragazzi@comune.fi.it) or by calling ahead. Tel: 055.2768224

 A symbol of Florence for more than 700 years and designed by Arnolfo di Cambio (one of the leading architects of the time), **Palazzo Vecchio** was built by the priors who ruled the city before the Medici family took over. A dramatic, impressive, and majestic town hall was essential for demonstrating Florence's power to its neighbours, so in 1298 the town took upon the challenge of building this monumental hall that would send a clear message to neighbouring towns. The massive form wasn't just a stylish choice, either; the palace had to withstand attacks from the city's enemies. It was only in the 16th century, when Cosimo I moved to Palazzo Pitti on the other side of the Arno, that the palace's name was changed to Palazzo Vecchio. Today the palazzo still houses the offices of the mayor and the city council.

Start your visit from the outside and examine the building's structure. Its famous 94-meter-high tower was initially part of an even older fortress that stood on the exact ground and was incorporated into the "new" building. The tower was also used as a prison cell at times, and two of its more famous "guests" were Cosimo I (during a brief period in which he was overthrown from power) and the fanatic monk Girolamo Savonarola. The impressive arches on the tower weren't just for decoration; they were used to drop boiling oil on the heads of invaders.

To enter the palace, you will pass through an elegantly decorated courtyard, featuring a lovely fountain designed by Verrocchio (Leonardo da Vinci's teacher) in its centre. The real experience begins on the second floor, where you will see the **Sala dei Cinquecento** (the Grand Hall), built under Savonarola's orders to house the city's governing body that replaced the Medici family (a total of 500 elected men). The lavish decorations were not Savonarola's doing, though. These were ordered and financed by Cosimo I, who took back power, got rid of the city's council, declared himself Grand Duke, and had Savonarola executed in front of a cheering crowd in Piazza della Signoria. The entire room was elaborately decorated by Giorgio Vasari (with the help of his assistants, of course) and is still considered one of the most impressive halls in Italy. The hall was originally to be adorned with works by two of the biggest names in the art scene at the time: Leonardo Da Vinci and Michelangelo Buonarroti. Both were invited to paint huge battle scenes (reaching 7 meters high and 18 meters long) that described glorious military moments from Florentine history, but each abandoned his work shortly after beginning. Da Vinci stopped because the new technique he was experimenting with (to substitute painting over wet plaster) failed, and Michelangelo was called upon by the Pope to work on the Sistine Chapel in Rome. However, recent research by a team of Italian scientists reveals that much more lies behind these walls...

# Leonardo's Mystery

Using advanced machinery and sophisticated tools such as heat sensors, endoscopes, and lasers, recent research has confirmed what art historians have long suspected: in a secret compartment behind one of Vasari's paintings (Battle of Manciano) lays Leonardo da Vinci's unfinished painting, Battle of Anghiari. Many believed that it was destroyed, but a mysterious hint left by Leonardo (a small writing on the wall that says, "those who seek find") led a team of scientists headed by Maurizio Seracini on a 30-year search for the painting. Several artists throughout history were also inspired to try to recreate the painting; the most famous attempt was Peter Paul Ruben's beautiful Battle of Anghiari, which is now displayed in the Louvre. Leonardo's painting cannot be seen, but researchers do hope to one day recover it without damaging the walls.

From here, continue your tour to the **royal apartments**. While not as impressive as those in Palazzo Pitti, they are still worth a visit to get a sense of how the Florentine aristocracy lived. **The Hall of Lilies** (Sala dei Gigli), which is completely decorated with the city's flower symbol, offers great views of the Duomo. Map-loving kids will find the **Hall of Geographical Maps** delightful as they explore how the world was slowly discovered, piece-by-piece, by brave sailors sent on missions around the globe.

Beginning in December 2014, a new attraction became available: a short tour of the archeological findings underneath Palazzo Vecchio. For a small extra fee you will be able to visit the Roman theatre hiding under the fortress.

🕐 Opening times: Friday-Wednesday, 9:00-19:00 (April-September, open until 24:00); Thursday, 09:00-14:00. The ticket office closes one hour before closing time. Children under 18 enter for free; children under six are not allowed to climb the tower. (Note that the tower is closed in inclement weather and that children under eight are not allowed to take part in the archeological tour.) Combo tickets are available for the museum, the tower, and the ar-

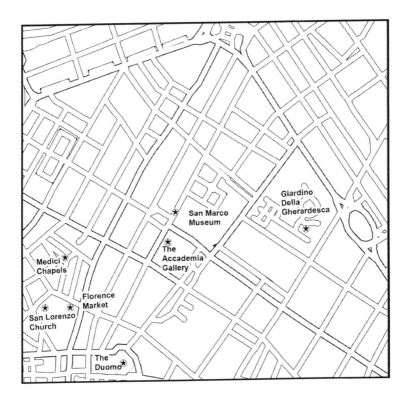

cheological site. Guided tours are available. For 5 euro, visitors can rent an audiovisual guide (recommended, especially for kids). Tel: 055.2768325, www. museicivicifiorentini.comune.fi.it/palazzovecchio

**Tip:** The Palazzo Vecchio is connected to Palazzo Pitti through the famous **Vasari Corridor**, built to give the Medici rulers a quick way to move around (and escape, if necessary) without being seen. Though the idea of walking along the corridor is exciting, there isn't much to see inside, and it is only accessible via advance reservations (and only open for part of the year). If you are especially interested in the corridor, check with the local tourist office to see if it's open during the time of your visit.

# Ponte Vecchio

**Ponte Vecchio** is Florence's oldest bridge and one of the best-recognized monuments in town. It is also the only bridge not blown up by German troops during WWII, allegedly because of a direct order from Hitler, who had visited Florence as a guest of Mussolini and was thoroughly impressed. Built in 1339

after a serious flood destroyed a previous, simpler bridge, shops were added on both sides to turn it into a lively medieval trade station. Though it may seem somewhat dodgy, the designs for Ponte Vecchio were actually quite precise, and according to official 14th-century documents, the bridge was set to be "32 arms long" (one arm is equal to about 58 cm). If you are wondering what all the locks in the middle of the bridge are for, remember that Italy is a romantic country. An age-old tradition states that lovers must come here, hook a lock to the fence, and throw the key into the river to signify their undying love. After officials decided they were tired of removing locks every week, the city began issuing a 50-euro fine to anyone caught following this tradition.

> **Tip:** The area immediately after crossing the bridge to the other side (known as Oltrarno) is the perfect place to relax and enjoy the view. Teenagers will be impressed with a cup of coffee (or non-alcoholic cocktails) at a chic little place overlooking the bridge, such as the **Golden View Open Bar** (cross the Ponte Vecchio, turn left, walk along the bank until you see the bar (bars in Italy aren't pubs, they are places which serve food and drinks, not necessarily alcohol). Check out the bar's website for a schedule of its regular live jazz concerts. Via dei Bardi 54 and 64, Tel:055.214502, www.goldenviewopenbar.com. A slightly pricier but incredible place worth the money is the SESTO restaurant and bar at **Hotel Excelsior**. Built to impress with its 360° view of the city, this is a perfect place to take sophisticated teenagers for lunch, coffee, or a non-alcoholic aperitivo and relaxation.www.westinflorence.com. Lastly, the ever popular **Terrazza Brunelleschi** also boasts a gorgeous view and tasty snacks. Book ahead a place on the terrace! www.terrazzabrunelleschi.it

# The Accademia Museum
# (Galleria dell'Accademia)

Though hardly as rich in monumental artwork as other museums in Florence, the Accademia is a must, if only to see one of the most famous sculptures in the world and one of the most popular attractions in Tuscany: **David** by Michelangelo Buonarroti. This incredible piece (moved here in 1873 from its original location, Piazza della Signoria) is a symbol of artistic perfection and political rebellion against any sign of tyranny and is considered one of Michelangelo's masterpieces. Other works in the museum (once a convent) include paintings by Renaissance artists Paolo Uccello and Domenico Ghirlandaio, a number of minor paintings by Botticelli, and a collection of antique musical instruments (which is included in the price of the ticket and might be of some interest to history-loving kids).

Michelangelo was only 26 when he was commissioned to create David from a flawed piece of Carrara marble that other artists had rejected. The result was described by Vasari in his rather poetic manner, "...nor has there ever been seen a pose so easy, or any grace to equal that in this work, or feet, hands and head so well in accord, one member with another, in harmony, design, and excellence of artistry. And, of a truth, whoever has seen this work need not trouble to see any other work executed in sculpture, either in our own or in other times, by no matter what craftsman".

Michelangelo wasn't the first choice to create David. The piece had originally been assigned to an artist named Agostino di Duccio, who was unable to finish it, and then passed on to another artist, Antonio Rossellino, who also gave up. Then stepped in Michelangelo, who had always claimed he was a tool guided by God, to create a truly unique sculpture.

Interestingly enough, Michelangelo chose not to represent David as a victorious hero with Goliath's head, which would have been a more obvious choice for such an iconographic sculpture, but instead focused on the intense moment of tension before the battle. Biblical David's battle against the giant Goliath was used as a case in point of the power of faith, resilience, and one man's ability to defeat a cruel oppressor. The sculpture was originally supposed to be put on top of one of the Duomo's buttresses, but when the Florentines saw the outstanding work by Michelangelo they decided it deserved a more prestigious setting. So that people could admire it, they put it in the Piazza della Signori, seat of the civic government, together with Donatello's *Judith and Holofernes*, another symbol of victory against tyranny.

🕐 Galleria dell'Accademia, Via Ricasoli 58. Opening: Tuesday-Sunday, 08:15-18:50; closed Mondays; ticket office closes at 18:20. Kids under 18 enter for free, will still have to pay the reservation fee (up to 5.50 euro). Children under six years old enter for free and don't need a reservation.

Buy your tickets in advance at www.ticketsflorence.com/en/museums-tick ets-florence/accademia-gallery. Alternatively, book a ticket in advance (with a 4-euro booking fee, per ticket) by calling 055.294883. Even if you haven't booked in advance, you can also make a reservation on the spot for a later hour in the day or the next day (this isn't always available and might be risky in high season) at nearby My Accademia Libreria, Via Ricasoli 105 (just across the street from the exit, www.myaccademia.com).

> **Tip:** Once you've finished touring the Accademia, you will find yourself right next to Piazza S.S Annunziata (designed by Vasari), a sunny vibrant little piazza with a supermarket and a number of Panini shops, in case you want to improvise a little picnic and rest. Alternatively, the Natural History museum and the botanical garden are right around the corner (Via La Pira 4).

# The Botanical Garden and the Natural History Museum

Just minutes away from the Accademia, and across the street from the San Marco museum, hide two delightful surprises for families. The first is the Botanical garden (Orto Botanico) and the second is the Natural Museum (Museo di Storia Naturale). Both are worth a visit, especially if you are travelling with younger children.

The **Orto Botanico** (closed at the time of this publication following damages from a storm, but should reopen in the summer of 2015) houses several medicinal plants along with beautiful flowers and trees. Founded in 1545, it is one of the oldest botanical gardens in the world. If you are looking to spend a calm afternoon outside, the garden is an option worth considering.

🕐 Orto Botanico, Via La Pira 10. Tel: 055 2756444/055 2756799. Open 1 April through 15 October, daily, 10:00-19:00 and 16 October through 31 March, Saturday-Monday only, 9:30-16:30.

Right next to the botanical garden you will find Florence's tiny, but interesting, **Natural History Museum**. To be exact, it is one of the three main sections of the Natural History museum in town (see details below about the second section). The Museo di Storia Naturale is one of the oldest museums of its kind in Italy and was founded more than 400 years ago. Today, only a small section is on display. The main attraction for families, without a doubt, is the collection of skeletons, including a few very impressive prehistoric elephant and bear skeletons.

🕐 Museo di Storia Naturale, Via Giorgio La Pira 4. Open Monday–Friday, 10.00–13.00, Saturday, Sunday, holidays: 10.00–17.00. Hours may vary off season. Tel: 055. 275.6444; edumsn@unifi.it.

The **second section** of the museum is located farther away, in Via Romana 4 (near the Boboli gardens and Pitti palace). Come here to see anatomically correct (and creepy!) wax models of corpses and thousands of skeletons of rare birds from across the world. Tickets to the museum in Via Romana can be combined with tickets to the Galileo Galilei Science museum.

🕐 Open Tuesday-Sunday, 10:30–17:30 (off season 9:30–16:30), Tel: 055 2756444/055 2755100.

# San Marco Museum

Though not a top-list destination (and often overshadowed by the nearby Galleria dell'Accademia), the ex-monastery of San Marco, which has been converted into a museum, is actually perfect for kids, who can explore its hidden angles and discover how monks lived more than 600 years ago. Focus your tour with kids on the second floor. The former monastery also houses some beautiful artwork.

Two very different people came out of this Dominican monastery: renowned artist Beato Angelico and infamous fanatical monk Girolamo Savonarola. One was known for his poetic, sweet art, while the other overthrew the Medicis, convinced Botticelli to burn his own paintings, and led Florence into a religious frenzy that ended with his execution in Piazza della Signoria (more on both later).

Start your tour at the ground floor and move counter-clockwise along the cloister. Enter the first room immediately on your right (the Pilgrims' Room). This room boasts beautiful paintings by Beato Angelico, such as *Marriage of the Virgin, Funeral of the Virgin*, the famous *Last Judgment* (*Giudizio Universale*, heavily influenced by Dante's *Divine Comedy*), and the *Tabernacle of the Linaioli* (designed by Lorenzo Ghiberti and painted by Fra Angelico between 1432-1433). Beato Angelico's real name was actually Guido di Pietro, but this Dominican monk's paintings were considered to be so serene and lyrical that he was nicknamed "Beato" (blessed). In 1982, he was actually made a saint by Pope John Paul II, becoming the patron saint of all artists.

• • • • • • • • • • • • • • • • • • • • • • • • • • • • • • • • • • • • • • • • • • •

**Mission 1:** Take a good look at the painting Last Judgment. How many people in this painting are holding books (not just pages)? How many are holding animals?

**Mission 2:** In the next room, there is a painting with flying baby heads. Can you find it?

**Mission 3:** In some other part of the ground floor (we won't tell you where, because that would be too easy...) you will find a huge metal object used to call the monks in times of prayer and danger. What is the object, and where is it?

• • • • • • • • • • • • • • • • • • • • • • • • • • • • • • • • • • • • • • • • • • •

As soon as you climb up the stairs to the second floor, you will see one of Beato Angelico's most well known paintings, *The Annunciation*, featuring a softly drawn angel whose wings literally shine (thanks to glitter mixed in with the paint) as he tells Mary of her impending motherhood. Beato Angelico became somewhat of a celebrity after he completed this painting and was invited to Rome to paint for the Pope (though he died shortly after and was buried in Rome).

**Mission 4:** Check out the monks' cells on the second floor. Can you see that many of them have a painting of Jesus in them, with a few lines written over Jesus' head? What language is that? Super bonus question: Do you know what the writing means?

**Mission 5:** There are two rooms with holes in the floor that you can peek through and see archaeological findings from Roman times. Which rooms are they?

At the end of the left row of the monks' cells, you will find two particularly interesting cells. The first belonged to Cosimo de Medici the Elder, the patron of this convent, who funded its renovation and was rewarded with a cell where he could be alone, pray, and repent for his sins as a banker and loan lender. The second is Girolamo Savonarola's cell, featuring his desk and some of his clothes.

**Mission 6:** Look at the clothes of Girolamo Savonarola. Do they look like clothes people today would wear? What can we learn from the size of his clothes about the size of men 600 years ago?

**Mission 7:** What is his shirt made of? Why do you think that is?

🕐 Opening times: Monday-Friday, 08:15-13:50 (ticket office closes at 13:20); Saturday-Sunday, 08:15-16:50 (ticket office closes at 16:20). Closed on the 1st, 3rd, and 5th Sunday and the 2nd and 4th Monday of each month. Children under 18 from the EU enter for free. Even if not from EU, ask whether your child is eligible for a free ticket. Piazza San Marco 13, www.polomuseale. firenze.it

## Savonarola and the Vanity Fire of 1497

Girolamo Savonarola was an extremely charismatic monk, who became a Dominican friar after hearing a sermon on repentance. He began preaching in the street of Florence, condemning humanistic arts, fashion, and just about everything the Renaissance represented. When the army of King Charles VIII of France invaded Italy, Savonarola convinced the King to expel the Medici family, and he took their place, establishing a strictly religious and almost totalitarian republic. On February 7, 1497, Savonarola and his supporters organized the great Vanity Fire, in which they burned any non-religious, beautiful object they could find, including artwork and priceless books. One of the most famous artists who was convinced by Savonarola's preaching was Sandro Boticelli. Botticelli, who had painted such world-famous masterpieces as Primavera and Birth of Venus, actually threw his own paintings into the fire before sinking into a solitary life of depression and study. Savonarola revealed himself to be more fanatical than anyone wanted and even managed to get himself excommunicated by the Pope. He eventually outgrew his welcome and in 1498, he was arrested, tortured, hung, and burned in Piazza della Signoria (the exact spot is still marked in the pavement). The Medici, who had obviously spent the entire time plotting their eventual return, did in fact come back, stronger than ever, and remained on their (metaphorical) throne for about 200 more years.

# San Lorenzo Church and the Medici Chapel

A visit to **San Lorenzo** consists of the church itself, the old sacristy designed by Brunelleschi, and the Laurentine Library (currently closed for renovations), designed by Michelangelo. All three should be visited if you have the time but probably won't be very interesting to kids. The adjacent **Medici Chapel** (which includes the wonderful "New Sacristy", designed by Michelangelo, and the Chapel of the Princes), however, is spectacular and in our opinion shouldn't be missed if you spend two or more days in Florence.

**San Lorenzo** is one of the oldest churches in Florence. It was consecrated in 393 and rebuilt in its current form by architect Filippo Brunelleschi during the first half of the 15th century. It is famous for being the parish of the Medici family, who also funded its transformation and decoration. In 1513, Pope Leo X Medici commissioned Michelangelo with the façade of San Lorenzo, the Medici Church. The artist drew the project but died before he had the chance to start working on it, and since nobody dared take over Michelangelo's task, the façade remains unfinished to this day. The church is named after San Lorenzo, the Medici protective patron saint. Much like the Medici family, San Lorenzo was known for his strong ties with the church, since he served as its financial manager (the Medicis were, among other things, the Pope's personal bankers). Unlike the Medici, however, San Lorenzo suffered a very unpleasant fate and was executed on a grill (!), becoming the patron saint to chefs and cooks (no one can say Catholics don't have a sense of humour).

Most of the Medici family members were buried in this complex, which is considered to be the very expression of Renaissance values and innovations: the architecture is rational and essential, and every element is intentionally related to the others by mathematical proportions.

The **Medici Chapel**, with its exaggerated but hugely impressive marble-cladded Prince's Chapel (that will squeeze a wow out of even the most reluctant teenager) and the New Sacristy, featuring two incredible Michelangelo sculptures, is one of Florence's finest attractions. The **New Sacristy** was supposed to contain four Medici graves, but after the Medici family was (temporarily) exiled from Florence and Michelangelo left for Rome to work for the Pope on the Sistine Chapel, the project was put on hold. Ironically, the two more important graves, those of Lorenzo the Magnificent, ruler of Florence, and his brother

Giuliano, were never even started, and the beautiful graves we see today are of two notably less important family members: Giuliano, Duke of Nemours, and Lorenzo, Duke of Urbino. The two wall tombs have a similar structure and each have an idealized life-size statue meant to symbolize the virtues of the ideal prince. Giuliano's statue expresses action, energy, and courage, while Lorenzo's represents caution and reflection. Though unfinished, this is one of the peaks of Michelangelo's art. **The Chapel of the Princes**, an incredible and wild feast of colourful marble plates and semi-precious stones, was designed by Matteo Nigetti in a dramatic and luxurious style, fit for the Medici family. Six more Medici family members are buried there.

· · · · · · · · · · · · · · · · · · · · · · · · · · · · · · · · · · · · · · · · · · · · · · · · · ·

**Mission 1:** In the New Sacristy, can you find a statue of a bird decorating one of the tombs? Is this bird a: pigeon, owl or parrot?

**Mission 2:** Can you find at least three examples of the Medici coat of arms in the Prince Chapel or in the entire complex? (Hint: The Medici emblem is a diamond and their coat of arms is six balls.) Use your binoculars if necessary.

**Mission 3:** Grab a pen and paper (or for bonus points, crayons or other colours) and design your very own coat of arms. One day, when you are the head of your own world-famous dynasty, you will need it to decorate your palace, won't you? Which symbols would you choose? Why?

· · · · · · · · · · · · · · · · · · · · · · · · · · · · · · · · · · · · · · · · · · · · · · · · · ·

**San Lorenzo:** 🕐 Opening times: March-October, Monday-Saturday, 10:00-17:00, Sunday, 13:00-17:00; November-January, Monday-Saturday, 10:00-17:00, closed Sundays. Last entry 30 minutes before closing. Kids under 11 enter for free. Piazza San Lorenzo 9, Tel: 055.216634

**Medici Chapel:** 🕐 Opening times: open year round, April-October, Tuesday-Saturday, 08:15-17:00, ticket office closes at 16:30 (the chapel is closed on the second and fourth Sunday of the month, and on the first, third, and fifth

Monday of the month); November-March, 08:15-13:50, ticket office closes at 13:20; EU citizens under 18 enter for free. Piazza Madonna degli Aldobrandini 6 (behind Piazza San Lorenzo, near the leather market). Tickets can be booked in advance (for a 3-euro reservation fee per ticket) at this number: 055.294883, www.polomuseale.firenze.it

# Santa Croce Church

Famous for its high concentration of artwork and for being somewhat of a Florentine Pantheon, **Santa Croce** is the most important Franciscan church in Florence and has many local celebrities buried within its walls. It is filled with medieval tomb slabs in its pavement as well as splendid Renaissance funerary monuments, making it quite tempting to play a little treasure hunt game of "find the famous man's tomb", beginning with Michelangelo (1475-1564), whose funeral was considered to be one of the most solemn events in the history of Florence.

**Mission 1:** Can you find Michelangelo's tomb?

**Mission 2:** Some say that in this very church you will find the statue that inspired the design for the statue of liberty! Can you find it?

**Mission 3:** Nearby, you will find the funerary monument of another very famous Italian scientist. (Hint: He invented the telescope and proved that the Earth moves around the Sun). Who is the scientist, and can you find his tomb?

**Mission 4:** Can you find the tombs of renowned historian, diplomat, and author Niccolò Machiavelli (1469-1527) and the world-famous composer Gioacchino Rossini (1792-1868)?

**Did you know?** Santa Croce also includes monuments to people who aren't technically buried there. Dante, for example, was honoured with a monument even though he was buried in Ravenna, since he was exiled from Florence due to political reasons.

A tour of the church can't be complete without appreciating the beautiful chapels, decorated with frescoes by Giotto and his pupils. The Peruzzi Chapel and the Bardi Chapel, named after the wealthy families who commissioned the frescoes, are among the most impressive, as is Donatello's **Annunciation** (near Michelangelo's tomb), known as **Annunciazione Cavalcanti**.

The frescoes in the main altar, depicting the story of the true cross, are considered a masterpiece, and were carried out by Agnolo Gaddi (the choice of theme isn't surprising, since according to Franciscan belief, relics of the cross were brought to the church in 1300).

Throughout the church are frescoes and statues of saints, placed there not just for decorative purposes but also to remind the Franciscan friars who came to the church daily that they should strive to be more like these role models. If you have time, step into the small but charming Pazzi Chapel, attached to the church. Stop at the Museum and Refectory as well, to admire Cimabue's Cross, which was severely damaged during a dramatic flood that hit Florence in 1966 and flooded the church (in fact, the water marks can still be seen on some of the walls). Restored during a long and extremely delicate process, Cimabue's Cross has become a symbol of Florence's resilience.

🕐 Opening times: Monday-Saturday, 09:30-17:30; Sunday, 14:00-17:30; the ticket office closes at 17:00, children under 11 enter for free, kids 12–17 pay a reduced fee, and family tickets (full price for adults and free entry for children under 18) are also available. Piazza Santa Croce 16, Tel:055.2466105, www.santacroceopera.it (see tip on the next page on how to avoid the line)

**Tip:** On Borgo dei Greci, the street connecting Santa Croce to Piazza della Signoria, you will find SIGNUM, the perfect one stop shop for souvenirs. Come here to find everything from medieval papers to swords to leather bound diaries. Borgo dei Greci 40, open daily, 09:30–19:30.

> **Tip:** Many people visit the **Leather School** (adjacent to the church) by themselves or with a tour and then buy a ticket to the Santa Croce Church from inside the school, to avoid the long ticket lines. The Leather School, an attraction by itself, is open daily, 10:00-18:00 (during the fall and winter months, the school is closed on Sundays). An organized tour costs 14 euro, but even if you tour it on your own, for free, kids will still enjoy the workshops, and savvy shoppers will appreciate the excellent quality (but very pricey) handmade bags (www. scuoladelcuoio.com). To enter the school (and then Santa Croce itself), simply walk from Piazza Santa Croce to Via S. Giuseppe 5r, visit the workshops, walk all the way to the end, buy a ticket for the church and go directly inside.

# Santa Maria Novella

Santa Maria Novella is arguably the most important Dominican church in Florence, with a façade designed by Leon Battista Alberti (1404-1472), an architect, writer, humanist, and one of the most influential figures in Renaissance art.

The church's Gothic interior is designed like a Latin cross, and is best known for its main altar (the **Tornabuoni Chapel**). On either side you will also find smaller but equally important chapels, named after rich and powerful families who financed their decoration, as was customary at the time. On the right is the elaborate **Strozzi Chapel**, decorated with a series of Filippino Lippi frescoes; on the left is the 13th-century **Gondi Chapel**, where you'll find Filippo Brunelleschi's Crucifix, the artist's only surviving wooden sculpture. Brunelleschi is famous for inventing linear perspective in art, engineering the Duomo's dome, and creating such pivotal works as the church of San Lorenzo and the historical Ospedale degli Innocenti.

If you've brought a pair of binoculars, now is the perfect time to use them to see details of Domenico Ghirlandaio's beautiful frescoes behind the main altar. The left section of the wall is dedicated to stories of the Virgin, and the right side features tales of Saint John the Baptist that took more than five years to complete. As with most church artwork commissioned by wealthy private families, these frescoes manage to express piety while also (fondly) memorializing their funders. For instance, a scene depicting the birth of Saint John the Baptist is set in a typical Florentine bedroom; next to the newly born Saint John stand not only servants but three women who just "happen to be" members of the rich and powerful Tornabuoni family.

Make sure not to miss the **main crucifix**, an early piece by Giotto hanging at the centre of the church. On the left wall toward the middle of the central nave rests what is probably the church's most notable piece of art, the *Trinity*, by Masaccio, which is considered monumental because of its once-revolutionary use of perspective to create the illusion of depth in a painting. If you stand close you will see the slightly disturbing writing in Latin at the bottom of the painting on the burial monument: "IO FU[I] G[I]À QUEL CHE VOI SETE E QUEL CH'I[O] SON VOI A[N]CHO SARETE." (I once was what you are and what I am you will also be).

**Mission:** How many people are in Masaccio's Trinity painting? How many are there if you count the skeleton, too?

🕐 Opening times: Monday-Thursday, 09:00-17:30; Friday, 11:00-17:30; Saturday, 09:00-17:00; Sunday, 13:00-17:00 (July-September, the church opens at 12:00 on Sundays). Last entry 30 minutes before closing. Children under five enter free. Piazza Santa Maria Novella 18.

> **Tip:** A visit to Santa Maria Novella wouldn't be complete without peeking into the nearby **antique perfumery**. Though absolutely touristy, kids will enjoy this museum-like store that is filled to the brim with vases, weird-smelling potions, and more—almost like something you'd find in Harry Potter's Hogwarts. Opening times: Friday-Monday, 09:30-19:30 (hours tend to vary, especially in August). Via della Scala 16.

# Orsanmichele

The church of Orsanmichele was built in the 1330s as a grain market, but in the 15th century the building was modified, its arches were closed, and it was transformed into a church. For several years, Orsanmichele served as a playground for local guilds, who competed in showing off the marvellous artwork they managed to acquire and commission. The church's niches quickly filled up with bronze statues and priceless paintings, some of which have been moved to the second floor (where you will find the Orsanmichele Museum).

🕐 The Orsanmichele Church (ground floor) is open daily, 10:00-17:00 (during August, the church is closed on Mondays). The Museum of Sculptures (1st and 2nd floor) is open year round on Mondays, 10:00-17:00. Via dell'Arte della Lana, Tel: 055.284944.

# Bargello

The **Bargello** dates back to 1255, when it served as the town hall (and later as a prison). In the 19th century, it was turned into a museum. It may not host the most famous collection in town, but it is charming, kid friendly, and easy to tour, and therefore popular with families. The courtyard on the first floor is filled with fun statues and dramatically decorated walls, and the top floors (sometimes closed, especially off season; ask before you buy a ticket) offer collections many kids will appreciate, from Islamic artefacts to armour and tapestries. Among the well-known pieces of the museum, you will find Donatello's *David*, three sculptures by Michelangelo, and several works of Tuscan ceramic masters Luca and Andrea Della Robbia.

🕐 Opening times: open daily, 08:15-13:50 (ticket office closes at 13:20). Closed on the 1st, 3rd, and 5th Sunday, and 2nd and 4th Monday of each month. Via del Proconsolo 4, www.polomuseale.firenze.it

# Museums and Attractions on the Other Side of the Arno River (Oltrarno)

## Palazzo Pitti and the Boboli Gardens

The Pitti Palace is the main monument on the other side of the Arno, a huge Renaissance-style palace built by a rich banker named Luca Pitti and later purchased by the Medici family to be turned into their version of Versailles. The palace consists of a number of museums but visiting all of them can take up an entire day and isn't recommended for families (it's exhausting even for seasoned art lovers). The most famous part is the Galleria Palatina, which hosts an impressive art collection, but our personal recommendation is that you skip the museums altogether, or, alternatively, visit only the collections that will impress the kids, such as the Costume Gallery (which features a number of dramatic clothes from the 16th century)

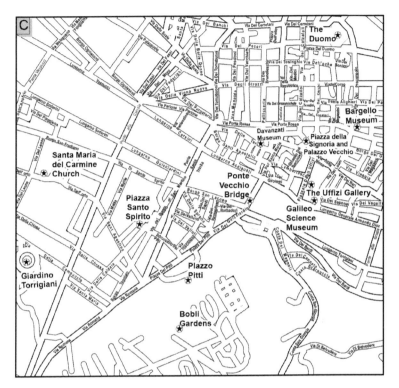

or the Carriage Museum (which is closed at the moment; check to see if it has reopened by the time of your visit).

The highlight of Pitti Palace for families with children is, without a doubt, **the Boboli Gardens**. These are the most famous gardens in Florence and a refuge for tired families in dire need of a place to rest (or to run around freely). The Boboli Gardens, built for Eleonora di Toledo, Cosimo de Medici's wife, are filled with antique statues from the Medici collection and also feature a fountain and an amphitheatre. You can either remain in the area around the palace or climb towards the Rose Garden and Belvedere Fortress for an impressive view of the city (though not as impressive as the view from Piazzale Michelangelo, which is further up the hill).

🕐 Opening times for **Boboli Gardens** and **Costume Gallery**: open daily, 08:15-18:30 (until 19:30, July-August; until 17:30, October and March; until 16:30, November-February). Closed on the first and last Monday of each month. Last entry an hour before closing.

🕐 Opening times for **Royal Apartments** and **Palatine Gallery**: Tuesday-Sunday, 08:15-18:50 (closed on Mondays). Ticket for all four attractions is 11.50 euro (more when there are special exhibitions) or free with the Firenze card. Combo tickets just for the Royal Apartments, the Palatine Gallery, and the Boboli Gardens are also available. Piazza Pitti 1, www. polomuseale.firenze.it

# Gardens in Florence

Sometimes kids just need to run around on the grass, as far as possible from any sort of museum or church. If you've already visited the most famous garden in town—Giardini Boboli (Boboli Gardens), adjacent to Palazzo Pitti—there are a number of other options to explore. **Le Cascine Park** in Via della Catena is a very popular choice, with a playground, a pool, and a pizzeria in the park. It is quite close to the centro storico, and you can reach it in about 15 minutes on foot from the main train station. Right next to it is the garden surrounding Fortezza da Basso, an ancient fort at the outskirts of the historical center, which today hosts several cultural events a year.

The **Giardino dell'Orticultura** is fun to explore, and in the summertime you will usually find some sort of event going on, including live music shows at night. Not far from this popular garden is the smaller, but lovely, **Orti di Parnaso**: a small park with a dragon-shaped fountain. Lastly, the garden in **Villa Vogel**, in Viale Antonio Canova is quite pleasant and is open year-round. It offers visitors ample space to run around, a playground, and a basketball court.

# Santa Maria del Carmine and The Brancacci Chapel

Decorated with Masaccio and Masolino da Panicale's frescoes and housed in the Santa Maria del Carmine Church, the Brancacci Chapel is a real treat for art lovers. If you have already crossed the bridge to visit Palazzo Pitti, and have leftover time and patience, then don't miss this little gem, which can even be visited in less than 15 minutes if you are in a hurry. Luckily, the frescoes are low and clear enough for kids to see and enjoy (assuming you will manage to convince them to go see yet another fresco...). Booking your visit in advance is advised, especially during the high season.

**Santa Maria del Carmine** was built as a Carmelite church in 1268 along with a convent, both of which are still standing today. The church was seriously damaged over the years, leading to its eventual renovation in an 18th-century Rococo style. A rich merchant named Felice Brancacci commissioned the frescoes in the chapel in 1423, but the whole project was cursed with bad luck from the get-go. Masolino, who was hired to decorate the chapel with his protégé, Masaccio, died shortly after receiving the commission. Masaccio took over, completed most of the work, and then died too. After opposing the Medici family, Branacci was himself expelled from Florence, leaving the chapel untended. Only years later was Filippo Lippi, another great painter, brought in to complete the job, managing to complement the beautiful Masaccio style.

On the left wall of the **Brancacci Chapel**, you can see the most famous part of the work, *Expulsion of Adam and Eve from Paradise*, their faces heavy with grief and tears. The scenes on the central wall describe episodes of St. Peter's life, and on the right wall you will find two frescoes by Masolino and three by Filippo Lippi (again, describing scenes from St. Peter's life).

As was the case for his contemporaries, newly rediscovered Greek and Roman art influenced Masaccio's work, and his drawing of Eve (*Expulsion of Adam and Eve from Paradise*) is based on the famous classical statue *Venus Pudica* (a version of which can be seen in the Uffizi). He also incorporated people he knew into his pictures; some researchers believe the man without pants who is paying a sum of money is Masaccio's friend, Donatello.

**Mission 1:** There is one fresco that pictures Adam and Eve standing next to the tree, with a snake beside them, but something is very, very strange about that snake. Can you find the painting and discover what is so strange about it?

**Mission 2:** Find the scene called Baptism of the Neophytes. You can use your binoculars if you need them. (Hint: The scene takes place in the river, where the men are being baptised). How many dressed men are in this scene?

**Mission 3:** Take out a piece of paper and a pen. Take a good look at the mosaics and then, without peeking, try to draw three kinds of typical medieval hats, just like they appear on the frescoes. Check your drawings when you're done. Were you successful?

**Mission 4:** There is one fresco with a man hanging upside down. Can you find it? How many people are standing on his left?

Opening times: Monday, Wednesday-Saturday, 10:00-17:00; Sunday, 13:00-17:00. Closed: Tuesdays, 7 January, Easter Sunday and 16 July (in addition to the usual closing days of all other monuments in Italy). Reservations may be required. Last entry 30 minutes before closing; children from the EU under 18 enter for free (ask anyway whether you are entitled to a free ticket). Piazza sel Carmine 14, Tel: 055.2382195, www.museicivicifiorentini.comune.fi.it/brancacci/

## On Masaccio

Tommaso di Ser Giovanni di Simone Cassai, known among his contemporaries as Masaccio ("clumsy" Maso), was a star who rose quickly and disappeared just as suddenly when he died at only 27 (thus perhaps founding the "27 Club" made up of famous artists who died at that cursed age, including Jimi Hendrix, Janis Joplin, Kurt Cobain, and Amy Winehouse). He earned his nickname, as Vasari explains in his biography of the painter, "not, indeed, because he was vicious, for he was goodness itself, but by reason of his so great carelessness, and with all this, nevertheless, he was so amiable in doing the service and pleasure of others, that nothing more could be desired". Masaccio is considered by many to be the first great painter of the Renaissance, thanks to his innovative use of geometric perspective, rigorous definition of space, revolutionary realism, and essential figures, which brought life and un-seen-before drama to the stories he told with his brushes. Vasari defined his work in the Brancacci Chapel as "the school of the world", because "all the most celebrated sculptor and painters since Masaccio's day have become excellent and illustrious by studying their art in the chapel".

The best place to relax after visiting the Pitti Palace and the Brancacci Chapel is Santo Spirito Square. The piazza often hosts little markets, live bands, and (sometimes) street artists. There are a number of cafés to sit in to enjoy a cold drink or a glass of white wine surrounded by students, locals, and happy tourists.

# Piazzale Michelangelo and San Miniato al Monte

Piazzale Michelangelo is probably the best-known spot in town to enjoy a magnificent view of Florence. There are a number of other places from which to enjoy a bird's eye view, such as the tiny town of Fiesole, but that requires taking bus number 7, driving for about 20 minutes, and then walking up a somewhat steep

road to get to the really good views. The observation "deck" from the Duomo's dome, Giotto's Bell Tower and Palazzo Vecchio's tower offer good views, as well, but then you can't see the Duomo or Palazzo Vecchio, obviously, and you have to climb over 400 steps. Piazzale Michelangelo, however, offers an easily accessible panoramic view of the whole town, and you can reach it by bus, with hardly any walking, which makes it perfect for younger children and toddlers too.

Named after the great Michelangelo Buonarroti, the Piazzale, which was built in a neo-classical style in 1869, is decorated with replicas of his sculptures (including a huge David).

**Mission 1:** Take a look at the view. Can you recognize any of the sights in front of you? Can you find: the Duomo? Palazzo Vecchio? Ponte Vecchio? How about Santa Croce?

> **Tip:** The walk up to Piazzale Michelangelo is hard, but the walk down is pleasant. If you have some extra time, it's a nice way to pass half an hour and let the kids run for a while before moving on to your next destination.

The walk up to the piazzale can be very long and tiring, especially for younger kids, so either take a bus (number 12 or 13 from the SMN station: 12 is better because it stops both at the piazzale and San Miniato al Monte) or a taxi. While you are up there, consider visiting two other attractions nearby: the beautiful and ancient church of San Miniato al Monte and the Rose and Iris Gardens. The San Miniato complex features a monastery, a monk-run pharmacy, and, if you come on time, Gregorian chants. The Rose and Iris Gardens, which extend on either sides of the piazzale, are especially worth visiting when in bloom.

**San Miniato al Monte** (meaning "on the mountain") is a splendid Romanesque church, built during the 11th century and dominating Florence from the top of a hill. It is run by Olivetan monks, who still live in the adjoining monastery. The church is named after San Miniato, who, according to legend, was beheaded, got up, picked up his own head and slowly walked all the way up to the top of the mountain, where he died. The church was built over his remains, to commemorate him.

Both the exterior and interior of the church are characterized by the typical Tuscan alternation of white Carrara marble and serpentino (green marble from Prato). The most important artistic monument in the church is its impressive chapel dedicated to the Cardinal of Portugal, James of Coimbra, a member of the royal family, who died in Florence during his travels from Mantua to Rome when he was only 26. Once you've visited the church, head to the adjoining pharmacy, where you can purchase traditional monk-made liquors. Try to time your visit to the church to around 18:30 (17:30 during winter months) to be impressed by the **Gregorian Chants Mass** performed by the monks (kids will love the medieval, dramatic feel. Just to be on the safe side, call first to make sure hours haven't changed).

🕑 Opening times: open daily, 08:00-13:00; 15:30-19:00 (April-mid October open daily 08:00-20:00).
To get from Piazzale Michelangelo to San Miniato al Monte, walk for a few minutes along Via del Monte Alle Croci or take the number 12 bus from Piazzale

Michelangelo up one stop. Tel: 055.234.27.31, www.sanminiatoalmonte.it

# Museums for Kids

Aside from the kid-friendly attractions mentioned so far (the Duomo's dome, Boboli gardens, the Natural History Museum), there are a few more museums in town that are particularly suitable for children and are worth exploring.

## Davanzati Museum

If you have just two days in Florence, you may not have time to stop by Museo Davanzati, but it really does merit a visit. If you find a free hour, you will be rewarded with a charming and unique museum (an actual Renaissance home, still furnished) that will enable kids to peek into the past. The great views from the top floor terrace are an added bonus (but beware—you'll have to climb more than 100 stairs to get there. This will probably be too much for younger children).

Built by the family of a wealthy wool merchant named Davizzi in the 14th century, this museum is a typical medieval tower home and still maintains several of its original fixtures. Visit the great hall on the first floor, with its display of 16th-century objects, the charming Sala dei Pappagalli (Parrot's Room), the Renaissance-style bedroom, the third-floor kitchen and several other little surprises along the way. Organized tours in English can be booked in advance.

🕘 Opening times: open daily, 08:15-13:50; closed on the 2nd and 4th Sunday of every month, and the 1st, 3rd, and 5th Monday of every month. Children under 18 enter for free; ask whether you are eligible for a free or reduced ticket. Via di Porta Rossa 13, Tel: 055.2388610, www.polomuseale.firenze.it

# Galileo Galilei Science Museum

A favourite with families, this lovely Science Museum offers visitors the chance to explore and discover in the spirit of the famous 16th-century scientist Galileo Galilei. There are interactive exhibitions and regular activities for kids, as well as educational workshops, in English, that need to be booked in advance (check out their website at www.museogalileo.it and look for "Educational Workshops" under "Planning Your Visit"). You can also book in advance a fun guided tour, in English, or get an audio guide (recommended). To book a workshop or find out more call 055.2343723. Don't forget to find and visit Galileo Galilei's finger, one of the more surprising (but popular) exhibitis on display.

Start your tour with the Medici collection room and admire antique science books and 500-year-old scientific machinery and tools. Continue to the astronomy room and discover how astrolabes work. Kids will be impressed with the globe model in room 3, where they can find out everything they ever wanted to know about navigation, Galileo, telescopes, and inventions.

🕐 Opening times: Wednesday-Monday, 09:30-18:00; Tuesday, 09:30-13:00. Last entry 30 minutes before closing. Children 6-18 years old are eligible for a reduced ticket; under six years old enter for free. There is a family ticket available (two adults + max. two kids under 18). Piazza de' Giudici 1, Tel: 055.265311, www.museogalileo.it

# Stibbert Museum

Another favourite with families, this is THE place in Florence to admire armour, swords, and other exciting knight gear. Frederick Stibbert (1838-1906) was a Florence-born Englishman who built this impressive house, since turned into a museum (and garden—see box below), now filled with his armour, porcelain, clothing, and furniture collections. The Sala della Cavalcata room is especially impressive, with its Islamic armour ranging from North Africa to India and, of course, the collection of European armoury.

**GETTING THERE:** Unlike other attractions in Florence, this museum is not within walking distance from the centre. Take bus number 4 from SMN (direction CAPPUCCINI), get off at the GIOIA stop and from there, walk along Via Stibbert towards the museum (about 10 minutes). Alternatively— get a cab.

🕐 Opening times: Monday-Wednesday, 10:00-14:00 (ticket office closes at 13:00); Friday-Sunday, 10:00-18:00 (ticket offices close at 17:00). Closed on Thursdays. Closed 1 May, Easter, 15 August, Christmas, and 1 January. All children must pay for a ticket; price reductions available for those aged 0-3 and 4-12. **The visit is led by a guide of the museum and starts every hour. A group must be a minimum of 25 people or the tour won't leave. You can't tour on your own.** To visit the Japanese collection of armours, you must book in advance (currently the Japanese collection is open on weekends only. Tours leave: Friday, 15:00; Saturday, 11:00; Sunday, 15:00; hours may vary; check the website before booking). Tel: 055.475520, www.museostibbert.it

## Stibbert Garden

The garden adjacent to the museum is a charming place to relax after visiting the museum. There is a small greenhouse, a little lake, and a tiny Egyptian-style temple for the kids to run around. The garden is open daily, April-October, 8:00-19:00; November-March, 8:00-17:00 (closed Thursdays year round, and when the museum is closed). Free of charge.

Just a few minutes away, there is yet another garden called Giardino Baden Powell, which can also be accessed from Via Stibbert and is equipped with a playground for kids. Open daily from 07:00-20:00 (closes at 17:00 during the winter months).

## Leonardo da Vinci's Machine Collection

This small but popular exhibition is dedicated entirely to the machines designed by Leonardo da Vinci. The machines have been created in full-scale, and kids of all ages will enjoy touching them, operating them (when possible), and exploring the ingenius ideas da Vinci came up with. The exhibition is located in Galleria Michelangelo, in Via Cavour 21, just two minutes from the Duomo. Open daily, 09:30-19:30. Find out more here: www.macchinedileonardo.com

Alternatively, there is a competing da Vinci exhibition in via dei Servi 66, called the Leonardo da Vinci Museum. This exhibition also houses some large models of the machines. Both are fun to explore, but personally we prefer the museum in via Cavour.

# KIDS'CORNER

## More About... The Duomo!

We all know the Duomo in Florence is BIG, but just how big is it? And how tall is that tower standing next to it? The Duomo is the third largest church in the world (after Saint Paul in London and Saint Peter in Rome), and its dome is 45.5 meters wide. That's like 4 school buses parked in a row or 189 iPads! To get to the top, you have to climb 463 steps. The Duomo itself is 153 meters long and 38 meters wide, with arches that are 23 meters high, which is like 13 average men standing on top of each other's heads. But that's nothing compared to Giotto's Bell Tower, which is 84.70 meters high and 15 meters wide. If you wanted to cover it with toilet paper, you would need more than 120 rolls!

# KIDS'CORNER

## More About... Death Masks!

Though they were first used thousands of years earlier (in Roman times), death masks were a popular object in Renaissance times. When someone famous died, mourners would lay his body on a bed and make a special mask of his face so that it would remain forever. Masks were made for Lorenzo the Magnificent, the all-mighty ruler of Florence, and Brunelleschi, the architect who designed the dome. These masks weren't only used to decorate public places or tombs of the dead. They were placed in private homes, too, which means you could easily find a typical Renaissance family sitting down for dinner and above the fireplace would be Grandpa's face, staring at them all...

## More About... The Medici Family!

Everywhere you go in Florence, you will find something that has to do with the town's most famous family, the rulers of Tuscany and patrons of the arts, the Medici family. The Medici family had a huge influence on Italian history. They were successful bankers who accumulated large amounts of money and power. They were skilled politicians, too, managing to place their family members in important religious and political roles (Lorenzo the Magnificent's son, for example, was elected to be Pope). But things didn't always go so smoothly for the Medicis. They were kicked out of town by their enemies more than once, and rival families even tried to murder them! The most famous attempt on their lives was called the "Pazzi Conspiracy".

# KIDS'CORNER

## The Pazzi conspiracy

Rival families hated the Medici, who ruled Florence with an iron fist for a very long time, and waited for moments of weakness to attack. When Lorenzo Medici (known as Lorenzo the Magnificent, or Lorenzo Magnifico) got in trouble with the Pope, the Pope agreed to look the other way while the Pazzi family attacked. It all happened on a sunny Easter morning in 1478. Lorenzo and his brother were in the Duomo, wait-

ing for Mass, when two assassins jumped them. Though Lorenzo escaped with injuries, the assassins managed to murder his brother, Giuliano. Lorenzo ran to Palazzo Vecchio, while word of the attack quickly spread throughout Florence, and his supporters rushed to save their leader. The attack failed, the Medici family stayed in power, and Lorenzo showed no mercy towards those who had betrayed him. Those who organized the plot were caught, tortured, and executed in front of the cheering crowd.

# KIDS'CORNER

## More About... How Frescoes were made!

So many churches in Florence (and in all of Italy, actually) are filled with frescoes, but exactly how were they made? Did people during medieval times have colours like we do today? And why did they need to break eggs and squash bugs? Let's find out!

People usually use the word "fresco" when they talk about paintings that are applied directly on a wall (instead of a canvas, or a piece of paper, for example), but the word actually refers to the technique of (quickly!) painting over a fresh layer of plaster before it dries (in Italian, "fresco" means "fresh").

Artists living during medieval and Renaissance days couldn't just go to the store and buy any colours they wanted; they had to make their own colours using natural substances, including minerals, plants, and even animals to produce the hues we see today. Before artists could buy minerals in special shops, they had to make the colour blue, for example, from the leaves of a plant called woad (also used to dye clothes). Before red minerals were available (like iron oxide), ref was produced by squashing an insect called kermes, which lived in oak trees, and using its blood and shell as a pigment. Alternatively, artists could also extract colour from red plants and flowers.

Once the painters had squashed enough bugs and minced enough plants and minerals to produce their colours, they needed to mix them with a substance that would serve as a binder, otherwise the colour would never stick to the wall. The solution? Egg whites! It may seems strange, but egg whites were the perfect binder, and colour mixed with egg whites (this mix-

# KIDS'CORNER

ture was called Tempera) lasts for hundreds of years.

Frescos were considered hugely popular, and the perfect way to decorate houses and churches, but they did have one big disadvantage—artists had to paint very quickly or else the plaster would dry and the fresco would be ruined. Some artists— Leonardo da Vinci, for example—hated working quickly. In fact, Leonardo disliked it so much that he even tried to invent new techniques that could be substituted for the popular art form, but he wasn't very successful.

Because it takes up to ten hours for plaster to dry, artists would divide their frescoes into sections and complete the artwork in pieces every day. Experienced artists knew how much they could manage to paint in one day and were able to apply just the right amount of wet plaster on the wall. That amount of plaster was called "giornata", which means "one day" or "one day's work" in Italian.

## More About... The Fashion and Beauty world of Florence!

Clothes were a very important part of Renaissance culture.

Medieval and Renaissance societies were divided into classes, and because clothes were the main way of demonstrating a person's position, status, and patrimony, you couldn't just wear anything you wanted. There were laws prohibiting the poor from wearing certain colours (red, for example, was reserved for the rich and powerful) or extravagant items, such as golden-belts or shoes decorated with pearls. In Pisa, for example, the law prohibited any woman who wasn't the wife of a doctor or a

# KIDS'CORNER

knight from wearing velvet clothes.

The fashion industry in Florence was world famous. Rough wool would be sent via ship from England and worked until it became a precious delicate fabric, which was then used to make incredible dresses fit for royalty. The rich owned some extraordinary items that would make the best fashion designers today blush with shame.

Let's look at Beatrice, a typical teenager from a noble family in Renaissance Florence. What would she wear and how would she prepare for a party? Beatrice would start off by taking a bath.

Her maid would help her, of course, by pouring water that had been warmed over hot coals into a basin. Then, her maid would rub and clean Beatrice's body with soap made from plants and animal fat and perfumed with flowers. Then Beatrice would put on her beautiful dress and attach her sleeves (back then sleeves weren't a part of the dress but were attached with buttons). After she was dressed, she would call another maid to braid her hair in a fashionable way.

After Beatrice was dressed and had her hair done, it was time to put on some make-up.

# KIDS'CORNER

Renaissance women liked to keep their faces very pale (only people who had to work outside had a tan; noble women had fair, pale skin). Make-up was prepared with substances we today know are harmful and even poisonous. WARNING: Do not try these at home. Leaves and roots of nettle, or iris roots, were boiled and the water was used to whiten skin, while red sandalwood and distilled wine were used to create blush. Pieces of cloth soaked in a chamomile and honey concoction were placed on the gums to strengthen them, and a combination of olive juice and onion juice was used to seal cavities. Borax water was used to encourage hair to grow stronger. Water, in which wheat had been soaked for 15 days, was also used to whiten skin, and dried squashed flowers were made into lipstick.

# Special Guides

## The Ultimate Guide for Art Detectives

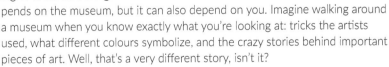

Walking around a museum can either be interesting or it can be boring. Sometimes which it is depends on the museum, but it can also depend on you. Imagine walking around a museum when you know exactly what you're looking at: tricks the artists used, what different colours symbolize, and the crazy stories behind important pieces of art. Well, that's a very different story, isn't it?

Exploring a museum with that knowledge might just be fun... So before we hop into the Uffizi, let's start with some insider's info that can help you see medieval and Renaissance art in an entirely new light.

## What does "medieval art" mean?

Everyone seems to talk about medieval art. "Oh yes, you can see amazing and beautiful medieval art in Tuscany," they say. But what does that mean, and what are the Middle Ages? The middle of *what*? The answer is simple: the Middle Ages refers to the time period between the fall of the Roman Empire (in the year 476, over 1500 years ago) and the discovery of America (in 1492, over 500 years ago). Medieval art is the artwork that was produced during that span of time.

## Why do people in medieval paintings look so weird? They don't look real at all!

That's absolutely true, but it's for a good reason. During medieval times, a painting was supposed to be symbolic, so no one cared whether the people or animals looked realistic or even if the colours were real. Medieval artists weren't bad painters or unable to hold paintbrushes. They were actually very talented; they just cared about other things entirely. In fact, most of the art produced during medieval times was religious and paintings were used to pass on messages or ideas, not to look natural. No one really minded if a man was painted flat, floating in space, bigger than a house, or if dogs seemed bigger than horses...

## Why did they always paint religious scenes? Why didn't they paint flowers or people?

Artists during the Middle Ages didn't sell their artwork in the same way that artists do in modern times. Instead, they found patrons—people who ordered and paid for paintings—who would pay them to create art. Most patrons were religious men from the Catholic Church, including the Pope, religious orders, monasteries, etc. And they were obviously interested only in religious art, which was used to educate people and to decorate churches. Even when families ordered paintings, they used them to decorate private places of worship, like family chapels.

## Why is there so much gold everywhere?

Precious materials were extremely important in medieval art. Today we judge a painting by how good the artist is, but back then a painting was considered good if the painter used a lot of really expensive materials, such as gold, gems, and a colour called ultramarine blue (which was made with a very expensive mineral called lapis lazuli). The more gold the painter used, the better the painting! So a painting rich in gold and precious materials like

Cimabue's *Madonna di Santa Trinita* (see room 3 in the Uffizi) would be a huge hit, but a painting that today we consider to be one of the most beautiful paintings in the world, like *Primavera* by Botticelli (see rooms 10-14), would be considered absolute rubbish. "This is terrible," a medieval art critic would say. "Arrest this painter immediately!"

## But why do people look so flat in medieval paintings?

That's because artists were very influenced by Byzantine art and traditions, which depicted flat-looking people on a gold surface. It's actually more complicated than that, though. When you think about it, three-dimensional figures are meant to represent the real world, right? When you paint a person, you paint him in three dimensions, not flat. But medieval artists, who were painting God or Jesus most of the time, wanted to emphasize that they weren't painting real life. They were painting the sublime, the super-terrestrial world, and the heavens. So, by using gold (which was considered to be God's colour) and by painting flat figures, they were basically saying, "I have created a shape that has no mass, no physical existence, no real space"—the closest thing possible to a divine form. When we look at paintings from medieval times, like those in the first rooms at the Uffizi (rooms 3-7), we are basically looking at paintings that were all about symbolism, ideas, and very expensive materials.

## Why does the art after the 15th century look different? And what was so special about the Renaissance?

Ahhh, good question. Well, during that period there was a dramatic change in the art world. First, paintings became much more realistic. How did this happen? A famous painter named Giotto came along and started changing the rules (if you've been to the Santa Maria Novella Church, you've seen his ground-breaking work). "Ladies and gentlemen, I refuse to continue painting paintings filled with gold, where people float in the air and are as big as houses," he declared. "No, no, no, this just won't work. I want to create art which will be much more natural, more real," he said, and that's exactly what he did. Giotto is considered to be the first artist to start the Renaissance movement, which is about realistic, classical shapes that take human proportions and presence seriously. But it didn't end there!

Next, Filippo Brunelleschi came along and dropped another game-changing bomb. "Enough, this is ridiculous," he said. "I want to see perspective. I want to be able to create a realistic illusion in my painting, and I want the people in my paintings to look like actual human beings, with volume." So he invented linear perspective, which means that if something is standing far away from you, it will look small, and if something is standing right next to you, it will seem big. "Duh!" you must be thinking. It seems so obvious to us today, but it was a crazy idea back then, and it took people some time to get used to it.

Thus the Renaissance began. Figures were suddenly three-dimensional, not flat. Light became important and people were painted proportionally in natural poses. According to a man named Vasari (one of the most important artists and architects in Renaissance Florence, and the man who built the Uffizi), this huge change reached its peak with an artist whose name you already know: Michelangelo, of course, the most famous Renaissance painter (together with Leonardo da Vinci). His work was so good, and so impressive, that Vasari claimed that no one could improve Michelangelo's work, and that the best anyone could hope for was to copy him.

### Did medieval artists have museums like we have today?
No, and honestly, if they were to wake up from their graves and join us right now in the Uffizi Museum, they would be SHOCKED. Why? Because to them art wasn't something that had a value on its own. You didn't have museums or exhibitions, and the idea that someone could value art just because of its aesthetic or historical value would seem crazy!

# How Medieval and Renaissance Artists Worked-A Look Behind the Scenes

It is important to bear in mind that Renaissance or medieval art was not supposed to embody the individual artist's personal beliefs or experiences. The artist did not work to express his innovative ideas or bare his soul. He had a workshop, open to the street, like the ones you can still see on Ponte Vecchio. These were no different from other shops, and in fact the word "artist" was scarcely used: a painter was simply called a painter, and he was considered a craftsman, nothing more. When a painter or sculptor were hired by a patron, the two men entered into a contractual agreement, which specified what the patron wanted, how much he would spend, and the quality and quantity of the more expensive materials the artist had to use, such as gold, silver, or ultramarine blue.

The number and importance of the commissions an artist received depended on his reputation and his ability. Some artists were extremely talented, like Paolo Uccello, but they spent more time studying perspective than schmoozing, networking and obtaining important commissions and thus remained poor. Others were very talented but also well connected, like Donatello, who did quite well.

Every artist had apprentices who worked in his bottega, or shop, as well as the bottega master, who was in charge of obtaining commissions from patrons, paying bills, and keeping the books. He was also in charge of a number of apprentices, aged 13-14, who came to learn and become skilled craftsmen one day.

Collaborating on a painting was a big honour for an assistant, but before he could get his hands dirty with paint, he was first sent to do more humble jobs, like sweeping, preparing wooden panels for painting, or preparing pigments. Artists did not buy colours that were ready to be used; they bought mineral pigments that had to be prepared. This was typically a task for one of the youngest apprentices. As an apprentice's skills grew, he would begin to copy the master's drawings, and then begin to sketch, paint, and cast sculptures. Finally, when he was an advanced apprentice, he would assist the master himself, contributing to the very same artwork the teacher was working on, by painting the background or minor figures while the master painted the main figures (see, for example, Andrea del Verrocchio's Baptism of Christ, in the Uffizi, in which Leonardo most certainly painted the angel on the left). Apprenticeship in a bottega was long; Cennino Cennini (author of the Craftsman's Handbook, a comprehensive technical manual written by a working artist in the early 15th century and a primary source on the artists' life and work) recommends at least six years of meticulous study. No party colleges were available. The apprentices lived with their masters, forming somewhat of an extended family. Botticelli, for example, was Filippo Lippi's apprentice, and they were very close. Many years later, when Filippo died, Botticelli took Lippi's son—Filippino, into his workshop, and instructed him in painting.

Every independent artist (usually the head of a workshop) was a member of a guild. A guild was like a union, an association of people working in the same field; their purpose was to regulate their work and trade, to maintain certain standards, and to protect the interests of the members (even to support them in case of accidents or illness). Guilds started to develop all over Europe in the 12th century, organizing every aspect of economic life during that time.

In Florence, guilds were called Arti, meaning arts. Today we use this word to indicate artistic practice, but then it was used in its etymological sense, meaning the ability to do something.

In the Middle Ages, artists did not have specific guilds. They belonged to guilds depending on the materials they used in their work. Painters, who used minerals (for pigments), belonged to the guild of the Arte dei Medici e degli Speziali (a guild of physicians and pharmacists). Goldsmiths and battiloro (literally "who hammers gold", the ones who prepared the golden backgrounds in medieval paintings) belonged to the Arte della Seta (guild of silk weavers and merchants). Sculptors and architects belonged to the Arte dei maestri di Pietra e di Legname (guild of the master stonemasons and woodcarvers). In 1350, painters and miniaturists founded a confraternity, called the Compagnia dei Pittori (Company of the Painters).

The idea that an artist was unique in some way started to develop only in the 16th century. It was then that painting and sculpting stopped being considered a physical job and became intellectual occupations, and artists started defining themselves as such. They were encouraged to study literature and history, to deepen their general knowledge, and to behave as social role models and gentlemen. This new attitude would eventually lead to the present-day conception we have of artists.

# The Uffizi's Insider's Guide

Welcome to the Uffizi, one of the best-known museums in the world. Once an office space for the Medici family, today the museum is a can't-miss stop in Florence and host to some truly incredible art.

**Note:** The Uffizi is currently undergoing an extensive rennovation, and some of the artwork has been temporarily moved into other rooms. As of February 2015, the art from rooms 3-7 has been  moved to rooms 43-45. Rooms 8 and 10-14 remain the same. Leonardo's work can be found in room 15. Michelangelo's work is on display in room 35. Since the renovations are ongoing, the numbers of the rooms indicated in this guide may not be accurate during the time of your visit.

## ROOM 2 (Currently rooms 43-45)

Our tour of the Uffizi begins in room number 2, with three of the greatest masters of medieval Italian art: Giotto di Bondone (best known as Giotto), Benvenuto di Giuseppe (known as Cimabue), and Duccio di Buoninsegna. All three were known for challenging the traditional schemes of their times and introducing new elements into painting, such as realism, naturalism, and illusionism. In particular, Giotto's contribution of introducing three-dimensional painting and creating the illusion of depth in a realistic way was a vital step towards Renaissance art. Take a look at **Cimabue's** *Maestà of Santa Trinita* **(1280-85)** and **Duccio's** *Madonna Rucellai* **(1285)**. These two altarpieces, among the most famous masterpieces of medieval art, were created for two Florentine churches: Santa Trinita and Santa Maria Novella. The subject is both is the same, a very traditional one in Christian art: the Madonna in Maestà (Italian for majesty). The Virgin usually wears a red or white dress in these paintings: white is symbol of purity, while red is, in this case, a regal attribute, inherited from classic iconography. You'll notice that Mary also always wears a blue robe or mantel, and that is hardly a coincidence. Blue (ultramarine blue) was a very important colour in medieval and Renaissance art. It was made with a semiprecious stone called lapis lazuli, which cost more than gold and had to be shipped from Afghanistan (its name, ultramarine, meaning "over the sea", indicated the path it passed before reaching the artists' workshops). Though the blue has darkened over the last 700 years, it was once quite brilliant, and as you may have read with your children in our "Ultimate Guide for Art Detectives", it was used for the most important figures in the painting.

Both altarpieces are solemn and were largely influenced by Byzantine art. Note, for example, the gold striations of the drapery (**lumeggiature** in Italian, from the word **lume**, light) in Cimabue's altarpiece. These were painted to create a glittering effect that would overwhelm the religious observer, who was looking at the painting in its original setting, the Santa Trinita Church, illuminated by only candlelight. The four men at the bottom of the painting are all biblical figures: prophets Jeremaiah and Isaiah, who spoke of the Messiah in their prophecies, and Abraham and David, as if to indicate that Jesus is their offspring, as was promised in the prophecies.

The same solemn Byzantine iconography can be seen in Duccio's **Madonna Rucellai**. Mary is seated on the throne, and the star on Mary's forehead is a reference to the name Saint Jerome gave Mary ("Stella Maris"—Star of the Sea, in Latin) to emphasize her role as guide to the faithful. Just as impressive is Giotto's realistic portrayal of the same scene (**Madonna di Ognisanti**), creating the illusion of depth through his use of perspective.

**Mission 1:** There are a number of paintings in this room with the same scene—Mary holding baby Jesus, surrounded by angels or people. But which of the paintings has the highest number of people or angels around Mary's throne?

**Mission 2:** In one of the paintings, an angel gives Mary a vase with flowers (lilies, a symbol of Mary's purity). Can you find the painting?

## ROOM 3 (Currently rooms 43-45)

Some real treasures of the Sienes School hide in room number 3. Possibly the best known among them is Simone Martini's and Lippo Memi's gothic *Annunciation* (1333). This triptych was brought to the Uffizi from the Duomo in Siena, a clear symbol of Siena's defeat in the fight against mighty Florence. In the centre of the panel, we can see the Archangel Gabriel telling the Virgin Mary she will be the mother of God (notice the golden vase of lilies in the very centre of the painting, symbolizing Mary's purity and virginity). Mary, sitting on a wooden throne, is surprised by Gabriel's arrival while she is reading a passage by the prophet Isaiah that announces the arrival of the Messiah. According to Isaiah, the Messiah will be a prince of peace, and therefore, the angel is holding an olive branch. Gabriel's apparition is sudden, and Simone Martini painted the angel as if he were touching the ground in this very moment, with his plumed wings still open and his cloak still flowing.

The technique is extremely refined: the wings are painted with colour on a layer of golden leaf, and then the gold is scratched to mark highlights. The words pronounced by Gabriel, "Ave gratia plena dominus tecum" ("Greetings most favoured one! The Lord is with thee"), are actually written on the painting, as if the angel were pronouncing them now, in front of us, and we are witnesses of this divine apparition. Surrounding Mary and Gabriel, we find two saints, as was traditional when designing medieval altar panels (the narrative scene would be in the centre, and the standing saints in the side panels). Saint Ansano is holding a palm branch, a symbol of martyrdom, and Saint Massima is holding a cross and a palm branch.

**Mission 3:** One of saints is wearing clothes that clearly indicate he's from Siena. If you've already visited Siena, you should be able to answer this question: Which saint is from Siena, and how do you know?

**Did you know?** Saints were usually portrayed with a specific attribute, or item, which was relevant to their story, so that the public would immediately recognize them (as these paintings were often used for educational purposes). Saint Peter, for example, usually holds the keys of the kingdom of heaven; Saint Catherine of Alexandria is represented with a sumptuous dress, because she was a princess, and a wheel, which was the instrument of her torture; and Saint John is usually painted with a book in his hand.

Don't miss the paintings by Ambrogio Lorenzetti (and his brother, Pietro Lorenzetti), who is responsible for some of the most beautiful artwork in Siena (see Palazzo Pubblico in the Siena Itinerary). Ambroggio Lorenzetti's style is so original, personal, rich, and vivid that he manages to tell a story like few others. In Storie di San Nicola, for example, Lorenzetti tells of St. Nicholas and his miraculous actions: he saved flour bags that fell to the sea thus sparing the town of Mira from hunger, he brought to life a boy strangled by the devil (see the upper left panel), and he eventually became a bishop. The anger, despair, and gratitude are clearly visible in the protagonist's expressions.

**Mission 4:** There's a painting in this room with several ships in it. Who painted it?

**Mission 5:** There's another painting in this room with a woman holding a book and a feather. **Question 1:** Can you find the painting? **Question 2 (bonus question):** Why is she holding a feather? What do you think she used it for?

........................................................................

## ROOM 4 (Currently rooms 43-45)

Of the different paintings representing 14th–century Florentine art in this room, Giottino's **Pieta** is probably the most touching, thanks to its realistic, human tones. Giottino (a.k.a. Tomaso di Stefano) earned his nickname because of the way he closely studied the works of Giotto, whom he admired.

## ROOMS 5 and 6 (Currently rooms 43-45)

Rooms 5 and 6 offer the viewer some dramatic and luscious Gothic paintings. Gentile di Fabriano's impressive Adorazione dei Magi, for example, brings to life the story of the three Magi who followed a star to find baby Jesus through colour and dynamic figures. This painting was commissioned by one of the richest men in 15th-century Florence—a banker, politician, and well-known enemy of the Medici family named Pala Strozzi—who paid an incredible 30,000 florins for the painting (nearly eight times the annual average salary in Florence). If you look closely, you'll find Pala in the painting. Say hello to the man with the red hat in the front row!

## ROOM 7 (Currently rooms 43-45)

Room 7's biggest attraction is Paolo Uccello's **Battle di San Romano** (1438), a dramatic portrayal of the Florentine victory over army forces from Lucca, Siena, and Milano in San Romano in 1432. The panel is one of three; the other two were sold in the 19th century and are now in the National Gallery in London and the Louvre in Paris. Leonardo Bartolini Salimbeni commissioned all three paintings, probably as a wedding gift for himself and his new bride. The problems started after Leonardo died. His two sons inherited the painting, but the new ruler of Florence, Lorenzo-refuse-me-not-Magnifico, expressed his deep interest in it (the way mafia bosses express their deep wish that you pay them protection money) and offered to buy it. When he was refused, he simply used his power to steal the painting and displayed it in the Medici Palace, where it remained until it was moved to the Uffizi.

Paolo Uccello's interpretation of the battle is interesting. Blood, violence, and pain seem to be completely missing, and the whole scene seems more like a tournament than that of a real military battle. Uccello was famous for having devoted his life to the study of linear perspective, calling it "his sweet mistress" (which thoroughly annoyed his wife), and this painting reflects that interest, even if the actual result is sometimes odd and lacking. Vasari summed it up nicely, writing: "This man, endowed by nature with a penetrating and subtle mind, knew no other delight than to investigate certain difficult, nay, impossible problems of perspective."

Also worth noting in this room are Masaccio's *Madonna col Bambino* and Masolino and Masaccio's severe and sophisticated *Madonna col Bambino, Sant'Anna e angeli*.

## ROOM 8

Room 8, a favourite for many, features the beautiful, delicate, and poetic work of Filippo Lippi. It's hard not to fall in love with Lippi's elegance, which manages to be romantic and sweet without falling into excess.

Of the many artists in the Uffizi, Filippo Lippi probably had the craziest and most controversial life. Born to a family of humble means, he was orphaned at an early age, and with no one to take care of him, he was sent to a Carmelite convent when he was 14. From the very first day, it was evident that Lippi was much more interested in painting than studying. Luckily, he was given the chance to explore his artistic talents, and he quickly blossomed. Lippi left the convent to open his own workshop, but he was still contractually obligated to the convent and continued to serve as a chaplain there to pay his debt. At one point during his travels, he was actually abducted and enslaved by pirates, yet he managed to negotiate his release thanks to his artistic skills. He then fell in love with a young girl named Lucrezia Buti who had posed for one of his paintings. Whether this love was reciprocated is unclear, but the end result was that Lippi kidnapped her, despite the nuns who closely guarded her at all times. They had a child together, Filipino Lippi, who became a famous painter like his dad.

Lippi had a huge influence on several of the artists of his day. Botticelli was his pupil (you can compare their work to find the similarities and differences). Lippi is one of the most popular Renaissance artists, and his paintings can be found in the most important museums in the world. Especially worthy of attention are the beautiful *Madonna col bambino e angeli*, the *Coronation of the Virgin*, and *Adorazione col Bambino*. It is also interesting to compare the style of father and son—a number of Filippino Lippi's paintings are in this same room.

The second best-known painting in the room is Piero della Francesca's double portrait of Count Federico III da Montefelto and his wife, Battista Sforza (of the famous Sforza family in northern Italy). In this painting, the husband is on the right side of the painting, instead of the traditional left, and both faces are portrayed in profile, which was usually reserved for sinners and demons, not noble men and women. The peculiar position is explained by the fact that the Count had lost an eye and part of his nose in a tournament a few years before this painting and was trying to hide his injury. His wife, so peaceful and regal, was already dead when this painting was made (it was probably commissioned in her honour by her bereaved husband).

The combination of the profiles with panoramic landscapes, as well as attention to the smallest detail, recalls the influence of Flemish painting, though the light palette is definitively Italian. Della Francesca carefully described the details of the rich damask sleeve of the duchess and her sumptuous jewels, especially the big pearls that show her high status and at the same time contribute to highlighting her white skin, not to mention her elaborate hair (in the Renaissance, a high and smooth forehead was considered fashionable, and women used to shave their foreheads to achieve a high profile).

Interestingly, the diptych is painted with oil, not with tempera (almost all the paintings you've seen so far were made with tempera), a technique that hadn't been used in Italy before the 15th century. To see more of Piero della Francesca's work, go to Arezzo, in southern Tuscany, where you will find his world-famous cycle of frescoes in the San Francesco Church. See the Arezzo Itinerary for more details.

**Mission 7:** There's a painting in this room by a painter named A_____ B_____, featuring a woman and an angel. Can you find the painting? What's the painting called?

**Mission 8:** Take a look at Filippo Lippi's beautiful and famous painting Madonna with Child and Angels. How many faces can you count in the painting? Hint: One face is hiding...

## ROOMS 10-14

These rooms, dedicated mostly to the work of Botticelli, are among the absolute highlights of the Uffizi Museum. If Giotto and Duccio laid the path to realism and three-dimensional figures, and others followed by introducing perspective and realistic vitality to their work, Botticelli and the artists in the next rooms

(Michelangelo, Leonardo, and others) brought this theme to a new height, the Renaissance as we know it. Several exquisite paintings compete for the viewer's attention: the world-famous *Birth of Venus* and *Primavera*, of course, but some minor gems are here as well, such as *Madonna del Magnificat*, *Ritorno di Giuditta dal Campo Nemico* (Judith's Return from the Enemy's Field), *Madonna della Melagrana*, and *Alegoria della Callunia*.

*Primavera* (Allegory of Spring) was commissioned to Botticelli by Lorenzo il Magnifico (Lorenzo the magnificent) as a wedding gift to his cousin, Lorenzo di Pierfrancesco de' Medici in 1482. This painting is considered one of Botticelli's most allegorical. The bluish winged figure on the left is Zephyr, the spring wind, who takes the nymph Chlorys as his spouse, giving her the power to generate flowers. Peonies and cornflowers sprout from her mouth while she turns into Flora. The smiling young woman dressed in white and covered in carnations, daffodils, and roses is the personification of Spring, and the whole scene fizzes with life and nature (Botticelli incorporated 190 different kinds of flowers and plants into this painting, 130 of which have been identified so far). Venus presides over this mythical realm, standing in front of a myrtle tree, a symbol of love, while on the right the three Graces dance together, and Mercury dissipates the clouds with his caduceus to preserve the eternal spring. On the top, Cupid shoots his love arrows, flying among the oranges, a symbol of the Medici family, and orange blossoms, a symbol of love and weddings in Renaissance times.

The painting was strongly influenced by classical literary works by the Latin poet Ovid (a practice that became popular during the Renaissance, as people were enthusiastically rediscovering the Greek and Roman cultures) as well as more modern writers, such as Agnolo Poliziano, a Florentine poet at the Medici court, and even Lorenzo il Magnifico himself. Another interpretation is that the mythological figures embody ideas taken from the Neoplatonic philosophy which was very much in vogue in those days, and that the whole painting should be seen as an allegory of the power of love, elevating the human soul.

Botticelli was at his prime when he painted the *Birth of Venus*, probably commissioned by the Medici family. The story was inspired by a Latin text that was widely known and appreciated during the Renaissance, Ovid's *Metamorphosis*, as well as by Angelo Poliziano's poem, *Stanze per la Giostra*. Botticelli's interpretation of Venus, the Roman Goddess of Love, coming ashore on a shell is stunning. She has just been born (from the foam of the waves, as delicate as can be) and is already a woman. The model for Venus herself remains a mystery, though many believe it was Simonetta Vespucci (a relative of Amerigo Vespucci, the famous seaman who discovered America). Botticelli was probably in love with her and used her as a model for several of his paintings, but any physical relationship was out of the question, as she was Giuliano Medici's mistress.

## More on Botticelli

Alessandro Filipepi, better known as Sandro Botticelli (1445 - 1510), was destined to be an artist from a very young age, and after an apprenticeship with a goldsmith, he became Filippo Lippi's pupil (many years later, when Lippi died, Sandro taught Lippi's son, Filippino Lippi, how to paint).

By age 25, Botticelli owned his own workshop. He spent more than a decade painting his principal masterpieces, and his style evolved into one characterized by a calligraphic linearity, defining delicate and graceful figures, while maintaining a gentle and vivid style. He often worked for the Medici family, who highly appreciated his work, and Pope Sixtus IV invited him to Rome to help decorate the Sistine Chapel in the Vatican.

But this promising career was followed by a profound spiritual crisis. Botticelli was heavily influenced by Fra Girolamo Savonarola's preaching (see the San Marco Itinerary in this chapter), which called for penitence and urged for Christian renewal. When Savonarola organized the infamous Bonfire of Vanities in 1497, Botticelli threw his own paintings into the fire, seeking atonement. Considering that Botticelli's *Primavera* and *Birth of Venus* are among the most famous Italian paintings in the world, and that they are widely considered to be the embodiment of Renaissance itself, it is incredible to think that Botticelli could have just as easily disappeared into oblivion..

**Mission 9:** Two of the most famous paintings in the world hang in these rooms. One is called Primavera (which means spring, in Italian) and the other is called Birth of Venus. Question 1: What's the name of the artist who painted both of these paintings? Question 2: In Primavera, there is a man picking a fruit from a high tree. Which fruit is he picking? Question 3 (bonus question): What's the name of the angel at the top of the picture who is shooting arrows? (Hint: these are arrows of love...)

**Mission 10:** Take a look at the beautiful painting, Birth of Venus. Question 1: What is Venus standing on? Question 2: In what year was this piece painted? Question 3 (bonus question): Which of the paintings in this room is your favourite and why?

## ROOM 15

Room 15 houses three paintings by genius Renaissance painter, architect, engineer, and inventor Leonardo da Vinci. Though these are not his masterpieces, they are interesting paintings, especially the **Annunciation**, an early work da Vinci painted in 1475-1480 that sets the tone for the master's future style. Da Vinci sets the scene in the quiet hortus conclusus (enclosed garden), an allusion to Mary's virginity, with the angel bowing before Mary to offer her a lily, another symbol of purity. The angel's wings reflect Leonardo's attention for nature and for birds, which he liked to observe, studying the characteristics of their flight while dreaming of one day building a flying machine. The same scientific eye is evident in the detail of the flowering grass lawn, a translation into images of his botanical interests. Flemish artists Leonardo knew in Florence probably inspired the level of detail in the background landscape.

To see another example of a young da Vinci work, take a look at **Battesimo di Cristo** (Baptism of Christ) by his teacher, Verocchio. The angel on the left was almost certainly carried out by Leonardo. You might also wish to take a closer look at the angel on the right. Some researchers believe it was actually painted by a third artist, Sandro Botticelli.

**Mission 11:** How many of the paintings in this room feature babies? How many paintings are there by Leonardo da Vinci? Bonus question: Can you name two more very famous paintings by Leonardo da Vinci?

**Mission 12:** There is one painting in this room with an angel flying and holding a cup. Can you find it? Who painted it?

**Tip:** Would you like to know more about the fashion and beauty world of Renaissance Florence? Check out the Kids' Corner in this itinerary!

## ROOM 35

Room 35 is another of the Uffizi's highlights, featuring the work of genius painter and sculptor Michelangelo Buonarroti (to enjoy more of Michelangelo's work, go to the Galleria dell'Accademia and the Medici Chapel, both described in this itinerary). The most famous piece in the room is the *Tondo Doni*, (1507) which is named after the rich wool merchant Agnolo Doni who commissioned it and paid 140 scudi for it. Michelangelo worked on this painting approximately during the same time he was working on his most famous sculpture, David (now in the Accademia Museum).

The tondo is an evolution of the "desco da parto", a decorated wooden tray filled with food that was brought as a gift to a woman who had successfully given birth (not a trivial matter in those days, when so many births ended with the death of the mother or the child or both). The desco da parto wasn't thrown away, but often hung on the wall as a memento.

In this tondo, Michelangelo depicts the Holy Family, one of the most traditional subjects in the arts, but completely revolutionizes its iconography. He adapts his composition to the circular shape of the tondo, by creating something completely new: the Virgin, an unusually muscular young woman, hands the Child to Saint Joseph by turning towards him in a complicated and unnatural movement. The rotation of Mary's body and arms gives the composition a spiral movement that would inspire many artists in the following years. The interaction between the figures is expressed by the way their bodies interact and intertwine with unexpected dynamic energy.

Behind the Holy Family, we find the small figure of Saint John the Baptist (easily identified, thanks to the cross he holds), and in the background are five nude youths. According to some, these figures represent pagan men before the arrival of Christ or perhaps Christians disrobed in order to receive Baptism.

The wooden frame was designed by Michelangelo and probably carved by a member of the Tasso family (a famous woodcarving family in Florence). Interestingly, the large frame not only displays the coat of arms of both the Doni (lions) and the Strozzi (three crescents. Doni's wife, Maddalena, was born to the Strozzi family) families, as can be expected, but also contains certain features (five heads, two prophets, two sibyls) taken from Lorenzo Ghiberti's Gates of Paradise (the bronze door of the Baptistery, next to the Duomo), a masterpiece we now know Michelangelo adored and thoroughly studied.

## ROOM 26 (Currently room 66)

Room 66 continues our tour into the high Renaissance with works by another great artist of the time, Raphael. His beautiful **Madonna del Cardellino** (recently restored after 10 years of work) was a wedding gift for his patron Lorenzo Nasi and is executed with sheer elegance and charm.

In this room you will also find the Portrait of Pope Leone X (born Giovanni de' Medici, son of Lorenzo il Magnifico), which was commissioned by the Pope himself. Like so many other paintings in those days, every single object portrayed in the painting has a meaning and reason for placement. The unusual point of view Raphael chose shows the Pope sitting at his desk, in front of a precious illuminated book, identified as the Hamilton Bible. The illuminated Bible, the golden magnifying glass, and the wrought silver bell are all there to let the viewer identify the Pope as a Medici; the bell bears the Medici coat of arms, while the parchment code is open at the beginning of the Gospel of Saint John, the Pope's namesake.

These fine (and costly!) objects were also meant to remind the viewer of the Pope's refined taste, only natural for a pope who came from the Medici family, who prided themselves on being patrons of the arts.

## ROOM 28 (Currently room 83)

Room 83 houses the not-so-Florentine but absolutely wonderful works of Titian, including the world-famous painting **Venere di Urbino** (Venus of Urbino). Named **Venus** because of the position in which the model is lying in this painting and believed by some to be a portrait of a courtesan, this is more likely a nuptial painting of a young lady who is looking directly to the only viewer who was supposed to see the painting: her husband. The roses she holds in her right hand are a symbol of love; the dog at the end of the bed represents fidelity; and the myrtle in the vase, close to the window, is both sacred to Venus and a symbol of eternal love and marital fidelity. Titian painted an adjoining chamber in the background, paved with marble and decorated with brocades hung on the walls, where two maidens are preparing a splendid dress for their mistress. The girl in white is searching for something in a carved and painted cassone, a typical chest in which clothes were kept in the Renaissance.

••••••••••••••••••••••••••••••••••••••••••••••••••••••••••••••••••

**Mission 13:** What were your three favourite pieces? Why?

**Mission 14:** Once you end your tour, go to the bookshop and see if you can find a postcard of these three works. If not, can you find postcards by the same artists of other works you liked? (Parents—after such hard detective work, by such brilliant detectives, you might want to buy the favourite postcards, or at least one!)

••••••••••••••••••••••••••••••••••••••••••••••••••••••••••••••••••

There are several other interesting paintings in the remaining rooms, and a number of lesser-known works by big names, such as Rembrandt and Velasquez, which you can easily skip if everyone is tired. The one room you really shouldn't skip is the **Caravaggio Hall (room 90, right next to the exit).** Though he had very little to do with Florence, Caravaggio is one of the undisputed geniuses of Italian painting, and this is an opportunity to see three of his great works. One of these is the shockingly dramatic **Sacrifico di Isacco** (the Sacrifice of Isaac), with the unforgettable expression on Isaac's face, rendered even stronger by the technique Caravaggio was famous for: combining harsh realism with chiaroscuro (juxtaposing light and dark tones to set a mood in a painting).

# Eating in Florence

Florence offers some great food and wonderful restaurants, but finding a kid-friendly option may be slightly more challenging, and there are so many restaurants, trattorias, osterias, bars, and tavole calde that it's easy to get lost. Here are a few basic recommendations, to help you navigate your way:

- Trust your instinct, as there is no point in dragging the whole family across town just to stick to the recommendations in this guide. If the food looks fresh, it's probably good. If you are too close to a tourist attraction, if only tourists are sitting inside, or there's an eager waiter standing on the street trying to convince you to come in—it's probably bad. Though frustrating for foodies who want to try typical Italian dishes, most places that kids will love serve the basics—pizza, some more pizza, pasta, and salads. Oh yes—pizza too...

- If your kids aren't that fussy about their food, you will find that most restaurants are actually friendly and accommodating (simply avoid the high-end places). The adults can enjoy the more complicated dishes and order a plate of pasta con salsa (pasta with tomato sauce) for the kids. After all, there is no point in spending 15 euro for a fancy dish for a kid who thinks the sauce is "weird" and doesn't care whether the pasta was personally crafted by the owner's grandmother or came from a frozen bag. If the restaurant won't serve any plain pasta with tomato sauce, you can still order patatine fritte (French fries), which are featured in most restaurants' menus (under "Contorni", which means side dishes), to keep kids happy.

- Many tourists find that eating in a restaurant every day can be not only very expensive but also stressful for the body. If you are looking for a lighter lunch, there are several little places serving Panini (sandwiches) or slices of pizza to go. It might actually be a good idea to save the restaurants for dinner, when everyone is calmer. Instead of a heavy lunch, you might enjoy dotting your day with ice cream stops that will keep everyone happy and refreshed.

# **Quick-fix** Restaurants

## NEAR THE MERCATO CENTRALE

For a quick lunch, try the restaurants in front of the Mercato Centrale (five minutes from the Duomo), or the restaurants in the upper floors of the newly rennovated market. Prices are slightly high, but the quality is good. Outside the market complex there are a number of simple but reasonable restaurants, but only one is worth mentioning - **Trattoria Mario** is a Florentine institute, reasonably priced and delicious, but there is always a line and not much time to linger around, and it's not very kid-friendly (or vegetarian-friendly, for that matter; almost everything on the menu contains meat). However, if you come early and see an opening, walk right in; it's worth it. Open daily for lunch only (12:00-15:30); closed on Sundays. Cash only and no reservations accepted. May be closed during parts of August. Via Rosina 2 (if you stand on the stairs with your back to the market, Mario will be at your two o'clock). Tel: 055.218550, www.trattoria-mario.com

## NEAR THE DUOMO

**Ristorante Self-Service Leonardo** is a very simple place (cafeteria), but it offers ample seating and dishes kids will probably enjoy. Open Sunday-Friday, 11:45-14:45, 18:45-21:45. Via de' Pecori 11, right behind Giotto's Bell Tower, Tel: 055.284446

A better option than a cafeteria, in our opinion, would be a pizzeria. One of our go-to quick-fix restaurants near the Duomo is **Gusto Leo**. This simple pizzeria offers some pasta dishes and salads, too, and prices are reasonable, despite the central location (Pizzeria yellow, just across the street from Gusto Leo, isn't bad either). Via del Proconsolo 8, Tel: 055.285217, www.ristorantegustoleo.com. Open daily, 9:00-23:00.

Alternatively, about 3 minutes from the Duomo hides another great pizza place: **Pizzaeria O'Vesuvio**, that serves real, traditional Neapolitan pizza to satisfy any palate. Their extended opening hours mean you can have an early or late lunch, if you want. Via dei Cimatori 21, Tel: 055.285.487, www.ovesuvio-firenze.com. Open Tuesday-Sunday, 11:30-16:00, 19:00-23:45. Monday open for dinner only.

**Mr Pizza**, right next to the entry to the dome (if you are standing in front of the Duomo, facing the doors, Mr. Pizza will be on your left) offers pizzas and salads, as well as outside seating, overlooking the stunning Duomo. Open daily, 11:30-midnight. Piazza del Duomo 5, ww.mrpizzafirenze.it, Tel: 055.386.0311

A few meters away, at the intersection between Piazza Duomo and Via Martelli, you will find **Snack Bar Bottegone**. This is more a cafeteria than a restaurant, and the food is very simple, but there is ample seating, and a few basic dishes that kids will like.

As you walk along Via dei Calzaiuoli, the main street connecting the Duomo to Piazza della Repubblica, you will find yet another quick fix cafeteria - **Snack Self Service Marchetti**. The food, as can be expected, is simple and somewhat pricey, given the location, but if you are looking for a simple solution - this might be it. Via dei Calzaiuoli 102, Tel: 055 210805, not far from the Disney shop.

## NEAR SANTA MARIA NOVELLA
**Trattoria il Contadino** is a simple and tasty little place near the station and just 10 minutes from the Duomo), kid friendly and reasonably priced. It is open daily, all day long, which means as early or as late a lunch as you please—a rare privilege in Italy. Monday-Friday, 12:00-22:30. Via Palazzuolo 69, Tel: 055.2382673, www.trattoriailcontadino.it

**Ristorante Spada** is a popular venue. The food is not bad (but not exceptional, either), but if you happen to be visiting Florence on a weekday, and the restaurant is offering its lunch deal - walk right in. For 11 euro per person you will enjoy a very satisfying meal. Via della Spada 62, Tel: 055.218757, www.laspadaitalia.com. Open daily, 12:00-15:00, 19:00-22:30.

## NEAR SANTA CROCE AND PIAZZA DELLA SIGNORIA
**Osteria de' Benci** offers a modern and tasty twist on Tuscan classics. The pasta dishes are very good, as is the meat, especially the tagliata - grilled and sliced sirloin, and the Bistecca. Watch out - they serve their steak bloody! Via dei Benci 13, Tel: 055.234.4923, www.steriadeibenci.it. Open daily, 12:30-15:30, 19:30-23:00.

If you are looking for a sandwich to eat on the go, then **Via dei Neri** is the street for you. Located Half way between Piazza dela Signoria and Piazza Santa

Croce, this tiny street boasts three popular panini shops (one of them is the most famous sandwich shop in town - **L'Antico Vinaio**) and some delicious ice cream (Gelateria dei Neri - see description below). While L'Antico Vinaio has many fans, and rightfuly so, we'd like to point out that the shop across the street, **La Fettunta**, offers some mighty sandwiches of its own. Skip their mediocre pasta dishes and go straight for the massive porchetta (fire roasted pork) sandwiches, served in delicious focaccia bread. One of these, with a glass of their red wine (or a coke, for the kids), will be more than enough to keep you going! Via dei Neri 72, Tel: 055 094 8930. Open daily.

Lastly, if you are looking for a place to buy reasonably priced but tasty sandwiches, the area behind Piazza della Signoria and the Uffizi offers a good selection. **Mangia Pizza** is a small but elegant sandwich shop, with a fantastic selection. All the sandwiches are made with quality produce. (If you want sometihng simpler - pop next door, to 'Le Tre Comari', where they'll make you a very tasty and amusingly large sandwich for 3 euro). Via Lambertesca 24/26. Tel: 055.287.595, www.mangiapizzafirenze.it. Open daily, 10:00-19:00

If you are looking from some very good but pricey burgers (Italian style, with locally grown beef and gourmet extras, like truffles), try this kid-friendly place: **Lungarno 23**. Open Monday-Friday, 19:00-23:00; Saturday-Sunday, 12:30-15:30, 19:00-23:00. Located in Lungarno Torrigiani 23 (in front of the Galileo Science Museum, on the other side of the river), Tel: 055.2345957, www.lungarno23.it

Another place that serves tasty hamburgers, and is just a minute or two from Piazza Santa Croce, is **Soul food**. Take the kids here if they have had enough with pasta and pizza. The design is modern, prices are reasonable, and the food is very good. Come here for lunch on a weekday. At dinnertime, and on weekends, the restaurant is less of a family venue and more of a cool night spot for locals. Via dei Benci 34, Tel: 055.2639.772, www.soulkitchenfirenze.it Open Monday-Friday, 11:00-02:00, Saturday-Sunday, 18:00-02:00.

# **More Serious** Restaurants

If you only have a few days in Florence, with or without kids, you will probably want to try at least one good Italian restaurant (you can always order, as suggested before, a plate of patatine fritte or promise them two desserts if they behave). For more serious dining, try one of these options, which all serve good, modern, and very tasty local dishes. If there is a specific restaurant you like (not just from this list, but anywhere in Florence), we highly recommend **booking in advance**. All the good places fill up very quickly, and if you don't reserve a place you will have to settle for mediocre options.

## NEAR THE UFFIZI AND THE DUOMO
**Ristorante Frescobaldi** hides just off Piazza della Signoria. It might take you a few minutes to find it, but it is very much worth the search, as the food here is quite delicious. Prices aren't low, but they aren't ridiculously high, either, considering the quality of the food and the location. Try their 'primi' - we like the spaghetti with sea urchin, prawns and tomato sauce, the oven baked pasta served with a rich ragu, and the fresh tagliollini with truffles. Meat lovers will enjoy the braised veal cheek, and the steak, naturally. Via dei Magazzini 2. Tel: 055 284724, www.deifrescobaldi.it.

The recently opened **Da Vinci** restaurant offers light lunches in an informal bistro, or a more formal dining experience. The restaurant is located at the top floor of the Eataly complex (an entire palazzo dedicated to Italian food and food culture), just half a block from the Duomo. The food is innovative and the presentation modern. Alternatively, try the more easy-going **food court** on the first floor. There are plenty of options to choose from.
Via Martelli 22, Tel: 055. 0153603, email: Ristorantedavinci@eataly.it

Lastly, a personal favourite: just two minutes from the Duomo and Eataly, you will find the hugely popular **Il Desco trattoria.** This charming place offers fresh and modern Tuscan dishes as well as a number of vegetarian options. The decor is lovely: there is a small patio and garden, and the owners are very friendly. Try their pasta dishes, and their antipasti, which are especially good.
Via Cavour 27, Tel: 055.288330, www.ildescofirenze.it. Open Monday-Saturday, 12:20-22:30 (reservations are recommended, especially for dinner).

## NEAR THE MERCATO CENTRALE
**Osteria Pepo** serves tasty, modern dishes, based on traditional recipes. Open daily, 12:00-14:30, 19:00-22:30. Via Rosina 6r, Tel: 055.283259, www.pepo.it

## NEAR PALAZZO PITTI
**Il Santo Bevitore** offers great traditional dishes and a vibrant elegant atmo-

sphere. Not really suitable for younger children; foodie teenagers, however, will appreciate this chic place. Open Monday-Saturday, 12:30-14:00, 19:30-23:00; Sunday open for lunch only. Via di Santo Spirito 64r (halfway between Pitti Palace and Brancacci Chapel), Tel: 055.211264, www.ilSantobevitore.com

## NEAR THE ACCADEMIA AND SAN MARCO

**Ristorante Accademia**, overlooking the quaint little San Marco Piazza, serves some delicious localities (try the meat dishes) that will satisfy demanding palates. Open daily, 12:00-15:00, 19:00-23:00. Piazza San Marco 7r, Tel: 055.217343, www.ristoranteaccademia.it

## NEAR SAN LORENZO AND MEDICI CHAPELS

**La Cucina del Garga** offers modern personal interpretations of the classic Tuscan cuisine. Monday-Saturday, 12:00-14:30, 19:30-22:30; Sunday closed. Via San Zanobi 33r, near the San Lorenzo market, Tel: 055.475286, www.garga.it

## NEAR SANTA CROCE

**Ristorante Dino** serves traditional, tasty, and hearty Tuscan-style food. Monday 19:30-22:30; Tuesday-Sunday, 12:00-14:30, 19:30-22:30; closed Sundays. Via Ghibellina 47r, Tel: 055.241452, www.ristorantedino.it

If it's meat you are looknig for, and some delicious pasta, then **La Maremma** is the place to go. Aptly named after Tuscany's most southern region, which is famous for its meat production, La Maremma offers some tasty yet not overly-complicated dishes, such as pork chop stew with chestnuts, pici pasta with sausage and porcini mushrooms, a very good 'tagliata' steak, trippa (cow's stomach), and more. Via Giuseppe Verdi 16, Tel: 055.244615, www.ristorantelamaremma.com.

Another great option for those looking for a typical Tuscan trattoria is **Del Fagiolo**. The portions are generous, the meat is excellent, their steak is famous, and they treat their pasta with the respect it deserves. This place is always full, which can be a bit exhausting, but if you have the patience to wait in line, del Fagiolo deserves a visit. Corso dei Tintori 47, Tel: 055.244285. Open Monday-Friday, 12:30-14:30, 19:30-22:30.

# Ice Cream!

The debate over Florence's best ice cream (gelato) has been going on for years and we, mere mortals, shall not presume to resolve it. The simple truth is that it really does depend on how you like your ice cream. Kids will usually love the ice cream in the touristy places (those high heaps of colourful ice cream in the shop around the Uffizi and Ponte Vecchio), because it comes in impressive containers, it's shiny, and the tastes are subtle, never aggressive. But don't worry — even if you buy ice cream from the most touristy gelateria, it will still be reasonably good.

If you are looking for great, not just reasonably good ice cream, check out these places, all well known and armed with fanatic fans ready to defend their favourite gelateria's reputation.

Traditional ice cream lovers, who look for the old fashioned, rich, creamy, and deep flavours, will be impressed with one of our personal favourites—**Grom**—which hides away in a tiny little alley called Via del Campanile (from Giotto's Campanile turn to Via del Campanile and walk 50 meters. It's hard to miss the line). Open daily, 11:00-24:00. Tel: 055.216158, www.grom.it

**Vestri** also offers some very good ice creams made with traditional ingredients, as well as an assortment of delicious chocolates that will get the sugar pumping. The tiny shop is located in Borgo degli Albizi (from the Duomo, walk along Via del Proconsolo, turn left onto Via dell'Oriuolo, and turn right onto Piazza Salvemini). Open Monday-Saturday, Tel: 055.2340374, www.vestri.it

**Perche' no!** is also comfortably located near the sights (just a few meters from Piazza della Signoria) and offers fresh, tasty ice creams and granitas in both traditional and original flavours. Via dei Tavolini 19r (walk from Piazza della Signoria along the main street leading to the Duomo, Via Calzaiuoli, and turn right onto Via dei Tavoini.) Open daily, 11:00-21:30 (Saturday open late until 22:30; Tuesday closes early at 20:00). Tel: 055.2398969, www.percheno.firenze.it

**Gelateria dei Neri** is not only a local establishment, but our perosnal favorite gelateria in town. We have yet to taste such intensely flavorful, creamy ice creams as the ones served here. That said, we realize that this may not be the best ice cream for kids, who might prefer simpler tastes. There is onlt one way to find it - try their ice cream, and if you don't like it, walk half a blck in the firection of piaza Santa Croce to Gelateria La Carraia, and buy a new cone there...

**Gelateria Carabe** brings the Sicilian tradition to Florence with fresh, fruity flavours, tasty ice creams, and Sicilian pastries and granitas. Via Ricasoli 60r (literally 20 seconds away from the Accademia). Open daily, 10:30-24:00. Tel: 055.289476, www.gelatocarabe.com

Last but not least, try the extremely popular **Gelateria La Carraia**, strategically placed just off the La Carraia bridge (there is a second location in Via dei Benci 24, half way between Piazza della Signoria and Piazza Santa Croce). Kids will love this friendly place, and enjoy the view of the Arno river. Piazza Nazaro Sauro, Open daily, Tel: 055 280695, www.lacarraiagroup.eu

# Sleeping in Florence

There are literally hundreds of accommodation options to choose from in Florence and the area. Apartments are a popular choice for families, especially if you plan on staying in Florence for a number of days/weeks and taking day trips to other destinations like Siena, San Gimignano, and Pisa. Before booking, check out websites like www.tripadvisor.com, www.booking.com, and www.venere.com for comments, hotel ratings, and bargains.

## IF YOU ARE LOOKING FOR AN APARTMENT HOTEL

**Signoria Apartments** offer a number of comfortable apartments for the whole family in the heart of Florence. Tel: 055.2381857, Cell: 338.9137450. www.Signoriaapartments.com

**Residence Michelangelo** is an elegant liberty-style villa divided into comfortable apartments. Tel: 055.6811748, www.residencemichelangiolo.it

**First of Florence** apartment hotel offers equipped apartments within walking distance of the Duomo. Via dei Servi 38, Tel: 055.218442, www.firstofflorence.it

**Residence Hilda** is an elegant and well located apartment hotel in Via dei Servi 40. Tel: 055.288021, www.residencehilda.com

The following websites list several apartments in Florence, depending on the number of people and your budget: www.friendlyrentals.com, www.florenceaccommodation.com, www.waytostay.com, www.gowithoh.com/vacation-florence-apartments, and www.apartmentsflorencerental.com. Before placing your reservation, try to cross-reference the apartment with other websites to see A) if you can get a better deal and B) what other travellers had to say.

## IF YOU ARE LOOKING FOR A HOTEL OR A B&B

**La Dimora degli Angeli** offers modern and inviting rooms just a minute away from the Duomo. Via de Brunelleschi 4, Tel: 055.288478. www.ladimoradegliangeli.com

**Hotel l'Orlogio** is a great choice. A modern hotel, perfectly located, and serves a nice buffet breakfast in a dining hall overlooking the view. Piazza Santa Maria Novella 24, Tel: 055.277380, www.hotelorologioflorence.com

**Hotel David** offers comfortable rooms and simple décor with friendly service and reasonable prices. Within walking distance from the centre. Viale Michelangiolo 1, Tel: 055.6811695, www.hoteldavid.com

**Hotel Davanzati** is an excellent choice: modern, reasonably priced, and a great location. Via Porta Rossa 5, Tel: 055.286666, www.hoteldavanzati.it

**Hotel Alessandra** is another reasonably priced option, with modern rooms and a great location. Borgo SS. Apostoli 17, Tel: 055.283438, www.hotelalessandra.com

**Residenza il Villiono** is a quiet, inviting place, with comfortable rooms (there's also a family suite) and a little garden to play in. Via della Perfola 53, www.ilvillino.it

## SLEEPING OUTSIDE OF FLORENCE, TOWARDS THE CHIANTI REGION

**Le Massucce** is a reasonably priced, charming place. Simple but comfortable and just 15-20 minutes from Florence (by car). Apartments with amenities; lovely garden but no pool. Via Cassia 18, San Casciano Val di Pesa, Tel: 055.828397, 333.1459279, www.lemassucce.com

**Le Torri** is a 13th-century villa with family rooms. Only 25 minutes from Florence (by car), it overlooks the Chianti Hills. Via Poppiano 88, San Quirico in Collina (Montespertoli), Tel: 0571.670952, 338.5406164, www.letorri.com

## Special Events in Florence

Though the best medieval courts take place in other towns (Monteriggioni, Volterra, Arezzo and Massa Marittima, see later itineraries for more detail), Florence does offer one world-known event. Calcio Fiorentino is a famous Florentine football match that takes place every June in Piazza Santa Croce and draws a huge crowd. It can be a rather violent ordeal (like American football but without protective gear) but is very impressive to watch. This early form of football (soccer) originated in the 16th century and was played in Piazza della Signoria until it was moved to Piazza Santa Croce. Today, four teams compete for the title, each representing a different Florentine quarter: Santa Croce (blue uniforms), Santa Maria Novella (red uniforms), Santo Spirito (white uniforms), and San Giovanni (green uniforms). The costumes and excitement in the air also make for a unique experience. Check out YouTube videos (look for Calcio Fiorentino) to decide whether this is the event for you (or if it's too violent). Tickets sell out very quickly (start looking for them in May) and tend to be expensive, so book in advance. Info: www.calciostoricofiorentino.it Tickets: www.boxofficetoscana.it

> **Tip:** There are numerous small events in Florence all year: wine tasting, food and ice cream festivals, open-air concerts in parks, and much more. Check with the local tourist office to find out about special events happening while you're visiting.

## Special Activities in Florence

Special activities are a sure-fire way to excite kids and even keep hard-to-please teenagers entertained. Florence is an incredible place, but kids might not necessarily appreciate its art and history as much as adults do. Combining your exploration of the city with a Segway tour, cooking class, or fun out-of-town activity will make for memorable moments children will love. Add a few ice cream breaks and a visit to the park at the end of the day to relax and unwind, and you'll have a winning recipe for enjoying Florence with kids.

## COOKING CLASSES

Cooking classes are a great idea for families. Even if your kids initially balk at the prospect, they will definitely remember the experience. The classes can be pricey, though, so call ahead and ask about family rates. Also make sure to find out whether kids are welcome—some classes are geared more towards adults. If the prices are too high, consider taking classes in a less touristy destination. You'll find a number of kid-friendly cooking classes in San Gimignano, Lucca, and Cortona (see later itineraries for detailed options). Unfortunately, not all courses have phone numbers you can call for information; some can only be contacted via their websites. **In any case, courses are popular, so book in advance!**

**Accidental Tourist** offers moderately priced cooking lessons for the whole family in an 800-year-old villa. The hands-on course is especially recommended for children, but it's also immensely popular—be sure to make reservations well in advance. And don't forget a camera to capture the flour-y moments. A half-day cooking class costs about 80 euro per person. Tel: 055.699376. www.accidentaltourist.com/activities/cooking-class

Another good option for families is **Tuscany Cooking Class**, which offers courses in a charming villa just outside of Florence. Run by Italian chefs, these classes are also geared towards children; talk to the staff about your kids' ages to decide upon the most suitable options. www.tuscany-cooking-class.com

**Cooking Tuscany** is a "foodie" favourite, meant for those who love and appreciate Italian cuisine (which also means it might be more suitable for older children and teenagers), in a medieval setting near the Arno River in Florence. www.cookingintuscany.net

Yet another option is participating in a **hands-on cooking fiesta** at an actual Florentine family home, where you'll make authentic dishes and get a real feel of the town. www.tuscany-cooking.com

Are you looking for a **private lesson** with a chef or a guided tour of the market? Try one of the activities organized by www.vinaio.com/cooking-programs/private-cooking-activities.

**Chefs Ginny and Fiamma** also offer private lessons. They can come to your rental apartment (provided it is properly equipped) or you can attend one of their lessons in the Chianti Region, which is less than an hour from Florence.

www.kitchencheznous.com

## ADVENTURE PARKS NEAR FLORENCE

There's no rule that says you have to spend your entire trip to Florence within its city limits. If you need a break from museums, churches, and even the Tuscan charm, a half-day in an adventure park can be a welcome change of pace, and you can always return to Florence for a tasty dinner and a lazy, relaxed stroll along the city's streets.

Adventurous kids ages three and up will love **Parco Avventura il Gigante di Albero Vivo**, which offers a chance for them to jump, climb, complete obstacle courses, and navigate rope ladders between trees. Arrive at least three hours before closing time to get the full experience, and note that kids must be wearing sports clothes and closed-toe shoes to use the tracks. Opening times: March-April (weekends only), 10:00-sunset; May-September, open daily (except Mondays), 10:00-sunset. October-November (weekends only), 10:00-sunset; Closed for bad weather, closed during the winter. Parco Avventura Il Gigante, Via Fiorentina 276, Vaglia (a few km from Florence), Tel: 320.3261243, www.parcoavventurailgigante.it

**Tree Experience** near Fiesole is another great option for the adventurous and features tarzaning, rope bridges, and a soft air range. Just a few km from Florence. Opening times: June-September, open daily, 10:00-19:00; April-May, open daily, 10:00-18:00; March and October, weekends only, 10:00-18:00. Closed during the winter months. Fiesole, Tel: 055.3984036, www.treeexperience.it

# PISA and LUCCA

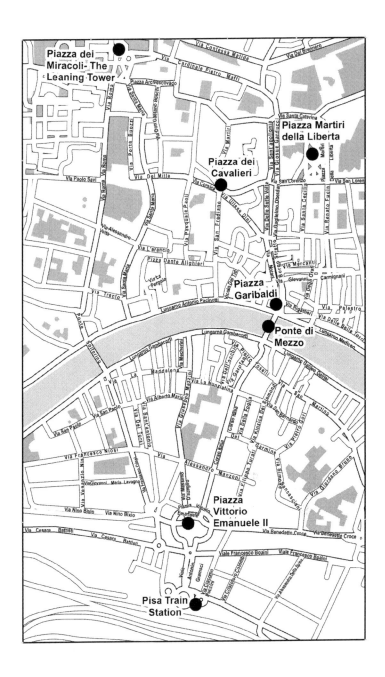

# Chapter 2

# Pisa and Lucca

Situated only 20 minutes away from each other, Pisa and Lucca combined make for a fun, action-packed day trip, sure to please both toddlers and teenagers. Pisa is known for its Leaning Tower, where each family member can pose for photos as they pretend to "hold" the Tower. Lucca offers elegant little streets, opportunities for bike rides along medieval ramparts, and a generally tranquil atmosphere. It's the perfect place to end your day trip, relaxing with a glass of wine while the kids lick ice cream and play in one of the town's many traffic-free piazzas.

If you plan to see both cities in the same day, it's best to visit Pisa first for three reasons. First, if you intend to spend the night in the area, Lucca offers a better selection of hotels and B&Bs. Second, Lucca is even nicer during the afternoon than in the morning. Third, there is always a line at the Leaning Tower, so unless you make a reservation (not a bad idea, by the way), you'll have to stop by the ticket office and book a spot for later in the day (im-

mediate openings are rare during the high season). If you don't arrive until the afternoon, you risk not being able to climb up the Tower at all.

## Top 5 Family Activities

1. Rent a bike and ride along the wonderfully preserved ramparts in Lucca (especially beautiful during sunset).

2. Twirl around Lucca's completely round Piazza Anfiteatro.

3. Climb up Pisa's world-famous Leaning Tower and then take a picture of yourself pretending to hold or push it.

4. Visit the beautiful Livorno Aquairum.

5. Jump around in one of the many parks and adventure parks in the area.

# Pisa

## GETTING THERE

**BY CAR:** Neither Pisa nor Lucca require a car during your visit. In fact, both town centres are ZTL and closed to non-resident traffic. From Florence, you can get to Pisa in under an hour via the toll free Fi-Pi-Li (also known as the SGC Firenze Livorno). Park at the **Pietrasantina** parking lot where you'll also find a gas station, small restaurant, and tourist information office. From there, a shuttle called **Navetta**, or the regular bus called the **LAM Rossa** will take you directly to the Leaning Tower of Pisa.

**BY TRAIN:** Both express and regional trains run regularly from Florence to Pisa (express trains take 50 minutes, while the regional takes just over an hour). Pisa is also well connected via train with several other major cities in Tuscany, as well as with Rome and Milan. Trains from Pisa to Lucca (a 20 minute ride) leave every 30 minutes (the last train leaves at 21:50).

**BY PLANE:** Pisa has a growing airport with several regular and low-cost flights arriving and departing daily. Both Ryanair and Easyjet use Pisa as their base in Tuscany. Though the airport is small, it is comfortable and very close to the city. There are also direct flights from Pisa to New York (via Delta) and connecting flights (with Alitalia and other companies) to just about any destination in the world.

**Tip:** If you plan to explore Pisa before heading to Lucca, or if you're just stopping by for a few hours and then heading back to Florence, you can leave your luggage in the Pisa train station (note that you can't leave any luggage bigger than a backpack in the Leaning Tower's cloak room, so if you are travelling with a suitcase and plan to climb up the Tower, the train station is the place to leave it). Look for the sign saying "deposito bagagli" on the far right end of platform number 1 (next to the police station). This service is available daily, generally from 06:00-21:00 (though hours may vary, ask before leaving your bag to avoid unpleasant surprises). Each platform at the station has an elevator at its far left side, which is especially useful if you are carrying heavy bags and can't carry them up and down the stairs (elevators operate daily between 06:00-22:00).

**TOURIST INFORMATION OFFICES:** In addition to the small office in the Pietrasantina parking lot, there is a newly refurbished information desk in the Pisa Airport ☺ (open daily, 09:00-23:00; also offers on-the-spot hotel booking services; Tel: 050.502518), and another tourist office is located on the left corner of Piazza Vittorio Emanuele II, just two minutes from the train station (open daily, 09:00-19:00; Sundays and off-season, 09:00-16:00; Tel: 050.42291).

Pisa is often overlooked by tourists who rush to the Leaning Tower and then dash back to Florence on the first available train, but it is actually a lovely town, fun to explore with kids, and a great place to eat a reasonably priced and tasty Tuscan meal. Pisa also offers a number of popular annual events (see the end of this chapter for details) which shouldn't be missed if you are in the area. A former local maritime empire which once dominated the Mediterranean Sea with its skilled navy and impressive fleet, Pisa today is known mostly as a quiet university town (and the alma mater of one famous fellow, Galileo Galilei). If you have only two hours in Pisa, skip the scenic walk suggested in this itinerary and head straight to the Leaning Tower. But if you do have the time to wander around, we suggest exploring the other attractions near the Tower (in the area known as Piazza dei Miracoli), as well as the town itself, either by foot or on a family bike.

## A Cool Way to Tour Pisa

Booking a novelty ride can be fun for the whole family and especially exciting for kids. You can rent bikes, tandem bikes, or rickshaws and wildly navigate the streets in **Toscana in Tour** in Via della Faggiola Ugguccione 41 (next to the Leaning Tower; Tel: 333.2602152, www.toscanaintour.it) , www.ecovoyager.it).

## GETTING TO THE LEANING TOWER

**BY BUS:** Exit from the train station and take the bus called LAM Rossa from the stop **in front** of the train station, directly outside the NH Cavalieri Hotel; it will leave you just outside Piazza dei Miracoli. Bus tickets may be bought in advance in the station or more expensive tickets are available on the bus (if you have exact change). Don't forget to validate your ticket in the little machines on the bus, or you may be fined.

**BY TAXI:** There's a taxi station outside of the train station, on the left.

**BY FOOT:** If you have the time, the most enjoyable way to reach the Tower is by foot. This will allow you to partake in the views Pisa has to offer, especially those around the river. You can also sample delicious ice cream on the way and engage in some fun window shopping. It's hard to get lost, and it's an easy 25-30 minute stroll.

**Our tour of Pisa begins** at the train station. Walk straight ahead across a very large piazza called Piazza Vittorio Emanuele II (notice the colourful Keith Haring mural just to the left of the piazza) and then continue along the main road, Corso Italia. Keep walking along this road (which features plenty of shops to grab a teenager's interest), until you reach the river and the main bridge, Ponte di Mezzo. This is one of the prettiest points in town, with a great view of the river and the elegant buildings along its banks.

**Did you know?** Much like Ponte Vecchio in Florence, during medieval times the Ponte di Mezzo was home to dozens of tiny artisans' shops.

**Tip:** Though foodies won't deem it to be the best ice cream in Pisa (that honour belongs to **de Colteli**, at Lungarno Pacinotti 23, open daily from 12:00, www.decoltelli.it), the **Bottega del Gelato** in Piazza Garibaldi, immediately off the bridge, is the most popular ice cream shop in town. Kids love it, thanks to its wide selection of chocolate- and cookie-based ice creams, and the quality is good too.

**Tip:** If you don't plan on spending money at a restaurant and prefer a picnic instead, there is an good Panini shop right off of the bridge (to your right, in Piazza Cairoli) called **Il Crudo** (open daily from 11:00). Pack your sandwich to go, and after your visit to the Leaning Tower, you can stop for lunch by the Tower itself. Alternately, you can buy a tasty sandwich once you get to the Tower—try Paninoteca **il Canguro** at Via Santa Maria 151. If you want to get away from tourists, head to Pisa's prettiest piazza, Piazza Santa Caterina (also known as Piazza Martiri della Liberta'), just five minutes from the Tower.

Once you've crossed the Ponte di Mezzo bridge, you'll find yourself in Piazza Garibaldi, Pisa's main square. From there, walk along the boutique-filled main street (Borgo Stretto). Shopping lovers will find an interesting but pricey selection of modern Italian fashion and shoes for every taste. Continue on Borgo Stretto and turn left just before the pharmacy, at Via Ulisse Dini, to reach Piazza dei Cavalieri (if you want to skip this part, continue walking straight along Borgo Stretto, winding with it as it turns left, and you'll reach the Leaning Tower directly).

**Piazza dei Cavalieri** (the Cavaliers' Square) is named after the knights of Santo Stefano's Order, an order founded by the Grand Duke of Tuscany, Cosimo de Medici, to protect the coasts of this region from vicious attacks by pirates. The Grand Duke's friend and personal architect, Giorgio Vasari, designed this impressive piazza, which is surrounded by some of the most beautiful buildings in town, including the graceful sgrafito-covered **Scuola Normale**, built by Napoleon and considered today to be one of the best universities in Italy.

**Mission 1:** How many roads lead to this piazza?

**Mission 2:** Whose statue is in the middle of the piazza?

Exit Piazza dei Cavalieri through Via dei Mille, turn right onto Via Santa Maria and walk for about five minutes until you reach Piazza dei Miracoli and the impressive Leaning Tower. Piazza dei Miracoli is the poetic name given by (the slightly insane) Italian writer Gabriele D'Annunzio to Pisa's Duomo square, a large area to the north of the city which includes the Duomo, the Baptistery, the Leaning Tower, and the Camposanto, all supreme examples of the Pisan Romanesque architectural style.

The Leaning Tower of Pisa

is one of the world's most famous buildings. The first stone of this unique bell tower was set on 10 August 1174 by architect Bonanno Pisano. While building the third floor, it became clear that the Tower was leaning, though the reason was unknown. The construction was halted for one century, until architect Giovanni di Simone added four floors in the 1270s and tried to compensate for the deficiency by bending the Tower to the other side. Construction was eventually completed about a century later, and a bell chamber was ceremoniously added, but it was becoming difficult to ignore the fact that the Tower was noticeably leaning to its side. It took 700 years for architects to understand that the problem was not the Tower itself but the earth beneath it—the soft clay soil was causing the foundation to settle unevenly, forcing the structure to tilt more and more. In 1990, the Italian government closed the Tower to the public, and an independent and international committee of structural and geotechnical engineers, architects, and art historians was assembled to find a solution. Counterweights were placed on the north side, and temporary cables were installed to steady the Tower. Slivers of soil were drilled out from the northern side of the Tower, allowing gravity to coax the structure back upright. These extraordinary measures were officially concluded in 2001, and today a limited number of tourists can visit the Tower daily, climb its 294 steps, and enjoy a unique historical experience as well as a great view of the town.

**Mission 3:** Take a photo of yourself holding the Tower up with your hands, your head, your legs, and your bottom.

Interestingly enough, there are actually two additional (smaller) leaning towers in Pisa—one is the tower of the San Niccola Church (a tiny but charming church on the banks of the Arno, just two minutes from Piazza Garibaldi), which has tilted with time, and the other is the bell tower of the San Michele of Scalzi Church, which was once straight but was deformed by the famous 1966 Arno flood. Want to find out more fun facts? Check out the Kids' Corner at the end of this itinerary!

**Tip:** Though parents might find them tacky, kids tend to love the souvenirs found in Piazza dei Mircaoli. From little statues of the Tower to cups and magnets, there are several knickknacks from which to choose. All the souvenier stands are concentrated together right outside the piazza, near the McDonalds/Sbarro. Unlike Florence, you won't be able to find cheaper souvenirs in other areas of town. Pisa is very small, so if you want to buy something, this is the place to do it. Also - avoid eating in the restaurants around the Tower. There are a number of good restaurants in town, but none of them are in this area (see "Eating in Pisa" at the end of this itinerary for the best options).

Pisa's impressive **Duomo** stands proudly next to the Tower. The construction of the Duomo, dedicated to Santa Maria Assunta (Saint Mary of the Assumption) was begun in 1063 by architect Buscheto, whose name and work is celebrated in the inscription on the façade of the church. This was an extremely rare honour in the 11th century, and you can see the inscription if you look left of the main entrance. The design of the Duomo is clearly influenced by Roman basilicas, but some oriental influences are visible as well. This isn't as surprising as it may seem, since Pisa (as a leading maritime city) was involved in trade and the crusades, and so was heavily exposed to styles and cultures from all across the Mediterranean. The manicured grass that surrounds the Duomo today is quite different from what the medieval inhabitants of Pisa saw, though. Back then, the area was dotted with ancient sarcophagi (stone tombs), most of which were later moved to the Camposanto.

 **Mission 4:** Today we can still find inscriptions on the marble around the Duomo perimeter, showing the locations of underground medieval tombs that weren't moved. Can you find any?

Inside the Duomo, you will find the pulpit decorated with stories of Christ, created by one of the greatest Gothic sculptors, Giovanni Pisano (c. 1248-1315). The apse, decorated with a precious 14th century mosaic, depicts the Virgin and Saint John the Evangelist. Saint John's face was the last work completed by Cimabue (who died in Pisa in 1302).

The **Baptistery** was begun in 1152 by Diotisalvi as a central-plan Romanesque building, and it took two centuries to complete. In 1260, Nicola Pisano was appointed headmaster of the project and added some Gothic elements, such as cusps, tabernacles, and sculptures, which were created by his son, Giovanni Pisano. If you take a close look at these sculptures, they will seem strange and out of proportion, but that is entirely intentional. Giovanni Pisano took into consideration that proportions change according to one's point of view. Since he believed that most people would be looking at the Duomo and the Baptistery from afar, he designed the statues in such a way that they would seem proportional when viewing the entire piazza from a certain distance.

The most incredible thing about the Baptistery is its unusual **acoustic effect** (before you leave for your trip, watch a video on Youtube demonstrating this effect, so that you can reproduce it with your kids when you visit!). Basically, because of the unique structure of this building, notes last for a very long time, enabling you to sing and accompay yourself at the same time. In high season, the guards often demonstrate this cool little effect.

Lastly, the **Camposanto** is a historical cemetery and the last monument to be built in Piazza dei Miracoli, between 1278 and 1464. Traditionally, it was believed that sacred soil from Golgotha in Jerusalem was brought to the Campo after the second Crusade. This soil gave the field its name (campo santo = holy field) and started a series of legends, including a common belief that bodies buried here would rot within 24 hours.

**OPENING TIMES AND TICKETS FOR ALL PIAZZA DEI MIRACOLI MONUMENTS:**
**The Leaning Tower**: 🕐 Open daily, January-February, 10:00-17:00; March, 09:00-18:00; April-September, 09:00-20:00; October, 09:00-19:00; November-24 December, 10:00-17:00; 25 December-6 January, 09:00-18:00. (Mid-June-late August, open until 22:00.
**The Baptistery (Battistero)**: 8:00-20:00 (off season: 10:00-17:00)
**The Duomo**: 🕐 From 10:00 daily (from 13:00 on holidays).
You can buy online tickets for the Leaning Tower in advance up to 20 days prior to your visit, and pick them up from the Ticket Office at least 30 minutes before your tour begins. Order tickets here: www.opapisa.it. Note that **children under the age of eight cannot climb the Tower**, and children between the ages of 8-18 must be accompanied by an adult. Check all bags in advance in the Ticket Office lockers (only normal-sized backpacks are accepted; don't bring strollers or luggage with you).

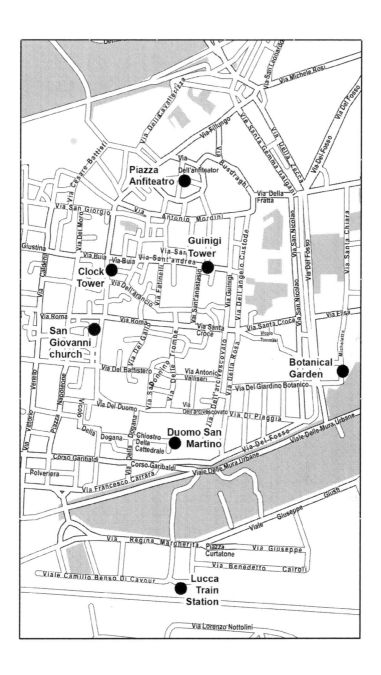

If you plan on visiting the other attractions in the piazza, you might want to buy a combined ticket (entrance is free for children under the age of ten). The ticket for the Leaning Tower, however, must be bought separately, and it isn't cheap (as of this publication, it costs 18 euro per person to climb up). If you haven't booked your tickets online, buy them at the ticket office behind the Leaning Tower or at the entrance to the Museo delle Sinopia (near the Duomo; look for the yellow signs).

# Lucca

A small romantic town with 100 churches and several lovely little piazzas, Lucca is the perfect place to pass an afternoon. Since the historical centre is closed to most traffic, it's safe for children to walk around freely and explore (but do watch out for the occasional car). Lucca was founded by the Etruscans and was one of the more

important medieval towns in Tuscany, an inspiration to writers and poets such as Dante Alighieri, for example (who spent a few years in the area). For several years, Lucca thrived thanks to a booming silk trade and banking industry, and it was protected from invasions by its massive walls. In fact, it wasn't until Napoleon's army came knocking on the door that the city surrendered for the first time. During the 19th century, Lucca became a favourite with romantic tourists, and it inspired composers such as Puccini (his Lucca home can be visited, but it isn't as impressive as his villa in Torre del Lago, 20 minutes away).

## GETTING THERE

**BY CAR:** Driving to Lucca from Pisa is not only easy but also a very pleasant drive along the countryside (don't take the highway; take the SS12). There are several parking lots outside the old city walls where you should leave your car (don't drive into Lucca itself; it is almost completely ZTL, and you'll get a fine if you even try). Park in one of the many parking lots and spaces surrounding the walls. Make sure you bring about 15 euro in change with you, as the parking meters don't acept notes.

**BY TRAIN:** This is probably the easiest way to reach Lucca. From **Pisa**, take the regional train (there's a train every 30-40 minutes, and the ride takes about 20 minutes). The train from **Florence** to Lucca can take up to two hours. Some trains are direct, while others require you to change in Pisa's main station (Stazione Centrale).

**TOURIST INFORMATION OFFICE:** Lucca's tourist office is the place to find out more about local events and itineraries, not just in Lucca itself but in the surrounding area too (Bagni di Lucca, Versilia, and Vale del Serchio). 🕐 Open Monday, Wednesday, Friday, 09:00-13:00; Tuesday, Thursday, 09:00-18:00; Closed on Weekends. Piazza Santa Maria, 0583.919931

# Our tour of Lucca begins at the train station. From here, walk

out towards the ramparts, or city walls (they are hard to miss, since they're in front of you as soon as you leave the station). Cross the street and follow the white path along the grass. The path will lead you to a hidden crossing point under the wall and into the city. This is your chance to admire the impressive walls (14 meters high and 12 km long; they took more than 100 years to build) which protected Lucca from numerous threats for hundreds of years.

Almost as soon as you enter the city, you will see on your left one of Lucca's best-known churches, the **Duomo** dedicated to **San Martino**. Built in 1063 by Bishop Anslem (who later became Pope Alexander II), the Duomo boasts three especially notable works of art: Jacopo Tintoretto's *Last Supper*, Dome-
nico Ghirlandaio's *Madonna and Child with Saints Peter, Clement, Paul, and Sebastian*, and  Fra Bartolomeo's *Madonna and Child*. Just as beautiful is the *Volto Santo di Lucca* (meaning "The Holy Face of Saint Luke"), a little wooden temple positioned in the right nave which, according to the locals, dates back to the year 742. The life-like sacrofage of Ilaria del Carretto, the young wife of Lucca's ruler, Paolo Guinigi, who died at 25 and was commemorated in this work by Jacopo della Quercia, is beautiful, too. If you have some extra time, a small ca-

thedral museum (next door) boasts a number of little treasures and illuminated manuscripts.

**Mission 5:** If you look closely (best to use your binoculars!), you will discover that all of the columns decorating the Duomo's façade are different from each other. How many different kinds can you count?

Legend has it that the columns are all different because the city decided to save some money by inviting different artists to a fictional competition. The artists were told that he who who offered the best design would be hired to design the whole façade, but instead they just used the columns the artists made for the competition and hired no one!

**Mission 6:** Some of the columns are decorated with animals. Which animals can you find?

🕐 Opening times: **Duomo**, open daily, 09:30-16:45; March-October, until 17:45, free of charge. **Museum**, 15 March-2 November, open daily, 10:00-18:00; 3 November-14 March, Monday-Friday, 10:00-14:00, Saturday, 10:00-18:00, Sunday,10:00-17:00; 1 January, 13:00-18:00. Combined tickets to the Museum and the Church of San Giovanni (see next) are available. Piazza Antelminelli, Tel: 0583.490530, www.museocattedralelucca.it

**Tip:** Just seven minutes away from the Duomo is Lucca's sweet little Botanical Garden, a perfect stop for those who wish to get away from the crowds. July-August, Open daily, 10:00-19:00; mid-March-May, open daily until 17:00; May-July, open daily until 18:00; mid-September-November, open daily until 17:00; closed during the winter months. Combined tickets with the Clock Tower (see later) and the Guinigi Tower (see later) are available.

From the Duomo, keep walking along Via Duomo towards Lucca's most interesting church, especially for children, **Chiesa di San Giovanni**. You'll find it tucked away in a small piazza by the same name. Though the façade doesn't promise much, the church hides a secret—its ancient base is still accessible, as are the remains of the Roman temple that stood under it. Walk to the far end of the church and down the stairs to discover the Roman structure. The "newer" part of the church is beautiful as well; the ceiling is decorated with elegant wooden carvings, and the simple but spacious design, combined with the cold, heavy, and solemn stones, transports visitors back in time.

◑ Opening times: 15 March-2 November, open daily, 10:00-18:00; 3 November-14 March, Monday-Friday, 10:00-14:00. www.museocattedralelucca.it

**Mission 7:** What kinds of Roman antiques did you find in the underground part of the church? Did you find any mosaics? Describe one of the mosaics you found.

**Tip**: In Piazza San Romano 4, just a few minutes away, you will find Lucca's Comics Museum (Museo del Fumetto). It is very small and could use a make-over, but younger children might enjoy it. Open daily (except on Mondays), 10:00-18:00

From Chiesa di San Giovanni, turn right to Via Roma and then left to **Via Fillungo**, Lucca's main street filled with shops, boutiques, and cafés. Some of these shops have been drawing in the crowds for more than 150 years.

About halfway along Via Fillungo is the **Torre delle Ore** (Clock Tower), which rings four times an hour due to a mechanism installed in the 18th century that is still visible today (they really did make things to last back then). Engineer-loving kids might enjoy climbing the 50-meter-high (207 steps!) tower and exploring the apparatus themselves. As all good clock towers do, this tower boasts a legend. It is believed that, once upon a time, a local woman named Lucida Mansi made a deal with the devil. In exchange for remaining young and beautiful, the devil would return in thirty years to take away her soul. On the very last night of those thirty years, just as the clock was about to strike midnight, Lucida raced up and tried to stop the lancets, but she was too late. The devil won, and her soul was lost forever. Before climbing up the Tower, we hope more quickly than poor Lucida Mansi, make sure the mechanism is working and open for visitors.

🕐 Opening times: Open daily, April-May, 09:30-18:30; June-September, 09:30-19:30; March and October, 09:30-17:30; closed November-February. Children under six enter for free. Children under 14 pay a reduced fee. Combined tickets with the Botanical Garden and the Guinigi Tower are available.

Follow via Filliungo until you reach Lucca's best-known piazza—Piazza dell'Anfiteatro. The piazza's unique closed circular shape (and name) derives from the fact that it stands above what was once the town's Roman amphitheatre.

••••••••••••••••••••••••••••••••••••••••••••••••••••••••••••••••••••

**Mission 8:** How many roads lead to this piazza? (Hint: Count its large stone entries.)

**Mission 9:** There is a stone with a cross marked on it at the very centre of the piazza. Step one: Find the stone. Step two: What do you suppose it marks? (Hint: Based on its position, what do you think it could indicate?)

••••••••••••••••••••••••••••••••••••••••••••••••••••••••••••••••••••

Just three minutes from the piazza (walk along Via delle Chiavi d'Oro) is another attraction kids might enjoy, the **Guinigi Tower.** Built by one of Lucca's richest and most powerful families, it is probably the prettiest tower in town and offers not only impressive views of the city but also a charming little garden at its top (though there really is no need to climb both the Clock Tower and the Guinigi Tower. Both have their fans; the choice is up to you).

🕐 Opening times: open daily, June-September, 09:30-19:30; November-February, closes at 16:30; March and October, closes at 17:30; April-May, closes at 18:30. Via Sant'Anfrea 41. Combined tickets for the Botanical Garden, the Clock Tower, and Guingi Tower are available. Kids under six enter for free. Kids under 14 pay a reduced fee.

Spend some time exploring the hidden streets of Lucca and admiring the tiny houses and medieval alleys before you head to the town's most popular attraction for families: **the ramparts** (the walls of the city). Renting a bike and riding along the ramparts while enjoying wonderful views is definitely the best way to end your tour in Lucca and is a favourite for many. Bastions (*baluardi* in Italian) along the wall serve as access points to the top of the ramparts. There are 11 of them, and they were all built during the Renaissance to protect the town from canons, a popular new weapon at the time. In fact, the bastions themselves were heavily armed and equipped with more than 100 canons.

# To rent a bike, try one of these options

**Bike Rental in Tuscany,** in Via Elisa 26, is one of our favorites. The service here is serious and professional, and they offer a number of rental options, from simple bikes to tour the town, to professional MBX for those who want to ride in the countryside (or even all the way to Pisa). GPS units are available and guided tours can be organized, if booked in advance. The shop is

located just minutes from Piazza Anfiteatro and Via Filungo. Find out more here: www.bikerentalintuscany.com.

**CHRONO'BIKE**, in Corso Garibaldi 93, next to Teatro Giglio and a few minutes away from the Duomo, www.chronobikes.com.

**Punto Bici**, in Via Del Crocefisso 8, next to Piazzzale Verdi, www.puntobici.Lucca.it.

**Antonio Poli**, in Piazza Santa Maria 42, Tel: 0583.493787 (or other shops around Piazza Santa Maria).

# KIDS'CORNER

## More About...
## The Leaning Tower!

You may have seen photos of the Tower or heard stories but nothing prepares you for the moment you see it with your own eyes. But wait! Before you climb up this historical monument, let's start with seven fun facts about the Tower…

1. The Leaning Tower is 55 meters high, which is about as tall as 30 grown men standing on top of one another.

# KIDS'CORNER

2. The Tower is made of marble and limestone and weighs an astonishing 14,453 tons! That's like 45,160,625 average-sized golden retriever dogs put together, or 2064 buses! No wonder it started sinking!

3. The outer diameter of the Tower is 19.58 meters; that means it would take about 12 adult men to stand around it in a circle to hug it.

4. The inclination (or tilt) of the Tower is about 10%.

5. There are seven bells at the top, so if you wanted to, you could ring a different bell every day of the week.

6. The Tower was almost bombed by the Allies during World War II, when the Germans were using it as an observation post. Thanks to a special spy who was sent to check the field and understood the importance of the Tower and its beauty, the Tower was saved!

7. Of the 45,000 students who study each year at the university of Pisa, none (yes, nobody) dare climb up the Tower. Why? Because of a local superstition that says any students who climb the Tower will never finish their studies or earn their degree.

## More About... Pirates!

If you've visited Piazza Cavallieri, you know that Pisa needed an Order of Knights to protect it from terrible pirate attacks. But wait! What do pirates have to do with Pisa? We have two words for you: sea trade.

# KIDS'CORNER

One thousand years ago, during the 10th and 11th centuries, Pisa was much more than a sleepy little university town. It was a strong and powerful republic by the sea that traded with many countries all around the Mediterranean, and its sailors and army leaders were well known and feared.

Controlling the sea meant controlling trade routes that brought food, fabrics, gold, silver, slaves, and spices to the area, and that was a very lucrative business. No state would easily give up that power, and some very dramatic and bloody battles took place between the maritime republics (Pisa, Amalfi, Genova, and Venice) over control of the most profitable sea paths.

That wasn't the only problem Pisans had to deal with, though; there were also plenty of pirates. Pirates have been around since the invention of boats. Egyptian pirates, for example, were roaming the shores of Cyprus more than 2400 years ago, and Greek pirates terrorized merchants in Ancient times. In fact, the word "pirate" comes from ancient Greek and means "to light", because pirates would burn down ships after they ravaged them.

The medieval period was no different. Actually, it was different. It was much worse. The more goods that were transported across the sea, the worse the raids got, and pirates always

# KIDS'CORNER

seemed to come up with bigger and crazier plans to take control of the ships. At one point, the pirates came up with the idea of lighting fires on abandoned rocky beaches at night, so that the sailors would think they had arrived at a safe beach lit by a lighthouse. When the sailors tossed down the ship's anchor, it was usually too late. The ship would crash on the sharp rocks and the merciless pirates would jump out from their hiding places and loot everything. Things got so bad that local Pisa merchants actually left money in their wills so that the city would build a real lighthouse and no other merchants would suffer a similar fate.

What did a trade ship look like and how did it navigate the Mediterranean Sea?

The most popular kind of ship back then was called the Galea. The Galea was a wooden war and trade ship that was based on an improved design of ancient Greek ships. Surprisingly enough, wind wasn't used to move the ship (it didn't have sails). Instead, human rowers sitting in the bottom of the hull moved the ship. The rowers worked very, very, very hard. In fact, most rowers were either convicted felons or slaves. The felons were sentenced to work in the ship (especially war ships) instead of going to prison, but both the felons and the slaves suffered a terrible life of hard physical work and abuse. By the way—anyone could become a slave! If an enemy ship caught you, they would either kill you or turn you into a slave (unless someone paid for your release).

Even if you weren't a slave or a prisoner, it still wasn't easy living on a ship. Drinking water had to be disinfected with vinegar to prevent it from going stale. Food was usually limited to dry meats and dry bread (an occasional hot meal could be cooked inside a metal barrel, but only very carefully, because you didn't want to burn the ship down), and there were no fruits or veg-

# KIDS'CORNER

etables. Before long, the crew would become ill with a disease called scurvy and their teeth would fall out! Scurvy is a terrible disease caused by a lack of vitamins (remember, the sailors had no fresh fruit or vegetables), but it wasn't until the 20th century that people understood this connection.

## More About...
## Galileo Galilei!

Pisa's most famous son just happens to be one of the greatest scientists ever. Would you like to know why?

Galileo Galilei was born in Pisa in 1564, the eldest of six children. Shortly after he was born, the whole family moved to Florence, which enabled young Galileo to receive an excellent education. Galileo is considered to be one of the most brilliant astronomers and physicists in history and has even been given the title of "the father of modern science". He is responsible for many scientific advances, including:

1.    Proving Copernicus's theories that the earth revolves around the sun, and not vice versa, as the ancient Greeks believed.

2. Discovering the four largest moons of Jupiter (known to this day as the Galilean moons).

3. The invention of the telescope (which he built in 1609).

Like many other students of his time period, Galileo studied the physics of Aristotle. Unlike other students, however, he was not convinced by what he read. He decided to write down his thoughts and, in the process, revolutionized scientific thinking. People who knew Galileo realized he was a genius, but the Roman Catholic Church was very upset by his theories. When Galileo claimed that the Danish astronomer Copernicus was right and that the Earth revolved around the Sun (as opposed to the Sun revolving around the Earth, as the Church claimed), not even his powerful friends from the Medici family could protect him. Galileo was questioned by the Inquisition, accused of heresies, and eventually sentenced in 1633 to house arrest in his home in Florence for the rest of his life. He gradually grew weaker (and blind) and died nine years later, in 1642. Galileo's personal life was just as complicated. He never married, but he did father three illegitimate children. He sent his two daughters to live in a convent as they didn't have much of a chance of getting married, but he maintained a special contact with one them, Virginia, who is better known by her religious name—Sister Maria Celeste.

# Eating in Pisa and Lucca

### PISA

If you are looking for a cheap and quick fix, see earlier recommendations for Panini shops in town (there's also a McDonald's near the Leaning Tower, but we cannot in good faith recommend that tourists choose an international fast food chain over the local food, no matter how much kids may love Happy Meals). As far as restaurants go, there are a number of good options from which to choose.

**Il Campano** is a personal favourite; it's a family-run, reasonably priced restaurant with great seasonal dishes. ⊙ Open daily, 12:30-15:00, 19:30-22:45; closed on Wednesdays; closed for lunch on Thursdays. Via Cavalca 19, Tel: 050.580585, www.ilcampano.com

**Osteria alle Bandierine** offers simple but delicious pasta dishes. Open daily (for dinner only) from 19:30. Via Mercanti 4, Tel: 050.500000, www.ristoranteallebandierine.it. Monday closed.

**050** is a tiny little restaurant offering local, seasonal, and mostly organic dishes. Try the delicious risottos and the pastas (the meat is better in other places). ⊙ Open Tuesday-Sunday, 12:30-14:30, 19:30-21:30. Via S. Francesco 36, Tel: 050.543106

**Trattoria La Taverna di Emma** is right next to the Leaning Tower and has gained a solid reputation as one of the most popular eateries in the area. The food is simple but tasty, and prices are usually reasonable. Via Carlo Cammeo 50, Tel: 050.555003. Open Monday-Saturday, 12:30-16:00, 20:00-22:30.

**Osteria San Paolo**, open daily, 12:00-14:30, 19:30-22:30; may be closed on Sundays off season. Via San Paolo 16, Tel: 050.501194, www.osteriasanpaolo.com

For great pizza, try **Bella Napoli**. ⊙ Open daily, 12:00-15:00, 19:00-24:00; closed on Mondays. Via del Borghetto 44 (10 minutes away from the centre; from Piazza Garibladi, Pisa's main square, simply walk along Lungarno Mediceo and turn left at Via del Borghetto), Tel: 050.578520, www.bellanapoli-pisa.it

Another great pizza place is **Pizzeria Funiculi-Funicula**. Open daily, 20:00-23:00. Lungarno Mediceo 43 (on the river, three minutes from Piazza Garibladi and the Ponte di Mezzo), Tel: 050.580201, www.pizzeriafuniculiPisa.it

In both cases—book in advance; these pizza spots are extremely popular with the locals!

## LUCCA

If you are looking for a reasonably priced and tasty slice of pizza, try **Pizzeria Bella Mbriana**, a real and delicious Neapolitan pizza spot. Open Monday, and

Wednesday-Friday, 12:30-14:30, 18:30-23:30. Via della Cavallerizza 29, Tel: 0583.495565

Another popular pizza place, specializing in steamy and delicious slices, served with a piece of *cecina* (a chickpea-based dish) is **Pizzeria da Felice.** Open daily, 10:00-20:30; closed on Sundays. Via Buia 12, Tel: 0583.494986

For a more sophisticated meal, try **Osteria San Giorgio.** Their homemade pasta, grilled meats and tasty desserts make this pleasant trattoria a stop worth making. Via San Giorgio 26, Tel: 0583.953.233, www.osteriasangiorgiolucca.it. Open 12:00-15:00, 19:00-23:00. Booking in advance is advised.

Alternatively, try **da Pasquale**, an unassuming but delicious little place, favoured by the locals. Via del Moro 8, Tel: 0583.496.506, www.dapasquale-lucca.com. Open Wednesday-Monday, 19:00-22:30

**Ammodonostro** is a charming little restaurant with a reasonably priced and tasty menu, with some gluten-free and vegetarian options. It also has a pleasant little garden for sitting. Open daily, 11:00-14:30, 19:00-22:30; closed on Tuesdays. Via della Fratta 20, Tel: 0583.953828, www.ristoranteammodonostro.it

**La Pecora Nera** is a small and simple kid-friendly place (take one look at the décor and you will understand why toddlers like it) with a mostly pizza-based menu. Their forte is their kid-meals: small portions of dishes which will appeal to kids. The food here is a little too simple, in our opinion, and prices are a little high, but for families with very young children, looking for a spacious restaurant that accommodates toddlers, this place is worth considering. Alternatively, try the Pizzeria located on the same piazza (town square) as Pecora Nera. It's called **Mara Meo**, and it offers some very tasty pizza and sandwiches for very reasonable prices. The added bonus of both restaurants is their location, overlooking the huge piazza, which means the kids run around freely before continuing the sightseeing tour.
La Pecora Nera, Piazza San Francesco 1, Tel: 0583.469738. Wednesday-Friday, open for dinner only. Saturday-Sunday, 13:00-15:30, 19:30-22:30. Monday-Tuesday closed.
Pizzeria Mara Meo, Piazza San Francesco 17, Tel: 0583.467.084, in high season open daily, 10:00-22:00/23:00 (24:00 on weekends).

# Sleeping in Pisa and Lucca

## PISA

As mentioned before, Lucca has a better range of hotels and B&Bs, but if you do want to stay in Pisa, there are a few options.

**Villa Theresa** is a tiny and charming bed and breakfast, situated at the heart of Pisa's historical centre. A 15-minute walk from the leaning tower, and a two-minute walk from the main shopping street of Corso Italia, this is one of the best options in town. Book well in advance, as this popular spot fills up quickly!
Via della Foglia 13, Tel: 050.49159, www.villatheresa.it.

**Hotel Bologna** is centrally located next to the Leaning Tower and offers comfortable modern rooms, making it one of Pisa's more popular choices. Via Mazzini 57, Tel: 050.502120, www.bologna.Pisahotelsitaly.it

## LUCCA

**Tip:** Lucca has some lovely little B&Bs within the ancient walls, but bear in mind that many of them are in ZTL areas and are therefore inaccessible by car. Speak with your hotel in advance, and make sure they can issue you a temporary ZTL pass for the time of your stay.

**La Boheme** is comfortably located in the centre of town and offers elegant rooms in an inviting setting. Via del Moro 2, Lucca, Tel: 0583.462404, www.boheme.it

The **Lucca in Villa San Marco** apartment hotel is very popular with travellers and for good reason. Well-located, comfortable and modern rooms, helpful staff, and reasonable prices make it a good deal. Via Farnesi 266, Lucca, Tel: 0583.080268, www.Luccainvilla.it (Note: The same family owns another good place—Villa Elisa & Gentucca—near the railway station.)

**Casa Paolina** is another popular apartment hotel with good amenities, location, and staff for a comfortable night in town. Piazza XX Settembre 2, Lucca, Tel:

0583.495823, www.casapaolina.it

**Al porto di Lucca** is a popular B&B, offering Wi-Fi, modern rooms, and elegant décor. Via Nottolini 10, 55100 Lucca, Tel: 0583.53516, Cell: 328.6778927, www.alportodiLucca.com

**Locanda Sant'Agostino** is charming, and though it is slightly pricier, it is worth the cost to enjoy the old-world elegance and charm throughout the hotel. Piazza Sant'Agostino 3, Lucca, Tel: 0583.443100,  www.locandasantagostino.it

If you are looking for a place outside of Lucca, surrounded by beautiful nature, calm ambiance, and a pool for the kids, try **Le Murelle Farm**. It is a lovely little farm, inviting and well positioned, with great views. This farm is also known as Azienda Agricola Moretti. Via per Camaiore, traversa V, Cappella, Ponte del Giglio (Lucca), Tel: 0583.394306, 0583.394055, www.lemurelle.com

# Special Events in the Area

## PISA

**Luminara**: This festival is a magical moment that celebrates Pisa's saint protector, San Ranieri. During the Luminara, more than 70,000 candles are lit, the streets are filled with people and vendors, and concerts and other events are held throughout Pisa. The next morning, on June 17th, fun medieval processions cross the town, accompanied by drums and people in lively costumes. The Luminara lights up Pisa on June 16th, at Piazza Garibaldi and the streets next to the river (called Lungarno).

**Regata delle Repubbliche Marinare**: Once every four years, this event draws in a crowd of more than 100,000 people. Antique boats from the four ancient maritime republics—Pisa, Amalfi, Genova, and Venice—compete in an exciting rowing match. The event is accompanied by vivacious medieval processions and music. Contact the tourist office to find out when the next regatta will take place in Pisa. You will find all the action along the Arno River (come early to catch a good spot, around the Ponte di Mezzo).

**Giocco del ponte** (Battle of the Bridge): on the last Saturday in June, an antique game is set on the main bridge in town, Ponte di Mezzo. Even more interesting is the medieval court that walks around town, delighting locals and tourists with music and vivacious medieval costumes.

## LUCCA

**Palio di San Paolino** (known also as Palio della Balestra) is a medieval feast dedicated to the ancient art of crossbow shooting, accompanied by medieval processions and music. Enjoy the feast on July 12th at Piazza San Martino. For more information, go to www.Luccaturismo.it.

On the third Sunday of every month, a **delightful antique market** (one of the largest in Tuscany) fills the streets between Piazza Antelminelli and Piazza San Giovanni. Kids love the old and weird artefacts! The precise day and time of the market may vary, check with the local tourist office before your visit to confirm.

# Special Activities in the Area

## COOKING CLASSES

Cooking classes can be fun for the whole family and an experience kids will remember. Chef Paolo Monti offers a variety of classes adapted for young chefs, at about 85 euro per course. Book in advance! Via Per Sant'Alessio 3684, Carignano, Lucca, Tel: 0583.329970, www.cucina-italiana.com

## PARKS AND ADVENTURE PARKS

Though Pisa and Lucca provide a full day of adventures, there are a number of parks in the area that can be easily combined into the itinerary, especially if kids are growing tired of museums and churches. The following options each require about half a day, including the drive.

**Livorno Aquarium**: Just 20 minutes from Pisa, this is the largest aquarium in Tuscany and is a popular and highly recommended destination for families. Here you will find over 3000 animals (and over 1700 species) including turtles and tropical fish. Children under 12 pay a reduced entry fee, children under 1.5 meters enter for free. Opening times: June, September, open daily, 10:00-19:00; July-August, open daily, 10:00-21:00, April-May, open daily, 10:00-18:00 (until 19:00 on weekends); During the winter months the Aquarium is open on weekends only (10:00-18:00), but hours may vary, check the website before leaving. Tel: 0586.269111, www.acquariodilivorno.it

**Pinocchio Park Collodi:** This well-known park, named after Carlo Collodi, author of *Pinocchio*, is just 35 minutes away from Pisa and is considered one of the main attractions for children in the area. Unfortunately, the park isn't very well kept, and though some parts of it are still charming (especially the gardens) other parts leave great room for improvement, especially considering its high entrance fee. We cannot recommend it wholeheartedly, but those who do venture to the park will be rewarded with a few good attractions for toddlers and younger kids (the main target age of this park). Face painting and mask making are available at no additional cost between 1 March and 31 October (call before arrival to make sure the activities do actually take place on the dates that interest you; some of these activities need to be booked 10 days in advance, Tel: 3396.491097). There is also a fun playground and the world's largest Pinocchio statue. If you are looking for more of an amusement park, there are two closer, cheaper, and better options that older kids will enjoy more (Piccolo Mondo and Parco Pitagora; see below for their descriptions). Opening times: March-November, open daily, 08:30-sunset; November-February, open weekends only, 10:00-sunset. Parco di Pinocchio, Via S. Gennaro 3, Collodi (Pescia), Tel: 0572.429342, www.pinocchio.it

**Parco Pitagora:** Unlike the Collodi Park, this attraction has no historical value, but it is modern and fun. With bouncy castles, slides, playgrounds, trampolines, and more, both toddlers and older kids will find something to do. Located 20 minutes north of Pisa, it is open year round, from 10:00-19:30 (June-August, until 24:00). Closed on Tuesday. The playground closes for a lunch break between 12:30 and 15:30. Via Aurelia, Lido di Camaiore, Tel. 0584.611008, www.parcopitagora.com

**Cavallino Matto:** Located one hour south of Pisa (and also featured in the Etruscan Beach Itinerary), this is a fun little place that younger kids will love (kids older than 12 probably won't be impressed with this place). Canoes, face-painting, carousels, an African village, a funicular (cable car), and more will make for a much-needed break from the sightseeing. Opening times: mid-April-late June, open on weekends only, 10:00-18:00. July-mid-September, open daily, 10:00-18:30. Cavallino Matto, Via Po 1, Marina di Castagneto, Donoratico, Tel: 0565.745720, www.cavallinomatto.it

**Piccolo Mondo:** Even though it's smaller than the other parks, Piccolo Mondo is located just outside of Pisa and offers fun attractions, like bouncy castles, go-karts, trampolines, and a pool (bring your bathing suit!). Opening times: mid-June-mid-September, open daily, 10:30–after dinner; the last two weeks of September, Tuesday-Sunday, 15:00–sunset; October and March-May, Tuesday-Friday, 16:00-sunset (on Saturdays and Sundays, the park opens at 15:00). Opening times may change, so check the website in advance. Piccolo Mondo, Strada Provinciale 9, San Giuliano Terme (Pisa), Tel: 338.7726711, www.piccolomondo.it

**Parco Avventura Villa Basilica:** The best option for more active kids and teenagers is this adventure park, located just 10 minutes away from the Pinocchio Collodi Park, featuring such attractions as climbing tracks and rope ladders. You can also rent mountain bikes. Opening times: July-August, open open daily, 10:00-19:00; June and September, Sunday only. Tel. 333.7105636, www.sospesonelverde.it. Pizzorne (Lucca province). GPS coordinates: N. 43.92632°; E. 10.62109°

# THE GARFAGNANA

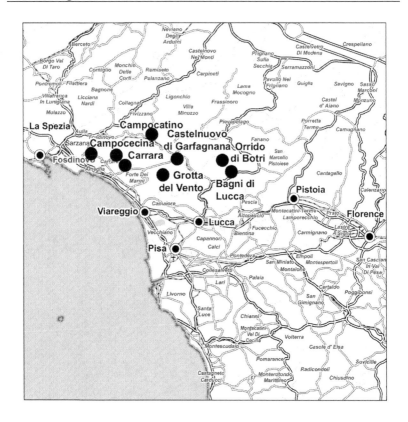

## HOW LONG WILL IT TAKE TO GET THERE?

Lucca to Bagni di Lucca: 45 minutes
Lucca to the Orrido di Botri: about one hour
Lucca to the Grotta del Vento: about one hour
Lucca to Fosdinovo Castle: 50 minutes
Fosdinovo to Campocecina: 45 minutes

Chapter 3

# The Garfagnana

When travelling with kids, incorporating fun, outdoor activities is a must or they will get bored (and drive their parents insane). A trip to the Garfagnana area in northern Tuscany is the perfect solution not only for those looking for a break from all the art and museums in Florence and Siena, but for any family that enjoys spending time outdoors. Whether you plan on staying in the area for a number of days—soaking in the crisp mountain air, hiking, biking, and touring around the majestic Apuan Alps—or you're just passing by for a day and looking for family-friendly activities, the Garfagnana area has a lot to offer. From caves and natural reserves to adventure parks and quarries, you will find it all here. The many attractions in this area have been divided into two itineraries and (as always) can be easily mixed and matched. However, before doing so, take the time to study the maps. This is a very hilly area, and what may seem like a measly 20-km ride between two towns can turn out to be an hour-long drive down a very winding (and sometimes stressful) road.

## Top 5 Family Activities

1. Get wet and enjoy the wonderful nature in Orrido di botri Canyon.

2. Admire the stalagmites and stalactites in Grotta del Vento.

3. Visit the quarry near Carrara to discover where Michelangelo got his marble.

4. Hike to Campocatino or Campocecina to enjoy the spectacular Apuan Alps view.

5. Visit the ancient Fosdinovo Castle and stop at the nearby Adventure Park.

**Our first itinerary** focuses on the Carrara Marble Caves (quarry), Fosdinovo Castle (and the Fosdinovo Adventure Park), and Campocecina, ending with dinner on the beach. The Carrara Marble Caves are where the best marble in Europe has been quarried for hundreds of years. It has been used in the homes of noble families, castles across Europe, and of course, for some of the most famous sculptures in the world (like Michelangelo's *David*). Touring the quarry and caves will be exciting for kids, who will be impressed with the machines, enormous space, and dramatic scope of the marble hills themselves. From here, continue to Fosdinovo Castle, high up in the Apuan Alps. This is one of the few castles still open to visitors, and much of its original décor has been preserved. Next to the castle, you will find the popular Fosdinovo Adventure Park, a perfect stop for bouncy adventure-seeking kids. If you still have some energy left, and you don't suffer terribly from carsickness, climb up the very windy (but safe) road to the village of Campocecina. The view is spectacular, and the whole family can enjoy a picnic surrounded by majestic mountains on one side and the sea on the other. Don't bother driving up on foggy days, though, as you won't be able to enjoy the view. Alternatively, end your day at the beach enjoying seafood pasta or pizza in one of the pleasant restaurants in Marina di Carrara or Forte dei Marmi.

# For our second itinerary, we recommend combining a visit to the Grotta del Vento—a cave filled with colourful stalagmites and stalactites—with a trip to a quaint little town called Bagni di Lucca, including a hike up to the flowering meadow of Campocatino. Alternatively, you can skip the caves and combine your trip to Bagni di Lucca with a half-day (and wet!) hike to the popular Orrido di Botri canyon. Combining the canyon with the caves, though tempting, isn't recommended because it can be too physically intensive for just one day. But if you insist, it's best to hike the Orrido very early in the morning, then head to the Grotta later in the day.

Our suggestion, for a relaxed visit of the area, is to choose one of the following combinations:

1. Hike along the Orrido di Botri, then eat dinner in Bagni di Lucca and take a pleasant stroll along its promenade.

2. Start your day in Bagni di Lucca, take a short hike up to Campocatino, and then drive to see the Grotta del Vento.

3. Combine a visit to the Grotta del Vento with one of the many exciting outdoor activities in the area, such as rafting, hiking, or horseback riding. (See "Special Activities in the Area" at the end of this chapter for some ideas.)

**Tip:** For those who are looking for a short, scenic hike, we would recommend a hidden little corner of the Garfagnana, known as Isola Santa. The tiny and half-deserted village of Isola Santa sits on a spectacularly blue lake, and is surrounded by majestic nature. If you are lucky enough to visit this area in the spring or in the autumn, you will enjoy some of the most beautiful views the Garfagnana has to offer. Getting here is easy: use Google Maps to reach the exact spot, and walk down to the lake.

# General Tips and Gear for the Entire Garfagnana Area

The longest route through the Orrido di Botri isn't recommended for kids under 12 (the trek requires walking in water over slippery surfaces), but there are easier paths that are suitable for younger children (at least seven years old). The Grotta del Vento is suitable for all ages, but if you or your kids suffer from very serious carsickness, the Garfagnana area itself may not be for you. Consider limiting your visit to sights that can be easily reached from the main road without driving up the windy little paths. The Fosdinovo Castle and Adventure Park, for example, can be reached from Sarzana (a town by the beach) without having to drive along any particularly narrow and winding roads (see the itinerary). The marble quarries are relatively easy to reach, too. Alternatively, visit Isola Santa and hike in the surrounding area.

If you do decide to mix and match itineraries, try not to visit the Marble Quarry and Grotta del Vento or the Grotta del Vento and Fosdinovo Castle on the same day; they are on different sides of the Apuan Alps, and the drive can be stressful. If you plan on visiting the Orrido di Botri, make sure you pack comfortable water-resistant walking shoes (regular sandals won't do; it's a slippery area) and a change of clothes. If you plan on visiting Campocecina and the Grotto del Vento, bring a sweater; it gets chilly. Pack snacks and anti-carsickness medicine, as well, just to be on the safe side.

**ITINERARY 1:** The Marble Quarry in Carrara, Fosdino-vo Castle and Adventure Park, Campocecina, and a Night by the Beach

# The Marble Quarry in Carrara

The best (and only) way to visit the quarry is with a tour. The most popular option is the **Marmo Tour** (Marble Tour), which will allow you to visit the quarry from the inside. The tour, which lasts 30 minutes, will take you along a quarry carved deep into the mountain to see huge cavernous rooms and learn about the marble extraction process.

🕐 Opening times: April, September, and October, 11:00-17:00 (until 18:30 on weekends and holidays); May-August, open daily, 11:00-18:30. Children aged 6-12 are eligible for reduced tickets. Piazzale Fantiscritti 84, Miseglia (near Carrara), Tel: 339.7657470, www.marmotour.com

If you are willing to splurge, the most exciting way to visit the quarries is with a personal guide, in a jeep. Gabriele, the owner of Cave di Marmo Tours, offers excellent excursions (www.cavedimarmotours.com). Alternatively, try the Carrara Marble Tour, which offers some cheaper options www.carraramarbletour.it

Once you've finished admiring the caves, go back to Carrara and get on the SS1 road towards Sarzana (don't take the SS446dir directly from Carrara heading north). This may seem like a detour, but it is far easier to reach Fosdinovo this way, avoiding the tiny, windy Garfagnana roads. Drive west toward the beach, and once you've reached Sarzana, follow the signs for Fosdinovo. Take the Via Paghezzana and then the SS446 road up the hill (the borgo and the castle are just 2 km away; follow the signs).

> **Tip:** On the way up from Sarzana to Fosdinovo, you will notice a very particular restaurant on your right, filled to the brim with motorcycles of every sort. This unique space is absolutely worth a visit if you are a car or motorcycle fan, but keep in mind that the food leaves much to be desired. If you do stop here, stick to a drink and a sandwich, just enough so you can sit inside and enjoy the décor.

# Fosdinovo Castle and Adventure Park

Built in the second half of the 12th century, the Malaspina Castle in Fosdinovo is one of Tuscany's best-pre-served castles; today, it hosts a museum and an arts centre. Don't miss the arms room, the panoramic terrace, and the ramparts. The museum is open daily (except for Tuesdays), and all tours are guided. You can book a guided tour in advance with a guide dressed in medieval costumes (for a minimum group of six people; this service may not be available year-round) or join a nightly spooky tour of the castle (on Fridays, at 22:00; depends on the number of people who have booked the tour). 🕐 Opening times: May-September, tours start at 11:00, 12:00, 15:30, 16:30, 17:30, and 18:30. Off-season (October-April) tours start at 11:00, 12:00, 15:00, 16:00, and 17:00. Closed year-round on Tuesdays. Via Papiriana 2, Fosdinovo, Tel: 0187.680013, www.castellodifosdinovo.it

**The Fosdinovo Adventure Park** is just 1 km farther north (drive along the SS446). This is quite a popular park, with adventurous activities for children ages five and up, including rope bridges, bungee trampolines, and mountain bike courses, as well as obstacle courses that will challenge teenagers, too. If you do visit the adventure park, calculate a minimum of three hours for a standard visit.

🕐 Opening times: mid-March-May, weekends only, 11:00-17:30; mid-June-late August, open daily (except Tuesdays), 10:00-19:00; September, weekends only, 10:00-19:00; October, call first; the park is often closed due to bad weather. Entrance allowed until 2.5 hours before closing time. Via Cucco, Fosdinovo, Cell: 320.9060749, www.parcoavventurafosdinovo.com

# Campocecina

If you have time or energy left and want to get a unique view of the Apuan Alps, Campocecina is a secret the locals like keeping to themselves. Overlooking the majestic Apuan Mountains on one side and the Mediterranean Sea on the other, Campocecina is the perfect place for relaxing, hiking, or a delicious picnic. Alternatively, try the (only) restaurant in the area, fittingly named **Ristornate Belvedere** (meaning "the Panoramic Restaurant"). 🕐 Opening times: mid-June-October, open daily, hours may vary, but the restaurant is usually open all day long; October-mid-June, open on weekends, 09:30-18:30. Calling ahead is advisable. Piazzale dell'Acquasparta, Campocecina, Tel: 0585.841973, www.campocecina.altervista.org

To reach Campocecina, follow the SS446 from Fosdinovo, and after about 1.4 km, take a sharp right turn to SS446dir. After about 5 km, turn a sharp left to SP59 and follow the road until you reach Campocecina and the restaurant. From here you can explore by foot and settle at the best viewpoint. From Fosdinovo the drive up to Campocecina will take about half an hour.

# Night By the Beach

If you don't plan on sleeping up in the Garfagnana area, you can end your day at one of several locations by the beach; enjoy the cool, salty breeze and relax after an adventure-filled day. A picnic with a glass of wine for the adults and tasty snacks for the kids will go wonderfully with the front-row view of the sunset. To reach the beach, drive back toward Fosdinovo and down the hill toward Sarzana and from there to the beach. Marinella di Sarzana and Marina di Carrara both offer a number of typical beach-town food stalls and family pizzerias along the promenade. For a more serious, authentic dining experience, check out our recommendations under "Eating in the Area" at the end of this chapter.

## ITINERARY 2 Bagni di Lucca, Campocatino, Orrido di Botri and the Grotta del Vento

# Bagni di Lucca

## GETTING THERE

The easiest way to reach Bagni di Lucca is with a car (also essential for the other parts of this itinerary). From Lucca, drive north along the SS12. You'll pass several little towns on the way that seem almost identical; you'll know you've arrived once you see the strange triple-arched, asymmetrical stone bridge (known as Devil's Bridge) at the entrance to town.

**TOURIST INFORMATION OFFICE:** The friendly local office is located in Via Umberto 197, and is open daily (though hours may vary, especially off season). Tel: 0583.805745, www.turismobagnidilucca.com

Bagni di Lucca was once a favourite vacation destination for European high society, attracting both literary figures (Elizabeth Barrett and Robert Browning) and royalty (Napoleon's sisters, Paolina Borghese and Elisa Baciocchi) to its thermal baths and calm surroundings. Today, Bagni di Lucca has lost much of its former glory, but it is still a nice stop to make on the way north to Garfagnana, if only to take a photo by the Devil's Bridge or take a pleasant walk along the promenade.

Start your tour with a quick photo next to the ancient 93-metre-long Devil's Bridge, "il Ponte del Diavolo". Built in 1100, the bridge is considered a local treasure and is protected by law; it is illegal to cross it with heavy machinery or vehicles that might damage the structure. Legend has it that the bridge earned its name after a local builder struck a deal with the devil. The devil would help him finish the bridge in one day and, in return, would receive the soul of whoever first crossed the bridge. But as the hours went by, the builder felt guilty about what he had done. He talked with the town elders, and they came up with a plan the ASPCA (or the RSPCA) wouldn't much appreciate. A dog was sent to cross the bridge, and the devil was forced to take the canine's soul.

Engineers will also appreciate the next bridge along the river (one of the first suspended bridges built in Italy, as early as 1841, by architect Lorenzo Nottolini). Once you've entered Bagni di Lucca, you might enjoy touring the area (there are historical buildings elegantly decorated on the inside, such as the old casino) but, honestly, kids won't find the area particularly interesting, and there are much better sights to see farther north.

# Campocatino and the San Viano Eremo

If you are looking to pass a few hours touring the area and admiring the views with a pleasant hike, try driving from Bagni di Lucca to the town Vagli di Sotto, and from there up to Vagli and Campocatino. It's a 25-minute drive up the mountain to an area that hasn't changed much in the last 400 years. Park your car and hike a few hundred metres until you reach a little fountain and see the flowering meadow.

**Tip:** Other popular hiking options in the area are Campofiorito and Montefegatesi. Consult the local tourist office to find out more about both and to find out whether the road leading to these sights is open and accessible.

# Orrido di Botri

Before leaving, make sure you pack comfortable, water-resistant walking shoes (not sandals or beach slippers), a towel, and a change of clothes. There's plenty of water, and you will get wet! Please note that this trail is not suitable for very young children.

## GETTING THERE

From Bagni di Lucca, drive towards Tereglio, continue along the SP56, and follow the directions towards Ponte a Gaio-Orrido di Botri. From there follow the signs to the Orrido. The ride can be steep at times. The area is clearly marked, but if you are having trouble finding it, set your GPS to Ponte a Gaio, and continue from there.

This is one of the most impressive canyons in Tuscany and hiking it is fun. The massive canyon walls have been sculpted for millions of years by water coming from the Pelago River, creating a unique form that has inspired many (even Dante, when he described the entrance to Hell in his masterpiece, *Divina Commedia*). Once you reach the Orrido, you will pay a small entrance fee and receive helmets, which are obligatory for the whole track. There are three different routes available. The shortest and easiest one—"Guadina"—lasts about 30 minutes (and another 30 minutes to walk back); it's only 80 metres long and is suitable for children as young as six. The second route—"Prigioni"—is slightly longer than the first, follows the narrowing torrent, and includes a 500-metre walk in the water. We recommend that if you are in reasonable shape you at least choose this path or kids may be disappointed they didn't get to splash around. The most complete course—"Salto dei Becchi"—includes a longer walk along the impressive excavated walls and leads you to a little pool at the end. This course takes about four hours to complete, requires a professional guide, and is not suitable for children under 12 or anyone in poor shape. In any case, don't go beyond this point unless you are a certified mountain climber carrying the proper gear.

Information regarding all the routes is available at the ticket office at the park's entrance, and during the high season, you can also call in advance: 0583.800020. The Orrido di Botri Park is open between June and October. In years past, the Bagni di Lucca Tourist Office (Pro Loco Bagni di Lucca) has organized guided excursions of the Orrido di Botri every weekend. These tours last four hours, cost about 14 euro per person, and begin at 09:30 in Ponte a Gaio, near the entrance to the Orrido. The fee includes a helmet and the entrance fee to the reserve. Kids under 11 pay half price. All tours must be booked in advance via email, **info@ufficioguide.it**, or find out more here: **www.ufficioguide.it/programma/botri**. Call and find out if a tour is leaving when you are visiting the area: 0583.805745.

Alternatively, book (in advance) a guided and reasonably priced tour with Associazione il Bivacco. Tel: 339.2429589, **www.ilbivacco-toscana.it**, **info@ilbvacco-toscana.it**

# Grotta del Vento (Cave)

## GETTING THERE

The quickest way to the Grotta del Vento Cave is to drive from Bagni di Lucca along the Serchio Valley (road SS12) towards Castelnuovo di Garfagnana. After passing Ponte a Moriano, Borgo a Mozzano, and Gallicano, you will see signs directing you to the cave (which is about 12 km from Gallicano). The area is clearly marked, but if you are having trouble finding it, use these GPS coordinates: Lat. 44°02'03" N (Decimale: 44,0341° N), Lon. 10°21'27" E (Decimale: 10,3575° E).

The Cave is a highly recommended activity for the whole family, as long as your kids are old enough to walk for an entire hour without stopping.It's impossible to push a stroller along the narrow and humid trails of the cave. The Grotta del Vento is easily reached, requires no hiking, and is suitable for all ages (though children younger than five-six may find it scary).

The Apuan Alps are rich in Karst phenomena (a landscape formed when rocks such as limestone and dolomites are dissolved by water), and no place is better to appreciate these complex, millions-of-years long processes than the Grotta del Vento (meaning "the cave of the wind"). The cave combines limestone walls, which have been carved by extreme weather conditions, with beautiful stalactites and stalagmites. The tour consists of three mini-itineraries (sections) and lasts about three hours (an hour for each section). You can choose to visit just the first part, if you don't want to spend the entire morning there. It is impressive even on its own, thanks to a rich display of stalactites and stalagmites. This is also a good idea for toddlers who won't last for more than one hour in a cave.

You can also combine just the first and the second parts. In the second part, you will see impressive mud formations and a little underground river. The third part of the tour consists of visiting a vertical shaft that leads to an underground canyon. This is impressive but not suitable for people with claustrophobia.

🕓 Opening times: The Grotta del Vento is open year-round (except for Christmas). April-November, guided tours of the first itinerary leave at 10:00,

11:00, 12:00, 14:00, 15:00, 16:00, 17:00, 18:00. Guided tours of the second itinerary leave at 11:00, 15:00, 16:00, and 17:00. Guided tours of the three-hour, all-inclusive itinerary leave at 10:00 and 14:00. For tour times outside high season, check the Grotta website. On busy days, to avoid overcrowding and long waits, groups will enter as soon as they reach the maximum number. Children under 10 are eligible for discounted tickets. Via Grotta del Vento 1, Vergemoli, Tel: 0583.722024, www.grottadelvento.com

## An Alternative to Grotta del Vento

There is another cave filled with stalactites and stalagmites in the area – the **Antro del Corchia**, which is also quite impressive. The main disadvantage is that this cave is farther north, and requires additional driving along the Garfagnana roads.

So which cave should you visit? Both caves are impressive, but the Grotta del Vento is probably a better choice. The Antro del Corchia is slightly less accessible, because you can't reach the cave directly. You have to park your car at the lot in town and take a free shuttle to the cave. You also can't take photos inside, whereas you can at the Grotto del Vento. If you do choose to visit this cave, bring a sweater, as it's only 7.6ºC (45ºF) inside. Don't forget comfortable walking shoes with a rubber sole, either; it's slippery inside.

The cave has variable opening times, so check their website to make sure they are open on the date of your arrival. Generally speaking, during high season (July-August) guided tours of the cave leave at 10:00, 12:00, 14:00, 15:00, 16:00, and 17:00. Additional tours may be added during peak season (mid-August) at

11:00 and 13:00. The rest of the year, the cave is open weekends only (occasionally on Fridays), and tours leave at 10:00, 12:00, 14:00, and 16:00. The cave may be closed during winter months; check in advance. Antro del Corchia Cave, Apuan Alps Park, Via IV Novembre 70, Levigliani di Stazzema, Tel: 0584.778405, www.antrocorchia.it

# KIDS'CORNER

## More About... Italian Food!

Tuscany isn't just about travel and beautiful sights; it's about food, too! If you've been travelling for a while, you've probably come across a few Italian delicacies. If not, this quick guide will be helpful.

## Know Your Dough: A Quick Guide to Pizza, Calzone, and Piadina

- If it's flat and you put sausages, cheeses, and vegetables on it and then roll it or fold it like a tortilla, it's a piadina.
- If it started off like a pizza but then got folded over and now looks like a chubby half-moon, you have a calzone on your hands.
- If it's a round piece of dough with toppings and (optional) tomato sauce, alert the media: we have a pizza in the house! (It's true, you can get a pizza with no tomato sauce;

# KIDS'CORNER

it's called pizza bianca or white pizza.)

 **Mission 1:** How many types of pizza do you know?

## Do you know what these pizzas are?

- Pizza Margherita
- Pizza 4 Formaggi
- Pizza con Prosciutto e Funghi

In case you don't know, here is our complete guide to Italian pizza. If nothing else, this guide will make you the No. 1 expert in your family on anything pizza-related!

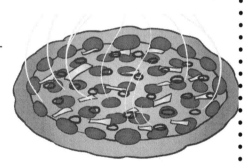

- Margherita: tomato sauce, mozzarella
- Marinara: tomato sauce, garlic, oregano
- 4 Stagioni (4 seasons): tomato sauce, mozzarella, artichoke, mushrooms, ham, spicy sausage
- 4 Formaggi (the 4 cheeses): mozzarella, stracchino, gorgonzola, and grana. This is considered a pizza Bianca: (a white pizza), because there is no tomato sauce.

# KIDS'CORNER

- Porcini: tomato sauce, mozzarella, porcini mushrooms
- Capricciosa: tomato sauce, mozzarella, prosciutto cotto (ham), salsiccia (sausage), mushrooms, artichokes, olives
- Verdure (pizza with vegetables): tomato sauce, mozzarella, zucchini, eggplants, radicchio, grilled peppers
- Napoli: tomato sauce, mozzarella, anchovies, oregano
- Cotto (pizza with ham): tomato sauce, mozzarella, prosciutto cotto
- Funghi (pizza with mushrooms): tomato sauce, mozzarella, prosciutto cotto, mushrooms
- Wurstel (pizza with hot dog slices on top): tomato sauce, mozzarella, hot dog slices
- Tonno & Cipolla (pizza with tuna and onions): tomato sauce, tuna, onions, mozzarella
- Bufala: tomato sauce, mozzarella di bufala, basil. The mozzarella di buffalo, in case you wondered, is the REAL DEAL. This is mozzarella that is made of buffalo milk, not cow milk.
- Speck & Rucola (pizza with a type of sausage called speck, and rocket, a slightly bitter-tasting leaf): tomato sauce, rocket, mozzarella, speck
- Crudo (pizza with a type of ham called Prosciutto crudo): tomato sauce, mozzarella, prosciutto crudo
- Rossa: pizza with tomato sauce and nothing else
- Rucola: pizza with rocket and mozzarella

# KIDS'CORNER

Some of the most popular pizza toppings in the USA, like sweet corn or pineapple, don't exist in Italy!

## Pass the Pasta!

Take our Chef Luigi's challenge to see if you are truly the greatest expert who's ever lived on all matters pasta!

1. What is pasta made of?
   a. Alien residues
   b. Durum wheat and water (sometimes wheat water and egg yolks)
   c. Pasta isn't made; it's created by the almighty pasta Gods

2. What are ravioli?
   a. How should I know?
   b. Little square pockets of pasta filled with a stuffing like ricotta and spinach, mushrooms, or meat and served with a tasty sauce
   c. A nickname for revolutionary soldiers in Mexico

3. True or false: Italians eat about 28 kg of pasta a year (each!).
   a. True
   b. False
   c. Can you repeat the options?

4. True or false: Italy is the world's largest pasta producer and exports more than 1.7 million tons of pasta each year. That's like

> **Bonus Question: Name 5 pasta shapes!**

# KIDS'CORNER

850 million bags of pasta!

a. Naaaah, I think you're lying
b. True! It's true!
c. I want to believe you... do you have proof of this?

## super mission for smart detectives:

You are Cosimo de Medici, ruler of all of Tuscany, and you are worried about the latest Ottoman pirate attacks near the port of Livorno. You want the St. Stephen knights to operate immediately, and you need to get a secret message to the knights, but you are stuck far away, between the high mountains of the Garfagnana. You must find a way to pass an encrypted message to your knight in Florence, but you know that you can trust no one, not even your own servant. So you decide to write an encrypted message and seal it with your wax seal. But how can you do that? Let's find out!

How to make a secret encrypted message

## can you make your own?

# Eating in the Garfagnana

## BAGNI DI LUCCA

Thanks to its traditional menu—including homemade pasta and meat dishes—**Buca Di Baldabo'** is popular with the locals. Try the gnocchi, which are quite good. Open weekdays for dinner only, 19:30-22:30; weekends, 12:30-14:30, 19:30-22:30; closed on Tuesdays. Booking in advance is advised. Via Prati 11, Vico Pancellorum, Bagni Di Lucca, Tel: 0583.89062

**Trattoria Borghesi** is centrally located and is perfect for a quick but tasty lunch. Via Umberto 85, Bagni Di Lucca, Tel: 0583.87219, www.barborghesi.it

**Ristorante Circolo dei Forestieri** is another good option; it is near the entrance to town and overlooks the river (book a place on the terrace in advance). Open daily, 12:00-14:30, 19:00-22:30; closed on Mondays; Tuesdays, open for dinner only, 19:00-22:30. Piazza Jean Verraud 10, Bagni Di Lucca, Tel: 0583.86038, Cell: 329.7409058, www.circolodeiforestieri.it

## FOSDINOVO

If you are looking for a pleasant place to stop for lunch after your visit to the castle and adventure park, try **Agriturismo la Burlanda.** The food is good (and mostly organic), and kids will love the fact that you can pet goats and pigs in a little petting zoo on the premises. The agriturismo's restaurant is open on weekends, 12:00-15:00, 19:00-22:00; hours may vary, especially off-season. Call before driving up here. Thursday-Friday, open for dinner only, 19:00-22:00; Monday-Wednesday, by reservation only. Via Fabiano 6, Fosdinovo, Tel: 0187.628286, Cell: 333.6244525, www.laburlanda.com

## EATING ALONG THE BEACH

The popular **Osteria del Muraglione** serves meat and fish dishes to please all. Open daily for dinner, 19:00-23:00; closed on Mondays. Via Fivizzano 13, Marina di Carrara, Tel: 0585.857523.

**Ristorante-Pizzeria Venezia** will keep kids happy, with their simple and tasty pizzas. Open Wednesday-Sunday, 12:30-14:00, 19:30-22:00; Tuesdays, 19:30-22:00; closed on Mondays. Viale Amerigo Vespucci 30, Marina di Carrara, Tel: 0585.634453, www.ristorante-pizzeria-venezia.it

Farther south at Forte dei Marmi, a favourite resort for the rich (just 30 minutes from Pisa), you will find a few high-end (and, obviously, pricier) restaurants. If you are looking for an elegant seafood restaurant and are prepared to splurge on a Michelin-starred, top-ten kind of establishment, then **Lorenzo** is the place for you. This popular venue (book in advance!) has been serving some the best seafood dishes in Tuscany for many years. Open Wednesday-Sunday, 12:30-14:00, 20:00-23:00. Tuesdays, open for dinner only, 20:00-23:00; closed on Mondays. Via Carducci 61, Forte dei Marni, Tel: 0584.874030, www.ristorantelorenzo.com

**Perche' No** is yet another option in the area, serving classic Italian dishes (meat and fish) in Via Cugnia 381, Querceta and Forte Dei Marmi, Tel: 339.3574907

### CASTELNUOVO DI GARFAGNANA
Some of the best places for a tasty lunch or dinner in the heart of the Garfagnana are the deli shops in the town of Castelnuovo in Garfagnana, just 30 minutes north of Bagni di Lucca. There isn't much to see in town, but you will find a very friendly and knowledgeable tourist office (where you can get information about hotels and activities in the area) and great local produce (useful if you plan on going on a picnic). Park outside the town, near the little fortress, and walk in to taste excellent cheeses, sausages, and more in a well-known Tuscan establishment, **Osteria Vecchio Mulino**. Open daily, 12:00-21:00; closed on Mondays; open for dinner by reservation only. May be closed off-season. Via Vittorio Emanuele 12, Tel: 0583.62192, www.vecchiomulino.info

**L'aia dei Piero** is another popular (and tasty!) eatery just outside the historical centre. If you decide to stay for lunch, you'll be seated in a cave (which kids will adore). Open daily, 08:00-19:45. Tel: 0583.62519, www.aiadipiero.it

# Sleeping in the Garfagnana

If you plan on staying for a day or two in Garfagnana, it is best to sleep in the area around Bagni di Lucca or between Bagni di Lucca and Castelnuovo di Garfagnana so you will be surrounded by nature but still relatively close to most of the attractions.

**Pruneta** is a lovely little place, offering homey apartments, cooking classes, a beautiful view, and reasonable prices in the town of Torite, near Castelnuovo di Garfagnan. Pruneta di Sopra, Torrite, Castelnuovo di Garfagnana, Tel: 0583.88203, www.pruneta.com

**Agriturismo La Torre** is also a charming little place and great for families, with a pool, green grass to run around on, and lovely views. You can also rent mountain bikes to tour the area. Loc. La Torre-Fornoli, Bagni Di Lucca, Tel: 0583.805297, www.agriturismolatorre.it

**Park Hotel Regina** is located in a renovated historical building and enjoys a central location, comfortable rooms, and a pool. Viale Umberto 157, Bagni di Lucca, Tel: 0583.805508, www.coronaregina.it

# Special Events in the Area

There are a number of local events, such as town festivals and year-round markets, but if you only have time for one or two special events during your holiday, we recommend focusing on other places, such as Pisa, Monteriggioni, or Volterra, which offer more interesting options. If you visit Fosdinovo castle in July, the small (but fun) local medieval festival is worth exploring: www.fosdinovomedievale.it

# Special Activities in the Area

### HORSE AND PONY RIDES
Why not try a horseback riding tour while you are in the area? **Lucca Horse Riding Farm** offers a number of activities geared toward younger, inexperienced riders, and pony tours are available for younger children. Tel: 329.5727481, www.luccahorseriding.com

### RAFTING AND CANOEING
Rafting is perfect for those looking for an adrenaline rush. **Localita Pian di Fiume** (also a popular agriturismo) offers a number of rafting activities for the whole family. Choose from an hour-long, relaxed canoe ride for kids as young as four or an active and exciting rafting adventure for teenagers, ages 15 and up. In either case, this is not an activity for children who are afraid of water or

can't swim. Check on the website to see what special gear you might need to bring with you, and book in advance. Pian di Fiume, Localita Pian di Fiume 20, Bagni di Lucca, Tel: 333.1081168, 349.8557116, www.raftingh2o.com

Alternatively, check out the rafting activities offered by another local company, **Aguaraja Rafting**. They offer extreme rafting trips along the Lima River, near Bagni di Lucca. Località Cevoli, near Fabbriche di Casabasciana, Bagni di Lucca, Tel: 348.3301593, www.aguaraja.com

## QUADS

**Lucca Quad** offers the perfect activity for older, action-loving teenagers (Driver must be over 18, with a license). Passengers must be at least 12 years old. Book in advance. Tours leave from Via Cappella in San Cassiano Di Controne, Bagni di Lucca, Tel: 349.6087277, www.Luccaquad.com

## ADVENTURE PARKS AND BIKE TOURS

The Garfagnana is considered a sports lover's dream, with endless hiking options as well as adventurous sports. Most activities have to be booked in advance, but if you are looking for an adventure that requires no advance booking and allows the kid to have a good time jumping around the obstacle courses, try the **Fosdinovo Adventure Park** (see Itinerary 1 in this chapter) or the **Selva del Buffardello Adventure Park**. Please be aware that this second park is high up in the heart of Garfagnana, near the Orecchiella Nature Reservoir, and requires more than an hour and a half of driving on windy roads. If you don't plan on visiting that area, you may want to stick to the more accessible Fosdinovo Park. Selva del Buffardello Adventure Park is open daily during July-August and on weekends only in June. The park closes in bad weather. Children must be at least 1 metre high to access the obstacle courses, and all children under 18 must be accompanied by an adult. Selva del Buffardello, San Romano in Garfagnana, Località Prà di Lago, Cell: 347.7110433, 320.2469330, 328.5733095, www.selvadelbuffardello.it

Alternatively, try the **Ciocco Sport Village** in Barga, an excellent choice for families, offering activities such as bike tours, bow and arrow lessons, quad tours, horse rides, pony rides, Nordic walking, and much more that will delight kids and teenagers who want some adventurous fun. Booking in advance is recommended, especially for the quad tours. To drive the quad, you must be over 18 and have a license. Barga, Tel: 0583.719355, www.sportvillageciocco.it

## TREKKING

Trekking can be great fun and an excellent way to bring the family together, but it can also be intimidating to venture off all by yourself on a hike in an area you don't know very well (or at all). There is a simple solution: hire the services of a local environmental guide who will take you on a tailor-made excursion based on your tastes and physical abilities. These tours are much cheaper than you might think. You can find a list of guides at the local tourist offices, or join a group excursion led by such a guide. Both can be accomplished through the Associazione Garfagnana Guide, which offers full-day and half-day guided tours in the area at reasonable prices, as well as the names of private guides in the region. Find out more here: www.garfagnanaguide.it, or call 0583.65169.

Alternatively, book a guided trek with the Bagni di Lucca Hiking Association. Find out more here: www.bagnidiluccatrekking.com. (Tours must be booked at least three days in advance. Contact one of these numbers: 333.6402068 / 333.7294941.)

# VOLTERRA

# Chapter 4

# **Volterra**

Volterra is a beautiful medieval hill town that tends to be overlooked when visitors head off to the more famous San Gimignano or Montepulciano. But this 3000-year-old town has heaps of charm, history, and culture to offer and is far less crowded or touristy than San Gimignano. With an excellent Etruscan Museum, a Roman Theatre that kids can explore, great views, endless alabaster workshops and souvenir shops, Volterra has something for the whole family. It is also virtually traffic free (in its historical centre), so kids can run around most of the time (but do watch out for the occasional car). A visit to Volterra usually takes a half-day and can be combined with a visit to Monteriggioni (see the San Gimignano and Monteriggioni Itinerary), Pisa, or even San Gimignano (though combining it with either of the latter two would make for an intense day).

Our recommendation is to spend an entire morning in Volterra, and then head outside the town walls after lunch for some family fun. You will find a number of activities for all age groups listed at the end of this itinerary (see "Special Activities in the Area"). Toddlers, for example, will love the Peccioli Prehistoric Park, older children will enjoy the adventure park in Riparbella, and teenagers will have fun taking a horseback riding tour of the area. If you choose a family-friendly agriturismo with a pool (see the list of recommendations at the end of this itinerary) you will be able to spend the evening splashing around and relaxing after your fun-filled day. If you happen to be in Volterra during the third or fourth weekends in August, don't miss Volterra A.D. 1398, one of the best medieval festivals in Tuscany. To find out more, check out the "Special Events in the Area" section at the end of this itinerary.

## Top 5 Family Activities

1. Tour the Roman Theatre and discover Volterra's ancient past.

2. Discover the secrets of Etruscan culture in the Guarnacci Etruscan Museum.

3. Visit the Prehistoric Park in Peccioli.

4. Buy fun alabaster souvenirs.

5. Walk the medieval streets to Piazza della Liberta to enjoy the great view, or visit Volterra's Medieval Torture Museum.

## GETTING THERE

**BY CAR:** The easiest way to reach Volterra is by car. From Pisa, take the A12 autostrada and then the SS68 (take the SS439 only if you plan on visiting the Peccioli Prehistoric Park before you visit Volterra). You won't need a car in Volterra itself, but you will need one to tour the surrounding area and reach other attractions detailed in this itinerary (including your B&B, which will most likely be outside the town). Volterra is small, and even though there are 10 parking lots surrounding the city walls and inside the town itself, parking can be difficult at times. As always, make sure you don't enter the ZTL areas. Avoid parking lot number 3, which is reserved for locals only. Your safest bet is the large underground parking lot in Piazza della Liberta'.

**BY TRAIN AND BUS:** You can reach Volterra via public transportation, but it's a hassle, and you will most likely have to change buses mid way (there are very few direct buses to Volterra). All busses to the town will leave you at Piazza Martiri della Liberta'. Another problem with busses is that they aren't very frequent (some don't operate at all on Sundays and holidays).

**TOURIST INFORMATION OFFICES:** There are two tourist offices in Volterra; both are good, though we prefer the friendly and knowledgeable staff at the office in Piazza dei Priori 10 (next to the town hall, the building with the clock). 🕐 Opening times: open year-round, Monday-Saturday, 09:00-18:00; closed on Sundays. Tel: 0588.86150, www.volterratur.it.

# Twilight

For many *Twilight* fans, Volterra is best known as the setting for the second book in the Stephanie Meyer series, *New Moon*. Especially since the popular trilogy was made into movies, a steady stream of fans visits Volterra hoping to get a glimpse of some vampire magic (or Edward).

Though New Moon was actually shot in Montepulciano, crafty entrepreneurs do offer Twilight-themed tours of Volterra designed for teenagers, with entertaining (and slightly scary) little surprises along the way. Book in advance, as spots are limited, and the tours only happen on specific days. These tours can be expensive, but the price goes down if there are more participants. Contact the local tourist board responsible for the tour: www.volterratur.it Tel 0588.86099.

Alternatively, try booking a starlit tour of Volterra at night. It has nothing to do with *Twilight*, but it is still cool, and kids will enjoy it. Tours take place weekly from July-September. Children under the age of 14 participate for free. Check out available tours and book a spot by calling 0588.86099.

Volterra has been inhabited since Neolithic times, but it first became famous under the Etruscans, who transformed it into a flourishing city in the 4th century BC and surrounded it with a rock wall that was seven kilometers long (the wall was rebuilt and expanded in the Middle Ages). Volterra was one of the most important Etruscan cities in Tuscany, as is demonstrated by the richness of local findings. After years of constant fighting, Etruscans eventually surrendered to the Romans and were assimilated into Roman society, becoming equal citizens, but much of Etruscan culture can still be seen in this unique town.

## With so many Etruscan museums in Tuscany, how do you choose which ones to visit?

The Etruscans ruled all over Tuscany; in fact, this region was formerly known as Etruria, land of the Etruscans. There are numerous Etruscan tombs (necropolis), archaeological sites, and museums throughout the region, and though many of them are interesting and claim to offer a "unique experience", there is no reason to visit them all. The museum in Volterra is impressive and has some of the best exhibits, and even though they are sometimes poorly displayed in an outdated manner, it is nonetheless highly recommended. The Etruscan Museum in Cortona (see Cortona Itinerary) is one of the largest in Tuscany and much more user-friendly, but the artefacts themselves are less impressive than those in Volterra. The Archaeological Museums in Chiusi and Chianciano Terme (see Montepulciano and Chiusi Itinerary) are both small but charming. They are worth a quick visit if you are in the area and particularly interested in Etruscan culture. The best solution for families, who want to learn about the Etruscans in a fun and active way without overdoing it, is to combine a visit to one museum, like the one in Volterra, for example, with the activities suggested in the Montepulciano and Chiusi Itinerary (which include cool underground tours and a visit to richly decorated Etruscan tombs). If you are looking for a more active hike, consider combining a museum visit with a tour of the Etruscan Archaeological Park in Populonia (see the Populonia and Etruscan Beach Itinerary) or, better yet, the Archaeological Park near Sorano (see the Maremma Itinerary).

**Our tour of Volterra begins** in the town's main square, Piazza dei Priori. This charming square was originally known as the Bishop's Prato (Camp), but when the Bishop started losing power and Volterra became a free commune, it changed its name to **Piazza dei Priori**. On your right stands Palazzo dei Priori, an impressive medieval building planned by Maestro Riccardo, which took 49 years to complete. Like in so many other cases, the decorations on the outer walls tell us quite a bit about the history of the city itself. Note, for example, that the ornamental details include Florence's coat of arms (made of terracotta), which symbolize the town's years under Florentine occupation. Two Marzocco lions, another symbol of Florence, clear up any doubt about who the boss was in town.

**Mission 1:** One of the buildings in this piazza is known as Palazzo del Porcellino (the piglet building). Can you guess which one and why? Hint: Look up!

From here, walk along Via Matteotti, the town's main street; it is filled with fun little shops that will tempt you with their alabaster souvenirs (but you may want to wait until you visit the alabaster workshops described later in the itinerary). Turn left to Via dei Sarti and walk straight until you reach **Palazzo Viti**, one of Volterra's surprising attractions. Though not as dramatic as the Etruscan Museum or the Roman amphitheatre, this little regal mansion-turned-museum might interest history-loving kids. The lavish, dramatic décor, the chance to look at how people lived hundreds of years ago, and the small, intimate setting make for a nice quick visit. Interestingly, this modern palace is still inhabited by a member of the original noble family.

**Mission 2:** In one of the rooms in this little palace, the ceiling is decorated with portraits of four of the greatest poets who ever lived in Italy (including Dante Alighieri, of course). Can you find the room?

**Mission 3:** In one of the rooms, you will find a large and unique candelabrum decorated with dragons. Can you guess what it's made of?

🕐 Opening times: April–October, open daily, 10:00-13:00, 14:30-18:00. During the winter, open by appointment only. Kids under 10 enter for free. Via dei Sarti 41, Tel: 0588.84047, www.palazzoviti.it

> **Tip:** Palazzo Viti sometimes organizes art workshops for children. Check out their website for updates, and if you find something that interests you, book in advance.

From Palazzo Vitti, return to the main street and follow the signs (walking along the town walls) toward the **Roman Theatre** (or, to be more exact, toward the section of the wall that overlooks the theatre from above).

> **Tip:** On your way to the theatre, you will see signs leading to the Rossi Alabaster Workshop (and small factory), one of the largest in town, and a great stop with kids (another good workshop to visit is described later in the itinerary and is located next to the Etruscan Museum). Pop in to see the masters carve the alabaster or shine it with metal brushes. Both kids and adults will enjoy finding a little souvenir to take home. Rossi Alabastri Workshop and Shop, Via del Mandorlo, Tel: 0588.86133, www.rossialabastri.com

**The Roman Theatre** was built over 2000 years ago by the rich Ceicna family, an ex-Etruscan noble family who moved to Rome after the fall of Volterra. There they became prominent citizens and decided to honour their double identity by building a theatre in their hometown and dedicating it to the Roman Emperor, Augustus. This is one of the best Roman monuments in Tuscany, and an ideal stop for kids, who can run around between the ancient stone benches. Visitors can also walk on what is left of the stage, check out the changing rooms carved in stone, and imagine what shows were like back then, complete with aspiring actors and a cheering crowd (was it really that different from to-

day's *American Idol or Britain's Got Talent*?)

The Roman Theatre can be seen from above or you can go down to visit it (recommended). If you decide the latter, we suggest you first visit the other attractions in town, and only then walk back to your car and drive to the theatre (which is located below the town). Otherwise, you will have to climb all the way back up from the Roman theatre to town, and the steep walk will be hard·for kids. To drive to the theatre, set the GPS to Piazza Caduti Martiri dei Lager Nazisti.

🕐 Opening times: Mid-March-October, 10:30-17:30; November-mid-March, closes at 16:30. May close down entirely in bad weather. Tickets include the Roman Theatre and the Etruscan Acropolis. Cell: 328.0707834

> **Tip:** The **Etruscan Acropolis** is yet another archaeological site in Volterra, situated at the highest point in town (you'll see signs leading to it near the Etruscan Museum). The view from the Acropolis is nice (be prepared for a short but steep walk up), but there is really nothing much to see there. The remains of the temples are far from impressive and most of the site is closed because it is still under exploration. Personally, we recommend skipping it in favour of more interesting attractions. However, if you are looking for a place to picnic and relax in the sun, the Acropolis offers a large grassy meadow as well as a good view of the massive Medici Fortress.

From this point of the wall (overlooking the Roman Theatre from above), walk back to Via Matteotti. Turn to Via Gramsci and follow the signs to Volterra's famous **Etruscan Museum (Museo Guarnacci)**. One of the first museums in Europe, it was founded in 1761 by an eccentric antiquities' collector, Mario Guarnacci, who, upon his death, left his treasures to his native town. Inside, you will find a very rich, if sometimes poorly displayed, collection of urns, sculptures, mosaics, Etruscan artefacts (including those found in the Roman Theatre), bronze helmets, and much more. The main problem with the museum is that it offers very few explanations in English; consider renting the audio guide to complete your tour.

• • • • • • • • • • • • • • • • • • • • • • • • • • • • • • • • • • • • • • • • • • • •

**Mission 4:** List six different types of artefacts that you saw in the museum, and explain what they are.

**Mission 5:** Based on the exhibitions you just saw in the museum, can you guess the right answer for each of these questions?

**True or false:**

Most Etruscan vases were blue because that was the

most common colour in Volterra. T / F

The Etruscan lived 500 years ago. T / F

The Etruscans would burn their dead and put their ashes in beautifully decorated urns. T / F

........................................................................................

........................................................................................

**Mission 6:** In room number 29 (marked like this XXIX) you can find some interesting tools that the Etruscans used. Do you know (or can you guess) what they were used for? Hint: Think about the most famous type of rock in Volterra.

**Mission 7:** Throughout the first floor of the museum, you will find examples of

— — — — — — —

These were used by the Romans (who conquered Volterra) to decorate the floor and were made from several little colourful stones. Can you fill in the missing word?

**Mission 8 (Super Mission):** Can you design a vase in Etruscan style? Think about the illustrations the Etruscans painted on their urns, the style, and the colour. Do you think you can create something similar?

........................................................................................

🕐 Opening times: mid-March-October, open daily, 09:00-19:00. November–mid-March, open daily, 10:00-16:30 (may close earlier). Kids under six enter for free. Via Don Minzoni 15, Tel: 0588.86347

**Tip:** To find out more about the Etruscan culture, check out our fun Kids' Corner in the Montepulciano and Chiusi Itinerary.

Just a minute away from the museum, you will find the town's second largest **alabaster workshop** and shop, **Albarte**. Pop in for a visit; kids can see how the artists work and what amazing sculptures can be created from the elegant, delicate alabaster. Via Orti S. Agostino 28, Tel: 0588.85506, www.alabarte.com

# Alabaster

Alabaster, a soft stone that lends itself to the hands of the sculptor, has been a source of pride in Volterra since Etruscan times.

Over the years, some exquisite artefacts have been made by local artisans using ancient yet sophisticated techniques. There are several shops in town selling both alabaster items and Etruscan-style statues and jewelry. Look around before choosing items; though prices are similar throughout town, some shops offer better pieces.

Did you know alabaster is formed through a process that takes millions of years? Seawater crystallizes in caves and becomes this delicate stone, which means the souvenir you just bought is actually millions of years old! In the past, alabaster was used instead of glass (which was extremely expensive) for windows or for making bottles and jewelry for noblewomen. To colour the alabaster, it is mixed with other minerals.

Kids who are interested in absolute gore might appreciate a visit to the (horrifying) **Torture Museum**, just a few meters down from the Etruscan Museum. 🕐 Opening times: open daily, 10:00-19:00 (open weekends only during the winter). Piazza XX settembre 5, Volterra, Tel: 0588.80501

You can end your tour of Volterra in **Piazza Martiri della Liberta'**. Enjoy the beautiful view and explore the shops in the area (take a look at the alabaster souvenirs at Alabastro Ali shop near the piazza). Then have some lunch and drive down to the Roman Theatre for a close-up look.

# **Eating** in Volterra

For a quick, absolutely unpresumptuous fix, try **La Vecchia Lira**, a centrally located self-service cafeteria that offers simple but tasty food. You can also find gluten-free dishes. The cafeteria is open for lunch; for dinner you can sit down at their attached restaurant. Open daily, 11:30-14:30, 19:00-22:00; closed on Thursdays. Via Matteotti 19, Tel: 0588.86180, www.vecchialira.com

For a good slice of pizza, which makes for a kid-friendly and reasonably priced meal, try **Pizzeria Ombra della Sera**. Open daily, 12:00-15:00, 19:00-22:00; closed on Mondays. Via Guernacci 16, Tel: 0588.85274

Or sample the pizza at **Alla Vecchia Maniera**, open daily, 09:00-15:00, 19:00-24:00; closed on Tuesdays. Via Ricciarelli 38, Tel: 0588.88819

If you don't mind driving 5 minutes out of town, we recommend you head to **Agriturismo Villa Felice**, which is, in our opinion, one of the best restaurants in the area. The food here is simple but perfectly executed, and the view from the restaurant is extraordinary! If you are vising in high season, book a table in advance, as they are always full, especially on weekends.
Ristorante Agriturismo San Felice is located on the road to Volterra (SR68, km 44), Tel: 0588.39017/345.0671.489, www.villafelicevolterra.com. Open daily in high season, 12:30-14:30, 19:30-22:30. May be closed in the off-season.

# Sleeping in Volterra

**Agriturismo Diacceroni** is a great option for kids, with a little playground, horses, a pool, and organized activities for the whole family. Villamagna, Volterra, Tel: 0588.84064, 347.3556029, www.agriturismodiacceroni.com

**Podere Marcampo** is a comfortable option for families. Surrounded by spectacular views, you'll enjoy the simple but comfortable apartments in a relaxed atmosphere. Kids can play around in the pool. Localita San Cipriano, Volterra, Tel: 0588.85393, www.agriturismo-marcampo.com

**Park Hotel le Fonti** is a good choice, offering spectacular views, a pool, and comfortable family rooms. Via Fontecorrenti 8, Volterra, Tel: 0588.85219, www.parkhotellefonti.com

**Hotel Residence villa Rioddi** is another solid choice for families, with comfortable rooms, Wi-Fi, a pool, and a playing area. S.P Monte Volterrano 71, Volterra, Tel: 0588.88053, www.hotelvillarioddi.it

**Villa Porta all'arco** is a warm, charming place within walking distance of the town centre and offers reasonably priced rooms (but no pool). Via Mazzini 2, Volterra, Tel: 0588.81487, www.villaportallarco.it

Although slightly farther away from other options, **Il Cerreto** is a lovely alternative. An organic agriturismo, it was built in a charming little castle, featuring comfortable rooms, a biological pool (which means its water is treated with organic substances instead of chemicals), and an active farm. Loc. Il Cerreto, Pomarance, Tel: 0588.64213, www.bioagriturismoilcerreto.it

# Special Events in Volterra

If you are in the area toward the end of August, don't miss **Volterra A.D. 1398**. Volterra comes to life with warhorses, fearless knights, noblemen and ladies, artisans and merchants, common people and peasants, flag-wavers and crossbowmen, musicians, and jesters. The festival kicks off around the centro storico on the third and fourth Sundays of every August. www.Volterra1398.it

**Notti Bianche:** On the first Saturday of July and again on the first Saturday of August, music, food stands, and cultural events fill Volterra. Find out the exact events planned each year at the local tourist office.

**Volterragusto:** Every October for three weeks, you can enjoy specialties from the region, from white truffles and excellent cheeses to new wine and traditionally made sausages and breads. Several local restaurants take part in the activities, serving special mouth-watering truffle-based menus. The feast is always accompanied by cultural events, which are enjoyable as well. Check out the yearly program at www.Volterragusto.com. For more events, check out www.Volterratur.it

# Special Activities in the Area

## PREHISTORIC DINOSAUR PARK

**The Prehistoric Park in Peccioli** is a great destination for families with younger children and toddlers who are looking for less demanding afternoon activity. Some of the statues are slightly run down, but most kids would hardly mind that. Walk around between exciting statues of dinosaurs and explore a small playground, with lots of space to run around. Don't miss the "exploding volcano". Children under the age of three enter for free.

Open year-round, April-August, 09:00-19:00; September-March, 09:00-18:00. Via dei Cappuccini, Peccioli (the park is located about 1 km north of Peccioli, and 30 km north of Volterra), Tel: 0587.636030, Cell: 328.1785850, www.parcopreistorico.it

## HIKES AND EXTREME SPORTS

If you are looking for an adrenaline rush and enjoy canyoning, mountain biking, cave exploring or coasteering, try booking (in advance) an activity with **Tateam**. Canyoning is recommended for children older than nine. Activities are available year round but may be suspended during bad weather. Cell: 348.7911215, www.tateam.it

## HORSEBACK RIDING

**Manneggio 52 Area Park** is a local horse farm that offers horseback rides for older kids (over 14) and adults. Younger and inexperienced riders will be led on horse in nearby fields, whereas more experienced riders can set off to explore the charms of Tuscan nature. Book in advance. (This activity is also featured in the San Gimignano and Monteriggioni Itinerary, due to its proximity to both towns.) Via S. Margherita 47, Loc. Prato D'era, Volterra. Tel: 0588.42140, www.area52park.com

## ADVENTURE PARKS

One of the best ways to help kids blow off steam is to set them free to jump and explore in an adventure park. **Riparbella Giardino Sospeso** offers hanging ladders among the oak trees, acrobatic courses for kids over 110 cm, an archery course, a playground toddlers can enjoy, and a picnic area. Opening times: during high season, June-mid-September, open daily, from 10:00 until sunset; mid-September-November, weekends and holidays only, 10:00 until sunset; closed during the winter; March-June, open on weekends and holidays only, from 10:00 until sunset. Ticket office closes 2.5 hours before sunset. Children shorter than 140 cm are eligible for reduced tickets. Loc. Il Giardino, Tel: 335.7726323, www.ilgiardinosospeso.it

# CHIANTI

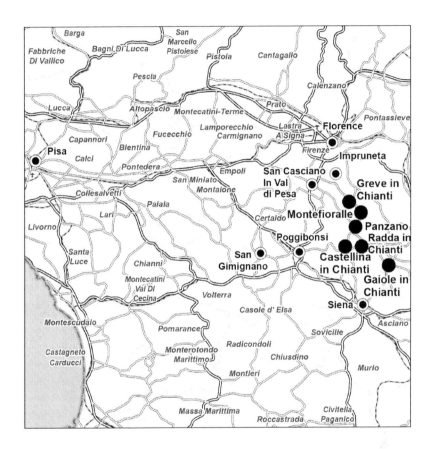

## HOW LONG WILL IT TAKE TO GET THERE?

Florence to Greve in Chianti: 50 minutes
Greve in Chianti to Montefioralle: 5 minutes
Greve in Chianti to Panzano: 15 minutes
Greve in Chianti to Radda in Chianti: 30 minutes
Radda in Chianti to Gaiole in Chianti: 15 to 20 minutes
Gaiole in Chianti to Siena: 40 minutes

# Chapter 5

# **Chianti**

The beautiful Chianti area, with its rolling hills and endless tempting vineyards, is a favourite destination for many couples who visit Tuscany. "But I have kids!" you may be thinking. "It's impossible to enjoy the charms of Chianti with kids." Well, that's not necessarily true. While it's not the most kid-friendly area, there are still a few possibilities for a fun day. By combining a more active wine tasting option with a tour of two towns and a fun afternoon activity for the whole family, a visit to Chianti can be enjoyable for all.

When choosing the location for your wine tasting, make sure it offers some entertainment for the kids; otherwise, you won't get any tasting done. A number of wine producers in this area are located inside ancient castles and offer the option of touring the castle as well as the vineyard, which allows kids to have fun, too (check out our recommendations at the end of this chapter, under "Special Activities in the Area").

There are four main towns in the Chianti region—Castellina in Chianti, Radda in Chianti, Greve in Chianti, and Gaiole in Chianti, as well as and several charming little 'borghi' (medieval vilages). We would recommned focusing your time on two of these borghi (mainly Panzano and Montefioralle, both of which are very close to Greve in Chianti) and one main town (Radda or Gaiole if you plan on doing any wine tasting, Greve if you've booked an organized tour).

Like always, we highly recommend working a special activity into the itinerary, using the list at the end of this chapter. A morning cooking class, for example, where kids can get their hands dirty with flour and sauces and prepare some of the dishes they have tasted throughout the trip could be a fun and memorable experience. Alternatively, you could also balance your day with nearby family-friendly attractions from other itineraries, like Monteriggioni (just 40 minutes away, described in the San Gimignano and Monteriggioni Itinerary) or the adventure park in San Casciano Val di Pesa (just 45 minutes away, described under "Special Activities in the Area" in the Florence Itinerary).

## Top 5 Family Activities

1. Have lunch or dinner in Radda in Chianti and enjoy the amazing view.

2. Tour the Sculpture Park near Castellina in Chianti.

3. Walk along the medieval streets of Montefioralle or Panzano in Chianti and imagine what life was like 800 years ago.

4. Taste wine and visit the impressive Brolio Castle (or the Meleto Castle).

5. Take a cooking class and cook like a true Italian!

# **Greve** in Chianti

## GETTING THERE

Though there are local buses connecting most of the towns and villages, the only way to properly tour the Chianti area is by car, especially if you want to do some wine tasting. From Florence, take the scenic SS222 road, head south, pass Imprunetta, and follow the signs to Greve in Chianti.

**TOURIST OFFICE:** Greve in Chianti's small tourist office is a good place to get information about local wineries and tours, as well as special events in the area. ⊙ Opening times: March-October, open daily, 10:00-19:00; November-February, open daily, 10:00-17:00. Piazza Giacomo Matteotti 11, ground floor of Palazzo del Fiorentino, Tel: 055.8546299

Right next door, you will find 'Discover Tuscany', a private tour operator, where you can book several tours, bike rides, and wine tastings in the area.

Greve in Chianti is the largest town in the Chianti region, but as far as tourism goes, there isn't much to see (there are two little museums but both can probably be skipped). Stop in Greve in Chianti if you are looking for a place to have lunch or if you happen to pass by on a Sunday when there's a small farmers' market. If you want to buy some meat, the well-known local butcher shop, **Falorni**, (www.falorni.it) has been serving local delicacies since 1729. (Adjacent to the butcher shop is a newly-opened cafeteria, run by the same owners, offering tasty dishes kids will like at very reasonable prices.)

If you haven't got the time to visit a winery but still want to try the local produce, try **Enoteca Falorni**, a beautifully decorated wine shop in the heart of Greve in Chianti, where you can buy a tasting card. Insert it into the temperature-controlled wine vaults and pour yourself some wine (charged per glass). ◕ Opening times: open daily, 10:00-19:00. Galleria le Cantine 2, Tel: 055.8546404, www.lecantine.it

Just a few minutes away from Greve in Chianti hides one of the loveliest borghi, or medieval fortified villages, in the area: the perfectly preserved **Montefioralle**. Like most other towns and villages in the area, there isn't much to do here except tour the narrow, medieval little streets, some of which are more than 1,000 years old. If you are looking for a place for lunch, **Ristorante Castellana** is a tasty option and just 500 meters from Montefioralle itself. The food is hearty and traditional, and kids will love the decor. ◕ Open daily, 12:00-14:30, 19:30-21:30; closed on Mondays. Localita' Montefioralle 1, Greve in Chianti, Tel: 055.853134. www.ristorantelacastellana.it (You can park your car in Piazza Santo Stefano, 50 metres from the restaurant.)

# Panzano

## GETTING THERE

Continue along the SS222 road, following the signs (alternatively try the SP118, for a change of view).

Panzano is a tiny medieval hamlet, overlooking an impressive view and situated about 8 km from Greve in Chianti. There isn't much to do at Panzano either, but much like Montefioralle, it is a nice place to stroll among cobbled alleys that haven't changed much since the 11th century and enjoy the medieval feel. The main attraction in town is probably the butcher shop (kids won't be interested). Dario Cecchini has made quite a name for himself, not just for the quality of his meat, but because every piece sold is accompanied with a quote from Dante's *Commedia Divinia* (www.dariocecchini.com). There are a number of good options for lunch in the area (but unless you are looking for a place to eat, you can easily skip Panzano altogether, in favour of more interesting destinations). Try **Ristorante Oltre il Giardino** and book a place outside on the terrace. ◷ Open daily, 10:00-15:00, 19:00-22:00. Piazza Bucciarelli 42, Panzano in Chianti, Tel: 055.852828, www.ristoranteoltreilgiardino.it

# **Castellina** in Chianti

## GETTING THERE

Continue south along the SS222.

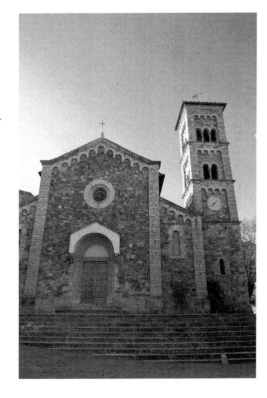

**TOURIST INFORMATION CENTRE:** Castellina's small tourist office is located in Via Ferruccio 40. ◷ Opening times: June–October, open daily, 10:00-13:00, 15:00-19:00; first two weeks of November, Saturday and Sunday, 15:00-18:00; December-mid-January, Friday, 10:00-12:00, Saturday and Sunday, 10:00-12:00, 15:00-18:00; end of March-end of May, Tuesday, Thursday, Saturday, Sunday 10:00-12:00, 15:00-18:00. Tel: 0577.741392, ufficioturistico@comune.castellina.si.it

Castellina in Chianti is probably the most pleasant of the Chianti towns (though it doesn't have the best view; that honour goes to Radda in Chianti). A rather small **archaeological museum** set in a 14th-century fortress in the main piazza educates visitors about ancient civilizations that lived in this area (visit only if you have some extra time). ◷ Museum opening times: June-August, open daily, 10:00-19:00; April-June, open daily, 10:00-18:00; September-November, open daily, 10:00-18:00; November-April, weekends only, 11:00-17:00; closed on most holidays, including Christmas and Easter. Tel: 0577.742090, www. museoarcheologicochianti.it

Even if you don't visit any of the sights in Castellina, it is still fun to tour around, and kids will enjoy walking along the medieval walls (the two Etruscan tombs outside of Castellina in Chianti, however, aren't worth a visit).

# Parco delle Sculture

## GETTING THERE
The park is about 40 minutes south of Castellina in Chianti. Head south along SP102 towards Pievasciata (the park is 4 km after the village).

One of the few child-friendly activities in the area is this artistic park, filled with unique sculptures created by artists from all over the world. It is a perfect place to walk around, admire art, and enjoy the fresh air. From June to August, there are weekly concerts (usually on Tuesdays at 19:00, although we recommend calling in advance) by classical and jazz musicians, who fill the park with smooth sounds. The combination of the view, the music, and the setting sun is truly magical. Arrive early to get a good seat. ◷ Opening times: March-November, open daily, 10:00-sunset. Tel: 0577.357151, www.chiantisculpturepark.it

# **Radda** in Chianti

## GETTING THERE
From Florence, drive south along the scenic SS222 and follow the signs to Radda in Chianti. From Castellina in Chianti, take the SS429 road, following the signs to Radda in Chianti.

**TOURIST INFORMATION OFFICE:** ☺ Radda's tiny office is open Monday-Saturday, 10:30-12:30, and 15:00-18:30; Sunday, 10:30-12:30. Opening hours may vary, especially off season. Piazza Ferrucci 1, Tel: 0577.738494

Radda in Chianti is a lovely little town and quite popular, even though there are very few activities to keep you busy. The good restaurants and incredible view surrounding the town, however, make it a perfect place to stop for lunch, dinner, or a picnic along the town walls.

When nearing Radda in Chianti, follow the signs to park your car along the medieval walls or in Piazza IV Novembre. In front of the main entrance to the centro strotico (historical centre), you will see a small park with a playground for kids. If you plan on enjoying a picnic, there is a good **delicatessen** nearby where you can buy a bottle of fine Chianti, bread, cheese, and high-quality local sausages. Try the Tonno di Radda, a delicate and tasty pork-based sausage, or some prosciutto. 🕙 The Casa Porciatti delicatessen is open daily, 08:00-13:00, 16:00-20:00; closed on Sunday afternoons year round and on Wednesday afternoons during the winter months. Piazza IV Novembre 1,Tel: 0577.738055, www.casaporciatti.it

Almost as soon as you enter Radda, you will see on your right the main church and in front of it, on your left, the town hall.

**Mission 1:** Take a good look at the town hall, in front of the church. There are a number of symbols covering it. What are these symbols? What do they represent?

**Mission 2:** One of these symbols is a hand holding a ...?

From here you can also travel along a medieval walking path that circles part of the town, called **Camminamenti Medievali**. These fortified walls were built in the 15th century by the Florentines, who wanted to protect this strategically placed town. Unfortunately, not much is left of the walls today, but you can still see some of their past glory around the garden area. Keep walking on this path to visit (from the outside) the ice house where, during the winter months, the Grand Duke ordered that snow be gathered and turned into ice.

**Mission 3:** For this mission, you will need a piece of paper, a pen (possibly some colours), and a lot of imagination. Now that you have seen a few medieval towns, do you think you could design your own?. Where would you build your medieval town? Think about your hometown—if you had to build a castle or a borgo, where would you place it? Why? How about the main piazza? Where would it be? What material would you have the builders build it from? In which style? Would the main

cathedral be like Pisa's Duomo, for example, or more like a small country church? How big should it be? What about the houses? Will they be more like Siena or Florence, or maybe like the houses in medieval towns in Chianti? Don't forget to design walls that will protect your borgo from unwanted visitors and enemy attacks. Design a central market place, too. Special and original ideas are worth bonus points!

# KIDS'CORNER

Italian is a fun and easy language, and after a few days in Tuscany you will surely pick up a few words. Here are a few useful sentences (and the correct way to pronounce them), the first step to becoming a perfect Italian gentleman or lady:

My name is Max / Jenny.
Mi chiamo Max / Jenny
(Mi kiamo Max / Jenny)

I am 7 years old. Ho sette anni (o sete ani)

| Age | Italian | Pronunciation |
|---|---|---|
| 7 | Sette | Sete |
| 8 | Otto | Oto |
| 9 | Nove | Nove |
| 10 | Dieci | di-echi |

# KIDS'CORNER

| 11 | Undici | Undichi |
|----|--------|---------|
| 12 | Dodici | Dodichi |
| 13 | Tredici | Tredichi |
| 14 | quattordici | Quatordichi |
| 15 | Quindici | ku-indichi |
| 16 | Sedici | Sedichi |

I come from the USA / the UK.
Vengo dagli Stati Uniti / Inghilterra
(vengo dallli stati uniti / Inghiltera)

Sorry, I don't speak Italian.
Mi dispiace, non parlo Italiano
(mi dispiache, non parlo Italiano)

Excuse me, where is the piazza/museum/hotel?
Scusi, dov'è la piazza/museo/hotel?
(skuzi, dove eh la piatsa / museo / otel?)

Excuse me, how much does this cost?
Scusi, quanto costa?
(skuzi, kuanto costa?)

One cone of ice cream please.
Un cono di gelato, per favore
(oon kono di gelato, per favore)

Excuse me, your dinosaur seems to be escaping.
Scusi, sembra che il suo dinosauro stia scapando

# KIDS'CORNER

(skusi, sembra ke il suo dinozauro stia scapando)

Good Morning! Buongiorno (buon-jorno)

See you later! Arrivederci (a-rive-derchi)

But Italians don't just use their mouths to speak; they use their hands, too. Gesturing is a very important part of an Italian conversation, so if you want to be a real Italian, you have to learn how to communicate using your face and hands perfectly.

Now that you are an expert in Italian, do you think you are up for a challenge?

Super challenge: Can you say these tongue twisters in Italian (they aren't easy, but what kind of super challenge would it be if it were easy?):

Bravo barbiere, sbaffami barba e baffi. **Pronounciation:** bravo barbiere, sbafami barba e bafi (Good barber, cut my moustache and beard).

Caro conte chi ti canta tanto canta che t'incanta. **Pronounciation:** caro conte, ki ti kanta tanto kanta ke tinkanta (Dear count, those who sing to you, sing so much that they enchant you).

And the most difficult one of all: Al pozzo di santa pazzia c' una pazza che lava una pezza, passa un pazzo con un pezzo di pizza, la pazza gli chiede «mi dai un pezzo di pizza?», il pazzo si arrabbia, il pazzo si infuria, prende la pazza, la pezza e la pizza e li piazza nel pozzo di santa pazzia protettrice dei pazzi. **Pronounciation:** al potso di santa patsia che oona patsa ke lava una petsa, passa oon patso con oon petso di pitsa, la patsa llli kiede "mi dai oon petso di pitsa?", il patso si arabia, il patso si

# KIDS'CORNER

infuria, prende la pastsa, la petsa e la pitsa e lii piatsa nel potso di santa patsia protetriche dei patsi

(At the well in Santa Pazzia there was a crazy lady who was washing a piece of cloth. A crazy man passed, holding a slice of pizza, and the crazy lady asked him, "Would you give me a bite of your pizza?" The crazy man got angry and took the old lady, her piece of cloth, and the pizza and threw them all into the well of Santa Pazzia, saint protector of the insane).

### tasty
(rotate your finger from right to left)

### i don't care
(move hand from under the chin towards the outside)

### How should I know / How is this possible?
(put your hands together and move towards your chest and then back down)

### This is expensive
(move fingers)

### you are afraid, aren't you?
(open and close your hand)

### let's go, let's leave
(move folded hand sharply from left to right)

# Eating in the Chianti Area

There are so many good dining options in the Chianti area that you can afford to be picky. The best food, as always, can be found in the tiny towns and villages scattered along the hills.

## GREVE IN CHIANTI

**Podere Le Fornaci** is a personal favourite. Right outside Greve in Chianti, this charming organic goat farm sells some of the best goat cheeses in Tuscany and also serves light lunches. Ideally, schedule a quick visit of the farm (great for younger kids) in the morning and buy some fresh cheese to nibble on later in the car before sitting down for lunch. Via di Citille 74, Greve in Chianti, Tel: 055.8546010, www.poderelefornaci.it

**Gallo Nero** is well known in Greve in Chianti. it isn't as cheap as the Falorni Cafeteria (see Greve in Chianti itinerary), but the food is good and the ambiance is inviting. Open Friday-Wednesday, 12:00-15:00, 18:30-22:00. Thursday closed. Via Battisti 9, Greve in Chianti, Tel: 055.853734, www.enoristorantegallonero.it

Another popular option in Greve in Chianti is **Villa Bordoni Restaurant** (reserve a table on the lovely terrace overlooking the view). The food is a modern version of Tuscan classics but be aware that the prices match the elegant feel. The restaurant also offers cooking lessons (book in advance). Open daily, 12:30-14:30, 19:30-22:00 (off season, closed on Tuesday). Via San Cresci 31-32, 50022 Greve in Chianti, Tel: 055.8547453, www.ristorantevillabordini.com

## CASTELLINA IN CHIANTI

**Osteria di Fonterutoli**, located just outside Castellina in Chianti, serves great food in a relaxed area of the Chianti region, with a garden kids can play in. Open daily, 12:30-14:30, 19:30-21:30 (closed on Tuesday, off season only). Via Puccini 4, Loc. Fonterutoli, Tel: 0577.741125 www.fonterutoli.com/Osteria-ita.

## RADDA IN CHIANTI

If you are looking for a simple pizzeria that also serves some pasta dishes, try the fresh and tasty food at **La Loggia del Chianti**. Open Tuesday through Sunday, 19:00-24:00. Via degli Ulivi 1, Radda in Chianti, Tel: 0577.738491 www.laloggiadelchianti.it.

**Ristorante Le Vigne** near Radda in Chianti offers some (usually) reasonably priced classic Tuscan dishes in an inviting setting. Ask for a table facing the view. Open from Easter until November, 12:00-22:00. Localita Podere Le Vigne, Radda in Chianti, Tel: 0577.738301.

Another delicious option outside of Radda in Chianti is **Osteria Le Panzanelle**, offering some homey and well-thought-out, delicious dishes. Open daily, 12:30-14:00, 19:30-21:30; closed on Mondays. Loc. Lucarelli 29, Radda in Chianti, Tel: 0577.733511, www.lepanzanelle.it

# **Sleeping** in the Chianti Area

**Mulino di Quercegrossa** is well known for its seven (yes, seven) connected pools. It also boasts a 150-meter-long river and a little waterfall, making it a perfect choice for water-loving kids. The B&B itself is simple but mostly comfortable (the restaurant, however, can be skipped). The B&B is located eight km from Siena, 35 km from Florence. Località Mulino di Quercegrossa, S.R. 222 Chiantigiana, Quercegrossa, Tel: 0577.328129, www.mulinodiquercegrossa.it

**Borgo Arentina** is considered to be one of the best B&Bs in the area between Chianti and Siena. Surrounded by beauty, it offers elegant, welcoming rooms and villas, cooking classes, and a terrace with a view (however, there is no pool). Gaiole in Chianti, Tel: 345.3537673, www.borgoargenina.it

**Le Bonatte** is positioned in an incredible area outside Radda in Chianti and offers large, inviting apartments, a pool, and great views. Azienda Agricola Le Bonatte, Loc. Le Bonatte 77, Radda in Chianti, Tel: 0577.738783  www.lebonatte.it

**Poggio d'oro** is an excellent choice. Just 30 minutes from both Siena and Florence, it has large, comfortably furnished apartments with a large pool overlooking the view. Via Valluccia 25, S. Donato in Poggio, Tel: 055.8072730, www.poggiodoro.com

**Agriturismo Il Colle** is another excellent option to consider. It's reasonably priced, and it offers large rooms, a pool, beautiful views, and a play area for kids. Via del Crocino 5, Greve in Chianti. Tel: 333,9078651 www.ilcolledelchianti.it

**Agriturismo Rifugium** is another popular choice. It offers comfortable rooms, a pool, and a playground for kids. Via di Casole 39/40 (loc. Casole - Lamole), Greve in Chianti, Tel: 3398565787, www.rifugiumagriturismochianti.com.

# Special Activities in the Chianti Area

## COOKING CLASSES

Cooking classes vary in length and price. Some are more suitable for children and some work better for teenagers and adults. Most require a minimum of participants (usually four) and all require booking in advance (we recommend booking as soon as you can, especially if travelling during high season). Before you pay a hefty sum, make sure it's the right class for you. Notify the chef of the ages of your children and ask what the menu is (especially if you have any special dietary needs). There are several more cooking classes in other areas of Tuscany. Check out the Florence, San Gimignano, and Lucca Itineraries for more options.

**Simonetta and Paola** offer a homey family-style cooking class at their kitchen in Gaiole in Chianti. The class can be adapted for kids as well (kids pay a reduced fee, usually about 85 euro). Localita' Poggio S. Polo 2, Gaiole in Chianti, Tel: 334.2476098, www.welcometuscany.com

**Guiditta** offers some hands-on experience in her cooking classes held near Greve in Chianti. A four-hour lesson, including dinner and wine, costs about 90 euro, and kids over the age of six are welcome (kids pay a reduced fee). Younger children can run around in the garden surrounding the villa, provided they are supervised. Via della Montagnola 110, Strada in Chianti, Greve in Chianti, Tel: 055.578620, www.itcooking.com

**Tenuta Casanova** offers not only wine tours around their agriturismo but also cooking lessons suitable for all ages. At the moment, two types of classes are available: a longer, full-day class, which costs 150 euro per person, and a shorter, half-day class for 100 euro per person. Both classes include a tour of the winery and lunch, and both classes offer discounts for children, depending on their age. Book at least three to four days in advance (much earlier during high season). Castellina in Chianti, Tel: 335.6150760, www.tenutacasanova.it

**The Volpaia Castle** agriturismo offers wine tasting tours and cooking lessons (it's a more elegant setting; this option is probably more suitable for teenagers, not for young children). Loc. Volpaia, Radda in Chianti, Tel: 0577.738066, www.volpaia.com

**Il Pintello** is an elegant but family-friendly agriturismo that also offers horseback rides, golfing, a spa, and cooking classes, but only for guests of the agriturismo itself. Via Volterrana 259, Chiesanuova, San Casciano Val di Pesa, Tel: 055.8242225, www.ilpintello.it

**Podere Campriano** is another elegant agriturismo which offers, among other activities, daily cooking classes emphasizing local traditions and tastes. Lessons cost about 60-90 euro per person and are suitable for children over eight years old. Viale Rosa Libri 36, Greve in Chianti, Tel: 055.853688, www.poderecampriano.it

The **Farm Cooking Together** cooking class offered by Fattoria Montagliari is yet another option, offering daily cooking courses in an 18th-century villa near Panzano (the owners have a restaurant too). A half-day cooking class costs about 130 euro per person, and in many cases kids may enter for free. Call at least a week in advance to book a place and to find out whether you'll need to pay for your children's spots. Via Montagliari 29, Panzano in Chianti, Tel: 055.852014, www.fattoriamontagliari.com

## HORSEBACK RIDING

The **Barardenga Riding School** offers day tours as well as moonlit night tours across rolling hills. Book in advance. Podere Santa Margherita, Strada del Ciglio 2, Castelnuovo Berardenga, Tel: 3398.318519, www.chiantiriding.it

**La Forra Farm** not only offers comfortable family apartments in Montegonzi, near Gaiole in Chianti, but also horseback riding tours. There are riding lessons (18 euro) available as well as 1.5-hour riding tours of the area (20 euro per person). Suitable for kids over six; book at least a few days in advance. Tel: 055.966091 or 3288.263542 (Sandro, the riding instructor), www.laforra.it

**Il Cipressino**, a lovely option for horse lovers, is a B&B that collaborates with the local Agrifoflio Riding Club to offer guests riding tours of the area. Località Cipressino, Barberino Val d'Elsa, www.cipressino.it

## HIKING AND BIKE TOURS

**Discover Chianti** offers custom-tailored bike tours of the Chianti area (remember that it is quite hilly, so it's probably too difficult for younger children and/or inexperienced riders). The company offers hiking tours too, which may be easier for children. If you are a bicycling fan, this is a great way to see the beautiful Tuscan scenery. Book in advance. Via I Maggio 32, Greve in Chianti, Tel: 328.6124658, www.discoverychianti.com

## WINE TASTING

Wine tasting is probably the most popular activity in the Chianti region and for good reason. Chianti is one of the most identifiable wines, not only in Tuscany, but in all of Italy.

The area between Radda in Chianti, Gaiole in Chianti, and Castellina in Chianti is nicknamed the "Black Rooster" area (thanks to the small illustration of a black rooster on each bottle of authentic Chianti), and is considered THE place to taste the local produce. Buy some bottles to take home or

back to your B&B/hotel/apartment to enjoy once the kids have fallen asleep (this way you can not only enjoy the Chianti wines without having to entertain the kids, but you also don't have to worry about waiting for your blood alcohol level to go down before you can drive to your next destination).

## Italian Wine Categories

Italian wines are divided into 4 categories:

1. VDT (Vino Da Tavola—table wine): usually a mediocre-quality, very cheap wine.
2. IGT (indicazione Geografica Tipica): wines that come from a specific region; these wines are simple but reasonable.
3. DOC (Denominazione di Origine Controllata): wines that come from a more specific part of a region, guaranteeing a certain product quality.
4. DOCG (Denominazione di Origine Controlata e Garantita): the highest recognition and quality control for a wine in Italy. Wines are not only subject to strict legal requirements (regulating the type of grapes used, for example, or the aging process) but are also subjected to blind tests to ensure even quality.
5. In Tuscany, we find another unique category called "supertuscans", made with a blend of local and non-autochthonous grape varieties. Though not considered DOC wines, they are extremely popular and one of the first supertuscan wines, the Sassicaia, is one of the most expensive wines in Italy.

# A (very) brief guide on how wine is made

A tour of Chianti, one of the most famous wine regions in Italy, can't be considered complete without a quick review of how wine is made. Though wine making has certainly changed over the last few decades (any farmer who would try today to squash his

grapes by stomping on them with his feet, as was done for hundreds of years in the past, would probably be arrested), and the different phases of production are now rigorously controlled by experts and scientists, for the most part, the production of wine is similar to the way the Etruscans and Romans did it more than 2,000 years ago.

Back then, just like today, great wines were a treat and a status symbol. The best wines were sent as a precious present to Popes and Emperors, and the sale of regular wine was controlled by the church and professional guilds. In Florence, for example, wine could not be (officially) sold to thieves and other criminals and some wines were only fit for royalty.

A good wine starts with good grapes, and most of the wine in

Tuscany is produced with Sangiovese grapes. Generally speaking, the taste of grapes depends on a number of factors, the most important of which are soil, water, and sun exposure. Once the grapes are picked off the vines, they are sorted and cleaned (in the past this was done by hand, but today a lot of the work is done by machines).

If the grapes are going to be used for red wine, they are sent to be pressed immediately with their skins still on. If the batch is going to make white wine, then the skins must be removed. At this point the grapes have to ferment for a while (in most cases other substances are added, to help the process, like yeasts). Once the wine has fermented, it is moved to huge wooden barrels (which usually contain about 230 litres), where it will mature. Most wines stay in the barrel and mature for at least a couple of months (or years) and then continue the aging process in the bottle. It's hard to buy very bad wine in Tuscany, and as long as you stick to DOC and DOCG wines (which are delicious and can cost as little as 4 euro in the local supermarket), you will usually enjoy good quality produce.

**Albola Farm** is a little winery set in a beautiful location and is a popular option for wine (and olive oil) tasting in the area, with the advantage of not having to book in advance. From April-November, there are daily tastings at 12:00, 14:00, and 17:00. Hours may vary, so check the website before leaving. Via Pian d'Albola 31, Radda in Chianti, Tel: 0577.738019, www.albola.it

**Meleto Castle** is set in a beautiful location about 1 km from Gaiole in Chianti and is one of the best-known options in the area. This is good for kids, too, because while you are sipping wine they can admire the castle. Built almost

800 years ago by Benedictine monks and remodelled and fortified in the 15th century, the castle can be visited before (or after) the wine tasting. Book in advance. Tel: 0577749217, www.castellomeleto.it

Another good option for families is **Castello di Brolio**, which today belongs to one of the best-known wine producers in the area, the Ricasoli family. Built by the Logonbards and purchased by the Ricasoli family almost 900(!) years ago, even kids will be impressed. The castle and impressive gardens can be visited as well (for a fee). ☉ The gardens are open daily from 10:00 to 19:00 during the high season. Check the website to see the different options the castle offers for visits (including sunset visits of the castle, picnics, and visits to the Ricasoli antique collection). Dinner and a wine tour can also be booked. Book in advance. Località Brolio, Gaiole in Chianti, Tel: 0577.7301, www.ricasoli.it/Tours (don't type Brolio on your GPS; use the coordinates as published on their "Contact Us" website page instead).

# SAN GIMIGNANO
## AND MONTERIGGIONI

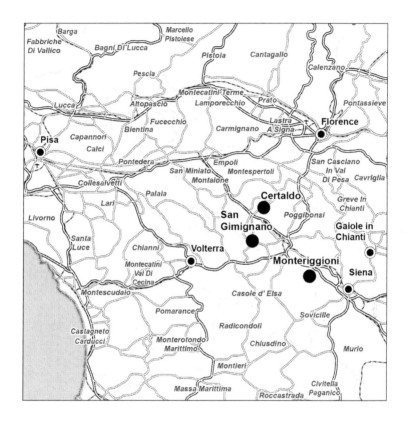

# HOW LONG WILL IT TAKE TO GET THERE?

Florence to San Gimignano - one hour
Siena to San Gimignano - 40 minutes
Volterra to San Gimignano - 40 minutes
San Gimignano to Monteriggioni - 30 minutes
San Gimignano to Certaldo - 20 minutes
San Gimignano to Greve in Chianti - one hour

# Chapter 6

# San Gimignano and Monteriggioni

Despite San Gimignano's undeniable charm, the Tuscan hill town is, quite frankly, somewhat of a tourist trap, and at any given moment there, you'll be surrounded by thousands of other people also attracted to its beauty. So why bother going? There are two reasons. First, San Gimignano is arguably the prettiest hill town in the area. Second, the town offers a combination of attractions that both children and adults are sure to love. Parents will appreciate the charming alleys and the lovely artisan shops that fill the streets, and kids will be impressed with the Big Tower (which they can climb on), the medieval setting, maybe even with the colorful local duomo. If you absolutely can't stand touristy spaces, then San Gimignano may not be for you, and you may want to try a calmer place, like Volterra, which is considered by many to be San Gimignano's older, more "sensible sister".

When planning your visit to San Gimignano, we recommend balancing it out with another less frenzied attraction. A calmer, nearby town, such as Certaldo (see brief description at the end of this itinerary), can make for a good stop. Better yet, book an outdoor activity that will get you away from the crowds (check out "Special Activities in the Area" at the end of this itinerary). If you are travelling with younger children, combine San Gimignano with a visit to a tiny village called Monteriggioni (35 minutes away) to create a complete medieval immersion day. Monteriggioni has an impressive medieval wall kids can climb on and an absolutely tiny (but fun!) museum where they can try on replicas of shields, helmets, swords, and armour. If you happen to tour the area during one of the medieval festivals in Monteriggioni in July, a visit to this village is a must (see "Special Events in the Area" at the end of this itinerary). Since Monteriggioni is centrally located, it can easily be combined with other itineraries in this book, such as Siena (only 20 km away), Volterra (40 km away), or even the Chianti region (Castellina in Chianti is only about 16 km away). If you feel like taking it easy, you can also spend the entire morning in San Gimignano, walking around and relaxing, and then head back to your B&B to splash around in the pool. In any case, this will surely be a fun and memorable day.

## Top 5 Family Activities

1. Climb up to the top of the Torre Grossa in San Gimignano and enjoy the beautiful view.

2. Visit one of San Gimignano's horrifying medieval torture museums.

3. Put on a helmet, grab a sword, and pretend to be a real knight at the Monteriggioni Museum.

4. Buy some ice cream in San Gimignano's Piazza della Cisterna before heading off to tour the town's wonderfully preserved streets.

5. Book a cooking class or a horseback ride in the countryside.

# San Gimignano

## GETTING THERE

**BY CAR:** As with most hill towns, the easiest way to get to San Gimignano is by car. From Florence, take the Raccordo Autostradale Firenze–Siena (going south towards Siena). Exit at Poggibonsi Nord and follow the signs to San Gimignano. Parking in town can be difficult, but if you're patient, you will eventually find a spot. Like most of the towns in Tuscany, all of San Gimignano's historical centre (centro storico) is closed to non-residential traffic and marked as ZTL. Luckily, there are several parking lots that are just a few minutes away from the centre by foot. If you are travelling with toddlers, and pushing a stroller, park in parking lot 3-4. There is an elevator connecting the lot to the historical centre, so you won't have to carry the stroller up a flight of stairs.

**BY TRAIN OR BUS:** There are no trains to San Gimignano (which means there is no train station to leave your luggage at, either, so don't come with any suitcases), but you can take a train or bus to Poggibonsi (from Florence, Pisa, or Siena) and then take the bus to San Gimignano (it's a 20 minute ride from Poggibonsi, and the bus leaves from the train station). If you do arrive by public transport, you should know that the schedule on Sundays and holidays is particularly sparse. The bus will leave you at the town's main entry, called Porta San Giovanni, and it's a quick walk from there up to the centre of town.

**TOURIST INFORMATION OFFICE:** Located next to the Duomo in Piazza Duomo 1, the local tourist office is easy to find. The staff are well informed about guide tours and activities in the area, and some activities can be booked on the spot (such as wine tours and guided tours of the town). ◕ Opening times: March-October, open daily, 10:00-13:00, 15:00-19:00; November-February, open daily, 10:00-13:00, 14:00-18:00. Tel: 0577.940008

San Gimignano is one of the most popular tourist destinations in the area. It has been called the Manhattan of Tuscany, thanks to its "skyscrapers" (medieval towers built by local rich families competing to see whose tower was the biggest), and is unanimously known as one of the best preserved medieval towns in the world. It was founded about 2300 years ago as an Etruscan village, and thanks to its desirable agricultural production (mostly wine) and its central position on the Via Francigena, it became an important destination during the 10th century. It blossomed until the mid-14th century, when everything came to a screeching halt after the town was badly hit by the plague. This was a disaster from which San Gimignano couldn't recover. For hundreds of years, it languished in obscurity (which is why it remained so perfectly preserved). After tourists rediscovered San Gimignano in the 19th century and were shocked to find it so unchanged by time, the town was quickly turned into a popular tourist destination.

# Our tour of San Gimignano begins at the town's main entrance, Porta San Giovanni (where the buses stop). From here, walk along Via San Giovanni, a street filled with little shops and cafés (but don't buy anything just yet; there are many more shops later in the tour). Continue straight until you reach **Piazza della Cisterna**, one of the best-known points in town. No number of tourists can ruin the fact that this little triangular piazza looks as if it were taken right out of a medieval fairy tale, with its famous octagonal well in the centre, and elegant 14th century palazzi overlooking it all. In medieval times, when San Gimignano was a favourite stop for pilgrims walking along the Via Francigena, this piazza was filled with inns and the well was the main water source.

**Mission 1:** Hundreds of years ago, this piazza was extended and expanded by one of the local governors, who also engraved his coat of arms onto the well. Can you find the coat of arms? (Hint: It's a simple symbol that you can climb on). Take a photo of the symbol.

Alongside the well stands a tall tower known as the Devil's Tower (**La Torre del Diavolo**). Legend has it that one day the owner of the tower returned to San Gimignano from a long journey to find that this possessed tower had grown taller in his absence. Two ice cream parlours in the piazza compete for the title of "Best Gelato in Italy". In our humble opinion, neither is the best in the land, but both are quite tasty. To be on the safe side, and so no one can accuse you of having left a rock unturned, we recommend trying both parlours yourself to see if the claims have any merit.

> **Tip:** There is no such thing as eating too much gelato while travelling in Italy, especially if you are travelling with children and spending the entire day walking around under a boiling Tuscan sun. A refreshing granita (a fruit- and ice-based dessert, similar to a sorbet) or a creamy scoop of ice cream can make all the difference, and, to be honest, we doubt that anyone ever lay on their deathbed regretting the amount of ice cream eaten during their vacation...

Next to the piazza, you will find the **Torture Museum** (there are actually two in San Gimignano; both are quite horrifying but seem to fascinate many children). The museum next to Piazza della Cisterna is bigger and better furnished, suitable for gore-loving teenagers.
🕐 March-October, open daily, 10:00-19:00; November-March, open daily, 10:00-17:00. Via del Castello 1, Tel: 0577.942243

The other museum is in Via Gan Giovanni. 🕐 Open daily, 10:30-18:30; during the winter months, the museum is open on weekends only. Via Gan Giovanni 125, Tel: 0577.940526, www.museodellatortura.it

From Piazza della Cisterna, continue straight ahead toward the main square, **Piazza Duomo**. Of the 72 towers which once loomed over San Gimignano, 14 remain and two of the most impressive ones are in this piazza. Stand facing the Duomo and look to the tower on your right. It was built by the Salvucci family, mainly as a way of showing off their power and wealth to their sworn enemies, the Ardinghelli family (who lived in the adjacent piazza and were building a "look how

mighty I am" tower of their own). In 1255, a city law finally put an end to the crazy building competition between families, stating that no tower could be taller than the tower of the Podesta (the governing body). The Salvuccis came up with a tricky solution: They built two towers, placing them at such an angle that, when viewed from a distance, they looked like one tower that rose up higher than all the others in town.

If you look behind you, you'll see Palazzo Chigi-Useppi, home of Teatro dei Leggeri (the local theatre, called the Theatre of Light), but until the end of the 14th century, it was a prison. On your left stands the **Town Hall** (with the tourist information centre on the first floor). This building was designed in 1289, and over the years, it was decorated with the coats of arms of powerful people who held official positions in town. Art lovers will enjoy visiting the upper floors, which currently house the Civic Museum and frescoes by artists such as Lippo Memmi and Benozo Gozzoli (you can peek inside the charming courtyard even if you don't go up to the museum). Adjacent to the Town Hall is San Gimignano's favourite attraction for kids: the highest tower in town (which you can climb!), called **Torre Grossa** (the Big Tower). This tower, built between 1300 and 1311, is made of brick and was originally 64 meters high, but after part of it collapsed, it was brought down to its current height of 54 meters. The view from the tower is spectacular.

**Mission 2:** Climb up the Torre Grossa and take a picture of the view.

🕑 Opening times: Town Hall and the Big Tower: April-September, 09:30-19:00; October-March, 11:00-17:30. If you intend on visiting all the civic museums in town (Museo Civico, Torre Grossa, Santa Fina's House, and the Archaeological Museum), combined admission tickets are also available. Children under six enter free, while kids between the ages of 6–17 pay a reduced fee.

> **Tip:** If climbing one tower isn't enough, you can also visit the Salvucci Family Tower (its entrance is near Piazza delle Erbe).

The last monument in the piazza is the **Duomo** itself, which merits a visit if you have the time. Though not an official duomo (there's no bishop in residence), it is one of the most lavishly decorated churches in Tuscany, and one of the reasons San Gimignano's historical centre was declared a UNESCO World Heritage Site. The frescoes on the right wall of the church are attributed to Lippo Memmi, who worked for eight years (1333-1342) to create these 22 lively scenes from the New Testament. Twenty-five years later, the painter Bartolo di Fredi was invited to decorate the left wall with 26 scenes from the Old Testament. At the ticket office, make sure you pick up the complimentary audio guide, and the special 4D glasses (yes, 4D, not 3D) They will give you a truly unique perspective of the Duomo's art!

🕑 Opening times: April-October, Monday-Friday, 10:00-19:00, Saturday, 10:00-17:00, Sunday, 12:30-19:10; February, March, first two weeks of November, and December-mid January, Monday-Saturday, 10:00-16:40, Sundays, 12:30-16:40.

**Mission 3:** Identify three of the scenes on the Duomo walls and write them down in your detective journal.

**Mission 4:** How many demons are there in Tadeo di Bartolo's Last Judgment fresco? Use your binoculars to get a better view!

Right behind the tower you will find San Gimignano's **1300 museum.** Sadly, since it moved to its new location, the museum has eliminated most of its exhibition, and the only thing that remains today is the large clay model of medieval San Gimignano (hence the name: San Gimignano 1300). Entrance is free. The museum is open daily, 10:00-17:00 (may close earlier off-season), Tel: 327 439 5165, www.sangimignano1300.com.

Alternatively, check out the antique cars in the small, but interesting **Peugeot Museum** right outside San Gimignano. Car lovers will appreciate the selection! Museo Gallerie Peugeot, Via per Fugnano, Tel: 335.65.67.417 / 0577.94.22.20, www2.peugeot.it/museo. Open Easter-mid November, 09:30-13:00, 15:30-19:00. Open by appointment only during off-season.

# Monteriggioni

The tiny village of Monteriggioni is just 35 minutes from San Gimignano and consists of two attractions: climbing and walking along the perfectly preserved (but short) walls surrounding the village, and visiting the small but fun medieval museum located near the walls (next to the main church), where kids can try on helmets, swords, and armour, pretending to be one of the Piccolomini Knights protecting Siena or a ferocious English Condottiere. You can easily spend an hour or two relaxing in Monteriggioni, before or after a visit to San Gimignano, Volterra, or the Chianti region. The absolute best time to visit the village is during one of the medieval events in July, when the whole castle comes to life (see "Special Events in the Area").

## GETTING THERE

The easiest way to reach Monteriggioni is by car. There is ample parking at

the entrance to the village (the village itself, consisting of one piazza and two streets, is ZTL). From San Gimignano, take SP1 towards Poggibonsi and then follow signs to Siena until you get onto the Raccordo Autostradale Firenze-Siena. Exit at Monteriggioni and follow SR2 to the village (there are signs to guide you). From Siena, take the Raccordo Autostradale Firenze-Siena and then the SR2. From Castellina in Chianti, take SP51 (towards Castellina Scalo) and then SR2 to Monteriggioni. From Volterra, take the SS68 going east towards Colle Val D'Elsa.

The **Monteriggioni Borgo** was built by Siena in the 13th century for a very specific purpose: to protect the Republic against constant attacks from its sworn enemy, Florence. Just 15 minutes from Siena, Monteriggioni overlooks the valley and, more importantly, the main road in those days, the Cassia (which was built by the Romans), so the soldiers stationed in this post could always see if some armed force were approaching. It took approximately seven years to build the 570-meter long walls and the 14 watch towers. To reach the museum, simply park your car, enter the walls, and walk along the main (and only) piazza (called Piazza Roma), until you come to the museum. Inside, you will find life-size armour from the 11th-16th centuries and medieval warfare models.

**Mission 1:** Take a picture of yourself holding a sword and pretending to charge, ready to defend the castle.

**Mission 2:** Take a picture of yourself dressed in armour and looking scary.

**Mission 3:** Take a picture of yourself looking even scarier!

🕑 Opening times (museum, walkways, and tourist office): April-September, 09:30-13:30; 14:00-19:30; November-mid January, 10:00-13:30, 14:00-16:00 (closed on Tuesdays); mid January-mid February, closed; mid-February-March, 10:00-13:30, 14:00-16:00 (closed on Tuesdays). The audio guide is an excellent source of information and worth the extra cost in this case, if you are interested in medieval warfare. Combined tickets for the wall walk and museum are available. Children under 12 enter for free, provided they are accompanied by an adult. Tel: 0577.304834, www. Monteriggioniturismo.it/en/museum-and-walkways

# Certaldo

When San Gimignano becomes a bit too much and you want to escape the crowds for an hour or two, Certaldo is a good option. Certaldo is a small town made up of two parts: the modern part, known as the lower city, and the medieval part, known as the higher city (Certaldo Alto) and can be reached with a cable car, which kids will love.

> **Tip:** The cable car (called funivia in Italian) leaves from the main piazza of the lower city. Make sure you buy a round-trip ticket (tickets purchased separately are almost twice the price).

Certaldo Alto hasn't changed one bit since the 15th century and is a perfect spot for a quiet afternoon stroll. There are a few little attractions in town as well (none of these merits driving especially to town):

1. The tiny and amusingly eclectic **Museo del Chiodo (the Nail Museum)** consists of a large hall filled with weird antique tools and machines. Unfortunately, there are no explanations in English (or Italian, for that matter), but kids are usually fascinated nonetheless. ◔ Opening times: summer, open daily, 09:30-13:30, 14:30-19:00; winter, 09:30-13:30, 14:30-16:30; closed on Tuesdays. The tourist office, in Via Boccaccio 16 (Tel: 0571.652730) has the keys for the museum; children under six enter for free.

2. **The Boccaccio family home:** Boccaccio was a famous Italian writer and poet. He was a Certaldo native, but because he was an illegitimate child, his exact place of birth is unknown. The Boccaccio family home may be visited, though there isn't much to see. The building was severely damaged and completely rebuilt in the 19th century, and because of this, the home offers no real treasures other than two pairs of 13th century shoes displayed in a glass cabinet on the second floor. There is, however, a nice view from the top floor, and on a clear day you can see the tower of San Gimignano right in front you.

3. You can also visit the **Palazzo Pretorio** (the City Hall) and wander the streets for a peaceful break before heading to your next destination.

# KIDS'CORNER

## More About... Living in Medieval Times!

It's easy to imagine life in medieval times when walking the streets of San Gimignano. It's no accident that this town and Monteriggioni (the next stop in this itinerary) were both featured in the video game "Assassin's Creed". But what was it really like to live back then? What would you eat? What would your day look like? And what happened if you were sick?

Let's take a look.

## More About... Crimes and Punishments in the 14th and 15th Centuries!

If you visited the Torture Museum (which isn't for everyone), then you learned about the punishments and torture used 500 years ago. During that time, being in jails, prisons, and dungeons wasn't considered a punishment but simply a place to keep people until they were punished or executed. If you think prison is bad today, imagine how terrifying it was then. Prisoners were kept in tiny damp cells filled with cockroaches and mice, with no fresh air or sunlight. Not everyone survived the jail experience, either; some became so ill because of the poor conditions that they died either while still inside prison or shortly after being released.

# KIDS'CORNER

People also believed in punishments that reflected the crime. If you stole something, your hand was chopped off. If you were blasphemous (spoke out against God), your tongue was cut off. Things got slightly better during the Renaissance, when more and more cities and kingdoms sentenced people to jail time instead of mutilation. In some cases, people could pay a fine instead of going to jail.

## More About... Medicine in Medieval Times!

Science wasn't very progressive in medieval times and was very much influenced by popular beliefs, superstition, and misconceptions. Doctors believed that the body was controlled by four humors (a Latin word meaning "liquids"): black bile, yellow bile, phlegm, and blood. If these weren't balanced, then you would become ill. This is why bloodletting became such a popular healing method; it supposedly rebalanced the blood humor in the body.

The phrases, "I'm not in the right humour" or "bad humour" comes from this belief. Men's humors were considered hot; women's, cold. The blood humor was probably the most important humor, and the techniques doctors used for blood-letting would make you run screaming for the hills today. One popular technique was to cut a vein and let the blood drip into a bowl. Another popular method was to use... **leeches!** Doctors would carry leeches in a little box in their bags and then put them on a pa-

# KIDS'CORNER

tient's body. The leeches would suck the blood and grow bigger and bigger. When they were nice and plump, the doctor knew they had ingested enough blood and would take them off.

If you needed an operation, had a broken leg, or had a big open wound, going to the doctor could be a very painful and dangerous thing. Many people didn't survive operations, because the anaesthetics the doctors used were primitive and dangerous. Typical anaesthetics were opium or hemlock, or even mandrake, a poisonous plant also used in mystical ceremonies. People believed that the mandrake had special powers and that if a human dug up the plant, he would die, so they sent dogs to dig out the root. Because these substances were unpredictable, some people never woke up from anaesthesia and others woke up crazy with hallucinations. Aren't we lucky to live in modern times with modern, safe medicine?

Back then, if a man was unlucky enough to have an open wound on the battlefield, a hot iron was sometimes used to burn and disinfect the wound so it would close. Sometimes, doctors used alcohol so people would pass out and feel nothing. Actually, these people were lucky to have doctors. Until 1215, surgeries were usually performed by monks. Because they were the only ones who could read the ancient medicinal texts written by Arab scholars, people came to them for help. Until the Renaissance, a lot of medicine was based on **magic** and **astrology**. People prayed to their saints, convinced sicknesses were due to curses. They went to "specialists" to get the curses removed, and many people believed in black magic and exorcism. Astrology was considered very serious business and useful for just about any aspect of life. Kings and emperors would decide the date of a wedding or a battle based on the position of the stars, and doctors checked the sky to understand why disease hit patients.

# KIDS'CORNER

Not all health problems required a doctor, though. People often used a popular tome called The Book of Secrets, which was a collection of herbal recipes, potions, and "magic" techniques to help cure smaller problems. Secret books were hugely popular in the 16th and 17th centuries, and you could find just about anything inside them, from ideas on how to cure a headache to tips on how to make perfume, alchemy, and mystical potions.

## More About... Food in Medieval Times!

Food in medieval and Renaissance times was very different than food today. First of all, there was no electricity, which meant no refrigerators and certainly no freezers, so you can forget about any precooked oven dinners, frozen fries, or ice cream. You can forget about any processed foods, like cereal or canned foods, too. None of these existed. Food was fresh and had to be eaten immediately or it would go bad. To conserve meat for the cold winter months, medieval families would cure or salt the meat, if they had any meat to cure. Many families were poor and could only eat simple foods, like bread and cooked vegetables. Many of the popular Italian dishes we love today didn't exist back then either, or at least not the way we know them now. Pasta existed, and Italians even invented lasagne as early as the 13th century, but their lasagne, for example, was just layers of pasta and cheese without any tomato sauce, because tomatoes weren't brought to Europe until 200 years later, when they were discovered in America.

Large festive dinners were very popular, especially when organized by noble families, and people loved to entertain their dinner guests with magic tricks. Filling a bottle with metal powder, for example, stuffing it into a roasted pig, and then running a magnet

# KIDS'CORNER

under the table to "make the pig dance" was a popular trick, as was emptying an egg, putting a cockroach inside, sealing the hole with some invisible white wax, and making the egg "dance".

## More About ... The Fearless Condottieri (Mercenaries)!

During medieval times, towns didn't have their own armies like we know them today. When a town had to defend itself, it would hire professional soldiers and assassins called condottieri: archers from Genova, soldiers from France and Switzerland, and explosive experts from all over Europe. Monteriggioni, for example, often housed such professional soldiers, who were used by the Piccolomini family from Siena to protect its land.

The condottieri were, in fact, soldiers for hire, or mercenaries, who were very professional but not that reliable. The problem with using an army of mercenaries is that they can't be trusted. Since they fought for money and personal glory, most of them would change sides and even betray their employers for the right price. Would you like an example? No problem. Let us tell you about a famous battle between Pisa and Florence in 1364. It all started when Florence wanted free access to Pisa's port and trade routes, so they declared war. The Pisan forces were led by a famous English Condottiere named John Hawkwood (Did you see the fresco in his honour in the Duomo in Florence?). They fought a very

# KIDS'CORNER

brave battle, and the Florentine forces retreated. Then the Florentines decided it was time to play dirty. They bribed John Hawkwood with a hefty sum in exchange for his word that the Pisan army would give the Florentines a five-month truce instead of crushing them and winning the war. This is exactly what Florence needed to recover, and indeed, they later won other battles and eventually the entire war.

An Italian Mission: These words didn't put their seat belts on and got all jumbled up on the flight to Italy. Can you rearrange the letters and figure out the original word? Hint: All the words have something to do with Italy: its art, culture, or food.

Azpiz                           _____

Synatuc                         _____

Smuesu                          _____

Icmedi                          _____

Amchilegol roranobuit           _____

Zalpoza cevicho                 _____

Omodu                           _____

Gansala                         _____

Laiop                           _____

Ganelin ertow                   _____

# Eating in San Gimignano and Monteriggioni

## SAN GIMIGNANO

If you are just looking for a sandwich or a slice of pizza to eat on the go or to use for a picnic, try the popular and tasty **Ricca Pizza**, 10 meters from the Duomo Square (open daily, 11:00-21:00, Via San Matteo 5; it will be hard to miss the line). You can also get tasty sandwiches in the **Enoteca-Delicatessen** at the corner of Via San Matteo and Via Cellolese. The service isn't great, but the cheeses are excellent and you can pick up a few extras to spruce up your picnic.

## Where to Picnic

Spending money on a restaurant isn't a necessity in San Gimignano. In fact, there are several pleasant spots to enjoy a tasty picnic instead. You can sit down for an improvised meal at any point along the wall, but it's much more comfortable eating in the little square next to the **Wine Museum**, or in its adjoining garden, where kids can run around on the soft grass. The museum itself is tiny with not much to see or do, but it is located inside the villa of the Rocca di Montestaffoli Complex (the ruins of a medieval fortress) and offers spectacular views of the area. The piazza in front of the museum often hosts live music shows during the summer months. To reach the Wine Museum, walk from Piazza Duomo towards Piazza delle Erbe (if you stand facing the Duomo, Piazza delle Erbe will be at 02:00 on your right) and follow the brown signs saying Museo del Vino/Museo Vernaccia. If you do decide you want to try a specific restaurant in San Gimignano, booking a place in advance is highly recommended, as they are always full in high season.

If you are looking for a restaurant or a trattoria, try **Locanda di Sant'Agostino**, which offers simple and reasonably priced lunch options (though nothing is actually cheap in tourist-crowded San Gimignano). This café-restaurant is strategically placed in Sant'Agostino Square, three minutes from the Duomo. You can order a salad or a pasta dish, even outside traditional lunch hours. Open daily. Tel: 0577.943141

Another option is the delightful **La Vecchia Nicchia-Renascimentho Farm Shop**, which offers a selection of rustic but delicious bruschetta with sausages and cheeses (you can also ask for take-out). Open daily, 10:30-19:00; closed on Thursdays. Via San Martino 12, Tel: 0577.940803

If you are looking for a stylish but reasonably-priced place with a vast gluten-free menu, try **Ristorante San Martino** 26, fittingly located at Via San Martino 26. Tel: 0577.940483, www.ristorantesanmartino26.it.

**Cum Quibus**, nestled away in an alley near Piazza Sant'Antonio, is the place to go if you want a serious culinary experience. While most restaurants in town are reasonably good, Cum Quibus is in a league of its own. Come here for their homemade pasta, smooth risotto, veal dishes, or anything with truffle. Book well in advance, and don't forget to try their desserts. The wine list is excellent, too. Open daily, 12:30-14:30, 19:00-22:00; closed on Tuesdays. Via San Martino 17, Tel: 0577.943199. www.cumquibus.it. Note that the restaurant usually closes off-season (mid January-mid March).

## MONTERIGGIONI
There are a few reasonably good eateries in Monteriggioni, but options are limited, so if you are looking for a more serious lunch, Siena (15 km away) is probably a better choice.
For a tasty sandwich in Monteriggioni itself, try La **Bettola dei Vinardi**, in Via Berrettini 38. For something more substantial, try Ristorante **Il Piccolo Castello**, right on the main piazza, Tel: 0577.304370, www.ristorantemonteriggioni.it. Open daily. Booking in advance is recommended in high season.

If you are looking for a more serious meal, **L'astronave** offers excellent pasta, good wines, and excllent cold cuts and steaks. This small family-run restaurant is geared towards locals, and offers a simple, very traditional menu, and generous portions. Located just a few minutes (by car) from Monteriggioni, in Scorgiano Near Colle Val d'Elsa. Book in advance during high season, it's very popular. Strada selvamaggio 80, Colle di Val d'Elsa, Tel: 0577 920116. Open 12:30-14:30, 19:30-21:30. May close off season.

## CERTALDO

**Osteria di Casa Chianti:** If you are looking for a real Tuscan dining experience, this is the place. Hearty, generous plates of meat will delight carnivores (vegetarians will probably better enjoy other places). Book a place in advance outside, in front of the beautiful view. The restaurant is located just 7 km from Certaldo, in the tiny village of Fiano. Open in the summer months, Tuesday-Saturday, for dinner only; open Sunday for lunch and dinner; closed on Mondays; The restaurnt usually closes down off-season. Loc. Case Nuove 77, Fiano, Tel: 0571. 669688, www.osteriadicasachianti.it

**Messer Boccaccio** is another excellent option. Try the pici pasta with pancetta; kids will like the pizza. Centrally located in the heart of town, the restaurant is open daily, 12:00-15:00, 19:00-23:30 (hours may vary off season, call in advance). Via Boccaccio 35, Tel: 0571.665122, www.damesserboccaccio.it

# Sleeping in San Gimignano

## SAN GIMIGNANO

There are several sleeping options in San Gimignano and the surrounding areas. If you have a car, you can easily book an excellent place with a pool and surrounded by lush nature 10 minutes from town .

**Voltrona B&B** is a great choice for families; it offers a pool, horseback riding lessons for kids and adults, a small lake to fish in, fabulous views, and farm tours for toddlers. Fattoria Voltrona, Loc. San Donato, San Gimignano, Tel: 0577.943152, www.voltrona.com

**Torre Prima** is another reasonably priced and good option for families, with a pool overlooking a beautiful view and lots of space in which to run around. Agriturismo Torre Prima, Loc. Cortennano 19, San Gimignano, Tel: 0577.941033, www.torreprima.com

**Casa Nova di Pescille** is beautiful; their apartments are comfortable and elegant, the restaurant offers tasty dishes and cooking lessons (which must be booked in advance), and the view is spectacular. Location is five minutes by car from San Gimignano. Azienda Agricola Casanova di Pescille, Loc. Pescille, San Gimignano, Tel: 0577.941902, www.casanovadipescille.com

**Forresteria del Monastero di San Girolamo** is one of the more reasonably priced choices in the area. Be aware that this is also an actual monastery run by Benedictine nuns. Via Folgore 30, Tel: 0577.940573, www.monasterosangirolamo.it

**Locanda Mandragola** is a charming little place, offering great value for your money and situated at the heart of San Gimignano (especially good if you don't have a car or want to spend the night in town). Via Diaccetto 7, San Gimignano, Tel: 0577.940454, www.locandalamandragola.it

**Agriturismo Santa Croce** is another lovely farmhouse that is comfortable, spacious, and just 400 metres from Porta San Matteo in San Gimignano. Tel: 0577.943073, www.agriturismosantacroce.it

## CERTALDO
**Hotel Certaldo** is a comfortable, elegant, hospitable option for families. Kids will love the pool, too. Via del Molino 74, Certaldo, Tel: 0571.651261, www.hotelcertaldo.it

# Special Events in the Area

## SAN GIMIGNANO
**Fiera delle Messi and Giostra dei Bastoni:** Every year, on the second or third weekend of June (check in advance), the streets of San Gimignano come to life with a medieval costume festival. The Knights of Santa Fina (San Gimignano's best-loved saint) re-enact the old harvest festival tradition, with colourful parades, jousting, dramatic wooden weapons and arms, street performers, and more. Several food stalls around town complete the festivities. Find out more at the local tourist offfice.

**Summer concerts:** San Gimignano welcomes the summer crowds with a series of open-air concerts and events located mostly around the Duomo. Find out if any events are planned during your visit by contacting the local tourist office (Tel: 0577.940008). Concerts usually run from June to late September.

## MONTERIGGIONI
**The medieval festivities in Monteriggioni** are worth the drive, especially if you are travelling with kids. The main events usually take place during the first two weeks of July when artists and performers fill the piazza. Stalls with medieval items and utensils, processions with men and women in medieval costumes, music and dancing all contribute to the festive atmosphere. Find out more and check for exact dates each year at www.Monteriggionimedievale.com.

## CERTALDO
Certaldo hosts two feasts worth visiting if you are in the area. In June, there is a medieval dinner, where all the staff and waiters wear medieval clothes, and the whole street is alive and decorated. Book in advance (Tel: 0571.663128, www.elitropia.org). In July, there is a feast with street performers and medieval games. Find out more at www.mercantiacertaldo.it.

# Special Activities in the Area

There are several excellent options for family activities in the San Gimignano area. Some need to be booked in advance (cooking classes, horseback rides, guided hikes), while others are just waiting for you to pass by. Scheduling an extra activity might seem excessive, but sometimes it's exactly the sort of thing that is remembered the most as a wonderful family moment.

## HIKING
Hiking by yourself can be intimidating, if you are worried about getting lost. Bruno Squartini, a licensed environmental guide, organizes daily 5 km hikes along the historical Francigena road. Book in advance, and let the guide know what you are interested in seeing, and what your level of fitness is. Bruno, Tel: 0577.940922 / 346.755.9908, bruno.squartini@libero.it.

## COOKING CLASSES
Cooking classes are one of the best activities for families, especially when you

find a class adapted for kids, too.

The **Chianti Cooking School** in Barberino di Val d`Elsa (25 minutes away from San Gimignano) offers hands-on courses for both beginners and more advanced aspiring chefs. One-day cooking classes are available for groups of at least 4-6 people and cost about 95 euro per person. Cooking classes for children are available. Book in advance. Loc: Sant`Appiano 16, Barberino Val D'Elsa, Tel: 055.807504, 335.6601381, www.chianticooking.com

**Cucina Giuseppina** is a little cooking school right outside of Certaldo where children are absolutely welcome. A three-hour class (between 10:30-14:00 or between 17:00-20:00) will cost about 95 euro for adults and about 50 euro for children under 14. Medieval cooking classes (yes, you read that right!) are also available. Book in advance. Cell: 348.0034869, www.cucinagiuseppina.com

## HOT AIR BALLOON

If you're celebrating a special occasion, why not commemorate it with a hot air balloon ride over the Tuscan fields? **Banda Balloons** offer rides for the whole family, creating an expensive but unique experience everyone will remember. The balloons leave from Montaione, 25 minutes north of San Gimignano. To ride the balloon, children have to be at least 1.2 meters high. If any of the passaengers weigh more than 80 kg, it's best to notify the organizers in advance. The flight lasts for 50-60 minutes and leaves early in the morning or late in the afternoon. Book at least a week in advance. Cell: 335.7656200, www.bandaballoons.com

## HORSEBACK RIDING

The **Vechhio Maneggio** is a friendly, comfortable and reasonably priced agriturismo that also offers pleasant horseback riding tours led by a former Palio Jockey. Children have to be at least eight years old to participate. A tour of about an hour will cost around 20 euro per person. Agriturismo Il Vecchio Maneggio, Loc. Sant'Andrea 22, San Gimignano, Tel: 0577.950232, www.ilvecchiomaneggio.com

**Area Park 52** offers horseback rides in a splendid setting that kids and teenagers will enjoy. Children must be at least 14 to participate in a riding tour. Activities with horses at the stables (not actual tours) may be available for younger children. Book in advance. The stable is located just 20 minutes from San Gimignano (near Volterra). Via Porta Diana 47, Loc. Prato d´era, Tel: 0588.42140, 3475.910373, www.area52park.com

# SIENA

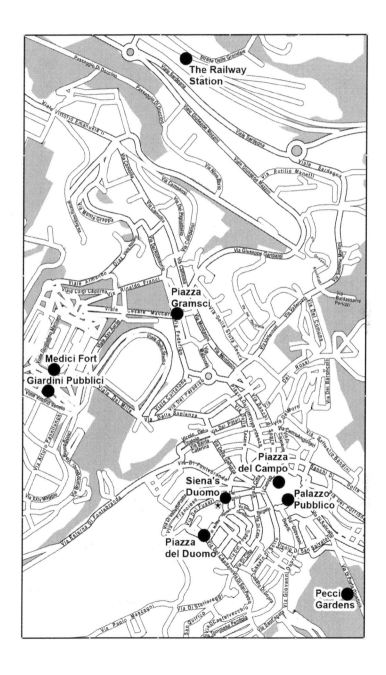

The Railway Station

Piazza Gramsci

Medici Fort

Giardini Pubblici

Piazza del Campo

Siena's Duomo

Palazzo Pubblico

Piazza del Duomo

Pecci Gardens

# Chapter 7

# Siena

Simply put, Siena is stunning. Its medieval red brick alleys, beautiful Piazza del Campo, overly dramatic but glorious Duomo (one of the most famous in Italy), and little shops and cafes all make Siena a must-see destination. Unlike Florence, which is so rich in monuments that it requires a tightly packed schedule of at least two days, Siena can be enjoyed at a much more leisurely pace, even if you have just one day to tour it.

Some travellers think Siena is an unnecessary stop if they've already seen Florence, but we disagree. The two towns are quite different; while Florence offers visitors the charms of the Renaissance, Siena celebrates the magic of medieval Italy. Much like San Gimignano, Siena never recovered from the plague (which hit the town in the 15th century), and after the city lost its ongoing battle with Florence it slowed down considerably. For tourists visiting Siena, this is a blessing, as the historical centre has changed very little over the past 500 years, and walking the streets of Siena feels like going back in time.

Much as they do with Florence, potential visitors often wonder how it's possible to tour Siena with children. If you have toddlers or kids who aren't particularly interested in museums and churches, we suggest focusing on three must-see attractions: first, the child-friendly, shell-shaped, and famous **Piazza del Campo**, where kids can soak in the sun, people-watch, and run around. Second, kids age eight and up can climb the **Torre del Mangia** (a popular tower located in the Piazza del Campo) to enjoy the beautiful view. Third, visit the **Duomo**, which is impressive enough to interest even reluctant kids. Once you are done, you can have lunch and walk around to discover hidden corners of the old town before moving on to your next destination. If you plan to spend less than a full day in Siena, we recommend passing the afternoon with either a special activity (see "Special Activities in the Area" at the end of this chapter) or a visit to other nearby attractions. At the end of this itinerary, you will find a list of four family-friendly attractions within an hour's drive of Siena. All four will nicely complement your tour of the town.

## Top 5 Family Activities

1. Climb the Torre del Mangia and get a unique view of the city.

2. People-watch in Piazza del Campo.

3. Visit Siena's incredible Duomo; notice the illustrated marble floors.

4. Check out the art in Museo dell'Opera and climb to the little panoramic terrace to get another view of the city.

5. Visit attractions outside of Siena, like Chiusdino.

## GETTING THERE

**BY CAR:** Reaching Siena by car is easy. From Florence, take the Raccordo Autostradale Firenze Siena. Exit the autostrada on Siena Ovest and follow the signs to the centro. However, most of the historical centre (centro storico) is ZTL, closed for non-resident traffic, so you'll have to park outside of this area. There are several options: **Parcheggio Stadio-Fortezza**, the biggest parking lot in town, is located next to the Medici Fortress, also known today as Fortezza Santa Barbara (from which there is a great view of Siena). **Parcheggio Stazione** in Piazzale Fratelli Rosselli is open 24 hours a day and is close to the train station. There is an escalator just outside that will bring you to the town's centre. **Parcheggio Santa Caterina** in Via Esterna di Frontebranda is also open 24 hours a day, and there's an escalator that brings you near the Duomo (escalators are necessary because Siena is located on top of a hill). If the escalators aren't working, take a local bus up to the town centre. See a detailed explanation about the escalators under 'By Train'.

**BY TRAIN:** Siena is easily accessible via train from most major cities in Tuscany. To reach the centro storico from the train station, you will need to take either the escalator or the bus to the city centre. Buy tickets at the newspaper stand in the train station (buy round-trip tickets so you won't have to find an open stand when you want to get back). To reach both the bus and the escalators, leave the train station, cross the road, and enter the shopping mall in front of you. **Escalator**: take the elevator to the top floor of the shopping mall, and from there follow the signs to the escalator. The escalator will bring you up the hill to Viale Vittorio Emanuele II, from which you can reach the historical centre in less than 5 minutes. **Bus:** leave the train station, cross the street and enter the shopping mall. Turn left, walk all the way to the end to reach the elevators, and go down one floor to find the buses. Almost all of the buses reach the historical centre, so it doesn't really matter which one you take (but to be sure, ask the driver when you get on board, 'Scusi, va al centro storico?' This meaning, 'Excuse me, are you going to the historical center?'). The bus will leave you either at Piazza del Sale or Piazza Gramsci, both of which are 5 to 7 minutes from Piazza del Campo. Don't forget to validate your ticket by pushing it into the little machine in the front of the bus.

**TOURIST INFORMATION OFFICES:** There is small tourist office in the train station where you can get updated museum opening hours and maps. ◷ Opening times: Tuesday-Friday, 09:00-13:00, 14:00-17:00; Mondays, 09:00-16:00. A larger office can be found at Piazza del Campo 56 and is open daily, 09:30-18:30 (off-season, especially during the winter, hours tend to change). Siena also has an expansive website with information about the town and the surrounding region: www.terredisiena.it.

## Siena in a Minute (A Brief History of Siena)

Local legend says that Senius, the son of Romulus (Remus and Romulus were the famous pair who were nursed by a she wolf and then founded Rome), is the founder of Siena. To this day, the symbol of Siena is a wolf nursing two babies. The reality was somewhat different; an Etruscan tribe (called Saina) arrived to the area some 2800 years ago and settled there. When the Romans conquered the Etruscans, Emperor Augustus founded the Roman city Saena Julia in the same exact spot, taking advantage of its strategic hilly position overlooking the entire area.

A small centre during Antiquity and the Early Middle Ages, Siena started growing when the Via Francigena became not only the most important path toward pilgrimage but also a principal trade route. Siena turned from a small town to a powerful local republic and constantly clashed with Florence, its nemesis from the north.

Siena was once a major banking and trade hub as well as a vibrant artistic and religious centre. It eventually lost most of its power in 1550, when Florence and the Medici family—with the help of the Spanish army—conquered the city. Today, Siena is a favourite tourist destination and home to a vibrant university.

**Tip:** If you plan on visiting only the main attractions in town, making a day trip to Siena from Florence is definitely a viable option. However, if you want to take your time and explore more than just the basics, a day trip may not be such a good idea. By the time you get there, park, and start your day, you will have lost most of the morning, and you'll have to dash through the main sights and battle against the closing times. To avoid this, either arrive early or arrive the night before, and wake up to calmly explore the town.

# Our tour of Siena begins at the bus stop of whichever bus

brought you up to town (if you've arrived by car, simply walk towards Piazza del Campo and start the tour from there). From here, follow the signs (and the constant flux of people) towards the town centre and Piazza del Campo. You will end up along the main road, Via Banchi di Sopra, lined with popular fashion shops. It doesn't take much to imagine that 700 years ago this street was bustling with a different kind of crowd: vendors from all over the area selling their live rabbits, cast iron pots, grains, and arrows.

Look for number 24 on your left. This is Pasticceria Nannini, a well-known local pastry shop owned by the family of one of Italy's most famous singers, Giana Nannini. In front of the pasticceria, at number 11, there is a relatively new shop, Gelateria Grom, where you can get some of the best ice cream in town (their chocolate ice creams are frozen decadence in a cup).

**Tip:** Just a few metres away, in Via Pianigiani 5, you'll find a shop run by Consorzio Agrario di Siena (Siena's agricultural producers union), where you can buy local specialities, excellent wine, and tasty pizza slices to nibble on as you explore the town or to pack up for a picnic later in the day.

Continue walking straight ahead; on your left you will see an impressive little piazza called Piazza Salimbeni. It houses a beautiful building that was once the home to the rich, powerful, and ruthless Salimbeni family. Today, it houses, the international headquarters of the oldest bank in the world (still operating), Monte Paschi di Siena, and isn't open to visitors.

**Mission 1:** Walk into the piazza to admire the building next to the bank up close. Look up and you'll see a creepy little surprise looking right back at you. Can you count the number of heads overlooking the piazza? Which is your favourite and why? If you have a pair of binoculars, this is the time to pull them out!

Continue straight ahead towards Piazza del Campo; two minutes later you'll reach Piazza Tolomei, where you'll see yet another impressive building which, interestingly enough, belonged to the Salimbeni family's worst enemy, the Tolomei family. The Tolomei and Salimbeni families spent years fighting for money and power before a family picnic was organized on neutral ground to bring peace to the situation. Both parties showed up, but as soon as the first course was served, the Salimbenis pulled out daggers they had hidden in their picnic baskets and murdered 18 of the Tolomei family members.

# Piazza del Campo

This world-famous piazza is Siena's best-known attraction and a perfect place for kids to run around, chase the occasional pigeon, soak in some sunlight, and admire the area's unique beauty. In the past, **Piazza del Campo**, the true heart of the city, hosted almost every public event, including markets, assemblies, and sporting events (jousting, carnival processions, hunting matches, and of course, the Palio). The unique shape of the piazza is meant to resemble Mary's Cloak and is divided into nine equal parts, representing the nine members of the council who ruled Siena during medieval times. To maintain the piazza's homogeneous look, all of its restaurants and cafés, even McDonald's, had to change their signs to match the brown colour of its surface.

The monumental **Gaia Fountain** is located at Piazza del Campo's highest point. Beautifully designed by Jacopo della Quercia, the fountain was meant for not only decorative purposes but also to serve as an important water source for the entire town. The fountain currently in the piazza is a 19th-century copy; the orig-

inal can be found in the Santa Maria della Scala Museum.

**Mission 2:** Take a photo lying down in the piazza.

**Mission 3:** Several animals decorate the fountain. Can you name at least five? (they can be real or fictional). Which is your favourite?

At the base of Piazza del Campo stands Siena's town hall, the **Palazzo Pubblico**, which hosts the beautiful Museo Civico (Civic Museum) on its top floor and has the most famous tower in Siena, the **Torre del Mangia** (also known as the **Torre Mangiaguadagni**). The Palazzo Pubblico was built by the "Nove Signori" (the Nine Lords, rulers of Siena) in 1310 and is considered one of the best examples of Gothic architecture in the world. In the past, it has served not only as a town hall but also as a prison (with damp, underground cells) and a storage facility. Note how its concave façade perfectly matches the convex profile of the Campo.

The beautiful **Civic Museum** occupies the top floor of the Palazzo Pubblico. It isn't very big, so even if you don't have much time you can still visit to enjoy some of the best works of art Siena has to offer. Most of the rooms are decorated with impressive frescoes, commissioned by the republican government (including a few dramatic and realistic battle scenes that will delight kids). Don't miss the room called Sala dei Nove (Room of the Nine), which was declared a world heritage site by UNESCO and features Ambrogio Lorenzetti's *Allegory of Good and Bad Government* frescoes. Also worth noting is Sala del Mappamondo (or the Great Council Hall), which features the *Maestà* and the battle fresco *Guidoriccio da Fogliano*, both by Simone Martini (1284-1344). The Sala del Risorgimento, the Sala di Balia, the Sala dei Cardinali, and the beautifully decorated Capella (chapel) and Anticapella (the room adjacent to the chapel), are all worth a quick visit. These rooms are perfect examples of how the constant competition between Florence and Siena turned out to be quite fortunate for the world of art and architecture. While the rich and power-craving men from both cities fought to demonstrate their superiority by financing the most incredible art money could buy, the world gained several churches, buildings, and works of art that are admired to this day.

As you tour the Civic Museum, you may notice that some of the frescoes aren't in very good shape. Some experts say this is because the salt that was once stored in the bottom cells of the Palazzo sucked water out of the walls, altering their shape and texture and thus damaging the frescoes.

## More on the Allegory of Good and Bad Government

The Council of Nine (an oligarchy of merchants who ruled Siena during the Middle Ages) commissioned Ambrogio Lorenzetti's masterpiece that decorates the Sala dei Nove. The large fresco, painted in 1339, carried a strong social message about the importance of republican government. Standing with your back to the windows, you will see on the left the "Good Government", a personification of the commune as a venerable old man dressed in white and black (the colours of the Balzana, Siena's coat-of-arms). He is sitting solemnly on a throne, surrounded by the Four Cardinal Virtues (Justice, Fortitude, Temperance, and Prudence). Above him are the Three Theological Virtues (Faith, Hope, and Charity) and below him stands the she-wolf with Romulus and Remus, a reminder of Siena's Roman origin. On his right side you will find Siena's army with its prisoners, and on his left, the allegory of Justice, as a woman, is seated on a throne. She is holding scales and looking at Wisdom above her. If you have a pair of binoculars, they will help you appreciate the details.

Looking at the paintings on the far left and right walls, it's easy to imagine which is meant to represent the impact a good government will have on city life and which depicts the devastating effects a bad government has on people. Notice, for example, the figure representing Tyranny on the left wall. Below it is the figure representing Justice, pale and immobilized. She watches the drought and pain around her that was brought on by bad rulers.

· · · · · · · · · · · · · · · · · · · · · · · · · · · · · · · · · · · · · · · · · · · · · · · · · · ·

**Mission 4:** As soon as you exit the Palazzo Pubblico, you will see a statue on your right. Can you find it? Pose just like it, making the exact same face as the statue, and take a quick photo.

**Mission 5:** Think about the difference in size between the Palazzo Pubblico (remember that this was once the most important building in Siena), and the size of town halls and courts today. Which are bigger? Why do you think sizes changed so much?

· · · · · · · · · · · · · · · · · · · · · · · · · · · · · · · · · · · · · · · · · · · · · · · · · · ·

🕐 Opening times, Palazzo Pubblico: mid-March-October, open daily, 10:00-19:00 (ticket office closes at 18:15); November-mid-March, 10:00-18:00 (ticket office closes at 17:15); combo tickets are available with the Torre del Mangia; children under 11 enter for free. Tel: 0577.292620

A visit to the Palazzo Pubblico can't be complete without visiting one of the most popular attractions in town, especially for kids: Torre Mangiaguadagni (popularly known as **Torre del Mangia**). The tower was once one of the highest in Italy and was named after the man who operated it, Giovanni di Balduccio, a big spender who eventually managed to earn the nickname "Mangiaguadagni" (Earnings Eater). The tower is 87 metres high, and you have to climb more than 300 steps to reach the top, but it's worth it; the views are spectacular. If you are wondering which tower is higher, the one in Siena or the one in Florence, the answer is Siena. And no, it's no accident...

• • • • • • • • • • • • • • • • • • • • • • • • • • • • • • • • • • • • • • • • • • • • • • • • • • • • • • • • • •

**Mission 6:** The earliest mechanism installed in this bell tower wasn't just thrown away after it was replaced with a modern one. Can you find where it is displayed? Hint: It is somewhere in the building itself, closer than you might imagine.

**Mission 7:** The tower doesn't just end normally; it has a big decoration on it. What shape is this decoration? What does it look like? Bonus question: Who designed it? You may use the Internet to find out.

**Mission 8:** Take a picture at the top of the tower, holding your fingers shaped like the letter "S", for Siena.

• • • • • • • • • • • • • • • • • • • • • • • • • • • • • • • • • • • • • • • • • • • • • • • • • • • • • • • • • •

🕑 Opening times, Torre del Mangia: March-mid October, 10:00-19:00 (ticket office closes at 18:15); mid-October-Feburary, 10:00-16:00 (ticket office closes at 15:15). An adult must accompany children under 14; combo tickets are available (with the Civic Museum); children under 6 enter for free (though the climb up might be too hard or scary for toddlers). Entry is limited to 50 people at a time, so prepare for a line. This attraction isn't for people who suffer from claustrophobia, or a fear of heights

Once you've had your fill of the piazza, walk along Via dei Banchi and then Via di Citta' towards Piazza Duomo (follow the signs) and turn right at Via del Capitano to find the Duomo on your right.

**Tip:** The museum system in Siena can be a little bit confusing. Some museums belong to the town, while others are religious or private, which means that you can't get just one combo ticket for them all. The Duomo is covered by the convenient OPA-SI combo ticket, which includes entrance to the Duomo itself, the Piccolomini Library (which is inside the Duomo), the Museo dell'Opera del Duomo (a small museum next to the Duomo that contains ancient artefacts and beautiful paintings and is worth a visit if you have some extra time), the crypt (which can be skipped), and the Baptistery (which is pretty but can be skipped). A separate ticket may be purchased if you want to visit the Santa Maria della Scala Museum (which is located in the same piazza as the Duomo but isn't covered by the OPA-SI ticket). The OPA-SI ticket can be purchased in the little booth on the Duomo's right, in front of the entrance to the Museo dell'Opera. A ticket to Santa Maria della Scala Museum (also sometimes known as Ospedale La Scala) can be purchased in the museum itself.

# The Duomo

One of the greatest Romanesque-Gothic cathedrals in the world and one of the five most impressive cathedrals in Italy, the Duomo of Siena is dedicated to Saint Mary of the Assumption. It was built during the 12th and 13th centuries on top of a pre-existing church, which in turn, had been built on top of an

Ancient Roman temple dedicated to Minerva (this was a common practice back then). Alternating black and white stripes (the colours of Siena's coat-of-arms) dominate the exterior and the interior, as well

as the impressive 77-metre-tall bell tower. Recently restored, the façade is stunning, with an intricate design of ornaments and sculptures; Giovanni Pisano (1250-1315) designed its lower part. His father, Nicola Pisano, one of the finest Gothic sculptors in Italy, created the splendid pulpit inside the Duomo, near the altar.

**Mission 9:** Look at the tower. Is it higher than the cathedral? [Remember to answer first, before reading the answer!] If you guessed no, you were right! Siena officials decided to make the stripes narrower as they went up, to create the illusion of a tower so high that it would make other cities (mainly Florence) jealous.

Once you step inside, admire the incredibly dramatic décor. Black and white colours dominate every corner, from the beautiful columns to the unique marble floor. The floor, in fact, is one of the Duomo's most famous features, a work of art that took more than 170 years to complete. It features a marble mosaic of episodes from Siena's history and biblical scenes.

**Mission 10:** Can you find any floor panels near the entrance that have to do with Siena's Roman past? (Hint: Think of wolves.) Bonus: Which animals surround the creature described in this panel?

**Mission 11:** It's time to take out the binoculars. Do you see anything peculiar at the tops of the columns? Do any of them have something... wild about them?

**Mission 12 (hard!):** Try to identify two of the scenes in the floor panels.

Walk toward the centre of the Duomo and look up to see its impressive dome. In front of you is Nicola Pisano's famous octagonal pulpit, built from the best marble available (from Carrara). It stands on a base of lions, with reliefs describing scenes from Christ's life and the judgment day. Directly in front of you, over the main altar, stands the Duomo's famous stained glass window, created by one of Siena's best-known painters, Duccio di Buoninsegna. This one is actually a copy; the original one, more than 800 years old, was moved to the Museo dell'Opera.

**Mission 13:** How many statues are holding candles in the main altar? On the floor in front of the altar, there are metal symbols. What is the fourth symbol from the bottom on the left side? What do you think it stands for?

Turn around, walk a few steps back toward the entrance, and you will see the **Piccolomini Altar** and **Library** on your right. The altar, featuring a sculpture by Michelangelo, was designed to serve as a tomb for Pope Pius II (who was originally a cardinal in Siena), but in the end, he was buried in the Vatican like most other popes.

Near the altar stands the **Piccolomini Library**, a charming little space that holds a collection of rare illustrated books and manuscripts. The library is entirely decorated with frescoes recounting the life story of Pope Pius II of the Piccolomini family, a true Renaissance man. Unlike at so many other places, these 550-year-old frescoes seem as bright and new as they did when they were completed. The reason is simple: since no candles were brought into the library (unlike the church itself), there was no heat or smoke to damage the paintings.

**Mission 14:** One of the panels describes a scene in which the young pope (who wasn't a pope yet) was made Cardinal. He kneels before the Pope and wears red clothes. Can you find it?

While leaving the Duomo, it's interesting to remember that the original plan was for this cathedral to be much bigger. In the 1330s, the city had an ambitious plan: to build a new, huge cathedral that was even bigger than Saint Peter's Cathedral in Rome. The existing church, far from being small, was going to be the transept of the new one. The project, however, was never completed, due to the enormous cost, political conflicts, and, most of all, the Black Death (plague) that devastated Siena, killing half of the town's population in 1438, including such artists as Pietro and Ambrogio Lorenzetti.

🕐 Opening times, Duomo, Piccolomini Library, Museo dell'Opera, Crypt, and Baptistery: March-October, 10:30-19:00 (on Sundays and holidays, the Duomo is open from 13:30-18:00); November-Feburary, 10:30-17:30 (on Sundays and holidays, the Duomo is open 13:30-17:30). Hours may vary during the holidays, last entry 30 minutes before closing time. Children pay a reduced fee - ask at the ticket office. To avoid the long line, you can walk up to the 'advanced reservation' box, pay one extra euro per person, and enter immediately. Several sections of the marble floor in the Duomo are covered throughout the year (to protect them) and are revealed for a few weeks only, usually during September and the first weeks of October. When the floor is revealed, the entrance fee to the Duomo is notably higher. Tel: 0577.286300

If you have extra time and the kids haven't lost their patience with "artsy stuff", the **Museo dell'Opera**, next to the Duomo, is worth a quick visit. Check out the original stained glass window up close, some works by Duccio di Buoninsegna, and climb up to the balcony that overlooks Siena. You could also visit **Santa Maria della Scala**, once a hospital and today a museum complex (currently parts of the museum are closed for renovation; check before entering to see what can be visited). This museum complex is famous for the well-known Pilgrim's Hall (Sala del Pellegrinaio), decorated with lively frescoes that tell the story of daily life in Siena in the 15th century. The complex also includes a children's art museum, but unless there is some special event or exhibition going on, it can easily be skipped.

🕐 Opening times, Santa Maria della Scala: March-October, open daily, 10:30-18:30; November-February, open daily, 10:30-16:30. Children under 11 pay a reduced fee. Tel: 0577.534571

# Relics, Missing Fingers, and Wet Nurses- Life in the La Scala Hospital

This 12th-century stone structure was once an important hospital, especially for pilgrims, who often became ill on their way to Rome. Pilgrims were a profitable business, and one of the ways hospital managers (yes, those existed back then, too) drew in the crowds was to offer the sick a chance to peek at religious relics. Pieces from the cross, relics of saints, and other items were huge selling points, and the better the relic, the more visitors and patients came. Obtaining the "good" relics wasn't easy, though, and the competition was fierce, which lead to gruesome scenes of businessmen running like maniacs around the bodies of recently deceased holy men and women, trying to get a tooth, or some hair, or possibly a finger that would later attract the crowds.

The cycle of frescoes decorating the main hall, (the Pilgrim's Hall, better known as the Sala del Pellegrinaio), was created by Domenico di Bartolo, Lorenzo Vecchieta and others. For many history lovers, this hall is a favourite attraction, because of the daily life scenes that it reveals. One scene, for example, describes a common feature of the hospital: when unwanted children were abandoned, wet nurses were hired to feed newborns and paid with silver coins or sacks of wheat (look at the panel before the last one, on the right and left walls). In truth, however, quite a few of these children weren't really abandoned. They were left at night in the hospital, and the next morning, their mothers would present themselves as wet nurses looking for jobs. So not only did these women get their children back, but they were handsomely paid for feeding them. In any case practice among middle-class and noble families during the Middle Ages and the Renaissance. Many children remained with their nurses until they were two years old and were then brought back to the family to be raised by their parents. A good wet nurse was hard to find; she had to be in her 30s, with a good bosom and a good temper (people believed a bad temper would contaminate her milk). Preferably, she would also have recently given birth to a boy (so her milk would still be good and "strong").

Upon leaving the Duomo (or the Santa Maria La Scala Museum), you may feel a craving for something sweet. If so, try the Antica Drogheria Manganelli, in Via di Città 71 (just two minutes from the Duomo). This well-known establishment is a popular choice for those who want to buy typical Siena-style cookies, called ric-caerlli (made with almond paste and topped with powdered sugar) or a nice slice of the local specialty, panforte (a heavy ordeal, filled with candid fruit and nuts; kids usually don't like it).

If you haven't got all day, your tour of Siena can end here. However, if you still want to explore this medieval town, there is more to see. First, stop for a quick lunch either at one of the restaurants suggested at the end of this itinerary or go for a picnic in the ever-popular **Pecci Gardens** (near the market square). To reach the gardens—where kids can run around and relax—walk back to Piazza del Campo, go behind Palazzo Pubblico, and walk towards Piazza del Mercato. Continue along Via porta Giustizia and then turn to Via del Sole to enter through the gate to the garden.

Other attractions in town are the **Medici Fort** (also known as the **Santa Barbara Fort**), from which you can enjoy an impressive view of Siena (and play in the adjoining public gardens), **San Domenico Church**, and **Santa Caterina's home** (Siena's patron saint). All are marked on the map that can be picked up at the tourist office. Another popular attraction is the **Old Jewish Ghetto**, a minute away from Piazza del Campo (though there isn't much to see, and the synagogue is only open on Saturdays).

# Gardens and playgrounds in Siena

Siena has a surprising number of lovely little gardens and playgrounds that younger children will love. The most famous and obvious choice is Peci Gardens, which are located behind Piazza del Campo (see Siena itinerary), but if you don't want to walk all the way there and are looking for a centrally located playground for the kids to run around, here are a few alternatives:

**The Medici Fort:** The Medici Fort is a huge space, just waiting to be explored. Kids can run around the fort itself or at the adjoining public gardens. There is a great view of the city, and  there are usually cultural events held in this area in the summertime.

**Giardini Lizza:** Right next to the Medici Fort and just two minutes from the NH hotel and Piazza Gramsci (where most buses stop), you will find the Lizza Gardens. This is the perfect spot for toddlers: there's a playground, a pond with ducks and swans, and lots of space to run around.

**On the corner of Via Sant'agata and Via Mattioli**, just a few metres from the popular Taverna San Giusppe restaurant and a short walk from the Duomo, you will find a small garden with a tiny playground and a nice view of the city.

**San Francesco:** Near the San Francesco Church you will find a small playground for toddlers, and a large piazza for them to run around.

## THREE FAVOURITE FAMILY ATTRACTIONS LESS THAN AN HOUR AWAY FROM SIENA

### 1.  CHIUSDINO

Chiusdino, just 40 minutes from Siena, is well known for its roofless fairy-tale-like rock church, the Abbey of San Galgano, surrounded by dramatically green meadows.

# Where's the Roof?

When the plague hit Tuscany in 1348, the monks suffered badly, not just from the disease but from crime that started to spread in the region. When the attacks persisted, several monks left the monastery, heading to Siena to escape

the bands of robbers who terrorized the area. The last of the monks left towards the end of the 15th century, and when lightning struck the bell tower in 1786 and it collapsed onto the abbey, destroying the roof, there was no one left to fix it. The abbey was believed to be beyond repair and was deconsecrated, but instead, thanks to its missing roof, it became a popular tourist destination in the area.

Once you have visited the abbey, you can either walk or drive up to the hermitage, a few minutes away (just look up the hill) where a famous sword-in-the-rock lies protected, a local (and less exciting) version of King Arthur's tales. The hermitage is where Saint Galgano, an ex-Chiusdino knight, retired to spend the rest of his life as a monk. He no longer needed the sword that had served him bravely, so he fiercely thrust it into the rock to symbolize his peaceful new life and his faith (the sword in the rock looked like a cross).

## 2. THE ROCK SCULPTURE PARK

If you have extra time, stop for a visit at a magical little place called Dreamwoods Sculpture Park, near Chiusdino, where artist Deva Manfredo creates unique sculptures using completely natural methods and by minimally manipulating the stone. There are also night visits to the park on the third and fourth weekend of every month (between May and October; the dates may change; always call and book in advance). 🕐 Opening times: March-November, weekends, 10:30-sunset; Tuesday and Friday, 14:00-sunset. The park is in Osho Miasto, Pod. S. Giorgio, near San Galgano. Cell: 333.4330183, www.devamanfredo-stoneart.com

## 3. TERME DI PETRIOLO

The free thermal springs of Petriolo (Terme di Petriolo) were frequented by locals for hundreds of years. Women would come from as far away as Florence, believing the water would help them become pregnant. Today, however, constant drilling in the area and general neglect have ruined much of the natural reserve. You can still visit it though, if you are a fan of open-air free thermal springs and you don't mind a somewhat rustic experience (since the terme are right by the river, locals, especially teenagers, love jumping back and forth between the river and the thermal baths). Don't drive here just for the baths, though; they are only worth a visit if you are simply in the area. To reach the Terme, drive about 38 km along the SS223 from Siena towards the tiny town of Santo. To find out more, check out this website (in Italian only, unfortunately): www.petriolo.org.

If you want a more organized experience of a spa resort with a pool fed directly by the thermal springs in the area, try the elegant Petriolo Hotel Spa, 20 minutes south of the free thermal baths, near Civitella Paganico. Note that children younger than 12 are not permitted into the thermal pools for health and safety reasons (the water has medicinal properties that might not be suitable for younger children, though local kids seem to ignore this advice). If you suffer from any health problems, you should check with your doctor before you enter the thermal baths. www.petriolospa.com

## 4. MONTERIGGIONI. Featured in the previous itinerary, is only 15 minutes from Siena, and makes for a very pleasant destination for an afternoon visit.

# KIDS' CORNER

## More About... Siena's Palio!

The Palio is a bareback horse race that takes place twice a year: on July 2nd and August 16th in Siena's main piazza, Piazza del Campo. It is also  one of the most famous horse races in the world. Siena is traditionally divided into 17 contrada (neighbourhoods), ten of which take part in this wild race, competing for a banner (the famous Palio). Tens of thousands of people come to see the Palio each year, thanks to the dramatic costumes (more than 500 people dress up for the occasion in traditional medieval clothes), and of course, the race itself! On the morning of the Palio, each contrada traditionally takes its horse to the neighbourhood church to have him blessed by the priest before the competition. Then the jockey, together with the horse and several inhabitants of that contrada, march ceremoniously to the piazza, waving their flags. Palios have been celebrated all over Tuscany for hundreds of years, and they are not limited to horses. In the past, Donkey Palios were also quite popular.

## More About... The Black Death!

The Black Death (a form of the bubonic plague) is probably the worst epidemic to ever hit Europe. It raced across Europe,

# KIDS'CORNER

Asia, and the Middle East, killing more than 25 million people, between a third and half of the population in certain areas. Can you imagine that? As if that weren't bad enough, symptoms included horrifying things such as buboes (the inflammation of lymph nodes, as a result of bacteria attacking them and making them swell up badly), gangrene, high fever, seizures, vomiting blood, and excruciating pain. The skin even began to decompose while the victims were still alive, exposing them to additional bacterial infections.

Scientific and medical knowledge in the Middle Ages was extremely limited (if you want to find out more, check out the Kids' Corner in Chapter 6, San Gimignano and Monteriggioni Itinerary, to learn some crazy facts about medieval medicine); most doctors and common people believed that the Black Death was a punishment for victims' sins. Others believed it was caused by "miasma", poisonous elements in the air carried around by the wind. Since astrology was considered a science and an integral part of medicine in those days, astrologers were called to "investigate" the matter and concluded that an unusual position of Jupiter, Mars, and Saturn in March 1345 was the plague's cause.

The real reason, of course, was quite different; the plague was caused by a strong bacterium called Yersinia pestis (named after one of the biologists who discovered it). The agent that carried it around was the common rat. Italian merchants who arrived by ship from China brought the plague to Europe, unknowingly carrying with them infected rats.

Today this disease can be cured if treated immediately with antibiotics, but

# KIDS'CORNER

in 1347, when the plague stormed across Europe, no cure was available. People developed several popular "remedies" and protections against the Black Death, from tying flowers around their noses to prevent the foul and dangerous odours from penetrating their bodies to carving crosses at the entrance of houses to protect their inhabitants.

As the plague progressed, the authorities took measures to try to stop it from spreading. Doctors wore special protective gear when treating the ill, and large gatherings of people, including popular feasts and religious processions, were prohibited by the Pope himself to prevent mass contamination. There were often so many dead that they were quickly buried, and their clothes burned.

## Eating in Siena

Picnics and pizzas aside, Siena does offer some good restaurants.

**La Taverna di Giuseppe** is one of the most popular restaurants in town, and it isn't hard to see why. The food is delicious, the setting is lovely, and the prices are reasonable. The restaurant is a short walk from both the Duomo and piazza del campo. Booking in advance is highly recommended. Via Giovanni Duprè 132, Tel: 0577.42286, www.tavernasangiuseppe.it. Open Monday-Saturday, 12:00-14:30, 19:00-22:00.

**Osteria Boccon del Prete** is a very good choice. Their menu is modern but rooted deep in the Sienese culinary tradition, prices are reasonable, and the restaurant is located just minutes from the Duomo. Book a table in advance, especially in high season. Via di San Pietro 17, Tel: 0577.280388. www.osteri-aboccondelprete.it. Open Monday-Saturday, 12:30-14:30, 19:30-22:30.

Via Franciosa 25-29, Tel: 0577.284.381, www.osteriadadivo.it. Open Wednesday-Monday, 12:00-14:30, 19:00-22:30.

**Orto de Pecci**, located in the Pecci Gardens, offers simple and tasty dishes kids will enjoy. Open daily, 12:30-14:30, 19:30-22:30; closed on Mondays. Via di Porta Giustizia 39, Tel: 0577.222201

**Trattoria Fori Porta** offers high-end, sophisticated, and excellent food (though it might not really tickle young children's palates), with a good selection of wines. Open daily, 12:00-14:30, 19:00-22:30, closed on Mondays. Via Tolomei 1, Tel: 0577.222100

# **Sleeping** in Siena

There are some lovely hotels within the walls of Siena, but you won't be able to reach them with your car as they are mostly in ZTL areas (theoretically, you can get a one-time permit to enter, but it's a complicated process and not worth the hassle). Consider either taking a taxi to help you with your luggage or choosing a hotel outside of Siena (or at least outside the centro storico, so you can reach it with your car).

**Le Chiarine B&B** is a clean, pleasant, reasonably-priced and well-positioned option in Via A. Pannilunghi 14, Siena. Tel: 0577.1655067, www.lechiarine.it

**Hotel Italia** is an excellent choice. This 3-star hotel is located right outside the historic center, in an area filled with little restuarants and pizzerias (perfect for a quick dinner before heading back to the hotel after a day of sightseeing). This comfortable and modern hotel offers large rooms (the junior suite can be used as a family room), parking (there is a small parking lot for guests, book well in advance as spaces fill up quickly), and an attentive reception desk. The same owners also run Hotel Garden (www.gardenhotel.it), which is slightly farther away but offers a pool, tennis court, a spa and ample parking for guests.

Viale Camillo Benso Conte di Cavour 67, Tel: 0577.44248, www.hotelitalia-siena.it.

**Sangallo Hotel** is just a few minutes away from Siena (by car). It is comfortable, reasonably priced, and—a bonus for families—has a pool. Strada di Vico Alto 2,

Siena, Tel: 0577.334149, www.Siena-hotels.com

**Tenuta di Monaciano** is about 20 minutes away from Siena and is surrounded by the beautiful vineyard-filled countryside. Here you will find a farmhouse converted into an agriturismo, cooking classes, and two pools (and, some nights, live music). Ponte a Bozzone, Siena, Tel: 0577.356805, www.monaciano.com

**Hotel Montaperti** will suit those who are looking for a modern, well-designed, and comfortable hotel just 12 km from Siena, easily accessible from the main road connecting Siena and Castelnuovo Berardenga. Asciano, Tel: 0577.36741, www.montapertihotel.com

If you are looking for a reasonably-priced B&B, **Agriturismo San Giorgio** is a good choice. Just five minutes south of Siena, this agriturismo offers beautiful views, comfortable apartments, and a pool. The kids will be delighted to find kittens, chickens and even a few sheep walking around the garden. Strada Radi 5866, Località Colle Malamerenda, Monteroni d'Arbia. Tel: 0577.378147 / 348.0541474. www.san-giorgio.net.

# Special Events in Siena

Though Siena is known for its Palio—Italy's most famous horse race, which draws a huge crowd—for a number of reasons we don't recommend attending it. First, standing with the crowds can be an intense experience and probably too difficult for children. It will be very hot and very crowded, and every year several people faint because of the heat and end up in the hospital. The only way to comfortably enjoy the Palio with children is to buy tickets for balcony seats in the buildings surrounding the Piazza del Campo (where the event is held); however, those seats cost about 300 euro **each**, which is way over budget for most families. If it is the actual Palio you are interested in, you might want to brave the crowds and find a place to stand in the piazza itself, but if it's simply a dramatic medieval event you want to see, there are several other (still crowded, but much less so) options in Tuscany, from the Giostra in Arezzo (see the Arezzo Itinerary) and Massa Marittima (see the Populonia and the Etruscan Beach Itinerary) to medieval feasts like the ones in Volterra, Monteriggioni, and Pisa (see the "Special Events" sections in all of the previously mentioned itineraries). **That said**, watching the colourful processions and impressive medieval courts in town on the day of the Palio is a recommended experience. Even if you don't see the actual race, you will still enjoy the festive feel in the streets around the Piazza.

# Special Activities in Siena

As always, adding a special activity into your itinerary can be a real treat. Whether you are looking for something more active, like a quad tour, or something relaxing, like a fun cooking class, Siena has something for you.

## COOKING CLASSES

**Scuola di Cucina di Lella** offers several cooking classes. Lella, who founded the first cooking school in Siena, runs courses which aren't adapted for kids, but family cooking classes (usually for a minimum of four people) can be organized if booked far enough in advance. Via Fontebranda 69, Siena, Tel: 0577.46609, www.scuoladicucinadilella.net

**Tenuta di Spanocchia Agriturismo**, near Chiusdino (consider combining with a visit to the abbey in Chiusdino), offers reasonably priced cooking classes that are fit for children, too (as well as comfortable apartments and tours of the farm). cooking classes adapted for children take place on specific days only. Book in advance, especially if you are interested in the special course for children. Tel: 0577.75261, www.spannocchia.com

**Ecco la Cucina Cooking School** in Siena offers hands-on cooking classes for all levels (but they are quite pricey; currently 150 euro per adult, 75 euro for teenagers, and 20 euro for kids, who won't do most of the cooking, but will eat the lunch cooked by the other participants). In a one-day course, you will make a four-course traditional Tuscan meal from scratch. This isn't the best choice for younger children; teenagers will enjoy it much more. Book in advance. Tel: 338.7745487, www.eccolacucina.com

## HORSE RIDES AND BIKE TOURS

**Centro Equestre Viamaggio**, located about 6 km from Siena, offers horse and pony rides, adapted for younger children, too. Book in advance. Strada Vicinale Viamaggio 15, Murlo (Siena), Tel: 333.5359296, www.ceviamaggio.com

If you'd like to tour Siena by bike, but are much less enthusiastic about the prospect of cycling up all those steep streets, **Siena Bike Tour** might just be for you. This small company offers electric bikes for rent, making Siena a little bit more accessible. Find out more here: www.sienamiketour.com

## ADVENTURE PARK

The **Saltalbero Adventure Park** (also featured in the Monte Oliveto Maggiore, Cortona, and Lake Trasimeno Itinerary), is about 45 minutes from Siena and offers just about everything your adrenaline-filled offspring will need—a playground, rope bridges, endless things to climb on, and even horse lessons (which need to be booked in advance). The park is open year-round (but may close due to bad weather) on Saturdays and Sundays only, 10:00-sunset. From June to mid-September, the park is open daily, 10:00-19:00. Loc. Fontemaggio 25, Rapolano Terme, Tel: 0577.725307, www.saltalbero.it

# Monte Oliveto Maggiore, Cortona and Lake Trasimeno

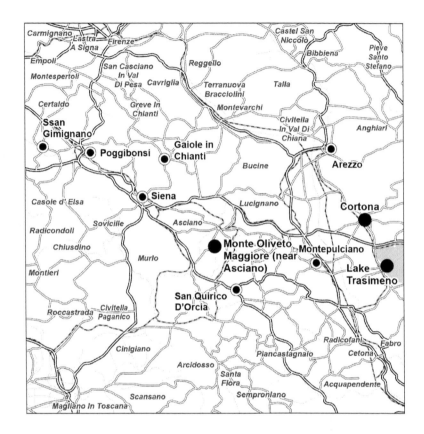

## HOW LONG WILL IT TAKE TO GET THERE?

Siena to Monte Oliveto Maggiore: 45 minutes
Montepulciano to Monte Oliveto Maggiore: one hour
Monte Oliveto Maggiore to Cortona: 1.2 hours
Cortona to Lake Trasimeno: 25 minutes
Cortona to Arezzo: 40 minutes

## Chapter 8

# Monte Oliveto Maggiore, Cortona and Lake Trasimeno

This next itinerary provides a relaxed day in the heart of Tuscany, combining the elegance of Cortona (a famous hill town), a visit to the beautiful Monte Oliveto Maggiore Abbey near Asciano, and an evening stroll along the shores of Lake Trasimeno, where both kids and adults can unwind. None of the attractions in this itinerary are "must-see" destinations, but they are all pleasant to explore, especially if you want to get off the beaten track. All three stops in this itinerary can be combined with other itineraries as well. Cortona, for example, is only 40 minutes south of Arezzo and 45 minutes west of Montepulciano. Monte Oliveto Maggiore is only 35 minutes away from Siena and only 40 minutes away from Pienza and Montepulciano. Lake Trasimeno is 45 minutes away from Montepulciano and Chiusi. As always, check out our "Special Activities in the Area" section for ideas—from cooking classes to horseback riding—that will help spice up your trip.

## Top 5 Family Activities

1. Explore Cortona's Etruscan Museum to discover the town's roots.

2. Visit the monks in Monte Oliveto Maggiore Abbey and listen to them chant Gregorian chants.

3. Book a ceramics workshop and design your very own plate in Cortona.

4. Pass the afternoon by Lake Trasimeno, and take the boat across it during sunset.

5. Enjoy one of the many summer events in Cortona, from concerts to medieval shows.

# Monte Oliveto Maggiore (Asciano)

## GETTING THERE

The Monte Oliveto Maggiore abbey is located in Loc. Chiusure, 14 km outside of Asciano (drive along the SS451, following the signs). Though it is nestled among hills and takes a while to reach, the drive isn't hard. If you're arriving from Cortona (about one hour away), take the Strada Provinciale 38 heading west. From San Quirico d'Orcia (about 30 minutes away), take the SR2 up north and then the SS451.

There are two well-known abbeys in Tuscany where visiting tourists often go to hear the monks chant Gregorian chants: **Sant'antimo**, near Montalcino (see the Val d'Orcia Itinerary), and **Monte Oliveto Maggiore**, near Asciano. Both are beautiful, and merit a visit. Sant'antimo is impressive from an architectural point of view— offering a beautiful Romanesque abbey in a stunning natural setting—and is more accessible (there is less walking and climbing, which may be an issue for toddlers). There are also at least four daily masses with chants celebrated in Sant'Antimo, but only one daily mass in Monte Oilveto Maggiore. Monte Oliveto Maggiore, on the other hand, is less touristy, and manages to maintain a much more authentic feel. With the beautiful frescoes (by Luca Signorelli and il Sodoma) decorating its cloister and the surrounding forests and rolling

hills gracing the landscape, you'll understand why the abbey is popular among locals and foreigners alike.

Monte Oliveto Maggiore was built in the 15th century and much of its original internal décor can still be admired. Try to time your visit to the abbey based on the Gregorian chants schedule, which can be found on the abbey's website.

🕘 Opening times: summer months, 09:00-12:00, 15:00-18:00; winter months, Monday-Saturday, 09:15-12:00, 15:15-17:00 (on Sundays, the abbey closes at 12:30). A Mass accompanied by Gregorian chants is celebrated on weekdays at 18:15 and on Sundays and holidays at 11:00. Tel: 0577.707611, www.monteolivetomaggiore.it

The tiny town of Asciano itself (14 km from Monte Oliveto Maggiore) makes a good stop for lunch, if you have the time. Truffle lovers will be happy to learn that Asciano is a central location for white truffle seekers. The expensive tuber (sold in specialty markets for about 2500 euro per kg) is the star of its own little museum (unfortunately, due to ongoing management changes, it will probably be closed during your visit).

## Terme Rapolano

Just 15 minutes from Asciano you will find one of the several thermal centres in Tuscany. There is a free section (though it is not as impressive as the one in Saturnia; see the Maremma itinerary, or the one in San Filippo: see the Orcia Valley itinerary) as well as a number of hotels with thermal pools that are not that expensive and very popular with locals on weekends and holidays. The infrastructure is lacking and somewhat outdated, but the thermal water is great, and kids probably won't mind that the resort isn't a five-star establishment (to be honest, it isn't four stars either). If you are travelling with teenagers, try the **Terme di San Giovanni night spa**; after dark, the area surrounding the thermal pool is lit by candles and colourful lights, and together with the warm water, the atmosphere is lovely. Terme di San Giovanni Rapolano, Via Terme San Giovanni 52, Rapolano Terme, Tel: 0577.724030, www.termesangiovanni.it. Another option worth checking out is **Terme Antica Querciolaia**, Via Trieste 22, Rapolano Terme, Tel: 0577.724091, www.termeaq.it.

# Cortona

Thanks to Frances Mayes's book *Under The Tuscan Sun* (which was turned into a movie starring Diane Lane), Cortona is now one of Tuscany's most famous hill towns. It is a delightful little place, more than 2500 years old, with a surprising number of attractions. Depending on your plans, you can spend half a day exploring the town and its surrounding area or breeze through in just two hours. Cortona has especially steep streets, and parts of it might not be suitable for toddlers. You'll be fine if you stick to the centre (which is relatively flat) but other attractions (such as the Via Crucis, which leads to the Medici Fortress, or the Public Gardens, mentioned later in this itinerary) require some serious uphill walking. Don't miss the Franciscan Hermitage just outside of town, where you can see monks working and praying in their medieval housing.

## GETTING THERE

**BY CAR:** To reach Cortona from Arezzo, head south along the SR71. From Asciano, drive east (towards Sinalunga) along the Raccordo Autostradale A1 Perugia (about 45 minutes away) and follow the signs. From Lake Trasimeno, take the SR71. Reaching Cortona with a car is definitely the easiest way, although there is one major drawback: parking. It can be a real challenge (a nightmare, really) during summer months, and you may have to circle the parking lots several times to find a spot. However, considering the lack of public transportation in the area, it's much easier to drive. Another important reason for taking a car is so that you can easily get from Cortona to other attractions in the area (in fact, following the suggested itinerary in this chapter without a car would be impossible). The largest parking lot in Cortona, called Santo Spirito Parking, is located at the lower part of town, and there's an escalator connecting the lot with Cortona's centrally located Piazza Garibaldi.

**BY TRAIN AND BUS:** The train service to the Camucia Station at the bottom of the hill, just 15 minutes from Cortona, is good, but the bus schedule from the station to the town itself is problematic. Buses leave once an hour or just twice a day on Sundays and holidays. Try taking a taxi instead. If you do take the bus, it will drop you off at Piazza Garibaldi. From there, walk along Via Nazionale (the only main road; it is filled with shops), and you'll quickly find yourself in the main square, Piazza della Repubblica.

**TOURIST INFORMATION OFFICE:** The tourist information centre (where you can stop to get a map of the town) hides behind the entrance to the Etruscan Museum in Piazza Signorelli. 🕐 Opening times: Monday-Friday, 09:00-13:00, 15:00-18:00; Sundays 09:00-13:00 (during the winter, the office is closed on Saturday afternoons and on Sundays). Tel: 0575.637223

## Our tour of Cortona begins at the lovely Piazza della Repubblica, Cortona's main square, which looks like it was taken out of a Disney movie. The piazza is dominated by the City Hall, which dates back to the 12th century. Just as in several other antique cities, the City Hall was built on top of the former Roman Forum (the centre of city life in ancient times). Though expanded and renovated in the 16th century, it still maintains its dramatic medieval look. The large bell set in its tower was rung to summon people to fight when necessary and to protect the town when it was under attack.

•••••••••••••••••••••••••••••••••••••••••••••••••••••••••••••••••••

**Mission 1:** How many stairs lead up to the City Hall's entrance?

**Mission 2:** This uniquely designed staircase is very wide, isn't it? In the past, things were measured using body parts to indicate their length, height, and weight (people used to say that a bridge was 30 feet long or 32 arms long, for example). Can you measure how wide the staircase is, using this ancient method? How many steps would it take you to cross it? How many feet is it? How many arms?

•••••••••••••••••••••••••••••••••••••••••••••••••••••••••••••••••••

**Tip:** There are a number of nice shops in Piazza della Repubblica. You can buy classic leather items at Maledetti Toscani, for example, and then pop in for a quick taste of wine and "stuzzichini" (little nibbles) at the Enotca Cacio Brillo, or try a glass of wine at the Caffe' la Post, both overlooking the piazza.

From here, walk towards the adjacent piazza, Piazza Signoreli, where you'll find Cortona's **Etruscan Museum (MAEC)**. The Etruscan Museum in Cortona is one of the largest in Tuscany (though not the richest in monuments; that honour belongs to the Volterra Museum). It is inviting and well organized, and it includes several audio-visual displays that kids will appreciate. The museum also houses a collection of somewhat interesting artefacts that tell the story of Cortona itself. Rooms 4-6 are dedicated to artefacts found during excavations of the Etruscan tombs of Tumulo I, II, and Sodo (all outside of Cortona and open to visitors), including funerary equipment, ceramics, and ivory sculptures.

Admission to the Etruscan Museum includes a visit to Sodo Etruscan Tomb, just outside of Cortona (when you drive out of town, you'll see signs clearly indicating the way to the tomb). Combination tickets for the Etruscan Museum and the Diocesan Museum (see below) are available as well. ⊕ Opening times: April-October, open daily, 10:00-19:00; November-March, Tuesday-Sunday, 10:00-17:00. Piazza Signorelli 9, Tel: 0575.637236, www.cortonamaec.org

Once you've had your fill of Etruscans, walk to the adjacent piazza (follow the signs to the Duomo) and you'll reach Cortona's **Diocesan Museum**. Unlike several other diocesan museums, which usually try to inflate the importance of a rather small collection of not-that-interesting local medieval artists, the Cortona Diocesan Museum is a little gem, popular with art lovers (though you can skip it if your kids are reluctant to see even one more painting or fresco). Once a church (Chiesa di Gesu', built in the 15th century), the building is small and inviting; it can easily be toured in half an hour if you don't have much time. Don't miss Fra Angelico's *Annunciation*, the rooms dedicated to Luca Signorelli (especially *Lamentation Over the Dead Christ* in Room 3), and the touching *Communion of the Apostles* (which once decorated the church's main altar). The lower floor (once the oratory) is beautifully decorated with frescoes carried out by the Lorenzetti family.

⊕ Opening times: April-October, open daily, 10:00-19:00; November-March, Tuesday-Sunday, 10:00-17:00; closed on Mondays. Combination tickets with the Etruscan Museum (above) are available. Piazza del Duomo 1, Tel: 0575.62830

From here, you can go back to the main square (about three minutes away) for gelato or a cold beverage before you continue on to tour Cortona's main street, **Via Nazionale** (connected directly to the piazza). Via Nazionale is small but packed with gift shops and cafés. Pasticceria Banalli is a personal favourite, thanks to its good selection of biscuits and cookies that go well with a steamy espresso. Caffe' degli Artisti is another popular option, known for its delightful design, and Caffe' Tucher offers reasonably priced light lunches as well as free Wi-Fi.

At the end of Via Nazionale, you will find Piazza Garibaldi (another main square, where all the buses stop) and signs directing you to the **Medici Fortress** high up at the top of Cortona. Because the path is lined with a series of statues and mosaics by local artist Gino Severini that imitate the Via Dolorosa, this (difficult!) hike is known as the Via Crucis. The path leads you to the most important church in Cortona, **Santa Margherita Church** (where the town's patron saint, Santa Margherita, remains preserved in a glass coffin, some 800 years after her death) and from there up to the Medici Fortress, known as Fortezza del Giorfalco (there isn't much to see in the fortress itself). It is a very steep and long walk; it will be quite difficult for young children and impossible to navigate with strollers. If you do decide to hike up, you'll be rewarded with an impressive view of the area. (Don't forget to take some water!)

🕐 Opening times for Medici Fortress: May-September, 09:00-13:00, 15:00-18:00; during the summer, it usually hosts cultural events; closed October-April.

---

**Tip:** Another possibility is driving up to the Santa Margherita Church and hiking from there to the fortress, provided you can find parking near the church.

# Why Not Design Your Own Clay Plate?

The dominant colour used by Cortona's ceramic artists is yellow, because this is the colour of Santa Margherita, the town's saint protector ("Margherita" means daisy). If you want to have a go at painting and imitating the local artists, why not book a ceramics class for the entire family? **L'antico Cocciaio**, a family-run ceramics shop, has been producing lovely items by hand for more than four generations and offers half-day workshops for creative kids and adults. You can make your plate or mug for a reasonable fee, but remember that whatever you make has to be baked.

Your items won't be ready for at least 5-7 days, so either pass by again to pick them up or have them sent to your current location (shipping fees apply). Via Bendetti 24, Tel: 0575.605294, www.lanticococciaio.com Book in advance.

At this point, you can either walk up and around town to discover other churches, monasteries and attractions in Cortona—the San Domenico Church, the Public Gardens (Giardini Parterre), or even Frances Mayes's house, which can be seen from the outside—or you can head out of town to visit an ancient Franciscan hermitage just a few minutes away. Unless you have a full day to spend in Cortona, we recommend limiting your visit to its lower parts, the museums, and Via Nazionale, and skipping the churches in its higher parts. As quaint as they may be, they hardly compare to the Franciscan Hermitage, or Monte Oliveto Maggiore.

If you've arrived in Cortona by car, reaching the Hermitage is easy: Simply follow the signs leading to a narrow, winding road immediately outside of Cortona (the drive down the narrow path takes about 10 minutes). The **Le Celle Hermitage** is a unique opportunity to see how monks lived more than 700 years ago, as the monastery hasn't been changed at all. Not only does it maintain all of its original features, it's still inhabited by monks. The Hermitage was founded by Saint Francis during his visit to the city in 1211 and was built inside little holes on

the side of the mountain. Today, you can visit Saint Francis's cell and see a little waterfall in front of the convent.

Like many other towns in Tuscany, Cortona has a rich Etruscan heritage. If you haven't visited (or don't plan to visit) other Etruscan graves, especially the ones in Chiusi, near Montepulciano (see the Montepulciano and Chiusi Itinerary), then you might like to visit Cortona's best-known Etruscan monument, the Sodo Tomb, which was made famous by an impressive marble staircase leading to it that was accidentally discovered by archaeologists. Much like the Hermitage, the way to the Sodo Tomb and other Etruscan tombs in the area is clearly marked with road signs around Cortona. A visit to the Sodo Tomb is included in the price of admission to the Etruscan Museum.

# Lake Trasimeno

Technically speaking, Lake Trasimeno is in Umbria, not Tuscany, but from a practical point of view, it's just 25-30 minutes away. Don't expect anything like what you'll find in the lake district of northern Italy (Lake Como or Garda). Lake Trasimeno is a far cry from those attractions, but it is still a great place for kids to run around and play. There are playgrounds, ice cream stalls, and a general relaxed atmosphere to keep the young ones happy. There is also a boat that connects the shore with a little island at the centre of the lake as well as with towns on the other side of the lake. If you are looking for a beach, Lido La Merangola-Lido Arezzo (Via Lungolago 49, just 300 metres from Castiglione del Lago´s historical center) offers a playground, ice cream booth and kiosk, and plenty of space to run around. Other recommended options are Zocco Beach (via Ghandi 37, S. Feliciano, Magione) and Sualzo Beach (right outside Passiganon sul Trasimeno). Alternatively, there is a small acquatic park called Aquapark di Tavernelle. This option is suitable for younger children, teenagers will probably find it too simple. The park is technically located in Umbria, not Tuscany, but from a practical point of view, it's just a short drive from Cortona. Via Pievaiola km.25, Tavernelle (PG). Tel: 075.832056. Open daily (in high season only), 09.30–19.00.

To get to the lake from Cortona, take the SR71 road heading south toward Perugia. Exit at Passignano Ovest and then take the Strada Statale Trasimeno towards the lake (less than 1 km). To find out more about the lake, visit its website: www.lagotrasimeno.net

# KIDS'CORNER

The word "monk" comes from ancient Greek and it means "being alone, solitary". Joining a monastery was very common in medieval times (either by choice or because people didn't have any other options).

Did you know? The first monastery—of the Benedictine Order—was founded in 520 AD and named after its founder, Benedictus. The three vows taken by the monks were poverty, chastity, and obedience.

What did a monk's life look like? Being a monk or nun wasn't easy. They lived by harsh rules—giving up things like love, having a family, and owning possessions—and lead a very religious life. This was especially difficult for women that were sent to a monastery against their will because their family couldn't afford to pay a dowry, which is a sum of money a woman had to bring with her to give to her husband and his family when she got married. If she had no money, becoming a nun was the only option. This happened to a number of women, including Galileo Galilei's daughter.

Life in a convent was simple (and could be boring). Some people dedicated their lives to taking care of the ill and worked in hospitals,

# KIDS'CORNER

while others grew incredible botanical gardens based mostly on medicinal plants. In fact, some convents still sell medicinal liquors, such as the Monks' Pharmacy in San Miniato a Monte in Florence or Camaldoli near Arezzo.

## Detective's Mission

You must have noticed that the clock on the tower in Cortona's main piazza doesn't have regular numbers on it. Instead it has what we call Roman numerals. These were numbers invented by the Romans and used in Europe for 1300 years until they were replaced by the numbers we use today. But in just about every corner in Italy, you can still find Roman numerals. As our chief detective, we have a bit of a challenge for you: Can you solve these Roman equations?

| Hint: | 1 = I | 2 = II | 3 = III | 4 = IV |
|---|---|---|---|---|
| | 5 = V | 6 = VI | 7 = VII | 8 = VIII |
| | 9 = IX | 10 = X | 20 = XX | 50 = L |
| | 60 = LX | 70 = LXX | 80 = LXXX | 90 = XC |
| | 100 = C | 500 = D | 1000 = M | |

Roman numerals are read from left to right, and if a smaller number is written before a larger number, it means you have to subtract it. For example: V is 5. I is 1. IV is 5 minus 1, or 4. Another example: C is 100. X is 10. So, XC is 90. Another example: L is 50. X is 10. So XL is 40. What if you want to write the number 44? No problem! First make 40 (L is 50, X is 10, so XL is 50-10=40) and then add 4 (IV) to make 44 (XLIV). To write 82, make 80 (50 +10+10+10= LXXX) and add 2 (II) to make 82 (LXXXII). To write 65, make 60 (50+10 = LX) and add 5 (V) to get 65 (LXV).

# KIDS'CORNER

### Easy:

Can you solve this exercise: M + III + VIII = ?

How about this one: X + XI + VII + C = ?

### Medium:

Can you solve this exercise: XD + VIII + LXX = ?

How about this one: CXXI + DIV − IX = ?

### Hard:

Can you solve this exercise: XCIX + IVC + MMVII − XD = ?

How about this one: (MDIII + CVII − III) * XLVII = ?

# Eating in Cortona and Monte Oliveto Maggiore

## CORTONA

There are a number of delicious dining options in Cortona. For a quick lunch on the go, try one of the shops that sells pizza by the slice around Piazza della Repubblica. You can also buy sandwiches (made on the spot) at the Despar Supermarket in Piazza della Repubblica, where you will find a number of cheeses and sausages on display. Kids tend to prefer the milder and sweeter taste of mortadella (a large, pink ham sausage) and prosciutto cotto (dry-cured, cooked ham), while the mozzarella and fontina cheeses are the most popular.

If you are looking for a classy restaurant, try **Osteria del Teatro**. The décor is odd, but the food is very good, especially the desserts. If you happen to pass by during truffle season, the rich, thick odour will convince you to order a steamy plate of pasta with white truffles before anything else. Open daily, 12:00-15:00, 19:00-22:00; closed on Wednesdays. Via Maffei 2, two minutes from Piazza Signorelli. Tel: 0575.630556

**Trattoria la Grotto** is another excellent (and more easy-going) option that serves traditional Tuscan dishes in a comfortable setting. Open daily, 12:00-14:30, 19:00-22:00; closed on Tuesdays. Piazza Balbelli 3, Tel: 0575.630271

## MONTE OLIVETO MAGGIORE

Only a couple of km from the Abbey you will find **Osteria il Pozzo di Chiusure.** The food here is tasty and authentic, and the location is charming. Come here to enjoy a pleasant al fresco lunch. Booking a table in advance is recommended. Piazza del Pozzo 5, Loc. Chiusure, Asciano. Tel: 0577.707148, www.ilpozzodichiusure.com. Open Wednesday-Monday, noon - 22:30. Tuesday closed. Opening hours may vary off-season.

Another tasty option can be found in the small town of Buonconvento, just 9 km from the Abbey. In addition to the local coffee houses and bar, where you can get a quick sandwich, you will find **Osteria la via di mezzo**, along the main road, offering tasty traditional and local dishes, in an elegant but not intimidating setting. Closed on Mondays, Via Soccini 53, Buonconvento. Tel: 0577.806320, www.osterialaviadimezzo.com

# Sleeping in Cortona and the Area

There are a number of good hotels in Cortona, but we recommend finding an agriturismo in the countryside. Daily walks up and down Cortona's steep alleys can be too much, and most hotels don't have pools or playgrounds.

**La Mucchia Casa Vacanza** offers a comfortable and inviting atmosphere, a large pool, lots of space for playtime, and a playground for kids. Loc. Mucchia 26, Cortona, Tel: 0575.604805 (They don't have their own website.)

**Agrisalotto** offers a charming space for a fun farm holiday, including a pool and reasonably priced apartments. S. Caterina di Cortona, Loc. Burcinella 88, Tel: 0575.617417, www.agrisalotto.it

**Margherita Holiday Home** offers a simple but inviting space surrounded by nature and overlooking beautiful views (as well as a few farm animals to liven up the atmosphere). It also has a medium-sized pool and reasonably priced rooms. N.A. Cegliolo 25, Tel: 0575.612648, www.margheritaholidayhome.com

**La Pievuccia** is an elegant choice and offers its guests visits to a vineyard, cooking classes, a pool, and a view. Located in the countryside between Cortona and Castiglione Fiorentino (an area surrounded by vineyards). Loc. S.Lucia 118, Castiglion Fiorentino, Tel: 329.6143882, 0575.1948450, www.lapievuccia.it

**Villa di Piazzano** is an excellent (though slightly pricey) option located minutes from Cortona. It features a pool with a view, impeccable gardens and services, and cooking classes. Loc. Piazzano 7, Cortona, Tel: 075.826226, www.villadipiazzano.com

# Special Events in Cortona

The **Archidado Joust** is the best-known event in Cortona. It dates back to 1397; both kids and adults will enjoy the decorated streets, men and women dressed in medieval clothing, and—of course—medieval "warriors" marching up and down the streets, flaunting their weapons and crossbows. The height of the feast is when two crossbow shooters from each of Cortona's five quarters compete in shooting an arrow at a target. This occurs the first Sunday of June at the Cortona centre. The Giostra dell'Archidado takes place in June. Find out more here: www.giostraarchidado.com.

The **Tuscan Sun Festival** is a popular local festival with a myriad of concerts (often by world-renowned artists), dances, and theatrical events all over Cortona during July and August. Some of these are suitable for children. Check the festival's website to see if any of the events might be suitable for your family: www.tuscansunfestival.com.

# Special Activities in Cortona and the Area

## ADVENTURE PARKS
If the kids are getting bouncy, half a day in an adventure park may be just the solution. **Saltalbero Adventure Park** in Rapolano Terme offers just about everything your adrenaline-filled offspring will need: a playground, rope bridges, endless things to climb on, and even horseback riding lessons (which you'll need to book in advance). The park is open year-round (but may close due to bad weather).

Opening times: Saturdays and Sundays, 10:00-sunset. From June-mid-September, open daily, 10:00-19:00. The park is located about 45 minutes from Cortona, near Asciano. Saltalbero Parco Avventura, Loc. Fontemaggio 25, Rapolano Terme, Tel: 0577.725307, www.saltalbero.it

## HORSEBACK RIDING
**Italia Trail** offers horseback riding lessons and treks in the Cortona area. Though younger children can't ride, they can pay a reduced fee and lead horses on foot. Call first to make sure this activity is right for you and to book in advance. Treks can be combined with wine tastings or other activities.
www.italiatrail.com

# Arezzo, Poppi, and Camaldoli

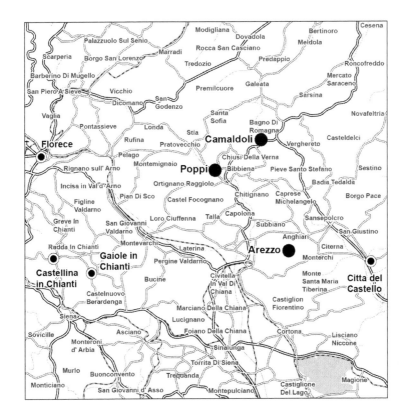

## HOW LONG WILL IT TAKE TO GET THERE?

Florence to Arezzo: one hour
Arezzo to Poppi: 45 minutes
Arezzo to Camaldoli Forest: one hour
Poppi to Camaldoli Forest: 25 minutes
Arezzo to Greve in Chianti: just over an hour

# Chapter 9

# **Arezzo, Poppi, and Camaldoli**

After spending time in Florence and the Tuscan hill towns, many travellers need a break from the crowds. The following itinerary focuses on an often overlooked town, Arezzo, and combines it with a visit to the Poppi Castle and the Camaldoli Forest (perfect for families who love to hike or even just walk around, enjoying the surroundings).

Art lovers won't want to miss Arezzo, where they'll find a world-famous cycle of frescoes painted by Piero della Francesca. The Medici Castle ruins and the medieval Central Piazza, which really come to life during the jousting festival known as "Giostra del Saracino" (see our "Special Events in the Area" section at the end of this itinerary), are also favourite destinations.

However, Arezzo might not be the ideal destination for families with younger children. The town is very steep, and walking may be difficult if you're carrying strollers or toddlers. Those simply looking for a bit of nature and a relaxed atmosphere can skip Arezzo altogether and head directly to Poppi Castle and Camaldoli Forest, possibly combining their visit with an outside activity (there are several to choose from; check out the "Special Activities in the Area" section at the end of this itinerary). Since Arezzo is close to Cortona, this itinerary can easily be combined with a visit there (see the Monte Oliveto Maggiore, Cortona, and Lake Trasimeno Itinerary).

## Top 5 Family Activities

1. See the Giostra del Saracino (jousting tournament) in Arezzo.

2. Have some ice cream while sitting in the beautiful Piazza Grande in Arezzo.

3. Be impressed with Piero della Francesca monumental cycle of frescoes in the church of San Francesco in Arezzo.

4. Visit the Poppi Castle, climb all the way to the top, and enjoy the view.

5. Hike in the beautiful and peaceful Camaldoli Forest, among 500-year-old trees.

# Arezzo

## GETTING THERE

**BY CAR:** From Florence, take the A1 autostrada heading south, to Rome; exit at Arezzo and park at the lot in Via Pietri, where you will find free and useful escalators that will bring you up to the top of the town at Piazza del Duomo. Note that there is a limit on how long you can park in this parking lot, so if you plan on staying more than a few hours, you'll have to come back and either put more money in the meter or find another spot.

**BY TRAIN:** Arezzo can be reached by train from Florence (trains leave every half-hour or hour, depending on the time of day) or from Siena (but you'll have to change trains in Sinalunga). Hourly trains connect Cortona (Camucia Station) with Arezzo. To get from the train station to the town centre, take one of the buses heading towards Piazza del Duomo (LF1D, LF9, or LF2—just make sure they are heading in the right direction; ask – *Skuzi, per il chentro storico*?). The problem with relying on the train is that if you want to get from Arezzo to Poppi and then on to Camaldoli, it will be very difficult using only public transportation. If you plan on following this entire itinerary, and not just visiting Arezzo, a car will make doing so much simpler.

**TOURIST OFFICE:** Arezzo's tourist office is surprisingly small and under furnished. If you are just looking for a map, you can skip the office and buy one at the tourist info point inside the shop immediately to your left after you get off the parking lot escalators. Otherwise, the tourist office is located on the first floor of the Palazzo dei Priori, at the top of the town and in front of Arezzo's Duomo. ◕ Opening times: November-March, Monday-Saturday, 10:30-12:30, 14:00-16:00, Sunday, 09:00-13:00; April-October, open daily, 09:00-13:00, 15:00-19:00. Piazza del Duomo 28, Tel: 0575.26850

Arezzo is one of the oldest towns in Tuscany. Like many other places in the region, it started off as an Etruscan settlement, grew during the Middle Ages to become a free city, and was eventually conquered by Florence (in 1384).

# Our Tour of Arezzo begins at the top of the town, at the impressive **Duomo** in Piazza del Duomo. You will find the elegant Gothic cathedral immediately to your right, just a few meters from the top of the parking lot escalators. The cathedral took more than 300 years to complete, and its façade was only relatively recently added (in the 20th century). In front of the cathedral, you will find Palazzo dei Priori, a distinctive medieval building dating back to 1333 that still houses the magistrates' offices and the town council.

From here, follow the signs in the piazza and walk toward the ruins of the **Medici Fortress**, the most kid-friendly attraction in town. You can enjoy a view of the city, play on the grass, and even have a little improvised picnic. Built on an existing fortress that dates back to the 10th century, the Medici family used this strategic point overlooking the whole area to build a defensive structure (which today is in the process of being restored).

Once the kids are done rolling and jumping, return to Piazza del Duomo and walk along Via Ricasoli toward **San Domenico Church**, where art lovers can admire the *Crucifix* by Cimabue, one of the most important Tuscan artists.

**Mission 1:** The San Domenico Church has a unique bell tower. Can you figure out what's special about it?

From San Domenico Church, continue walking down and turn left, following the signs to reach the **home of Arezzo native Giorgio Vasari**, a noted Renaissance architect, painter, and writer. Though it is not a huge monument, it's quite interesting for art and history lovers, and gives the visitor the opportunity to peek inside the home of a real Renaissance artist and imagine what his daily life looked like. Vasari only spent a few years in Arezzo (with his wife, Niccolosa Bacci, whom he married when she was only 14!), before being called to work in Rome and then Florence. While living in the town (from 1542–1548), he decorated his house in typical Renaissance fashion with the help of his students. A tiny garden outside the house is great for resting tired feet before continuing to your next destination.

🕐 Opening times: Monday-Saturday, 08:30-19:30; Sundays, 08:30-13:30; closed on Tuesdays. Via XX Settembre 55, Tel: 0575.409040

From here, turn to Via Cavour to reach Arezzo's best-known attraction, the **famous cycle of frescoes** carried out by Piero della Francesca in the **San Francesco Church**, known as *La Leggenda della Vera Croce* or The Story of the True Cross.

> **Tip:** Visits to the church have to be booked in advance, as there is a maximum number of visitors allowed in at any given moment. If you are travelling off season, you could probably book a tour on the spot or for later in the day (after lunch, perhaps), but if you are visiting during the summer months, it's best to call ahead and book in advance.

This unique fresco cycle was originally planned to be completed by Bicci di Lorenzo in 1447, but after his untimely death the project was entrusted to Piero della Francesca. The cycle is inspired by Jacopo da Varagine's *Legenda Aurea* (Golden Legend), the most popular religious text—after the Bible, of course—of the Middle Ages. The story of the cross, which fills the entire wall (use binoculars to get a better view; the story is painted from right to left) starts with

Adam's death, the first in human history. On Adam's tomb grows the tree of Good and Evil (look at the top square of the right wall). The tree is forgotten until one day the Queen of Sheba, who was going to visit King Solomon, walks on a wooden bridge and has a vision: The wood for the bridge came from the tree of Good and Evil, and with this wood, Jesus will be crucified. The queen tells King Solomon of her vision, and he decides to bury the wood to prevent it from coming true.

In the lower register, we find two symmetric supernatural events, both announcing Christ as Saviour —the Annunciation and the Vision of Constantine (the first realistic nocturnal scene in Italian art). After the vision, Constantine converts to Christianity. His mother, Helen, already a Christian, goes on a pilgrimage and finds the cross, proven to be the True Cross thanks to a miracle. On that very spot, Constantine decides to build the Church of the Holy Sepulchre. Notice in the background the city of Jerusalem, painted as if it were Arezzo (you can even spot the church of San Francesco itself —remember that most medieval art was used for educational purposes, teaching the masses about religion and morals; accuracy and anachronisms were far less important ...)

**Mission 2:** what do you think of Piero della Francesca's style? Do you like it better than other frescoes you've seen, or less?

The last episode of the cycle describes the war between Heraclius and Chosroes. Heraclius defeats the Persian King who has stolen the Cross; however, he does not make a triumphant entry into Jerusalem. Instead, he carries the Cross with humility, barefoot and following Jesus' example.

The Cross is the main character of this story, and even in the scenes where no cross is needed, Piero della Francesca emphasizes cross-like vertical elements (look at the Battle of Heraclius and Chosroes, for example, or at the Vision of Constantine). Upon completion, the frescoes were immediately considered revolutionary because of Piero's use of proportion in the Greco-Roman sense: classical, realist lines, emphasizing geometry and colour. They have been defined as much more than a simple work of art but as a theological declaration and request in a time of turbulence in the Church. An impressive crucifix at the altar, attributed to Duccio di Boninsegna, completes the church's unique atmosphere.

🕐 Opening times: Monday-Friday, 09:00-18:30; Saturday, 09:00-17:30; Sunday, 13:00-17:30. During the winter, the church closes at 17:30; during Easter, it closes at 16:00. Book a ticket either by phone or online. EU citizens under 18 enter for free. Piazza San Francesco, Tel: 0575.352727, www.pierodellafrancesca.it

Our next stop is Arezzo's well-known and impressive main square, **Piazza Grande**. The piazza is unusually shaped (like a trapezoid), characterized by a dramatic slope, and houses fairy-tale-like medieval buildings that overlook two of its most famous monuments, The Loggia and Pieve Santa Maria. The impressive 11th century Romanesque Pieve, with its distinctive round walls, has been

documented in a number of works of art, the most famous of which is Roberto Begnini's Oscar-winning film *La Vita e' Bella*. The Pieve can be visited daily. 🕐 Opening times: year round, 08:00-13:00, 15:00-18:30 (opening times may vary during holidays). Tel: 0575.22629

# Poppi Castle

## GETTING THERE

**BY CAR:** To reach Poppi from Arezzo, take the SR71. Once you reach Poppi, follow the signs to the castle.

Just 50 minutes north of Arezzo stands **Poppi Castle**, one of the area's more interesting and well-positioned castles, surrounded by lush, cool forests and rolling hills. Poppi Castle is quite small but well preserved, and it is an excellent stop for families with younger kids, who will enjoy exploring the different rooms (they may be especially impressed with the scary prison cells). The castle, which belonged to the Guidi family, was rebuilt and extended by Arnolfo di Cambio, the same architect who designed the Palazzo Vecchio in Florence. During a quick 20-minute tour, you will have time to visit the prison, courtyard, main hall, and library, which contains more than 25,000 antique books, including many that were transferred there for safe keeping from monasteries in the area (even the one in Camaldoli Forest). After the tour, climb up to the bell tower to enjoy the view!

🕐 Opening times: 7 January-15 March, 2 November-24 December, and 26 December-6 January: 10:00-17:00; 16 March-1 November: 10:00-18:00; 1 July-31 August: 10:00-19:00. Children under five enter for free; children under 12 eligible for a reduced ticket. Piazza della Repubbica 1, Poppi, Tel: 0575.520516, www.castellodipoppi.it.

**Tip:** If you are lucky, you will witness a real Falconiere (a man who hunts with the help of falcons, or other birds of prey, as noble men have done for hundreds of years). Gerardo Brami has been following this passion for years, and he spends hours every week flying the birds in the countryside around Poppi. During the summer, Brami often arrives at the castle to practice with his birds in a majestic manner that kids instantly adore (no actual hunting takes place). You can watch his videos and find out more about the precise dates of his performances via his website: www.gherardobrami.it. If you plan on staying in the area, you may even consider booking a private lesson.

> **Tip:** There is a small zoo near Poppi (you will find signs for it everywhere), but we don't recommend it.

# Camaldoli Forest

## GETTING THERE

**BY CAR:** From Arezzo, or from Poppi, take the SR71 up north, toward Bibbiena, and then merge into the SP67 (Camaldoli is about 15 km from Bibbiena).

From Poppi Castle, you can visit a unique **forest** that was considered sacred for many years. It makes an ideal starting point for a family hike. At the heart of the forest, you will find the Hermitage, founded 1000 years ago in 1012 by San Romualdo, to give monks a place of complete silence and calm for reflection and prayer. Stop for a quick visit at the famous **antique pharmacy (Antica Farmacia di Camaldoli)**, which has been run by the local monks for hundreds of years. Here you can buy traditional liquor, natural products, and medicinal remedies, as well as ceramic pieces. The pharmacy and the nearby church are open from 08:00-12:00 and 14:30-18:00. Antica Farmacia di Camaldoli, Camaldoli, Tel: 0575.556143, www.monasterodicamaldoli.it

The best way to discover the beauty of the forest is to walk around in it. Whether it's for an hour, including a light picnic at the forest's entrance, or for a long hike through the majestic forest, it's worth a stop.

> **Tip:** If you are looking for some serious hiking, there are a number of treks from which to choose based on your personal taste and fitness level. Consult the experts at the Centro Visite Badia Prataglia, in Via Nazionale 14 (Tel: 0575.559477 or check out www.badiaprataglia.com; unfortunately, the site is only in Italian). If you don't speak the language, click on "Itinerary Turistici" on the left section of the website's main page; Google Translate can give you a general idea of the hikes available. All itineraries leave from the tiny town of Badia Prataglia.

# KIDS'CORNER

## MORE About... JOUSTing!

Can you imagine what a jousting match was like? If you are lucky enough to see a match while you are in Tuscany (in Arezzo for example), you won't forget it. You can feel the drama in the air, the horses neighing impatiently, and the crowd tensely gathering around, just like they did 600 years ago, waiting for two knights to race down the field with spears, trying to knock the other opponent off of his horse. Jousting tournaments have existed ever since people learned how to fight, but the organized form started around the 12th century, when Richard the Lionhearted decided jousting would be good practice for his soldiers and knights before they left for the Crusades.

People loved watching jousting. It was like the reality show of the time, with glorious knights fighting for honour. The winners had it all—fame, money, and usually the heart of the women they loved, too.

Because the idea was to fight but not to kill each other, the knights used non-lethal weapons. Sharp blades that could cause serious damage were out of the question, for example. Tournaments and jousts were the best shows in town, with rich, important participants, usually from noble families. The knights wore beautifully decorated armour and helmets so the crowd could easily distinguish between them from afar. Sometimes knights chose crazy and freaky decorations that

# KIDS'CORNER

would scare their rivals (one knight went as far as decorating his helmet with whale teeth...). Jousting tournaments start with a warm-up, a fight between the contestants that doesn't use too much force. If it is a tournament between two groups (usually re-enacting famous fights from the past), each group tries to break the formation of the other in order to "take prisoners" and knock their opponents off the field.

## More About... Being a Falconiere!

Today when we are hungry, we can go to the supermarket and buy just about anything we want. But hundreds of years ago, things were different. If you wanted to eat meat, you had to hunt it down. Even when hunting was no longer a necessity, and people could go to local markets, it was still a status symbol. In fact, one of the favourite activities for noble and royal men, and in general the super-rich and powerful, was to go hunting with the help of three animals: a horse to ride on; a dog, who would help catch the prey or bring it to his master; and, if the man were very rich and important, a falcon. Falcons are natural hunters, fierce and quick, and they can be taught by expert trainers, called falconieri (singular: falconiere), to collaborate with man and hunt together. The falconiere was once one of the most respectable members of the King's court. He trained the falcons, took care of them, and taught them everything, waiting for the moment that they would be summoned by the King or the Lord. A good

# KIDS'CORNER

falcon would learn to trust his handlers and to jump as quick as lightning into the air at the sound of a command before attacking the prey and coming back to sit on his falconiere's arm.

## Did you know?

1. Falcons have two main ways to attack prey. They either fly in the sky until they spot a rabbit or another similar animal and then dive down at enormous speed directly onto their poor victim, or they fly very, very quickly and close to the ground (so shallow it's incredible they don't crash), between shrubbery and trees until they spot their  prey. Then they grab it and fly up to the sky.

2. Historically, not everyone was allowed to hunt, especially not with a falcon (which often cost more than a normal family made in a lifetime!). Hunting was a privilege reserved for nobility, and certain animals could only be hunted by the King or the most important men in the land.

3. Falcons don't trust their owners easily and at any given moment could try to fly away. One of the techniques falconieri used to earn a falcon's trust was to be their only source of food.

4. When a falcon eats, he eats everything, and we mean

# KIDS'CORNER

everything! If he catches a pigeon, for example, he will devour the entire bird: legs, head, eyes, feathers, and all. This is a risky moment; the falcon cannot have anything else to eat until he regurgitates the leftovers of his meal (he vomits a yellow-brown slimy ball, with whatever parts he didn't digest) or he could die.

5. To keep the falcons calm, a small leather hat was put on their heads to cover their eyes so they would sleep. This little hat was made of either dog or veal leather, and it was quite difficult to produce. It had to be light enough so that it wouldn't bother the falcon but strong enough so the falcon couldn't tear it (have you ever seen an angry falcon? Trust us, you don't want to, either).

6. The most important part of a falcon's training was the first few months, when he had to learn to accept the falconiere as his master. To do that, the falconiere would spend 24 hours a day with the falcon, seven days a week, for months. Can you imagine taking a bird with you to school, to the bathroom, or to bed? The falconiere and the falcon were literally inseparable; the falconiere would put a very thick leather glove on his arm, where the falcon would sit (if the falconiere didn't protect his arm properly, the falcon's claws could easily rip a piece of his flesh) as the falconiere would go about his day.

7. Falcons were very expensive and sensitive, and they had to be taken care of gently. One of their favourite activities was taking a bath. A large, flat bowl filled with water would be put in a room, and falcons would hop in to wash their wings, screaming with delight.

# Eating in Arezzo, Poppi and Camaldoli

## AREZZO

**Antica Trattoria della Badia** is a personal favourite, serving fresh and delicious local specialties in Via Cavour 70, just a few meters from the San Francesco Church. Try the scrumptious potato gnocchi with truffles and the delicate ravioli. In high season, book in advance. Open daily, 12:00-14:30, 19:00-23:00; closed on Wednesdays. Tel: 0575.356111

**Gastronomia Il Cervo** is another good option, focusing on traditional and local delicacies. Try the gnocchi and the rich antipasti plate. Open daily, 08:00-15:00, 19:00-21:00; closed on Mondays. Via Cavour 38, Tel: 0575.20872

For a quick lunch, kids will love **Crepe de Lune**. They offer tasty, sweet, and savoury crepes to go, ideal if you plan on having a big dinner in a restaurant that evening. Open Monday-Friday, 12:00-14:30, 16:30-20:30; Weekends open 16:30-20:30. Via Madonna del Prato 31, Cell: 338.8957070

If the kids want pizza, then (good) pizza they shall have! **Pizzeria 'o Scugnizzo**, a true Neapolitan pizzeria, also offers more than 200 types of beer for the adults. Open daily for dinner, 19:30-23:00; closed on Tuesdays (sometimes closed on Mondays instead; call in advance). Via de Redi 9, Tel: 0575.333300

## POPPI

**Osteria il Porto** is a simple but tasty family-run restaurant, offering good local dishes like tortelli in a ragu sauce and ribollita. Via Roma 226, Ponte a Poppi (just 8 km from Poppi itself), Tel: 0575.529233, Cell: 339.8960781

Alternatively, opt for a sandwich and ice cream in the central square (Piazza Garibaldi). Try **Gelateria ParadICE**, popular with the locals, in Piazza Garibaldi 5.

## CAMALDOLI FOREST

It doesn't look that impressive, but **Cafe' del Parco** has some of the best sandwiches and cantuccini (biscotti) in the area, hands down. The complex includes a pleasant hotel (called Locanda dei Baroni), a restaurant, and the aforementioned small café. Try anything with truffles, a shot of the local ancient monastery recipe liquors, and the cantuccini, of course. The café is open daily, 08:00-20:00, while the restaurant is open daily, 12:00-15:00 and 18:30-22:00. Via di Camaldoli 7, Tel: 0575.556015, www.alberghicamaldoli.it

> **Tip:** In front of the café, there is a tiny terrace with a little play area for toddlers. The hotel itself offers treks and horseback rides in the area as well.

# Sleeping in Arezzo and Poppi

## AREZZO

**Agriturismo Casette delle Erbe** is a great choice for families, a few kilometers from Bibbiena (near Arezzo), offering comfortable, homey apartments, a pool, two gardens (and a botanical garden), farm tours, and cooking lessons for its guests. Tel: 0575.511177 www.agriturismolacasettadelleerbe.it

**Podere Peciano** is lovely little agriturismo in the countryside between Arezzo and Cortona, offering simple and reasonably priced rooms. Ideal for those who like farm holidays (kids will adore the fact that there are rabbits you can pet, cows that will greet you in the morning, and goats to play with). Az. Agr. Chiovoloni, Via S. Pietro a Cegliolo 86, Cortona, Cell: 347.3099253, Tel: 0575.612917, www.poderepeciano.com

## POPPI

**Poggio a Poppi** is the perfect choice in the area, with large, welcoming, and reasonably priced rooms and apartments, a pool, and several activities for guests (including cooking lessons and hikes). Azienda Agricola Silvia Moneti, Via Magrete 13, Poppi, Tel: 0575.529886, Cell: 339.7772641, www.poggioapoppi.it

# Special Events in the Area

## AREZZO

**La Giostra del Saracino** is the most famous event in town and shouldn't be missed if you are in the area. The festival is based on the antique jousting matches that took place in piazzas during the Renaissance and in medieval Italy and dates back to the 13th century. During the day of the joust, the whole town comes to life with colourful processions and men and women in colourful medieval clothes. This occurs twice a year—on the third or fourth Saturday of June (the precise date changes annually; check the website in advance) and the first Sunday morning of September. Look for it in the Piazza Grande in Arezzo. For more information, visit the website: www.giostradelsaracino.arezzo.it.

> **Tip:** You can still enjoy the Giostra even if you arrive a few days early. The "knights" start practicing at least four days before the actual match around the areas of Porta S. Andrea, Porta del Foro, and Porta Crucifer. The final rehearsal (Thursday before the event in June; Friday before the event in September) tends to draw a crowd.

**Festa Meidevale Bianco Azzura** is another (smaller) local medieval feast. It is fun for kids to see medieval traditions come to life before their eyes. The feast starts at the end of May and runs through the beginning of June (on weekends usually). You'll find the event in Piazzale del Cassero in Castiglione Fiorentino (near Arezzo). For more information, visit the website: www.festamedievale.it.

**The Monthly Antiques Market** happens the first Sunday of every month around Piazza Repubblica and some of the lower streets as well. More than 500 stands fill the town for Tuscany's largest and most popular antique fair.

# Special Activities in the Area

Whether you plan a quick or a long visit to Arezzo, and even if you plan on skipping it all together, you should know that the surrounding area is filled with child (and teenager!) friendly activities that make an excellent diversion from the set tourist path. All of the activities below must be booked in advance.

**Skydive Toscana**, based in Arezzo, offers **skydiving** for everyone, even if you have no previous experience. If you feel like jumping out of a plane from 4500 meters in the air and want an adrenaline rush like no other, this might be for you. Participants must be at least 16 years old and at least 120 cm high. Via Francesco Baracca, Arezzo, Cell: 338.4360722, www.skydivetoscana.com

**Rendola Farmhouse** organizes horseback riding tours in the area (not suitable for children under 12 years old), as well as cooking classes in a 17th-century villa. Via della Fonte 45 Montevarchi (Arezzo), Tel: 055.9707045, www.rendolariding.it

Have all the medieval castles you've seen so far inspired your kids to go back in time and fight like real knights? Well, they can get pretty close; **Agriturismo Le Cregne** offers weekly, daily, and hourly courses in **bow and arrow shooting** (aspiring shooters have to be at least six years old). Cooking classes for kids, as well as horseback riding excursions for the whole family, are also avialble. Once you are done, you can also try their delicious organic produce. Azienda Ricola e Agriturismo Le Ceregne, Loc. Le Ceregne 74, Pieve Santo Stefano (Arezzo), Tel: 0575.791088 or 347.8439063, www.leceregne.it

If you are looking for something to bring a smile to your adventure-starved teenager, try **Cray Quad's Quad Tours**. Their basic, half-day, or whole-day activities will be something to remember. You must be over 18 and have a driving license

and an adventurous soul to get on this ride (children must be at least 12 years old to ride on the back). A three-hour tour will cost about 80 euro (for the driving parent) and 15 euro for the child sitting in the back. A one-hour quad tour will cost about 40 euro for the parent and 10 euro for the passenger. Via Nazionale Valdarno, 84, Loc. San Frustino, Pergine Valdarno (Arezzo), Cell: 335.7810988 (Maurizio), 333.5916457 (Francesco), www.crazyquadtoscana.it

Animal-loving children will enjoy the biological farm in the area. Called **"Friends of the Donkey" (Gli Amici del Asino)**, the farm offers family excursions on their stubborn but sweet and friendly donkeys, just like medieval people travelled through the mountainous areas. You can choose between a number of excursions, depending on the age and interest of the participants. An additional fee may be required to register for the donkey ride. Piazza del Mulino, 2 - 52015 Pratovecchio (Arezzo), Tel: 320.0676766 (Marta), 328.1933784 (Fabio), www.gliamicidellasino.it

# Populonia
# and the
# Etruscan Beach

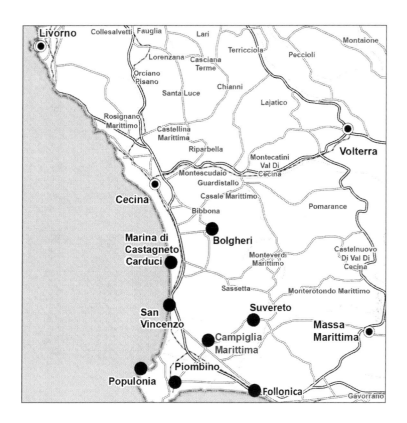

## HOW LONG WILL IT TAKE TO GET THERE?

Florence to Cecina: 1.5 hours
Siena to Cecina: 1.5 hours
Cecina to Bolgheri: 20 minutes
San Vincenzo to Populonia: 30 minutes
Follonica to Massa Marittima: 25 minutes

# Chapter 10

# **Populonia** and the **Etruscan Beach**

Many families skip over the Etruscan Beach, a fun-filled area of Tuscany stretching from Livorno to Follonica, simply because they don't know it exists. But if you're looking to incorporate a few more kid-friendly activities into your vacation—a half day at the beach, a visit to a water park, a tour of an archaeological park or an exciting

trip to the mines (little trains and helmets included)—then this is the area for you.

If you are travelling by car, you can easily reach many of the attractions in this itinerary and even combine them with other itineraries in this guide. The Follonica Water Park, for example, is about 90 minutes away from Siena, Volterra, and Pisa. Since there are several attractions along the Etruscan Beach (given its name by the many settlements built by the Etruscans along its shoreline), we've divided this chapter into two separate full-day itineraries that can be mixed and matched.

**The first itinerary** starts off with an attraction younger kids will love: the ancient mines in San Silvestro Park (near San Vincenzo). It then moves on to either Cavallino Matto Amusement Park or the beach itself and ends with a relaxing evening stroll along the medieval streets of Bolgheri.

**The second itinerary** focuses on the Archaeological Park in Populonia, which can be visited briefly or extensively depending on your level of interest and the activities available on the day of your arrival. This is followed by a short (optional) visit to the Etruscan and Archaeological Museum in Piombino and then off to the Follonica Water Park, where the kids can get some well-earned splash time.

> **Tip:** To best enjoy your days at the Etruscan Beach, make sure to pack the right gear. Hats, sunscreen, and comfortable walking shoes are a must, as are bathing suits, a change of clothes, and a sweater (for the mines). If you plan on visiting the Populonia Archeological Park and hiking along its trails (mostly an easy family hike), call in advance to ask if there are any active workshops being held on the day of your visit. The park sometimes organizes workshops for kids, usually held on Tuesdays, Thursdays, and Fridays during the summer months. Some of the workshops need to be booked in advance.

## ITINERARY 1:
## The Mines of San Silvestro (Temperino), the Cavallino Matto Amusement Park, and Bolgheri

# San Silvestro – Temperino Mines

## GETTING THERE

The best and easiest way to reach the San Silvestro Park Mines is by car. From Pisa, drive south along the SS1 (known as the "Aurelia") and exit at San Vincenzo Sud. Get on the SP20 towards Campiglia Marittima and follow the signs leading to the park.

A family favourite in the area, the Mining Museum is located in the San Silvestro National Park, near the medieval towns of San Vincenzo and Campiglia Marittima. The museum is relatively interesting, with exhibits covering mining tools, minerals, rocks, and excavation findings from the medieval town of San Silvestro, but the real attractions are the mines themselves. Kids (and adults) get to put on a yellow helmet and travel deep into the mines aboard a miners' train. The visit to the Temperino Mine includes explanations about how rocks were extracted from the land and a tour of the area. Unfortunately, tours of the mine can't be booked in advance (though we hope this will change in the near future), so if you arrive and the tour is full, you'll have to wait for the next tour to start or book a spot for a few hours later. Meanwhile, you can tour other smaller attractions in the area, such as Campiglia Marittima. Before booking, make sure a tour in English is available.

🕐 Opening times: July-August, open daily, 09:30-19:30; June and September, open Tuesday-Sunday, 10:00-18:00; February-May, open weekends only, 10:00-18:00. The park is closed from November-mid-January. Opening times may vary throughout the year, so call ahead (or email), or try and book a tour in advance. Children under six enter for free and families visiting both the mines and the Populonia Archeological Park (see later in the itinerary) are eligible for a special family discount. Guided tours of the mines are about an hour long and leave approximately every hour. Find out more about the San Silvestro Park and tours here: www.parchivaldicornia.it. Via San Vincenzo 34, Campiglia Marittima, Tel: 0565.226445, prenotazioni@parchivaldicornia.it

> **Tip:** Yet another fun option for mine-loving kids is the **Museo della Miniera** (the Mine Museum) in Massa Marittima, just 50 minutes from Populonia. Kids will love the 700-meter-long replica of a real mine, complete with gear and machinery, and will be impressed with the details of the miners' hard lives back in the day. Bring a sweater, as it can get chilly inside. Opening times: April-October, open daily, 10:00-12:45, 15:00-17:45; closed on Mondays (off season, the museum closes at 16:30). The museum can be toured with a guide only; tours leave approximately every hour (every half an hour in high season).

# Cavallino Matto Amusement Park

## GETTING THERE

**BY CAR:** The easiest way to reach the park is by car. From Livorno take the SS1, drive south toward Grosseto, and exit at Donoratico. Keep driving towards Marina di Castagneto (1 km).

**BY BUS AND TRAIN:** You can take the train from Pisa or Florence to Donoratico, and from there take a bus to Marina di Castagneto, Cavallino Matto. You will receive a 10% discount on entry if you show your bus/train ticket.

This is one of the largest amusement parks in the area (but don't expect Disneyland; when we say "large", we mean by local standards). It probably won't appeal to children older than 12, but for the younger crowd, it's a great way to pass a few hours on fun rides while still surrounded by nature and just a few minutes away from the beach. Most of the attractions are geared towards children taller than 110 cm, and you can check out the park website to mark your favourite attractions before you arrive. As an added bonus, most of the website is in English, too ...

🕐 Opening times: opening times vary yearly (check the website before leaving), but generally, the park is open daily from 18 May to mid-September, 10:00-18:00 (May-June, closed on Wednesdays). Children shorter than one meter enter for free and those shorter than 130 cm pay a reduced fee. Among the park's attractions are face painting, canoes, carrousels, gliders, a free-fall tower, and more. Via Po 1, Marina di Castagneto–Donoratico, Tel: 0565.745720, www.cavallinomatto.it

# Bolgheri

If you still have some energy left, and you don't want to end your day at the beach, make a stop at the tiny village of **Bolgheri**. The road leading to Bolgheri is one of the prettiest in the area, thanks to more than 2500 Cyprus trees planted along the 5 km lane in the 19th century. The endless vineyards (this area is known for its wine production) surrounding Bolgheri, the olive groves, and the soft, salty sweet breeze from the sea complete the experience nicely. There isn't much to see or do in this borgo, but it is nice to walk around and possibly stop for dinner (for recommendations check the "Eating in the Etruscan Beach" section at the end of this itinerary). The most famous monument in town is the fortress, built by the Gherardescas, a once-powerful medieval noble family who ruled over the entire territory. Today, the fortress is owned by a local agricultural company that offers wine tasting tours on the premises. Book in advance. Tel: 0565.762110, www.castellodibolgheri.eu

## ITINERARY 2:
## Populonia, Piombino, Follonica Water Park, and Suvereto

# Populonia

### GETTING THERE

The Populonia Archeological park is located just over an hour south of Pisa. To reach it, take the SS1 south, towards Piombino, exit at S.Vincenzo Nord, follow the signs toward Piombino, and then the signs to Populonia itself.

The Etruscans were not just landlubbers; they were also seafarers who developed maritime trade routes and went on conquering missions that inspired the ancient world. Many of their towns were built along shorelines, but Populonia was chosen for another reason: its iron-rich soil, which the Etruscans mined extensively. Populonia was one of the most important Etruscan towns in Tuscany, home to more than 18,000 thousand people at the height of its power (about

2600 years ago). The Etruscan necropolis in the area was discovered by accident in 1929, but only after years of research and digging did archaeologists realize the true extent of Etruscan settlement in the area.

A visit to the Populonia Park consists of a self-guided walking tour of the area, with a number of itineraries available, depending on the time you have and your level of fitness (some options are too difficult for younger children). The shortest tour will take about 1-1½ hours. All itineraries are clearly marked on the map provided with your tickets, which you can purchase at the ticket office. If you do tour the park, don't miss the 28-meter-wide Tomb of Carri (near the entrance) and the Iron Road (further into the park).

A second archaeological site, five minutes away by car from the Etruscan Park (follow the road signs) and directly under the ancient town of Populonia, is the Roman Archaeological Park, which also contains the remains of San Quirico's medieval monastery. Most of the objects found during the on-site excavations are now on display in the Piombino Museum or at the Archaeological Museum in Florence (you can thus skip the Populonia Archaeological Museum, which is tiny and has significantly fewer artefacts). Complete your visit with a quick tour of Populonia itself. There isn't much to see (except for a number of shops along the one main street), but at the very entrance there is a small fort you can climb upon to enjoy a view of the sea and the area. (If, at this point, you've seen more forts and castles than you care to count, feel free to skip it. It's fun to climb up, but it's a hardly a "must-do" activity.)

🕐 Opening times: March-May, October, open daily, 10:00-18:00, closed on Mondays; June, September, open daily, 10:00-19:00, closed on Mondays. July-August, open daily, 10:00-19:00; November-January, open weekends and holidays only, 10:00-16:00; closed 9-26 December.

> **Tip:** If you want to find out more about the Etruscans, check out the Kids' Corner in the Montepulciano and Chiusi Itinerary, dedicated to this interesting and ancient culture.

# Piombino

## GETTING THERE

The Archaeological Museum is in Piombino's historical centre, inside the medieval Spanish fortress by the sea and next to the promenade. From Populonia, follow street signs to Piombino, park near the historical centre, and continue on foot.

Though Piombino itself is a modern and not particularly attractive town, its Archaeological Museum is an interesting stop if you have free time on your hands. Built in the 19th century by Napoleon's sister, Elisa Baciocchi, the large museum houses several artefacts found in the excavations in Populonia as well as hundreds of other archaeological findings from the area. A kid-friendly section about Etruscan customs and the reconstruction of an Etruscan banquet are especially nice.

🕘 Opening times: October-February, open weekends and holidays only, 10:00-17:00 (October, closes at 18:00); March-May, open weekends and holidays only, 10:00-18:00; June-September, open daily, 10:00-18:00, closed on Mondays. Piazza della Cittadella, Tel: 0565.226445

# Follonica Water Park

## GETTING THERE

From Pisa, take the SS1 heading south towards Follonica, exit at Follonica Nord, follow the signs to Follonica and Castiglione della Pescaia (for about 4.5 km), and then the signs to the water park itself.

The Follonica Water (or Acqua Park) is extremely popular during the summer months, so prepare for massive crowds. With attractions such as 15-meter-high water slides, pools, and wave pools, everyone will be happy. Children under three enter for free; those under 11 are eligible for discounted admission. Anyone entering after 15:00 is also eligible for a discounted ticket. Via Sanzio, Zona Capannino, Follonica, Tel: 0566.263735, www.acquavillage.it

# Cecina Acqua Park

Another, slightly smaller, water park can be found in Cecina, 40 minutes north of Follonica (30 minutes south of Pisa; just 20 minutes north of the Mine Museum). The Cecina Acqua Park is in Marina di Cecina and offers similar attractions as its bigger brother in Follonica, from slides and chill-out areas to water slides and wave pools. It is probably a better choice for toddlers, who won't be able to use the high slides anyway, and you will be less cramped than in the Follonica Park. Via Tevere 25, Cecina, Tel: 0586.622539, www.acquavillage.it

## Suvereto

If you somehow have some energy left, you can spend a relaxed evening at one of the more charming medieval borghi in this part of Tuscany, Suvereto. Though mostly visited during town events (see "Special Events in the Area"), Suvereto is an inviting little village, surrounded by nature, and is the perfect stop for a family dinner overlooking the view. There is also a small doll Museum that features a collection of rare dolls from the 19th century until present day, which some kids may find interesting.

## **Eating** in the Etruscan Beach

### BOLGHERI
**Osteria Magona** offers tasty treats for those who venture all the way to Bolgheri. Open Sunday 12:30-14:00, 19:30-22:00; Tuesday-Saturday, open for dinner only, 19:30-22:00; closed on Mondays. Piazza Ugo 2, Tel: 0565.762173

### SAN VINCENZO
**La Barcaccina Restaurant** is located right on the beach, where you can enjoy a pleasant breeze and admire the sunset. The menu offers a number of kid-friendly options, as well. Advance reservations are advised during the

summer months, when the restaurant tends to fill up very quickly. Open daily, April-October, 12:30-14:30, 19:30-22:30. May be closed on Tuesdays. September-October and April-May closed on Wednesdays. October-April, closed. Via Tridentina 1, Tel: 0565.701911, www.barcaccina.com

## POPULONIA

Choices are limited in tiny Populonia, but if you do get hungry after touring the sites, try **La Taverna Di Populonia**, which offers rather simple pasta dishes and salads as well as outdoor seating. Open daily, Via San Giovanni, Tel: 0565.29541

# Sleeping in the Etruscan Beach

Finding a family-friendly apartment, B&B, or agriturismo in this area is very easy, since this is where all the locals go for their vacation—right to the beach.

> **Tip:** You can find several other options for resorts and tourist villages that cater specifically to families in this area (as well as further south, towards the Maremma, or up north, towards Pisa and Livorno) at the following websites: www.villaggituristicitoscana.com; www.villaggituristicitoscana.it; www.villaggitoscana.com

**Gli Etruschi Agriturismo** is 2.5 km from the beach, near Populonia, and offers family rooms, horseback rides for kids, a soccer field, a ping pong table, and a pool. Loc. Rinsacca 11, Piombino, Tel: 0565.276124, www.glietruschi.it

**Residence Villa Piani** offers furnished apartments by the sea as well as motorboat rentals, perfect if you want to head off to sea and explore the area. Renting a boat for a half-day costs about 80 euro. Corso Italia 44, San Vincenzo, Tel: 0565.705417, www.residencevillapiani.it

**Agriturismo Il Pelago** is a nice option for families, offering a pool, riding lessons, a playground for kids, and easy access to the highway (which is close). Loc. Bandita n. 345, Marina di Castagneto Carducci, Tel: 346.8511221, www.ilpelago.it

**Poggio all'Agnello Country & Beach and Residential Resort** is another great choice for families. As a resort village, they have several activities for children (which means you don't have to organize everything yourself), including everything from pony rides, art classes, and tennis courts to a playground, a pool, and rental bikes. You'll find it all, as well as simple, comfortable, and spacious family apartments close to the beach. Loc. Poggio all'Agnello 31, Piombino, Tel: 0565.297300, www.poggioallagnello.it

# Special Events in the Area

Forty minutes away from the beach lies the town of **Massa Marittima**, a pleasant destination on its own but especially popular when the **Balestro del Girofalco**, one of the greatest medieval feasts in Tuscany, is being celebrated. Watch the medieval processions, the colourful flags, and the wonderful decorations. Don't miss the arrow-shooting contest held between the ancient quarters of the town; the arrows are shot from a huge wooden instrument. This feast is far less crowded than other, more famous events, like the Palio in Siena (which is all but impossible to watch). The Balestro del Girofalco is celebrated twice a year, on the fourth Sunday of May and the second Sunday of August. You'll find it in the piazza in front of the Duomo. Find out more here: www. massamarittima.info/folklore/balestro.htm

**Le Serate Medievali** is yet another medieval feast, not as grand as the one in Massa Marittima but still enjoyable if you are in the area. The event consists of a series of smaller events, such as medieval processions, singing and dancing, and food stalls. You'll find this feast in the Suvereto historical centre throughout July. www.suvereto.net

# Special Activities in the Area

## AQUARIUM

A mining museum isn't the only attraction Massa Marittima has to offer. Younger kids will enjoy **Aquarium Mondo Marino**, a small but inviting aquarium that offers bi-weekly shark feedings (Usually Wednesday and Friday, 16:00) along with 30 tanks featuring 150 species of local fish (though the Livorno Acquarium, described in Chapter 2, is much larger and more varied, making it a better choice for families). ☻ Opening times: July-August, open daily, 10:00-20:00; June and September, open daily, 10:30-12:30,14:00-19:00; October-May, 10:30-12:30, 14:00-19:00, closed on Mondays. Via della Cava Valpaiana, Massa Marittima, Tel: 0566.919529, www.aquariummondomarino.com

## WATER SPORTS

If two water parks and a beach aren't enough, visit the **Tutun Club Surf and Sale** in San Vincenzo. They offer sailing and surfing lessons for children (starting at age six), banana rides, and canoe and pedal boat rentals. There is also a small quad track race for children three and up. Via Principessa 120, San Vincenzo, Tel. 0565.719537, Cell. 338.5430159, www.tutunclub.it

## HORSEBACK RIDING AND QUADS

**The Agriturismo Gli Etruschi** offers some pleasant horseback rides passing through vineyards in the tranquil setting of the Etruscan Beach (for teenagers and adults), or rides with an instructor inside the agiturismo (for children) Località Rinsacca 11, Piombino, Tel: 0565.276124, www.glietruschi.it

**Escursioni Quad Cecina** offers exciting quad road trips that will get the kids (especially teenagers) whipped up into a frenzy, allowing them to drive on the beautiful natural paths of the Etruscan Beach area. Regular quads can only be driven by adults with a license (kids can sit in the back), but mini-quads are available for children six and up (in addition to pony rides and organized treks). Via del Commercio, Localita' Poderino, Castellina Marittima, www.escursioniquadcecina.it (site in Italian only)

**Agriturismo San Marco** offers horse and pony rides for children ages 6–12. Tel: 0586.799380, www.agriturismosanmarco.it

There are several beaches in this area (the most popular are in San Vincenzo, Vada, and Baratti, right next to Populonia). But some of these beaches are filled with rocks instead of sand, and won't be suitable for children. If you are looking for a more "organized" experience, a place where you can rent beach chairs and find endless caffés and activities, head north to Viareggio, Lido di Camaiore, Forte dei Marmi and Pietrasanta (all four are small and hugely popular beach towns, located under 20 minutes from Pisa), where you will find several excellent options for the whole family.

# MONTEPULCIANO
## AND CHIUSI

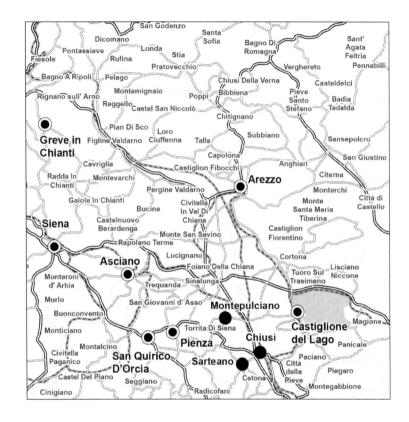

## HOW LONG WILL IT TAKE TO GET THERE?

Arezzo to Montepulciano: 45 minutes
Florence to Montepulcinao: 1.2 hours
Siena to Montepulciano: one hour
Montepulcinao to Chiusi: 30 minutes
Montepulcinao to Pienza: 20 minutes

Chapter 11

# Montepulciano and Chiusi

Montepulciano is a favourite Tuscan hill town for many travellers, mostly because of the excellent wines produced in the area (namely the Vino Nobile di Montepulciano and the Rosso di Montepulciano). Though it isn't an ideal destination for families (there aren't many child-friendly attractions in town and the walk up to the main piazza can be long and tiring), it is a charming little place, and if you have a few hours, it makes for a pleasant afternoon visit. Even if you don't spend your time hopping from one enoteca (wine shop) to the other, as many tourists do, you can still try one place (see our recommendations below), tour the main piazza (one of the prettiest in Tuscany), taste the famous local cuisine (perfect for meat lovers), and enjoy the view.

If you are visiting Tuscany toward the end of August, a stop in Montepulciano is a must to see one of the festivities that bring the town to life (see "Special Events in the Area" below). Ideally, combine a visit to Montepulciano with a fun-filled morning in Chiusi. Though it is often skipped, Chiusi is actually a perfect destination for families and offers underground historical tours and visits to Etruscan tombs.

Note that most of the attractions in Chiusi can be visited with a guided tour only (there are several every day; see details in the itinerary below).

The combination of the relaxed atmosphere and the good food in Montepulciano and the historical adventures that await you in Chiusi makes for a great day. If you still have some extra time, you could also Sarteano. Located just a few minutes from Chiusi, it houses some beautifully decorated Etruscan tombs.

## Top 5 Family Activities

1. Tour the mysterious and artefact-rich underground museum in Chiusi.

2. Explore the fun Porsenna Labyrinth in Chiusi.

3. Visit the colourful Etruscan tombs in Chiusi and Sarteano.

4. Walk around the elegant Piazza Grande in Montepulciano.

5. Taste the famous local Nobile di Montepulciano wine in one of the enotecas in Montepulciano.

# Montepulciano

## GETTING THERE

**BY CAR:** The easiest way to reach Montepulciano is by car. From Florence or Arezzo, take the A1, drive south towards Rome, exit at Valdichiana, follow the signs to Bettolle, then Torrita di Siena (SS327), and then the signs to Montepulciano (drive along SP135). There are a number of parking lots outside the historical centre of Montepulciano (which is, of course, ZTL). The closest one to the entrance is number 1 (near the tourist office), but it is almost always full. Your best chance of finding a parking spot is in parking lot number 5, situated near the bus station. It is quite far from the town centre, but don't worry, you won't have to walk all the way up the hill in the heat. Instead, use the elevator service connecting the bus station with the town (see explanation below, under "By bus"). On Thursdays, the local market is held in Piazza Nenni (near parking lot number 5 and the bus station), so the area might be a little congested.

> **Tip:** The walk up the main road (nicknamed the Corso), from the main entrance to town to the main piazza (Piazza Grande) can take nearly half an hour. Though pleasant, it will be hard on younger children (and on parents pushing strollers). If walking is an issue, use the little orange bus that goes from an (invisible) bus stop 50 metres before the town's gate up to Piazza Grande. This same bus will also take you from Piazza Grande to the San Biagio Temple (see later in the itinerary). Note that the bus is so small that it isn't suitable for strollers unless they are folded.

**BY BUS:** Two daily busses from Florence and eight from Siena (though none on Sunday) will take you to Piazza Nenni (near parking lot number 5). From there, walk toward the orange building and take two elevators (one elevator, a long corridor, then a second elevator) until you reach the Poggiofanti Gardens, which are just a few metres away from the main entrance to Montepulciano. From there, you can walk up the main Corso or the take the orange shuttle bus suggested earlier.

**TOURIST INFORMATION OFFICE:** There's a useful tourist office a few steps from the main entrance to town. Stand in front of the main entrance and look to your right. You'll see metal stairs that lead to a small parking lot and the tourist office. This is the place to buy a map of Montepulciano, book hotels, and purchase bus tickets (including the ticket for the little orange bus that goes to Piazza Grande). ☉ Opening times: May-September, Monday-Saturday, 09:00-12:30, 15:00-20:00, Sunday, 09:00-12:30; October-April, Monday-Saturday, 09:30-12:30, 15:00-18:00, Sunday, 09:00-12:30. Piazza Don Minzoni 1, Tel: 0578.757341

Montepulciano's origins are Etruscan (legend has it that the town was founded by King Porsenna, the same king who founded Chiusi), but the town only thrived much later. Today, it is admired for its majestic Renaissance buildings and quaint medieval alleys. Montepulciano was a long-time ally of Florence (thanks to its high position overlooking the valley and, more importantly, because it was close to Siena, Florence's nemesis to the south). Soon the trusted ally became a favourite vacation retreat for the Medici family, and Florence's involvement grew even greater during the 15th and 16th centuries, when court-appointed architects were sent to Montepulciano to redesign public buildings and render the town "more suitable" for the Medici taste.

# Our tour of Montepulciano begins at the town gate.

From here, begin your steady climb up, along the Corso, toward Piazza Grande. There are a number of interesting shops along the way; many are pricey but still worth checking out. The **Bottega del Rame**, for example, halfway up the hill, offers a lovely collection of mostly handmade copper utensils. Walking up the main Corso reveals the history of Montepulciano and its leaders; **Palazzo Bucelli**, for example (at number 73), was built to house writer and poet Pietro Bucelli's wide antiques collection and is decorated from the outside with archaeological findings from the area, which are incorporated into the house's walls.

A few metres ahead on your right stands the **Church of Sant'Agostino**, well known for its late Gothic/early Renaissance façade designed by Michelozzo di Bartolomeo (simply known as Michelozzo). Built in 1285 and completely redesigned during the 15th century, the church is simple but elegant. It's worth a quick peek to see the crucifix by Donatello and the painting *Crucifixion* by Lorenzo di Credi, Leonardo da Vinci's colleague (they both studied under the great Verrocchio).

Farther up the street, on your left, you'll see the **Torre della Pucinella Clock Tower**, decorated at the very end with a statue of Pulcinella (the clown from the *Commedia dell'Arte*, Italian comedy). Pulcinella means "little chick" and derives from the traditional long-beaked mask the clown wears during the comedy's performances.

Continue on and you'll reach the tiny, triangular **Piazza delle Erbe**, a traditional medieval town square where the town's three streets meet. In medieval times, this is where merchants would bring bags full of wheat to the local market. In fact, the building in front of you was known as **Loggia del Grano**, the wheat lodge, and served as the city's grain reservoir.

Take the left road (Via Voltaia) and continue walking up towards Piazza Grande. On the way, at number 27, you'll find the oldest and most famous dining establishment in the city, **Cafe Poliziano**, which is a great place to stop for a quick coffee. Keep walking straight ahead (the road changes to Via Poliziano), and at number 5, you'll find the **natal house** of Angelo Ambrogini (a.k.a. Poliziano), an influential Renaissance poet, philosopher, tutor to the Medici family and friend to Lorenzo Magnifico. Though Poliziano was born here in 1454, when he was still a child his father was brutally murdered, and Poliziano was sent away to study in Florence.

Just a few metres from here is Montepulciano's beautiful main piazza: **Piazza Grande**. Right in front of you is the tastefully designed **Palazzo Tarugi**, attributed to the mannerist architect Giacomo Barozzi da Vignola (known simply as Vignola), one of the most important Italian architects of the 16th century. In front of the Palazzo is one of the best-known symbols of Montepulciano, the **Pozzo dei Griffi e dei Leoni Well**. Probably designed by Antonio da Sangallo il Vecchio, the well testifies to the strong connection Montepulcaino once had with Florence. The well they designed (the pozzo) is covered with Medici family allusions (mainly lions, a Medici family symbol).

On your left is the elegant town hall (**Palazzo Comunale**), designed by Michelozzo and based on the designs for the Palazzo Vecchio in Florence. If you have some time you can climb to the top of the town hall and enjoy a great view of the whole area (on a good day you can see all the way to Siena). Open daily (may be closed on weekends off-season), 10:00-12:30, 14:30-18:00.

Last, but not least, is the somewhat sad-looking **Duomo**. It took 38 years to build this cathedral designed by Oppolito Scalza (1592-1630), but when the time came to create the façade—or at least cover the building with elegant looking travertine stone, like other buildings in the piazza—the budget ran out and the Duomo remained bare. You will notice that the **bell tower** does not seem to be designed by the same architect responsible for the church; in fact, the bell tower is the only remaining structure of the former church that was destroyed to build the Duomo. Art lovers won't want to miss Taddeo di Bartolo's impressive, golden *Ttrittico dell'Assunta* that decorates the Duomo's main altar inside (open daily, 08:30-13:00, 15:00-19:00).

> **Tip:** Just two minutes from Piazza Grande (near del Conte restaurant) is a **small park** called Parco Publico della Fortezza. There are very few activities, but there is a small bush maze to run around and shaded areas for relaxation.

## Wine Tasting in Montepulciano

Since Etruscan times wine has been made in the Montepulciano area. During the Middle Ages, the local production was so well recognised that it was exported, and during the Renaissance, Montepulciano wines were considered fit for the Pope. Today, this town is known for the ruby red, profound-tasting **Vino Nobile di Montepulciano DOCG**, made with a combination of Prugnolo Gentile and Canaiolo Nero grapes. The wine remains in the barrels for 24 months (30 months in the barrel and 6 more months in the bottle for the reserve wines) before it can be sold. Its less prestigious but delicious brother is the **Rosso di Montepulciano DOC**, made with the same grapes but following less strict regulations.

Wine tasting is a big part of visiting Montepulciano, but tasting it with kids in tow can be a challenge. They won't be patient, and they certainly can't try it themselves. The solution? Buy the kids something to nibble on while you taste the wines (consider ordering a plate of cheeses, so the kids can participate, too) and—more importantly—choose the right enoteca. Enotecas, or wine shops, can be interesting for kids; the walk down to the medieval cellar, the huge barrels, and the cold, musty air can all be used to your advantage.

Of the many enotecas in Montepulciano, two are particularly suitable for visiting with children. The first enoteca, **Contucci Cantina**, has an okay tasting room and an impressive basement (farther along the lane), where even hard-to-impress children will appreciate the 13th-century décor and huge wine barrels. The Cantina is near Piazza Grande (in Via del Teatro 1). It is open daily, and there is no need to book in advance. Daily hours: 08:30-12:30, 14:30-18:30; weekends, 09:30-12:30, 14:30-18:30. Tel: 0578.757006, www.contucci.it

The second enoteca, geared toward families with children, is **La Citta' Sotteranea**, strategically placed just a minute from the main entrance to Montepulicano (at Via di Gracciano, known simply as the Corso, number 82). Here you will find treasures such as Etruscan tombs, medieval weapons, artefacts, and tools that will delight kids while you taste local delicacies. There is also a garden where you can sit and enjoy food and drinks. Open daily, 09:00-19:30. Tel: 0578.716764, www.fattoriapulcino.it

**Tip:** If you are looking for a more extensive exposure to Montepulciano's wine culture, the local wine producers' organization (known as Strada del Vino) has an office in Piazza Grande where you can book a tour of an area vineyard or a wine-tasting tour. Opening times: Monday-Saturday, 10:00-13:00, 15:00-18:00; Saturday, 10:00-13:00; closed on Sundays. Hours may vary off-season. Tel: 0578.717484. Check out their website at www.stradavinonobile.it. Even if you won't be able to get any tasting done, you can still stop at any shop, pick up a bottle and take it home with you to your apartment or hotel. You can always enjoy it later, after the younger members of your clan fall asleep.

From Piazza Grande, either walk back to the town's entrance or—if you have the time—continue ahead and visit the beautiful **San Biagio Temple.** It can take about 20-30 minutes to get there and the walk down is pleasant for the whole family but climbing back up can be too challenging for adults, let alone children. Instead, consider walking down and taking the bus back up, taking the bus both ways, or walking from Piazza Grande back to your car, driving around Montepulciano, and then driving down to San Biagio (the temple is outside the historical centre and isn't in a ZTL area).

San Biagio, especially enchanting at dusk, is a beautiful example of Renaissance architecture and was designed and built by Antonio da Sangallo the Elder in 1518 for the noble Ricci family. Building the temple outside of Montepulciano wasn't a necessity but a choice made to express a clear separation between the medieval town and this high Renaissance temple.

# Chiusi

Chiusi is often overlooked by travellers who stick to the popular Montepulciano–Pienza–Montalcino route. Though this is a well-known and loved route, families will probably enjoy Chiusi much more. This tranquil little town offers its visitors a number of kid-friendly attractions, including two fun underground walking courses that will take you back 2300 years in time, and a visit to Etruscan tombs. This is also a great place to learn, in a fun way, about the Etruscan civilization, one of the more interesting and mysterious cultures in Italy (researchers are still trying to understand them today). At the end of this itinerary, you will also find a special box about Sarteano. Just 10 minutes (by car) from Chiusi, it is worth visiting to explore its impressive Etruscan tombs if you have the time (and if you are visiting the area on a Saturday).

## GETTING THERE

**BY CAR:** The simplest way to get from Montepulciano to Chiusi is by car. From Montepulciano, take the SS326 and head south.

**BY BUS:** You can take bus number FT4 (or FT2) from Montepulciano to Chiusi. There's a bus approximately every 90 minutes, but schedules change during holidays and on weekends. Make sure you get off at the centro storico of Chiusi, NOT at the station marked Chiusi Scalo.

**BY TRAIN:** There is a large train station in Chiusi Scalo (about 2 km from Chiusi's historical centre). Trains to Chiusi Scalo arrive from Siena (about once every hour). From the train station in Chiusi Scalo, take the bus up to Chiusi itself.

**TOURIST INFORMATION OFFICE:** The small but cordial office is in Piazza Duomo 1. ⊕ Opening times: April-September, open Monday-Saturday, 09:00-13:00, 15:00-18:00, Sunday, 09:00-13:00; October-March, open daily, 09:30-12:30 (hours tend to vary, especially off-season). Tel: 0578.227667

Chiusi's first settlements date back 4000 years, when farmers and shepherds were attracted to the local fertile land and decided to settle in the area. It was later inhabited by the Etruscans and flourished under the rule of King Porsenna, one of the best-known Etruscan kings, who was responsible for besieging Rome during the 6th century B.C. When Rome conquered the whole area, Chiusi (then called by its Latin name, Clusium) didn't fall into decay like so many other Etruscan towns, and thanks to its strategic position, it remained an important post. It was only later, when newer roads were built connecting Rome with Tuscany, that Chiusi became irrelevant. It remained an isolated town until tourists and explorers rediscovered it in the 19th century.

# Our tour of Chiusi begins at the entrance to town.

Once you've parked your car outside the city walls (Chiusi's centre, you've guessed it, is ZTL), walk along Via Porsenna toward the town's main square. Here, in Piazza del Duomo, you will find Chiusi's Cathedral, the Cathedral Museum, and most interestingly, Porsenna's Labyrinth, one of the best family attractions in the area.

> **Tip:** Tickets to the Labyrinth give you access to the Cathedral Museum too, which can be interesting if you have extra time. There are mostly Paleo-Christian artefacts, along with some medieval vestments and illuminated texts.

# Porsenna's Labyrinth

Kids can follow the footsteps of the great Etruscan King Porsenna in this small but adventurous Indiana Jones-style underground path. The Labyrinth is actually a 130-metre-long system of tunnels considered to be one of the most sophisticated water supply systems of ancient times in this area. The entire complex is based on Etruscan knowledge of how to take advantage of characteristics of the local stone to collect valuable rainwater in large cisterns.

Once you reach the central main cistern, look around carefully. A local legend claims that at the centre of the Labyrinth stood the tomb of Porsenna himself, coated in gold, held in a golden chariot carried by 12 golden horses and 5000 chicks made of gold. Perhaps one of the golden horses is still there?

🕙 Opening times: **The Labyrinth can only be visited with a guide** when the Cathedral Museum is open. Your ticket also enables you to climb up to the top of the cathedral's bell tower. During the high season (June to mid-October), tours leave daily at 10:10, 10:50, 11:30, 12:10, 16:10, 16:50, 17:30, and 18:10. During the autumn (mid-October to the first week of January) and spring (April to the end of May), tours leave twice a day at 09:45 and 12:45. During the winter, tours leave on Tuesdays, Thursdays, and Saturdays only at 09:45 and 12:45. Combined tickets for the Cathedral Museum and the Labyrinth are available. Ask whether you qualify for any reductions. Tel: 0578.226490

Once you exit the Labyrinth, you will still be in the Piazza (on the other side, near the Bell Tower). From here, cross the street, turn left onto Via Nardi dei Pietro, left again onto Via Lino Moretti, and right onto Via Santo Stefano, until you reach Via Cimina II and the **Museo Civico—La citta' sotteranea** (the Civic Museum and the underground city).

# La Citta' Sotteranea Musem

This museum is Chiusi's second main attraction for families and our personal favourite. The Civic Museum isn't particularly interesting (you can skim through it in 10 minutes), but the second part of the tour is quite exciting. With your guide (all tours require a guide), you will visit the "underground city", a series of tunnels filled with one of the largest European collections of Etruscan sarcophagi and tombstones. With a life-size model of an Etruscan canoe, typical vases, and the tour guide's explanations, this is a great visit for kids and teenagers alike.

🕐 Opening times: May-October, open Tuesday to Sunday (closed on Mondays); guided tours start at 10:15, 11:30, 12:45, 15:15, 16:30, and 17:45. November-April, open Thursday to Sunday. Thursday and Friday guided tours start at: 10:10, 11:10, and 12:10; Saturday and Sunday guided tours start at: 10:10, 11:10, 12:10, 15:10, 16:10, and 17:10. All tours start at the museum and then move to the underground city. Children under six enter for free; children under 14 pay a reduced fee. Tel: 0578.20915

If want to complete your Etruscan experience in Chiusi with a visit to the local Etruscan museum (especially if you haven't visited one of the bigger Etruscan museums, like those in Volterra or Cortona), stop by the Archaeological Museum (**Museo Archeologico Nazionale**). Small but interesting, the museum has a collection of items from the Etruscan settlements, including burial site models, vases, and mosaics. The museum is located in Via Porsenna 17 and is open daily, 09:00-20:00 (children under 18 from EU countries enter for free). The entrance ticket also includes a visit to two real Etruscan tombs just outside Chiusi. Since a guide will accompany you at the tombs, let the staff know that you are interested in visiting them when you buy the tickets, so you can book a tour. The two most important graves are the Tomb of the Monkey and the Tomb of the Pilgrim. Dating back to the 5th century B.C., **the Tomb of the Monkey (Tomba della Scimia)** was discovered in 1846 and consists of three rooms with coffins and traditional burial beds. There are a number of wall paintings as well, depicting scenes from Etruscan life, such as chariot racing, musicians mourning the dead by carrying the traditional palm leaves, and a small statue of a monkey, which gave the tomb its name.

••••••••••••••••••••••••••••••••••••••••••••••••••••••••••••••••••

**Mission 1:** Describe what paintings decorate the walls of the Monkey Tomb. Bonus: Why do you think these paintings were chosen? What can we learn from them? How do you think they were made?

••••••••••••••••••••••••••••••••••••••••••••••••••••••••••••••••••

**The Tomb of the Pilgrim** was discovered by accident in 1928 and is considered a good example of a family tomb with strong Hellenistic influences. You can still see most of the burial urns preserved inside. The lids of the sarcophagi in the last and main chamber were probably opened several hundred years ago, possibly by grave robbers (who were well aware of the Etruscan tradition of burying the dead with their most prized, and expensive, possessions).

🕐 Opening times: The graves can be visited year-round. March-October: Tuesday, Thursday, and Saturday; tour leaves upon request at 11:00 and at 16:00. November-February: Tuesday, Thursday, and Saturday; tours leave upon request at 11:00 and 14:30.

## Sarteano

If you happen to be visiting the area on a **Saturday**, and you have some extra time, don't miss this Etruscan necropolis (cemetery), one of the most colourful and elaborately decorated in the area. The visit has to be **booked in advance** through the local museum (which is also worth a quick visit if you have the time). During the summer months, tours leave twice daily, at 09:30 and 18:00. During the winter months, there's one daily tour at 11:30. Children under six enter for free; children under 18 pay a reduced fee. The museum is in Via Roma 24, Sarteano. Tel: 0578.269261, email (for booking): museo@comune.sarteano.si.it

If you are visiting the area in mid-August, you might also want to stop by and enjoy the local medieval feast and jousting match, which has been celebrated in town for hundreds of years.

# KIDS'CORNER

## More About... The Etruscans!

(Plus a special guide to the Etruscan alphabet, so you can write secret messages in code...)

Here are some quick interesting facts about the Etruscans (OR: everything you've always wanted to ask an Etruscan but couldn't... since there aren't any who are still alive).

- The Etruscans were the original inhabitants of Tuscany (that's why there are so many Etruscan museums around; they left remains, tombs, and mysterious objects everywhere). In fact, the name Tuscany is based on what the Romans used to call the Etruscans: "Trusci".

- Where did they come from? Researchers are still debating that question, but the answer is probably Asia.

## So what was it like to be an Etruscan?

If you were an Etruscan 2300 years ago, you probably lived in a clan, and your clan was probably organized into some sort of Etruscan local government or you had a king (like Porsenna). That gov-

# KIDS'CORNER

ernment or king had absolute power over your life.

1. Many of your friends and relatives would have been either warriors or seamen. Etruscans were famous as both. They would probably have left town every summer on missions to conquer land and open trade routes, returning with goods they had looted and even slaves (who were sometimes sacrificed to the Gods).

2. You would have lived on a high hill, as the Etruscans loved to build their towns up high for protection and near fertile land and water, so the society could grow and prosper.

3. If you were Etruscan, you would have believed in different Gods: Usil was the God of the Sun, Tivr was the God of the Moon, Turan was the God of Love, Laran was the God of War, Cel was the Goddess of the Earth, and Tin was the God of the Sky.

4. Most of your neighbours probably would have been farmers and shepherds. When there was a problem, you would have consulted the Aruspici, shamans who could predict the future by examining the internal organs of animals or human victims.

5. If you were an Etruscan woman, you would have been far better off than Roman or Greek women. Unlike those societies (which discriminated against women), Etruscan women were almost equal to men in several aspects. One indication of

# KIDS'CORNER

this is that we find the names of both fathers and mothers of the deceased on Etruscan graves.

6. If you were an Etruscan woman, you would have been able to conduct business, go to meetings and sporting events, dance in festivals, participate in religious festivals, read, and write.

7. If you were an Etruscan woman, you would have been known throughout the ancient world for your beauty. In fact, Etruscan women were known to take great pride in their looks, importing make-up and precious expensive oils for perfume.

8. If you were Etruscan, what would you have eaten for dinner? The truth is that not everyone enjoyed the same delicious meals. The poor couldn't afford many of the foods the rich could buy, but let's imagine for a second that you belonged to a well-off family and buying food wasn't a problem. In that case, you would have found the dinner table filled with wheat and vegetable dishes (meat and fish were rare). These were nutritious foods and very tasty. Sometimes Etruscans ate cheeses made with their sheep's milk, served with dried fruit and honey.

9. If you were Etruscan, what would have happened to you after you died? One of the things we know most about the Etruscans is what they did with their dead, because these are the monuments they left everywhere. The Etruscans (like other ancient cultures) put the dead in their necropolis (which literally means "city of the dead"). They would burn the deceased and bury his ashes with souvenirs and artefacts that represented that person's life story (jewellery, arrows, etc.) inside special funerary vases that were placed in the ground. Only later did the Etruscans

# KIDS'CORNER

start burying their dead in graves. The most prestigious members of society were buried in custom-built hills that

were a sort of ground-made pyramid, lavishly decorated with monuments and wall paintings (see, for example, the Etruscan tombs in Chiusi, Cortona, and Sarteano).

10. If you were Etruscan, what would you have believed in? As we said, the Etruscans (like the Greeks and Romans) believed in multiple Gods that represented the nature around them. They built temples for their Gods, and those temples were considered a home for the Gods on Earth. Religious shamans, the Aruspici, who could also read organs and predict the future, protected the temples.

11. If you were an Etruscan, would you have been able to read and write? Yes. The Etruscans developed an alphabet based on the Greek alphabet. They also wrote from right to left (unlike English, which is written from left to right).

## what did their alphabet look like?

### HOW to write secret messages in Etruscan

As you can see in the illustration, the Etruscan alphabet isn't very different from our alphabet. With just a little bit of practice, you can write secret messages in a 2500-year-old language that only you (and your friends, brothers, or sisters who learn the code) can understand.

Before we start writing, we need to know a little more about

# KIDS'CORNER

the Etruscan language. We wish we could provide you with a full dictionary, but the Etruscan language remains a big mystery, and researchers haven't completely cracked it yet, mostly

because they have very little material to rely on. The only remaining Etruscan book, for example, is called the Liber Linteus Zagrabiensis and most of it still hasn't been deciphered. In fact, the book only survived, instead of vanishing like the others, because it was written on fabric, and that fabric was later used to wrap a mummy in Egypt. When archaeologists unwrapped the mummy, they found the Etruscan book, too. A few other, shorter texts survived as well, and they have been partially deciphered. One of the most interesting surviving Etruscan texts is the Piacenza Liver, a life-sized bronze model of a sheep's liver, with names of Etruscan Gods on it. The text was probably used by the Etruscan priests in ceremonies (Etruscans, like many other ancient cultures, believed they could predict the future by reading internal organs).

Though we can't really read and write like the Etruscans did (learning the Etruscan grammar rules would take a very long time), we can still use Etruscan letters according to modern rules and create a smart but easy-to-use code. Just remember a few things: They wrote from right to left, and their words were <u>phonetic</u>, which means you spell words the way you hear them.

Now, using the illustration that shows the Etruscan alphabet, can you write your own secret messages?

**My cat likes playing the guitar.**

Being Etruscan rocks!

_____

Bring in the sheep, the wolves are coming.

_____

My name is XXX; nice to meet you.

_____

### A few REAL words in Etruscan

| | |
|---|---|
| I | Me |
| Un | You |
| An | He / She |
| Laut | Family |
| Pera | House |
| Pava | Boy |
| Talitha | Girl |
| Husiur | Children |
| Thamna | Horse |
| capu | Falcon |
| Usil | Sun |

# Eating in Montepulciano and Chiusi

## MONTEPULCIANO

It's easy to eat well in Montepulciano. There are at least five or six good restaurants, several great enotecas for wine tasting, and a number of cafés for lighter afternoon snacks.

**Osteria Acquacheta:** Steak lovers and hungry omnivores need look no further. This warm and welcoming place is known for its meaty dishes, especially the steak. Just be sure to book well in advance, as the restaurant is very popular, especially during high season. Open daily, 12:30-15:00, 19:30-22:30; closed on Tuesdays. Via del Teatro 2, Montepulciano, Tel: 0578.717086, www.acquacheta.eu

**La Grotta Montepulciano** is another highly regarded local establishment, pricey but delicious. Open daily, 12:30-14:15, 19:30-22:00; closed on Wednesdays. Via San Biagio 15, Montepulciano, Tel: 0578.757479 or 0578.757607, www.lagrottamontepulciano.it

**Osteria del Conte** serves simple but tasty food, with a good selection of Nobile di Montepulciano bottles. Try their "Conte" fixed menu. Open daily, 12:30-14:30, 19:30-21:30; closed on Wednesdays. Via San Donato 19 (a minute away from Piazza Grande), Tel: 0578.756062, www.osteriadelconte.it

**Osteria ai Quattro Venti** is a lovely place to sit down, relax, and enjoy tasty, simple local delicacies. Because it's right on the piazza, kids have room to move around and play almost freely (watch out for the occasional car!). Open daily, 12:30-14:30, 19:30-22:30; closed on Thursdays. Piazza Grande 2, Tel: 0578.717231

## CHIUSI

Whether you are staying in Chiusi for a quick lunch or a nice dinner, there a number of tasty reasonably priced options.

**Zaira** is an excellent choice, where you'll find delicious modernized versions of traditional Tuscan dishes. Try the meat (locally grown) and the antipasti plates. Open daily, 12:00-15:00, 18:00-24:00; closed on Mondays. Via Arunte 12, Chiusi, Tel: 0578.20260

**Ristorante Nonna Rosa** feeds the crowd with tasty rustic dishes, and kids will be impressed with the décor, which includes **antique Italian cars** inside the restaurant itself. Try the antipasti plate—it's rich and tasty. Open daily, 12:30-14:30, 19:30-23:00. Via Tulipani 1 (located in Hotel Rosati), Chiusi, Tel: 0578.274408

# **Sleeping** in Montepulciano and Chiusi

## MONTEPULCIANO

**Agriturismo Casagrande** is a good option for families. This charming place is located three km from Montepulciano itself, and offers seven apartments, a pool, and a large garden. Prices are reasonable, too.
Azienda Agricola Casagrande Via di Martiena 40, Montepulciano. Tel: 0578.756030 / 346.9554356, www.casagrande.siena.it.

**Il Greppo** is another very good choice. This charming property is surrounded by nature and offers guests large traditional apartments, a pool with a view, a playground, and some activities. Via dei Greppi 47,Abbadia di Montepulciano, Tel: 0578.707112, www.ilgreppo.it.

**Sant'antonio Resort** is a great choice for families; it includes comfortable apartments, a pool, and kid-friendly owners (book in advance if you want an apartment with a garden instead of a balcony). Via della Montagna 6, Montepulciano, Tel: 0578.799365, 348.7245126, www.santantonio.it

**Poggio Etrusco** is a lovely little agriturismo, offering not only comfortable and reasonably priced apartments surrounded by nature but also cooking classes for guests. Via del Pelago 11, Loc. Fontecornino, Montepulciano, Tel: 0578.798370, www.poggio-etrusco.com

**Palazzo Bellarmino** offers good value, with comfortable family apartments (but no elevator) near Piazza Grande. Via San Donato 10, Montepulciano, Tel: 0578.757155, www.palazzobellarmino.com

**Agriturismo La Bruciata** is a reasonably priced option, especially suitable for families, and located just 2 km from Montepulciano. It offers comfortable rooms, a huge garden in which to run around, and a pool. There's also a restaurant on the premises. Via del Termine 9, Loc. Poggiano, Montepulciano, Tel: 0578.757704,

Cell: 339.7815106, www.agriturismolabruciata.it

## CHIUSI

Most tourists don't stay to sleep in Chiusi and instead choose more traditional options nearby, but there are a few good options in and around town.

**Al Giardino degli Etruschi,** just a few minutes outside of Chiusi, is a popular choice with many, offering a pool, spacious rooms, welcoming hosts, and lots of room to run around. Loc. Dolcianello 32, Chiusi, 0578.20213, www.algiardinodeglietruschi.it

**Poggio Cantarello** is another good option, especially for those looking for a quiet and relaxing place surrounded by nature. This B&B also organizes walking and riding tours of the area, as well as olive oil and wine tasting activities, and it offers a large garden that will please kids (but there is no pool). Poggio Cantarello 94, Chiusi, 0578.274139, www.casavacanzatoscana.it

# Special Events in the Area

The **Bravio delle Botti** is Montepulciano's main summer event—a somewhat insane contest between the contrada (quarters or neighbourhoods) of the town. They fight over who can roll an 80 kg barrel almost 2 km uphill the fastest. This event, which dates back to 1373, was once celebrated to honour the town's patron, Saint John the Baptist. A medieval court, complete with decorations, music, and flags that kids will love, accompanies the event. This takes place on the last Sunday of August; arrive early to catch a place near Piazza delle Erbe or Piazza Grande or along the Corso. Find out more at www.braviodellebotti.com.

# Special Activities in the Area

There are a number of B&Bs and agriturismi in the area that offer private cooking lessons or horseback tours of the countryside, but if you are looking for extra activities, such as adventure parks, quads etc., there are more options farther down south (see the Maremma Itinerary). One possible attraction in the area (20 minutes away) is the Aquapark di Tavernelle near Trasimeno Lake (also mentioned in Chapter 8). Though this water-park is, technically speaking, in Umbria, not Tuscany, from a practical point of view, it's only 20 minutes away. The park isn't very large, but it is fun, and younger kids will have a great time. Via Pievaiola km.25, Tavernelle (PG). Tel: 075.832056. Open daily, 09.30–19.00 (in high season only). www.azzurrapiscine.it/aquapark-tavernelle.

# VAL D'ORCIA

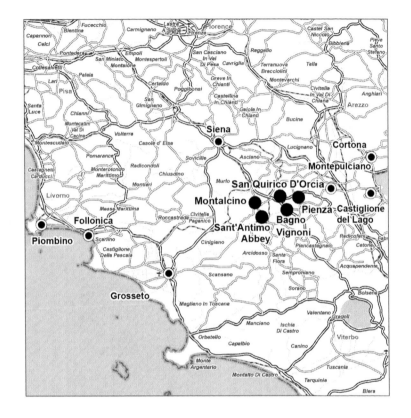

## HOW LONG WILL IT TAKE TO GET THERE?

Montepulciano to Pienza: 20 minutes
Florence to Pienza: 1.5 hours
Greve in Chianti to Pienza: 1.5 hours
Pienza to Montalcino: 25 minutes
Pienza to Sant'Antimo Abbey: 40 minutes
Montalcino to Sant'Antimo: 15 minutes
Pienza to Bagno Vignoni: 25 minutes
Pienza to Bagni San Filippo: 30 minutes

# Chapter 12

# **Val d'Orcia**

When you imagine "the magic of Tuscany", you're probably thinking of a place just like Val d'Orcia: a valley surrounded by majestic rolling hills, whose colour changes almost monthly, dotted with tall Cyprus trees and tiny, quaint little towns. If there is one area in the region that will stun you with its natural beauty, it's this valley, which has been recognized as a World Heritage Site by UNESCO. Numerous writers, poets, and artists have been inspired by the Val d'Orcia, as have many filmmakers. Among the movies filmed in the area are Franco Zeffirelli's *Romeo and Juliet*, Ridley Scott's *Gladiator*, and Anthony Minghella's *The English Patient*.

The best way to explore the Val d'Orcia is to simply take it easy, drive along the most scenic routes, enjoy the view, and stop in some of the towns featured in this chapter. Building an itinerary here can be tricky, though. Despite the fact that the area is beautiful and relaxing, it is likely that many of the attractions, even in popular and much-loved towns such as Pienza and Montalcino, won't really interest children.

## Top 5 Family Activities

1. Climb up the fortress in Montalcino and enjoy the beautiful view.

2. Soak and splash in the thermal spring water in Bagni San Filippo.

3. Run around the Horti Leonini Gardens in San Quirico d'Orcia.

4. Visit Sant'Antimo to hear the Gregorian chants and admire the beautiful abbey.

5. Try some tasty Pecorino cheese in Pienza.

Our personal recommendation is not to skip Val d'Orcia, which really *is* one of the more magical parts of Tuscany, but to simply balance it out constantly. If you dedicate an hour to driving around scenic roads (the area between San Quirico, Pienza, and Montalcino is particularly lovely), then make a stop at **Bagni San Filippo Natural Park** for a splash in the small thermal ponds. If you want to visit **Pienza** and taste some of the local Pecorino cheese, visit the **Sant'Antimo abbey** too, to hear local monks chant Gregorian chants. And if you can't resist a stop in **Montalcino** to taste the world-famous Brunello wine, combine it with a visit to the local fortress and climb all the way up and enjoy the view. If you want to make a stop for lunch,

choose a charming little town that also offers a garden for younger children to run around in, like **San Quirico d'Orcia**.

# Montalcino

## GETTING THERE

**BY CAR:** Montalcino can easily be reached by car. From Pienza or Montepulciano, take the scenic SS146. From Florence, take the Raccordo Autostradale Firenze-Siena and exit at Montalcino. There are a number of parking lots around town; choose the highest one—closest to the fortress—to avoid having to walk up. Note that Montalcino is quite hilly. If you are travelling with toddlers, or pushing strollers, this may not be the place for you. Opt for flat towns, like Pienza, instead.

**TOURIST INFORMATION OFFICE:** Montalcino's small office is useful for obtaining information not only about the town's attractions but generally about the Val d'Orcia. 🕐 Opening times: open daily, year-round, 10:00-13:00, 14:00-17:50; hours tend to vary off season. Via Costa del Municipio 1, Tel: 0577.849331, www.prolocomontalcino.it

Thanks to a growing interest in wine tourism, **Montalcino** has reinvented itself since the 1960s, going from a poor, unappealing town to a popular destination. The town's pride and joy, the delicious (and, by now, world-famous) Brunello wine, has put Montalcino on the map, and the surrounding beautiful views certainly don't hurt. However, this isn't a destination for families, so if you are not particularly interested in wine, you can skip it. Those who do want to taste some of the local ruby red magic can schedule a quick stop, perhaps for lunch (with the excuse that the family has to eat *somewhere,* you could try to sneak in a visit to an enoteca before the kids notice...). Ideally, combine a stop at a local enoteca with a visit to the town's impressive fortress, which kids will like. During the summer months, Montalcino becomes somewhat more family friendly, as it hosts several open-air concerts and theatre shows. Check with the local tourist office to see what concerts are available.

To reach the **fortress** (which is located at the highest point in town) walk along the main streets directing you to the "Rocca"—fortress. Once you've climbed this 14th-century fort up to its ramparts, you will enjoy an impressive view of the valley. If you have time, you can also stop at the popular wine bar at the heart of the fortress, but there are better and cheaper options elsewhere in town—look around if you have the time.

⊘ Opening times, **fortress and wine bar**: open daily, 9:00-20:00; closes at 18:00 from November-March. Rampart walk costs 4 euro (not cheap for such a simple attraction, so if you've seen other panoramic points, you may wish to skip this view).

## Brunello

The Brunello is a relatively new wine (invented in the 19th century), made exclusively from Sangiovese grapes, unlike other local wines that are often made with Canaiolo, Ciliegino, and Colorino grapes, too. Brunello was the first wine to receive the DOC certification (in 1966) and is considered by many, and certainly by the Italians, to be one of the best wines in the world. The production of the wine is subject to very strict norms and controls; a Brunello can't be sold before it has aged for two years in oak barrels and four months in the bottle (or six months, if it's a reserve bottle). The Brunello can be tasted in just about every corner in Montalcino. Simply walk around and enter whichever enoteca seems nicest. A glass typically costs around 5-6 euro.

# Pienza

## GETTING THERE

Pienza can easily be reached by car. From Montalcino or Montepulciano, take the scenic SS146. From Florence, take the A1 autostrada heading south (towards Rome), exit at Valdichiana, and follow signs to Sinalunga, along the SS327, and then to Pienza, along the SS146. Parking in Pienza can be an issue, especially during high season. Your best chance to find a space is in the main parking lot in town, located just off Via Mangiavachi 43 (also known as SP18. Watch for the small parking sign on the left.) outside the town; just make sure you don't park in a space reserved for locals only. Pienza itself is ZTL.

**TOURIST INFORMATION OFFICE:** Pienza's tiny office is open daily, March-November, 09:30-13:00, 15:00-18:30; December-February, open on weekends only, 10:00-13:00, 15:00-18:00. Piazza Dante Alighieri 18, Tel: 0578.748359, www.ufficioturisticodipienza.it

Pienza isn't a "must-see" destination, but it is considered by many to be a little jewel in the valley, thanks to its charming (and easy-to-walk, traffic-free) streets, spectacular views, and unique design, which is due to the Renaissance artistic and architectonic revolution. Once known as Corsignano, Pienza was the home of Enea Silvio (better known as Pope Pio II), who rebuilt his hometown according to Renaissance principles written by Leon Batista Alberti, inventor of the "ideal city". Pio II entrusted the project to one of Alberti's students, Bernardo Rossellino, who managed to transform the town in just five years. When the project was completed, the town was then renamed after the Pope—Pienza. The only problem with visiting the city today is that, during the summer, it can become so crowded with tourists it loses some of its appeal. If you happen to be visiting the area slightly off-season, though, it is absolutely lovely.

Your visit to Pienza will consist mostly of the town's main square, Piazza Pio II, where you will find the Duomo and Palazzo Piccolomini. The palazzo was the summer mansion used by the Pope on his vacations to his hometown and can still be visited today. As often happened, the Pope came from one of the richest and most powerful families in the area. In this case, it was the noble Piccolomini family, the same family that built the Piccolomini Library in the Duomo in Siena.

Guided tours of Palazzo Piccolo-mini will take you through rooms that still feature much of the original décor—some of which is more than 400 years old (though most kids may not find this quite so fascinating...). The gardens in the back, however, are lovely.

🕐 Opening times: mid-March to mid-October, open daily, 10:00-12:00, 14:00-18:00; mid-October to mid-March, open daily, 10:00-13:00, 14:00-16:30. First tour starts at 10:30; last tour at 18:00. The Palazzo can be visited with a guide only. Closed Mondays; closed 14-28 February and 16-30 November. Piazza Pio II, Tel: 0578.748392, www.palazzopiccolominipienza.it

The Duomo, with its oh-so-Renaissance façade, is charming and worth peeking inside (open daily, year-round, 09:00-13:00, 14:30-19:00). The Diocesan Museum, in Corso Rossellino, can easily be skipped.

**Tip:** Even if you don't visit the Piccolomini Palace, you can still walk behind it to enjoy a truly spectacular view (stand facing the Duomo, take the little alley between the Duomo and the Palazzo, and walk down a few metres).

## Cheesy, But in a Good Way

An important part of Pienza tradition is its delicate Pecorino cheese, which has been produced in this area since prehistoric times. There are several places to try the delicacy (and other tasty treats) all over town. Try **La Taverna del Pecorino**, hiding in an alley just off the main street. The service is pleasant and there is a good selection of local cheeses you can taste before buying. Via Condotti 1, Tel: 0578.749412, www.tavernadelpecorino.it

# Bagni San Filippo

## GETTING THERE

The best way to reach Bagni San Filippo is by car. From Pienza, head south along the SP18. Bagni San Filippo is just 30 minutes away.

Bagni San Filippo is without a doubt the best thermal park in the area, and a fantastic little stop for families.

Ideally, come here after having spent the morning touring some of the valley's towns and let the kids relax and unwind in the pools. Though it is not recommended to dip for more than 10-15 minutes at a time, you don't have stay in the water to have fun. You can dip in the smelly water (don't worry, this smell is perfectly normal and typical of thermal springs) and then hike along the small reserve. It is truly beautiful and fun to explore.

# Bagno Vignoni

## GETTING THERE

The best way to reach Bagno Vignoni is by car. Take the SS146 scenic route from Pienza or the SR2 from Montalcino.

**TOURIST INFORMATION OFFICE:** The friendly office will furnish you with information about the little park in Bagno Vignoni itself, as well as other attractions in the area, and nearby towns such as Castiglione d'Orcia (which isn't featured in this itinerary, and in our opinion, can be skipped). 🕑 Opening times: weekends only, summer months only, 10:00-13:00, 14:00-17:00. May, however, be closed during the winter months. Tel: 0577.888975

If you don't want to drive to Bagno San Filippo, then the second-best choice would be Bagno Vignoni, which is slightly closer to Pienza. Bagno Vignoni is a good place to get away from all the little medieval towns and run around freely. It isn't a destination on its own, nor is it worth a special visit, but it does

make for a good stop if you are travelling in the area with kids. Start your tour at the village's main (and only) square, which is actually more of a pool. This 49-meter-long and 24-metre-wide piazza is completely filled with warm thermal water (but you can't jump in!), coming from a depth of 1000 metres. If you look very closely, you will see bubbles in the water, indicating where the water comes from. Several famous people have visited the thermal water over the years, including the Medici family and Charles Dickens, and the town is still considered a popular spa retreat.

Stop by the tourist office (near the piazza) to get a map of the town and head off to the **Parco dei Mulini,** the town's main attraction. A pleasant walk will lead you to this small park, which consists of a number of ancient flour mills placed strategically along a path of thermal springs. The springs are clean, and if you aren't particularly fussy, you can take off your shoes (careful, it's slippery!), get in, and soak your feet. Unfortunately, by the time the water reaches the park, the thermal water has cooled down considerably, but it still has medicinal properties. Please note that thermal water may not be suitable for children younger than 12 (though the locals jump in with 5-year-olds) and should absolutely not be used as drinking water. Find out more about the area, the hotels, and the spas at www.termebagnovignoni.it.

# San Quirico d'Orcia

## GETTING THERE

The easiest
way to reach
San Quirico
d'Orcia is by
car. Take the
SR2 from Mon-
talcino or the
SS146 from
Pienza.

San Quirico is
a lovely place
to stop for
lunch or a cap-
puccino and

a snack when travelling through to Val d'Orcia. Surrounded by glorious views, San Quirico is nothing more than a tiny three-street hamlet, but it does offer two attractions for families. The first is the small but lovely **Horti Leonini Gardens**, created by Diomede Leoni in 1580 (open daily from 08:00-20:00; Tel: 0577.899711). The gardens are filled with little bushes trimmed like a maze, perfect for toddlers and younger children to run between and around. The second attraction is the impressive **Collegiata dei Santi Quirico e Giulitta**, a Romanesque church at the end of town, which makes for a pleasant afternoon stop (but isn't a must-see destination; visit only if you are in town for other reasons).

Once you've parked your car outside San Quirico d'Orcia (be careful not to park in resident-only parking spots and not to drive into the town itself, which is ZTL), start your visit in the Horti Leonini Gardens. Just over the wall you will also find a tiny playground with swings and a slide. Next to the gardens you will see a huge metal and wooden tool that dates back to the 13th century.

**Mission 1:** What is this tool and what was it used for?

From here, turn left and walk along the main road towards one of the most beautiful churches in the area, the **Collegiata dei Santi Quirico e Giulitta,** dedicated to a mother and son who became saints after they were viciously executed in the year 304. This church was built in the late 12th century and expanded during later years. The interior decoration, however, dates back to the 18th century. The great Tuscan sculptor Giovanni Pisano is said to have designed the first of the church's two lateral entranceways.

**Mission 2:** There are three entrances to the church, and they are all decorated with ferocious animals. Which animals guard the second entrance?

**Mission 3:** Next to the church there is an impressive well. There is a small metal flag above the well, and inside the flag there is a shape carved in the metal. What shape is it?

# Sant'Antimo Abbey

## GETTING THERE

The easiest way to reach Sant'antimo is by car. From Pienza, take the SS146 and then the Strada Provinciale della Badia di Sant'Antimo (toward Castelnuovo dell'Abate, the town nearest to the abbey). It's a 45-minute (slightly windy) drive. From Montalcino, take the Strada Provinciale della Badia di Sant'Antimo toward Castelnuovo dell'Abate; signs will direct you to the abbey, which is only 15 minutes away.

This enchanting Romanesque abbey is a favourite stop for travellers in the area, both for its beauty and for the Gregorian chants that can be heard a number of times during the day, recited by the Norbertine monks who live on the premises. Built during the 8th century atop an even older church, this abbey was once part of an important and rich complex, which included more than 90 churches and 85 religious buildings (monasteries, churches, and hospitals) in the area. According to local legend, the army of the Great Charlemagne stopped by the abbey, and many soldiers became very ill. During the night, an angel appeared before Charlemagne and told him he should prepare a potion for his soldiers, mixing the grass from the abbey with wine. Miraculously, the soldiers were healed after drinking the concoction, so Charlemagne decided to finance the rebuilding and extension of the abbey to its current size. To hear the Gregorian chants, you'll have to come at 09:00, 09:15, 12:45, 14:45, 19:00, or 20:30 during the weekdays, or at 09:00, 11:00, 12:45, 14:45, 18:30 or 20:30 on Sundays and holidays. To be on the safe side, check the website before you leave, to make sure that hours haven't changed. Abbazia di Sant'Antimo, Castelnuovo Dell'abate, Tel: 0577.835659, www.antimo.it

# KIDS'CORNER

## More About... Living in the Past!

Hey, here's a quick question for you. Did your parent chew your food before giving it to you when you were a baby? Was your tongue rinsed with salt and honey? No? Well, clearly you didn't grow up in the 16th century! But just to be on the safe side, take this questionnaire to find out when you were really born.

## How to Tell If You Were Born in the 16th Century: The Ultimate Questionnaire!

- As a baby, were you nursed by your mother, or were you sent away to a remote village and nursed by a wet nurse?

- When you started eating food, was it ground with a food processor, or was it first chewed by your mother and then given to you?

- When you started teething, did your dad rub your gums with a soothing lotion that he bought in the pharmacy or drug store or did he use rabbit brains or chicken fat?

- Do your parents give you special food to help you fight intestinal worms or are the only worms you see located in your garden?

# KIDS' CORNER

- Is Latin a popular subject in school or is English more your speed?

- As a young boy, were you expected to learn how to use a sword skilfully, or did your mother yell at you to put that sword down because somebody might lose an eye?

- Has an exorcist ever visited your house to remove evil spirits, or are Friday nights dedicated to simple family dinners?

- Is your tutor or teacher (if you are lucky and rich enough to go to school at all) allowed to beat you up with a stick if you behave badly, or are you sent to the principal's office instead?

- Do you go to school, or does a private tutor come over to teach you geometry, Latin, poetry, and rhetoric?

- Do your formal party clothes weigh more than you do, or do you mostly have jeans and T-shirts in your closet?

- Were you given diluted red wine to drink as a young child, or was it mostly water, juice, and sodas?

- Do you have your own bed, or do you sleep on a large bed with other family members?

- Do you have posters on your walls or frescoes and wood-carvings of scenes from the Bible?

- Does hot water come from the tap, or do you have to fill a metal basin and warm it up over a fire?

# KIDS'CORNER

- Do most of your friends live past the age of 15, or do at least a third of them die before they are five years old because of illnesses that have no cure?

- Is your city commonly under siege by mercenaries who try to conquer it in the name of the Pope or another empire, or are all the battle scenes you see in the movies?

- What time is it? If you answered "the second hour", your cover has been blown. You are from the past! The idea of a 12- or 24-hour clock is recent; people calculated time in a different way in the 16th century. The "first hour" was around what we call 06:00 today—time for the first prayer of the day. The third hour was about 09:00, the sixth hour was about noon, and the ninth hour was 15:00.

## Eating in the Val d'Orcia

### MONTALCINO
**Taverna al Grappolo Blu** is a popular option offering simple and tasty dishes (and good local wine, of course). Open daily, 12:00-15:00, 19:00-22:00, and located near the main square, in Via Moglio 1. Reserve a table during high season. Tel: 0577.847150

Another tasty option is **Re di Macchia** (kids will like the desserts). Open daily, 12:00-14:00, 19:00-21:00, closed on Thursdays. Via Saloni 21, Tel: 0577.846116

### SAN QUIRICO D'ORCIA
**Ristornate degli Archi** is a popular option among those stopping for lunch in town. Open daily, 12:00-15:00, 19:00-22:00, closed on Tuesdays. Via Dante Alighieri 24, Tel: 0577.899085

For a nice slice of pizza, try **Le Contrade.** Open daily, 12:00-15:00, 18:00-23:00, closed on Mondays. Via Nuova 18, Tel: 0577.898098

## PIENZA

There are several places in town in which you can buy a sandwich, or enjoy a quick snack, but if you are looking for a more serious meal, then head out to **Agriturismo Ristorante La Fonte.** Located just 3.5 km from Pienza (on the road leading to Chianciano Terme), this popular restaurant offers taditional Tuscan specialities in a lovely setting. The steaks and pasta are especially good here. If you want to dine outside, book a table in advance. Cooking lessons are available, too. Pod. Fonte Bertusi di Sopra 73 (SP146), Pienza. Tel: 0578.749142, www.lafonte.toscana.it

# Sleeping in the Val d'Orcia

There are several excellent options around the valley, suitable for those who intend on passing a few days in the area itself. However, if you plan on renting an apartment for a week and using it as your base for daily trips in other parts of Tuscany (visiting Siena, Florence, etc.), you should know that the roads, as beautiful as they may be, are windy, and you will waste a great deal of time trying to get from place to place. You would probably be better off choosing a different destination as a base for your daily trips (some place near a main road, between Siena and Florence, for example).

**Agriturismo La Fonte** near Pienza is a great option for families, with comfortable, reasonably priced apartments, a pool, a playground for kids, free Wi-Fi, and rental bikes. Podere Fonte Bertusi di Sopra 73, Pienza, Tel: 0578.749142, www.lafonte.toscana.it

**Agriturismo Bonello** is another reasonably priced option for families, with a pool, nice views, and a playground for kids. Strada Provinciale 146, Pienza, Tel: 0578.749928, Cell: 338.5824493, www.bonello.eu

**Poggio Istiano** offers reasonably priced rooms overlooking the valley, a pool, nearby fishing and horse farms, and cooking lessons. Azienda Agrituristica Poggio Istiano, Loc. Poggio Istiano, Castiglione d'Orcia, Tel: 0577.887046, www.poggioistiano.it

**Agriturismo Il Rigo** offers wonderful views, an elegant atmosphere, and activities such as cooking classes and horseback rides (organized with the nearby farm). Tel: 0577.897291, 342.3735370, www.agriturismoilrigo.com

# Special Events in the Area

**Festa del Barbarossa:** If you are visiting the area in June, don't miss the Barbarossa Medieval Festival, which has been celebrated by locals for more than 50 years and includes a medieval court, parades, and competitions. The festival takes place in San Quirico Val d'Orcia in June each year (check the website for exact dates). www.festadelbarbarossa.it

**Montalcino Jazz Festival:** Listen to some music under the clear, starry sky in one of Montalcino's open-air summer concerts, which kids might enjoy too. The concerts are in July; find out the exact dates each year at the local tourist office.

# Special Activities in the Area

Though there are a number of B&Bs in the area which offer cooking classes and activities for guests, the Val d'Orcia isn't the ideal place to find family-friendly activities such as adventure and amusement parks. For better choices, head north towards Siena or south towards the Maremma.

# MAREMMA

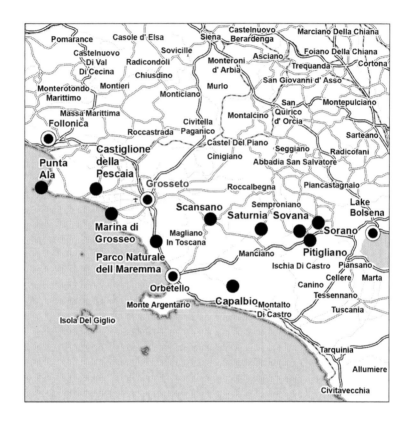

## HOW LONG WILL IT TAKE TO GET THERE?

Siena to Follonica: 1.2 hours
Montalcino to Follonica: 1.2 hours
Grosseto to Saturnia: 1 hour
Saturnia to Sovana: 30 minutes
Saturinia to Pitigliano: 30 minutes
Pitigliano to Lake Bolsena: 40 minutes
Maremma Natural Park to Capalbio Sculpture Park: 40 minutes

# Chapter 13

# **Maremma**

The Maremma spreads across the southern part of Tuscany below the Val d'Orcia and Senese hills. It encompasses several towns, the largest of which is Grosseto. For years, the Maremma was considered an undesirable area, rife with malaria and inhabited by poor farmers, but today this description couldn't be further from the truth. Visitors who venture there will discover a somewhat wild area offering tranquillity and rustic charm, tiny hill towns, beautiful natural reserves, fun parks, family-friendly beaches, and several outdoor activities. Though underappreciated, the Maremma is an excellent destination for families, as well as for those hoping to avoid the more crowded parts of Tuscany (such as Florence, Siena, and Pisa).

The two day-long itineraries offered in this chapter explore the best the Maremma has to offer, combining history, nature, fun, and adventure. Both itineraries are filled with more activities than you might manage in one day, enabling you to focus on what interests your family most and leaving the other options for another visit. You can even easily mix and match according to your preferences, not only within this chapter but also with the Populonia and the Etruscan Beach or the Montepulciano and Chiusi Itineraries.

Itinerary 1, for example, suggests a visit to the Saturnia Thermal Baths, the hill town of Pitigliano, and the Sorano Archaeological Park before ending with an evening at Bolsena Lake. However, you could just as easily skip the thermal baths and head for one of the many beaches in the area instead, or add a quick stop at Sovana (also detailed in Itinerary 1) rather than driving all the way to the lake. The same can be done with Itinerary 2.

Choosing what to take from these itineraries depends greatly on your family's personal tastes. Generally speaking, if you love nature, don't miss the Parco della Maremma (see Itinerary 2). You'll need at least half a day to visit it without rushing, though the track itself isn't difficult and is suitable for younger children, too. Adventurous kids will love the Sorano Archaeological Park (Itinerary 1), which combines light hiking with Indiana Jones-style touring between ancient monuments. Families who enjoy old towns and monuments won't want to skip Pitigliano (Itinerary 1) with its ancient Jewish museum and fortress. For a truly unique experience, don't miss the Capalbio Tarot Park (Itinerary 2), which will leave adults and kids alike with smiles on their faces. To mix things up, consider an outdoor activity such as an adventure park or a horse ride (very popular in this area). At the end of this chapter, you will also find a number of recommendations for the best family beaches in the area. Unless you live near the beach and enjoy it on a regular basis, this will be a real attraction for kids and an opportunity for parents to relax a little (constantly touring can be tiring, and sometimes we need a vacation from the vacation). Whatever you choose, the Maremma area is rich enough in charm and activities to ensure you have a wonderful time.

# Top 5 Family Activities

1. Visit the wonderfully colourful Capalbio Tarot Park.

2. Hike or ride like a professional through the Maremma Natural Reserve.

3. Take a dip in the thermal waters of Saturnia Terme.

4. Discover the secrets of the Etruscan culture in Sorano Archaeological Park.

5. Tour the ancient Jewish Museum in Pitigliano.

**ITINERARY 1:**
## Saturnia Thermal Pools, Pitigliano, Sovana, and Sorano (Optional: Lake Bolsena)

# Saturnia Thermal Pools

**Itinerary 1** begins with a quick dip in the Thermal Baths of Saturnia. To reach the site, drive for about an hour from Grosseto (the largest town in the Maremma, about an hour southeast of Siena) along the SS322 (toward Scansano). Once you've passed Scansano, continue another 30 km (following the road signs) until you reach Saturnia, the first stop of the day.

> **Tip:** Try not to schedule your visit to this area on Friday, Saturday, or Monday, as some of the attractions will be closed, and the Saturnia Thermal Baths will be very crowded.

**The Thermal Baths of Saturnia** are probably the best free thermal baths in Tuscany. They are extremely popular with locals and tourists alike and for good

reason (avoid them during holidays). Even though some of the water from the area has been diverted due to recent construction, this is still a pleasant stop, with 37°C water cascading from tiny waterfalls above to several small pools below in which you can sit and soak. The locals bring children of all ages, but some experts have advised that thermal baths are not suitable for children younger than 12. If you have any medical problems, you will want to consult your doctor before getting in the water.

The Saturnia thermal area is divided into two sections: a free part known as **Le Cascate del Gorello** and the hotels, which charge for entering and using their facilities. The free part can easily be reached by following the signs to Saturnia Terme. As soon as you see the (very) small sign saying Cascate del Gorello (Gorello Falls), turn in, park your car, change into your bathing clothes, and hop in the water!

If you are interested in the hotels, try the thermal pools in the Terme di Saturnia Resort (they also offer beauty treatments and a regular pool) - www. termedisaturnia.it

Once you've dried off, it's time to venture to what many call the gem of the Maremma: the ancient town of **Pitigliano**.

> **Tip:** Between Saturnia and Pitigliano hides a tiny hamlet called **Sovana**. There's nothing special to see there, but it is one of the prettiest towns in southern Tuscany. If you are looking for a place to stop for coffee or a bathroom break or to just walk along the (one) main street, this is it.

# Pitigliano

**GETTING THERE:** The best way to reach Pitigliano is by car. To enjoy the best views, take the Strada Provinciale Pian della Madonna (the main road) or the SS74 from Saturnia towards Pitigliano. As you get closer, the town will suddenly be towering above the gorge, entirely excavated in rock.

Parking can be difficult during high season. Either follow signs leading to the parking lot or take a sharp right turn as soon as you see the entrance to the historical centre and try to park on the roads above the town (just be careful not to park in a space reserved for residents). The historical centre itself is ZTL.

**TOURIST INFORMATION OFFICE:** Pitigliano's small office can be found in Piazza Garibaldi 51, near the fortress. 🕐 Opening times: April-May, Tuesday-Saturday, 10:00-12:30, closed on Mondays; June-September, Tuesday-Sunday, 10:00-12:30, 15:30-18:00, closed on Mondays. During the off season, the office is sometimes open on Saturdays but closed during the rest of the week. Tel: 0564.617111.

> **Tip:** A few hundred meters before the entrance to Pitigliano (when arriving from the aforementioned road), you will see a sign saying "Madonna delle Grazie". This is a popular panoramic spot, overlooking Pitigliano, where you can park your car on the side of the road, pop out and take some photos.

Pitigliano has been inhabited since Etruscan times, but it was during the Middle Ages that it truly flourished and even became a county capital. In 1293, it passed into the hands of the powerful Orsini family, who were interested in this strategically placed town mostly to help them in their constant battle against Siena.

Start your tour by walking toward one of the main monuments in town, **Palazzo Orsini** (look up, find its turret, and walk towards it). Originally built by the Aldobrandesca family, rulers of the area during the high middle ages, the fortress was restored and expanded during the 15th century by the Orsini's. Today, you can visit the fortress, see its rooms decorated in Renaissance style, and tour the local museum.

••••••••••••••••••••••••••••••••••••••••••••••••••••••••••••

 **Mission 1:** Even if you don't enter the fortress, take a picture in front of its entrance, and place your hand in such a way that it looks as though you are holding up the two arches that decorate the entry with your fingers (an optical illusion).

••••••••••••••••••••••••••••••••••••••••••••••••••••••••••••

🕐 Opening times: summer months, 10:00-13:00, 15:00-19:00; winter months,

10:00-13:00, 15:00-17:00; August, 10:00-19:00. Closed on Mondays. Children under six enter for free; children under 12 are eligible for reduced tickets. Tel: 0564.616074, www.palazzo-orsini-pitigliano.it

From the fortress, continue walking toward the main square (on your left will be the Medici Aqueduct, built between 1636-1639 and essential for supplying the town with fresh drinking water). Just a few metres ahead, the road splits into two—Via Roma on the right and Via Zuccarelli on the left. Walk along Via Roma; some of the town's nicest shops are on this road. Check out the artisan tableware at Paseggiando in Maremma (Via Roma 37), the antiques at Gianfranco Franci (Via Roma 49), or buy a beautiful handmade leather notebook next door at Officina Bartaria to use as a travel journal. Foodies will want to sniff around the many butcher shops towards the end of the street; Pitigliano is famous for its local boar sausages and boar sauce.

> **Tip:** In front of the tableware shop, there is a small bar with a little hall in the back. Though it doesn't look very promising, the mother and daughter who run the place serve simple but tasty and reasonably priced homemade pasta dishes, mostly to the locals who stop by for a quick lunch.

 **Mission 2:** Towards the end of Via Roma, there are a number of butcher shops. One of them has a very distinctive sculpture outside, so no one will get confused about what they sell. Can you find it? What is it?

At the end of Via Roma, turn left and left again to follow the parallel Via Zuccarelli (follow the sign "Synagoga"). The Pitigliano **Jewish Quarter** (or Ghetto) is unique in all of Tuscany and makes for an interesting visit even if you aren't particularly interested in Jewish culture (kids will love the mysterious rock-made rooms in the deceivingly simple-looking museum). Once home to a thriving community, today only one Jewish woman remains in Pitigliano to keep the tradition alive. The museum and the synagogue, however, still draw quite a crowd. Walk down to the museum (follow the signs) and start your tour at the "Mikveh", the ritual bath house carved entirely into the Tuff rock and resembling more of a biblical bathing house than something built during the Renaissance. Follow the marked itinerary and you will discover the rooms and artefacts which served the community for hundreds of years: a kosher slaughter room, a wine cellar, an antique matzo baking oven used during Passover, and more.

**Mission 3:** Enter the Mikveh and room number 1. Do you know what this room was used for? Once there was water here, which filled the little carved pools. Bonus: How do you think the water got here?

**Mission 4:** Room number 2 was once a cellar for kosher wine. What metal device do you see?

**Mission 5:** Room number 3 contains items from traditional Jewish life. Do you recognize any items? Do you know what they are used for?

**Mission 6:** Enter room number 5. Do you know what this oven was used for?

Built during the 16th century, many of these rooms were almost destroyed during World War II when the Allied forces bombed the area, but they were thankfully later restored. During your visit to the Jewish Museum, you can also climb up and visit the synagogue itself, which was built in 1598 and completely renovated in 1995. End your tour of the old Jewish ghetto with a few baked goods that you can buy next door at the Panificio del Ghetto (the Ghetto's Bakery).

🕐 Museum and synagogue opening times: April-September, open daily, 10:00-13:30, 14:30-18:30, closed on Saturdays; October-March, open daily, 10:00-12:30, 15:00-17:30, closed on Saturdays. Kids under six enter for free. Tel: 0564.614230

# The Jewish Community in Pitigliano

Pitigliano's small but vibrant Jewish community arrived during the 16th century after escaping from persecution and violence in neighbouring towns, which were controlled by the Papal states and filled with religious fervour as a result of the counterreformation. The Jewish community sought refuge in this territory controlled by the Orsini family and greatly contributed to the social and economic development of the town. The Jewish Ghetto was founded in 1622 and continued thriving under the Medici family rule, earning the name "Little Jerusalem".

Racial laws passed by Mussolini in 1938 changed everything for Jewish communities throughout Italy. Many families left Tuscany, seeking refuge in other cities or abroad. Others were caught and deported to concentration camps. Today, there are about 30,000 Jews living in all of Italy and a number of tiny Jewish communities in Tuscany (mostly in Florence, Pisa, and Livorno).

As you walk back toward the main piazza to conclude your visit, you will pass a model of an open-air archaeological "museum", meant to show a reconstruction of a typical Etruscan site in the area (you'll be able to see the real thing when you visit the Sorano Archaeological Park).

From Pitigliano, move on to **Sorano**, just 9 km away (follow the signs leading to Sorano). If you are interested in visiting the Archaeological Park, start your visit there (before visiting the town itself).

# Parco Archeologico Sorano

**GETTING THERE:** The park is just outside Sorano on a tiny road called Strada provinciale San Quirico. You will find a number of signs along the way directing you to Parco Archeologico Citta' del Tuffo—Sorano (some signs will direct you also to Parco degli Etruschi), but the entrance is very easy to miss, so drive slowly.

Though the monuments aren't incredible, they are very nice, and a tour of the park can be quite entertaining for kids, who will love the short hike and running between rock tombs and statues, pretending to be archaeologists revealing mysterious artefacts thousands of years old. Pick up a map at the entrance and head for the **Etruscan Necropolis** just north of the Calesine stream (all the paths are clearly marked, so you won't get lost), and then continue a little further until you reach the impressive **Ildebranda Tomb**, the park's main attraction. Don't miss the **Tomba dei Demoni alati** (the Tomb of the Winged Demons) nearby. Though not difficult, the path there does require some climbing and won't be suitable for toddlers or very young children.

🕐 Opening times: April-October, open daily, 10:00-19:00; October-November, open daily, 10:00-18:00. The rest of the year, the park is open on weekends only (hours may vary and the park might close down during the winter, so call first before arriving). Tel: 0564.633424, www.leviecave.it

Once you've had your fill of adventurous archaeological missions, it's time to explore Sorano itself.

# Sorano

Sorano is a tiny town, boasting one main attraction within its medieval walls—a **fortress** built by the Aldobrandeschi family (and then purchased by the Orsini family as a military stronghold). The fortress was mainly used as a food and water storage space (useful in case of a siege) and later turned into a gun powder production centre. The most interesting part of the fortress is the tour of its protected underground/shielded paths (called *camminamenti diffensivi*), which were built to allow soldiers to move from place to place without exposing themselves or being hit by enemies' arrows or firearms. As you tour the paths, you will notice little holes along the outer walls that were used to place arches and weapons and to shoot the enemy. The paths can only be visited with a guide, and tours need to be booked in advance at the (sometimes unfriendly, unfortunately) tourist office. Tours leave daily, year-round, at 11:00 and 16:00. The tour also includes a visit to the small museum, where you can see period clothes, Etruscan findings, and a few re-creations of machines invented by Leonardo da Vinci. To book a tour: Tel: 0564.633424, 0564.633767, email: info@leviecave.it

🕐 Museum and fortress opening times: April-September, 10:00-13:00, 15:00-19:00; during October, the fortress closes at 18:00; closed during the winter (except during holidays; check their website to see if the fortress is open during your visit off season); closed on Mondays (except for August and holidays). Bring a jacket, as it can get chilly inside.

If you have a few hours left and want to end the afternoon or pass your evening on a more relaxed note, consider driving to **Lake Bolsena** (which technically isn't in Tuscany but is only 45 minutes away, in Lazio). You will find a number of beaches, restaurants, and water activities along the lake shore that are suitable for children and make for a fun-filled afternoon for all. To get to the lake, take the SS74 from Sorano towards Gradoli and the lake, and then the SS489, following the signs to Lago Bolsano.

## ITINERARY 2:
## Parco della Maremma, Capalbio Tarot (Tarocchi) Park, Afternoon at the Beach

# Parco della Maremma

Itinerary 2 begins in the Parco della Maremma (Maremma Natural Reserve/ Park). Nature lovers won't want to miss this attraction, which offers some excellent guided tours and several itineraries for all levels, and a peek into a rich natural habitat, pinewood forests and wildlife. Consult the park's detailed and user-friendly website for more info (in English too!) at www.parco-maremma.it. Alternatively, call the Information Centre, Tel: 0564.407098.

**GETTING THERE:** From Grosseto, take the SS1 heading south exit at Alberese and follow the signs. The park is just 17 km from Grosseto. From Siena, head south along the SS223 (just an hour away). From Follonica, take the SS1 towards Grosseto, and from there, continue south to the Park.

The Maremma park is open daily year-round (though it may close down for part of the winter, check first), and can be toured either independently or with a guide and a group. Tickets should be bought at the Visitors' Centre, in the tiny town of Alberese (follow the signs leading to the centre). During the high season (15 June-30 September), the park operates several **highly recommended organized tours that kids will love.** Some, but not all tours are available off season too, so check the park website for available options during the time of your visit. These are some of the possible tours:

- **Night tours** (with compulsory guide): a cool experience for kids, teenagers, and adults, allowing you to enjoy the crisp air and listen for animals such as wild boars and foxes. Book in advance at the Alberese Visiting Centre. Via del Bersagliere 7, Albarese, Tel: 0564.407098, centrovisite@parco-maremma.it

- **Horseback tours:** only available for riders with some experience.

- **Chariot excursions:** a unique way to travel, and because chariots are silent (unlike cars), they will take you close to the animals without scaring them. Book in advance at the Alberese Visiting Centre.

- **Canoe rides:** in collaboration with the park, a private company (Silva Coop-erative) offers guided 2.5-hour excursions of the park in Canadian canoes. Book in advance, either through the Park Visitors' Centre or the Silva Co-operative. Cell: 331.5264929, www.silvacoop.com , info@silvacoop.com

**Tip:** Wear comfortable walking shoes, bring lots of water (there's no place to buy any in the park), pack some snacks, and make sure you have a hat and mosquito repellent. Since the park is a sanctuary for several animals, it is important not to make loud sounds (put your phone on vibrate and avoid yelling), litter (which animals could eat and become very ill), or light a fire (which is punishable with a very hefty fine).

If the morning has been dedicated to the natural beauty of the Maremma, it's a good idea to pass the afternoon doing something completely different, albeit still exciting, like the Capalbio Tarot Park.

# Capalbio Tarot Park (Giardino dei Tarocchi)

This park, which is one of the most unique and popular attractions in the area, was built by French artist Niki de Saint de Phalle and depicts the 22 major Arcana Tarot cards through enormous, delightfully colourful and original statues created by the artist.

**GETTING THERE:** The park is located just 45 minutes south of the Maremma Park (and one hour south of Grosseto). From Grosseto, or from the Maremma Park, take the SS1, heading south. Exit at Capalbio, and continue along the SP75 (toward Capalbio, Località Garavacchio) (a GPS can be useful).

🕐 Opening times: 1 April-15 October, 14:30-19:30. Kids under seven enter for free. www.nikidesaintphalle.com

**Mission 1:** Take a picture next to at least six statues and make a particular shape with your face and hands (a different shape for every sculpture!).

**Mission 2:** What was your favourite statue and why?

**Mission 3:** (Super Bonus Mission, worth double the points): Try to draw one of the statues.

# Maremma Beaches

 There are a number of well-known beaches in the area where you can go for a swim, spend a few hours playing in the sand, try some water sports, or even just have a family dinner and enjoy the cool salty breeze. You can also easily drive up north toward Follonica (about an hour and a half away), where there is an Aqua Park (see Etruscan Beach Itinerary). For the best family options, try one of these beaches:

- Bagno Bruna, at Castiglione della Pescaia, www.bagnobruna.it

- Tombolo della Giannella at Orbetello

- Principina al Mare Beach and Miramare (both near Marina di Grosseto) are two of the best options in the area for families.

- Punta Ala is further north but highly recommended (the beach is very long and divided into a number of private beaches; the part between Punta Hidalgo and Cala del Barbiere is great for kids, as are the beaches between Punta Ala and Follonica. There are also some fun little attractions in the area. Drive around and you will see playgrounds, golf, paddle boats to rent, and other activities. Older kids might enjoy water activities from www.puntaala-watersport.it

# KIDS'CORNER

## THE RIDDLE MISSION

The Grand Duke of Tuscany has created this riddle, which can be solved only by the most savvy   detectives. Are you up for the challenge? We can tell you right now—it isn't easy (but you can use the information in this guide or the internet to find the answers to any question)! Solve each question and then transfer the letters that are marked with a bold line under them (keep the order!) to discover the secret hidden phrase below.

1.   This is the most famous museum in Florence:

   __ __ __ __ __ __

2.   This world-famous painter painted masterpieces such as Primavera and Birth of Venus:

   __ __ __ __ __ __ __ __ __

3.   He was the famous Etruscan king who, according to legend, built the town of Chiusi:

   __ __ __ __ __ __ __

4.   This man was a true Renaissance genius. He was a painter, architect, engineer, and inventor. He is known for having painted the most famous smiling lady in the world:

   __ __ __ __ __ __ __ - __ __ - __ __ __ __

# KIDS'CORNER

5. Almost all the ceramics in the town of Cortona are painted with this colour, because this colour symbolizes the protective saint of the town

   — — — — —

6. This colour was reserved for important and noble people; only they could wear clothes dyed in this colour:

   — — —

7. He was the original architect for the Leaning Tower of Pisa:

   — — — — — — —    — — — — — —

8. This is the main and most famous square in Siena:

   — — — — —    — — —    — — — — —

9. In the past, these warriors protected royal courts and were organized in orders:

   — — — — — —

10. This word means "sun" in Italian:

   — — — —

WHAT IS THE HIDDEN PHRASE?

— — — — —    — — — — — !

# KIDS'CORNER

## THE ITALIAN CHALLENGE

CAN YOU FIND OUT WHAT THESE ITALIAN WORDS MEAN?

- PRIMAVERA  _____
- BAMBINO  _____
- AMORE  _____
- AVVENTURA  _____
- MACCHINA  _____
- MANGIARE  _____
- ALBERGO  _____
- BUONGIORNO  _____
- BUONA SERA  _____
- VACANZA  _____

# **Eating** in the Maremma

The best restaurants are in Pitigliano, Sovana, and Castiglione della Pescaia, but you can find delicious local dishes just about anywhere, especially if you are looking for beef- and boar-based specialties. All can be washed down with the local wine, Morellino di Scansano.

## PITIGLIANO

If you are looking for more of an upscale establishment, with excellent quality and local produce, try the **Hostaria del Ceccottino**. Open daily, 12:30-15:00, 19:30-22:00; closed on Thursdays. Piazza S. Gregorio VII (at the end of Via Roma). Tel: 0564.614273

**Il Tuffo Allegro** is another delicious, and somewhat more accessible option. Open Thursday-Monday, 12:00-13:30, 19:30-21:30; closed on Tuesdays; open for dinner only on Wednesdays; closed January-February. Vicolo della Costituzione 5 (just off Via Zuccarelli). Tel: 0564.616192, www.iltufoallegro.com

## SOVANA

The **La Taverna Etrusca** serves good quality (but sometimes pricey) modern versions of classic Tuscan dishes. Open daily, 12:00-14:30, 19:30-22:00 (opening times may change off season). Piazza del Pretorio 16, Tel: 0564.616531, www.tavernaetrusca.info

## SORANO

If you are looking for a nice pizza, try **Talismano**, well known for their thin crusts and within walking distance from the centro storico. Open daily for dinner only, 19:00-24:00; closed on Tuesdays. Via S. Marco 37, Tel: 0564.633281

# **Sleeping** in the Maremma

**Tip:** The Maremma is beautiful and wild, and its roads are sometimes windy. If you hate driving or are prone to car sickness, make sure you book a Bed and Breakfast near the areas you plan to visit in order to reduce driving time to a minimum. Alternatively, if you don't mind driving around, you can book a hotel at one of the resorts along the beach, a location that usually offers quite a number of activities for children. Then you can drive up to the heart of the Maremma whenever you want (consult more options listed in the Populonia and the Etruscan Beach Itinerary).

**Relais Vale Orientina** is a slightly more elegant choice just outside of Pitigliano. Instead of a traditional pool, you will find one built over a thermal spring, which pumps fresh thermal water into the pool all day long. Rooms are comfortable and the quiet forest surrounding the area adds to the charm. Tel: 0564.616611, www.valleorientina.it

**Agriturismo Il Girasole** offers comfortable apartments near the beach, with a swimming pool and pony riding lessons on its farm, near Grosseto. Strada Comunale di Montalcino, Loc. Barbaruta, Tel: 0564.401048, www.maresole.it

**San. Egle** is a new hotel and resort built in a 17th-century villa and surrounded by wonderful views. This place is perfect if you are travelling with teenagers (less suitable for younger children), who might better appreciate the locally grown organic meals, movies screened outside in the warm summer nights, and horseback riding activities (spa treatments are available as well). Agritursimo Biologico Sant'Egle, Sorano, Tel: 348.8884810, www.santegle.it

**Agriturismo Aia del Tufo** is a kid-friendly place, rustic but charming and full of animals kids can pet. In addition to a playground, the location offers educational tours of the farm (including a close encounter with the cows) and the vegetable gardens. S. Valentino, Sorano, Tel: 0564.634039, www.aiadeltufo.com

**Tenuta Agricola dell'Uccellina** offers simple but comfortable apartments on an active farm. Day trips and riding lessons, treks, wine tasting, and more are available. Tenuta Agricola dell'Uccellina, Località Collecchio 38, Magliano in Toscana, Tel: 0564.597104, www.tenutauccellina.it

# Special Events in the Area

There are a number of minor events in the Maremma, mostly town festivities and sagre (food festivals), which usually take place during the holidays or the grape harvest (October). Though they are fun, they are not particularly family oriented and can probably be skipped. If you do want to find out more about local events, we suggested consulting this website: www.turismoinmaremma.it.

# Special Activities in the Area

### ADVENTURE PARKS

There are several outdoor activities in the Maremma, but if it's an adventure park you are looking for, where kids can climb on trees, brave their way along rope bridges, and run wild, then **Parco Cieloverde** near Grosseto is the place for you. Opening times: mid-June to mid-September, open daily, 10:00-19:30; mid-May to mid-June, weekends only; mid-September to mid-October, weekends only. The park operates inside the Camping Cielo Verde at Marina di Grosseto, Via della Trappola 180, Grosseto, Cell: 338.8444996, www.parcoavventuracieloverde.it

### HORSEBACK RIDING

The Maremma has very a long and proud tradition of horseback riding and is considered to be the "Texas" of Tuscany, with the local cowboys called "Butteri". If you want to be like them, try the riding activities offered by **Hotel Prategiano**, an excellent three-star family hotel. It offers horse rides, mountain bike excursions, trekking, and exciting quad adventures (which teenagers will love). Book in advance. A two-hour horse ride (from 10:00 to 12:00 or from 14:00 to 16:00) will cost about 45 euro per person. Rides are available for children older than five. The farm and the hotel are located in Loc. Prategiano 45, Montieri. Tel: 0566.997700, www.hotelprategiano.it

If your action-hungry teenager (with a license) is looking for some road fun, **75 avventura** might be just what you are looking for. This local company offers exciting quad rides in the Maremma, as well as horseback riding in the deep valleys, archery lessons, hiking, and even lake kayaking. Horseback riding tours are available for teenagers (14 years and older), and riding lessons are available for children older than 10. Check out the different activities and book in advance at www.75avventura.com.

**Tip:** There are several riding farms in the Maremma, offering activities geared mostly toward experienced riders but sometimes meant for beginners, too (activities organized by agriturismi will often be for tourists and beginners, whereas stables offer more professional courses).

**The Ginestra Equitazione** offers riding lessons and trekking with horses in the wild paths of the Maremma, in addition to pony rides for younger children. La Ginestra Riding Centre, Strada delle Conce, Campagnatico, Cell: 335.7047106, 377.1971801, www.laginestraequitazione.com

The **Riding Centre Cavallo Maremma** offers fun riding and personalized riding tours of the Maremma and riding lessons, catering to children as young as five years old, as well as inexperienced riders. Cell: 331.4268904, www.centro-ippico-cavallomaremma.it

Horse lovers will love **Equinus**, local specialists in riding Butteri style and horse trekking. Most of their offerings are multi-day trekking tours for experienced riders. Check out their website to find out more about their activities and the shows they organize that draw a large crowd. Via dell'Unione 37, Grosseto, www.cavallomaremmano.com

Another popular horse farm, offering riding activities and trekking, mostly for riders with some experience (near Pitigliano) is **Maneggio Belvedere**. Located in Loc. Filetta, near Sorano, Tel: 0564.615465, Cell: 338.8100996, www.maneggiobelvedere.it

# Chapter 14

# Top of the Top

## Top 20 Family Attractions in Tuscany

Climb to the dome of Florence's **Duomo** (see Florence Itinerary).

Say hello to Michelangelo's *David*, one of the most famous sculptures in the world, in the **Accademia Museum** (see Florence Itinerary).

Stop by **Piazzale Michelangelo** for an incredible panoramic view of Florence (see Florence Itinerary).

Take a chariot, canoe, or just hike across the lovely **Maremma Natural Park** (see Maremma Itinerary).

Visit the huge and colourful tarot sculptures in **Capalbio**, and then head off to the beach (see Maremma Itinerary).

Tour the **underground city museum** and **Porsenna's Labyrinth** in Chiusi (See Montepulciano and Chiusi Itinerary).

Visit the colourful **Etruscan tombs** is Sarteano (see Montepulciano and Chiusi Itinerary).

Climb up the **Torre Grossa** in San Gimignano and enjoy the view (see San Gimignano Itinerary).

Dip in the thermal waters and discover hidden little pools in **Bagni San Filippo** (see Val d'Orcia itinerary)

☀ Try on a knight's armour and sword in the museum in **Monteriggioni** (see San Gimignano and Monteriggioni Itinerary).

☀ Climb to the Top of **Torre del Mangia** in Siena to enjoy a bird's-eye view of the city (see Siena Itinerary).

☀ Splash around in the **Follonica Water Park** (see Populonia and the Etruscan Beach Itinerary).

☀ Rent a bike and **ride along the** wonderfully preserved **ramparts in Lucca** (see Pisa and Lucca Itinerary).

☀ Climb up Pisa's world-famous **Leaning Tower** and take a picture of yourself pretending to hold or push it (see Pisa and Lucca Itinerary).

☀ Visit a vineyard and book a **family cooking lesson**, in the beautiful Chianti region (see the Chianti Itinerary).

☀ Get wet and enjoy the spectacular nature in the **Orrido di botri Canyon** (see Garfagnana Itinerary).

☀ Admire the incredible stalagmites and stalactites in the **Grotta del Vento** (see Garfagnana Itinerary).

☀ Visit the quarry near **Carrara** to discover where Michelangelo got his marble (see Garfagnana Itinerary).

☀ Hike to **Campocecina** to enjoy the spectacular Apuan Alps view (see Garfagnana Itinerary).

☀ Tour the Val d'Orcia and visit the beautiful **Sant'Antimo Abbey** to hear the Gregorian chants (see Val d'Orcia Itinerary).

# Top 3 medieval-themed, family-friendly festivals to visit while you are in Tuscany

**Volterra A.D. 1398** is when Volterra comes to life with warhorses, fearless knights, noblemen and ladies, flag-wavers and crossbowmen. The festival kicks off all around the centro storico on the third and fourth Sundays in August. www.Volterra1398.it

**La Giostra del Saracino** is the most famous event in Arezzo and is based on the antique jousting matches that took place in piazzas during the Renaissance and the Middle Ages. Join the colourful festivities which take place twice a year, on the third or fourth Saturday of June (the precise date changes annually, so check the website in advance) and the first Sunday morning of September. www.giostradelsaracino.arezzo.it

The **medieval festivities in Monteriggioni** are absolutely worth a visit to enjoy medieval stands, artists, vendors, and music filling the main square with a merry atmosphere. The main events usually take place during the first two weeks of July. www.Monteriggionimedievale.com

# Quick Review

## Three Fun Family Parks

1.  Admire the colourful tarot sculptures in **Capalbio Park** (see Maremma Itinerary).

2.  Tour the mysteries of the Etruscan civilization in the **Sorano Etruscan Archeological Park** (see Maremma Itinerary).

3.  Splash around and have fun in **Follonica Water Park** (see Populonia and Etruscan Beach Itinerary).

## Three Fun Family Hikes

1.  Admire the stalagmites and stalactites in **Grotta del Vento** (see Garfagnana Itinerary).

2.  Walk the fun and wet path along **Orrido di Botri** (see Garfagnana Itinerary).

3.  Hike, ride, or canoe along the popular **Maremma Natural Reserve** (see Maremma itinerary), and the **San Filippo thermal pools.)**

## Three Fun Towers To Climb

1.  Rush up the **Leaning Tower of Pisa** (see Pisa Itinerary).

2.  Climb up the **Torre del Mangia** in Siena (see Siena Itinerary)

3.  Huff and puff all the way along **Giotto's Bell Tower** in Florence (see Florence Itinerary).

## Three Places to Enjoy a Great Panoramic View

1.  Be wowed by the view from **Piazzale Michelangelo** in Florence (see Florence Itinerary).

2.  Enjoy an incredible view from **Campocecina** (Garfagnana Itinerary).

3.  Witness the natural beauty of the **Orcia Valley** from behind the Duomo in Pienza (see Val d'Orcia Itinerary).

## Three Fun and Adventurous Family Activities

1.  **Raft** along the Serchio River (see Garfagnana Itinerary).

2.  Tour the countryside aboard a **quad** (see the Cortona, Garfagnana, and Arezzo Itineraries).

3.  **Ride a horse** along the countryside (see San Gimignano and Monteriggioni Itinerary).

## Three Fun Activities for Toddlers

1.  Visit the **dinosaur sculptures** in Peccioli Prehistoric Park (see Volterra Itinerary).

2.  Ride the fun rides in **Cavallino Matto Amusement Park** (see Populonia and the Etruscan Beach Itinerary).

3.  Say hello to the **colourful tarot sculptures** in Capalbio Park (see Maremma Itinerary).

## Three Fun Places to Get Wet and Splash Around

1.  Make sand castles and jump in for a swim on one of the **beaches** along the Maremma (see the Maremma Itinerary).

2.  Splash in every possible direction in Follonica and Cecina **Water Parks** (see Populonia and the Etruscan Beach Itineraries).

3.  Enjoy the warm and medicinal thermal water in Saturnia **thermal baths** (see Maremma Itinerary).

## Three Places to Learn More About the Etruscans

1.  Explore two fun **underground museums** in the ancient town of Chiusi (see Montepulciano and Chiusi Itinerary).

2.  Check out the **Etruscan Museum** in Volterra (see Volterra Itinerary).

3.  Visit the modern **Etruscan Museum** in Cortona (see Cortona and Monteriggioni Itinerary).

## Three Great Museums for Kids

1.  Discover ancient skeletons and mummies in Florence's **Natural History Museum** (see Florence itinerary).

2.  **Try on armour and swords** at the museum in Monteriggioni (see San Gimignano and Monteriggioni Itinerary).

3.  **Discover your inner scientist** in the Galileo Galilei Science Museum in Florence.

# Photo Credits

### CHAPTER 1 - FLORENCE
Marc Scott-Parkin/Shutterstock.com; canadastock/Shutterstock.com; Timurk/Dreamstime.com; Coloubox (supplier: kavalenkava volha); Nikonaft/Shutterstock.com; Alessandro0770/Shutterstock.com; Oleg Znamenskiy/Shutterstock.com; canadastock/Shutterstock.com; Tobik/Shutterstock.com; Anton_Ivanov/Shutterstock.com; Superdumb/Dreamstime.com; wjarek/Shutterstock.com; Sorin Colac/Shutterstock.com; Tomasz Bidermann/Shutterstock.com; Renata Sedmakova/Shutterstock.com; Colourbox.com (supplier Paul Carlsen).

### CHAPTER 2 - PISA & LUCCA
Cristina Trif/Shutterstock.com; DrimaFilm/Shutterstock.com; Robert Hoetink/Shutterstock.com; Santi Rodriguez/Shutterstock.com; marcociannarel/Shutterstock.com; Kiselev Andrey Valerevich/Shutterstock.com; VectorShots/Shutterstock.com.

### CHAPTER 3 - GARFAGNANA
Claudio Giovanni Colombo/Shutterstock.com; JaySi/Shutterstock.com; Fotografiche/Shutterstock.com; Luca Grandinetti/Shutterstock.com; Clio85/Shutterstock.com; Santi Rodriguez/Shutterstock.com; Ammit Jack/Shutterstock.com

### CHAPTER 4 - VOLTERRA
Tobik/Shutterstock.com; Petr Jilek/Shutterstock.com; StevanZZShutterstock.com; Bertl123/Shutterstock.com; pincio/Shutterstock.com; Tom Davison/Shutterstock.com; Cathleen A Clapper/Shutterstock.com.

### CHAPTER 5 - CHIANTI
Tom Tom/Shutterstock.com; MauMar70/Shutterstock.com; Shaiith/Shutterstock.com; Teri Virbickis/Shutterstock.com; Steve Cukrov/Shutterstock.com; Roberto Cerruti/Shutterstock.com.

### CHAPTER 6 - SAN GIMIGNANO
Paolo Querci/Shutterstock.com; Sorin Colac/Shutterstock.com; stefano marinari/Shutterstock.com; MauMar70/Shutterstock.com.

### CHAPTER 7 - SIENA
Roman Sigaev/Shutterstock.com; wjarek/Shutterstock.com; stefano marinari/

Shutterstock.com; Roman Sigaev/Shutterstock.com; javarman/Shutterstock.com; Migel/Shutterstock.com; pisaphotography/Shutterstock.com; M. Rohana/Shutterstock.com; Colourbox (supplier: Sergey Yakovlev). CroMary/Shutterstock.com

## CHAPTER 8 - MONTE OLIVETTO MAGGIORE
Bertl123/Shutterstock.com; edella/Shutterstock.com, hipproductions/Shutterstock.com; Angelo Ferraris/Shutterstock.com; marcociannarel/Shutterstock.com; Frank Bach/Shutterstock.com; Sergiy Palamarchuk/Shutterstock.com.

## CHAPTER 9 - AREZZO
Marc Venema/Shutterstock; gkuna/Shutterstock.com; Panaccione Robertino/Shutterstock.com; Magati/Shutterstock.com; Malgorzata Kistryn/Shutterstock.com; Ariela Bankier; Chris Hill/Shutterstock.com; Dziewul/Shutterstock.com.

## CHAPTER 10 - POPULONIA
LianeM/Shutterstock.com; baldovina/Shutterstock.com; viki2win/Shutterstock.com; baldovina/Shutterstock.com.

## CHAPTER 11 - MONTEPULCIANO
newphotoservice/Shutterstock.com; nouseforname/Shutterstock.com; Wolfgang Zwanzger/Shutterstock.com; JaroPienza/Shutterstock.com.

## CHAPTER 12 - VAL D'ORCIA
Shaiith/Shutterstock.com; stocker1970/Shutterstock.com; Shaiith/Shutterstock.com; theskaman306/Shutterstock.com; Frank Bach/Shutterstock.com; DUSAN ZIDAR/Shutterstock.com; Andrea Izzotti/Shutterstock.com; Anna Biancoloto/Shutterstock.com; JCVStock/Shutterstock.com.

## CHAPTER 13 - MAREMMA
Shaiith/Shutterstock.com; Anna Biancoloto/Shutterstock.com; Davide69/Shutterstock.com; Tupungato/Shutterstock.com; Mikhail Bakunovich/Shutterstock.com.

## CHAPTER 14 - TOP OF THE TOP
moosa art/Shutterstock.com; Ariela Bankier. Studio Barcelona/Shutterstock.com

Graphic elements courtesy of Freepik.com; Colourbox.com (supplier: Stockwerk.dk)

Made in the USA
San Bernardino, CA
03 May 2016